THE
FUTURE OF
AMERICAN
FOREIGN POLICY

Senior editor: Don Reisman
Managing editor: Patricia Mansfield
Project editor: Robert Skiena
Production supervisor: Katherine Battiste

Manufactured in the United States of America.
65432
fedcba

For information, write:
St. Martin's Press, Inc.
175 Fifth Avenue
New York, NY 10010

ISBN: 0-312-06522-1 (cloth)
ISBN: 0-312-03574-8 (paperback)

Library of Congress Cataloging-in-Publication Data

The Future of American foreign policy / edited by Charles W. Kegley,
     Jr., Eugene R. Wittkopf.
          p.   cm.
       ISBN 0-312-06522-1 (cl.).—ISBN 0-312-03574-8 (pbk.): $13.50
     (est.)
          1. United States—Foreign relations—1989– I. Kegley, Charles W.
     II. Wittkopf, Eugene R., 1943– .
     JX1417.F88   1992   90-63555
     327.73—dc20   CIP

ACKNOWLEDGMENTS

Acknowledgments and copyrights are continued at the back of the book on pages 349–350, which constitute an extension of the copyright page.

 The text of this book has been printed on recycled paper.

CONTENTS

INTRODUCTION: SETTING PRIORITIES FOR A POST–COLD WAR WORLD

In the space of a few short years, world politics has undergone dramatic changes profoundly important to the future of American foreign policy. After a generation of intensive and extensive competition and conflict with the Soviet Union and its erstwhile allies, the United States suddenly confronts a radically new environment in which many of the objectives it has long sought through its foreign policy strategy of containment have been achieved. George F. Kennan argued in 1947 in his famous "X" article that "the United States has it in its power to increase enormously the strains under which Soviet policy must operate, to force upon the Kremlin a far greater degree of moderation and circumspection than it has had to observe in recent years, and in this way to promote tendencies which must eventually find their outlet in either the breakup or the gradual mellowing of Soviet power."[1] Now, more than forty years later, the breakup and mellowing seem to have occurred. Communism in the Soviet Union and Eastern Europe has collapsed, the Soviet Union's external empire has disintegrated and its domestic power has diminished, the Warsaw Pact is defunct, and the division of Germany has ended. The Cold War is over.

With the end of the Cold War, the United States for the third time in the century has been called on to confront its global destiny. The first came in the aftermath of World War I, when the nation reverted to its historic tradition of isolationism; the second followed World War II, when isolationism was rejected in favor of a policy of global activism. It was during this formative period that the United States evolved its grand strategy for combating the communist and Soviet menace, the elements of which are captured in the themes of globalism, anticommunism, containment, military might, and interventionism.[2] The third debate—sparked like the others by the end of war, albeit in this case a "cold" war—is concerned largely with the continued relevance of the grand strategy launched after World War II. Harvard po-

1

litical scientist Stanley Hoffmann captured the truly revolutionary nature of today's challenges when he observed, "There are periods of history when profound changes occur all of a sudden.... We are now in one of those periods, which obliges the United States to rethink its role in the world, just as it was forced to do by the cataclysmic changes that followed the end of the Second World War."[3]

It was amid this introspection in the United States and the profound geopolitical changes occurring in Europe that Iraq launched its invasion of Kuwait in August 1990. Soviet support of the U.S. position in the crisis over Kuwait and later in the Persian Gulf War—widely heralded, respectively, as the first post–Cold War crisis and a "defining moment" in the new post–Cold War order—symbolized the dramatic changes the world has witnessed in recent years. The Persian Gulf War may itself be the harbinger of the future, as the United States once more appeared willing to don the mantle of world policeman in widespread disrepute in the wake of the Vietnam War.

The crisis over Kuwait and the subsequent decision by the United States to resort to force of arms against Iraq stalled the third debate regarding America's world role, which by the summer of 1990 had become an extensive and lively exchange among policymakers and other elites about the future of American foreign policy in a post–Cold War world. Simultaneously with the unfolding of events in the Persian Gulf region, Soviet leaders undertook measures to deal with the convulsive changes sweeping the Soviet Union; many observers viewed these measures as a setback to the promise of a freer society and economy that Mikhail Gorbachev had husbanded since the mid-1980s. As a result, the outlines of the post–Cold War world were less clearly delineated than they had been as recently as November 1989, when the Berlin Wall came tumbling down. Still, as the United States approaches the millennium, the grand strategy of American foreign policy remains less certain than in any time in the recent past.

Policymakers today not only confront the most dramatic geopolitical changes in world order that have occurred in the previous half century; they also face another reality: the erosion of the political and economic supremacy in world politics once enjoyed by the United States. At the same time that new centers of power have emerged in Europe and Asia, widespread concern about the precarious state of U.S. fiscal affairs and its industrial, technological, and educational base shape a worrisome political climate at home. The United States is the most powerful nation in world politics today—a position affirmed by the desperate economic state of the Soviet Union, its nearest military competitor—but its ability to control outcomes at the international level now and in the future is seriously circumscribed.

Against this background, American foreign policymakers must confront critical questions as they assess the objectives of American foreign policy, the relationships of the United States with friends and foes, and the nation's foreign policy capabilities. At issue is whether the grand strategy designed to promote American interests and protect its security in the post–World

War II world will continue to serve the United States well as it looks toward the twenty-first century.

The purpose of this book is to provoke inquiry into the future of American foreign policy and the forces that will shape it. It is organized into three parts that emphasize *objectives, relationships,* and *capabilities.* Part I, Objectives, begins with a discussion of whether the United States should continue its global activism, revert to isolationism, or reorient its world role in other ways. This discussion is followed by a consideration of how the changing configuration of world power will impact the United States in a post–Cold War environment. Other essays in Part I propose alternatives to anticommunism and containment as foreign policy priorities and examine the impact that the post–Cold War world will exert on American domestic politics, where anticommunism and anti-Sovietism have heretofore been prominent in creating the domestic support necessary for active U.S. involvement in world affairs.

Part II, Relationships, focuses attention on the impact that a post–Cold War world can be expected to exert on U.S. relationships with its former adversaries and allies in Europe and Asia and on Third World nations once courted as potential partisans by the superpowers. The future of the North Atlantic Treaty Organization (NATO), the cornerstone of American foreign policy since early in the post–World War II era, figures prominently in the various discussions. The critical importance of economic issues in shaping U.S. security relationships with others is also highlighted.

Part III, Capabilities, critically examines ideas about the military means and intelligence capabilities appropriate to the realization of U.S. foreign policy objectives in the emerging global order. Issues that challenge American leadership in international economic affairs are also examined. Central to the discussion is the ability of the United States to match its capabilities to its commitments. We therefore conclude the book with three essays that explicitly focus on the heated debate about the alleged decline of American power in world affairs and its consequences for the future of American foreign policy.

NOTES

1. George F. Kennan ["X"], "The Sources of Soviet Conduct," *Foreign Affairs* 25 (July 1947), p. 582.

2. See Charles W. Kegley, Jr., and Eugene R. Wittkopf, *American Foreign Policy: Pattern and Process,* 4th ed. (New York: St. Martin's Press, 1991).

3. Stanley Hoffmann, "What Should We Do in the World?" *Atlantic* 264 (October 1989), p. 84.

Part I: OBJECTIVES

In 1941 Henry Luce, the noted editor and publisher of *Time*, *Life*, and *Fortune*, envisioned his time as the dawn of "the American century." The prediction was based on Luce's conviction that "only America can effectively state the aims of this war [World War II]," which included, under American leadership, "a vital international economy" and "an international moral order."[1] Fifty years later, in a State of the Union Address that followed shortly on the heels of the initiation of war against Iraq, George Bush spoke repeatedly of the "next American century" in which the "rule of law" would reign supreme in the "new world order." Like Henry Luce, Bush extolled America's leadership role, urging that "only the United States of America has the moral leadership, and the means to back it up." "As Americans, we know there are times when we must step forward and accept our responsibility to lead the world away from the dark chaos of dictators, toward the brighter promise of a better day."

Bush's vision embraced the tradition of moral idealism long evident in American foreign policy, but especially since Woodrow Wilson sought early in this century to create "a world safe for democracy." Bush's words also harked back to the 1940s when the United States and the Soviet Union stood shoulder to shoulder, first in opposing Nazi Germany and later in seeking to build a structure of peace premised on the continued cooperation of the wartime allies. Still, hubris in the belief that the United States alone now had a special responsibility for creating the new world order was only thinly disguised. Shortly after Iraq's invasion of Kuwait, for example, former Assistant Secretary of Defense Richard L. Armitage boasted that "those who so recently predicted America's imminent decline must now acknowledge that the United States alone possess [sic] sufficient moral, economic, political, and military horsepower to jump-start and drive international efforts to curb international lawlessness."[2]

In a similar vein, syndicated columnist Charles Krauthammer portrayed this as the "unipolar moment." "The center of world power [in the immediate post–Cold War world] is the unchallenged superpower, the United States," he wrote. "There is but one first-rate power and no prospect in the immediate future of any power to rival it. . . . American preeminence is based on the fact that it is the only country with the military, diplomatic, political and economic assets to be a decisive player in any conflict in whatever part of the world it chooses to involve itself."[3]

Arrogance about the unipolar moment paralleled the earlier exhilaration evident in the notion that communist ideology had failed and that democracy had emerged triumphant.[4] The theme, which was repeated often by members of the Bush administration during its first months in office, was given special intellectual currency by Francis Fukuyama, deputy director of the State Department's policy planning staff, who argued that political and economic liberalism had emerged the victor over its challengers. In consequence, he wrote, "What we may be witnessing is not just the end of the Cold War, or the passing of a particular period of postwar history, but the end of history as such: that is, the end point of mankind's ideological evolution and the universalization of Western liberal democracy as the final form of human government."[5]

The optimism about the future of American foreign policy implicit in these viewpoints must be tempered by another vision that comes out of the 1940s. This one is associated with the eminent political commentator and journalist Walter Lippmann who, in 1943, observed that "foreign policy consists of bringing into balance . . . the nation's commitments and the nation's power."[6] Coping with the "Lippmann gap," to use Samuel P. Huntington's felicitous phrase,[7] has become a widespread concern. As argued by James Chace, a former managing editor of *Foreign Affairs*, the United States "is becoming more ordinary, more like the others, and increasingly subject to unaccustomed constraints." Having failed for more than two decades to pursue a "solvent" foreign policy, Chace contends, "the central question now is how to manage domestic and foreign affairs to bring about a sustainable foreign policy."[8]

In a similar vein, historian Paul Kennedy provoked a storm of controversy about the ends and means of policy with his 1987 treatise, *The Rise and Fall of the Great Powers*, which became a national best-seller. "Although the United States is at present still in a class of its own economically and perhaps even militarily," Kennedy wrote, "it cannot avoid confronting the two great tests which challenge the *longevity* of every major power that occupies the 'number one' position in world affairs: whether it can preserve a reasonable balance between the nation's perceived defense requirements and the means it possesses to maintain those commitments; and whether . . . it can preserve the technological and economic bases of its power from relative erosion in the face of ever-shifting patterns of global production."[9]   The danger, he warned, is similar to that faced by hegemonic powers in earlier historical periods, notably the Spanish at the turn of the seventeenth century and the British at the turn of the twentieth.   "The United States now runs the risk . . . of . . . 'imperial overstretch': that is to say, decision-makers in Washington must face the awkward and enduring fact that the sum total of the United States' global interests and obligations is nowadays far larger than the country's power to defend them all simultaneously."[10]

Even those who reject the thesis of "imperial overstretch" worry about the solvency of the United States.   Krauthammer, for example, responds to the question "Can America long sustain its unipolar preeminence?"   with the observation that "an American collapse to second-rank status will be not for foreign but for domestic reasons. . . . America's low savings rate, poor educational system, stagnant productivity, declining work habits, rising demand for welfare-state entitlements and new taste for ecological luxuries have nothing at all to do with engagement in Europe, Central America or the Middle East. . . . What created an economy of debt unrivaled in American history is not foreign adventures but the low tax ideology of the 1980s, coupled with America's insatiable desire for yet higher standards of living without paying the cost."[11]

What should be the objectives of American foreign policy in the new world environment policymakers face abroad, given the constraints they encounter at home?   Fear of communism and Soviet expansionism galvanized domestic support for global activism in the years following World War II.   The radical geopolitical changes that have occurred since the late 1980s open these motivating objectives to scrutiny as the nation confronts its interests and purposes in a way not matched since the early years of the Cold War nearly a half century ago.

DEFINING AMERICA'S INTERESTS

For more than forty years, containment of the Soviet Union dominated the foreign policy of the United States.   The principle derives from President Harry S Truman's declaration in 1947 that "it must be the policy of the United States to support free peoples who are resisting attempted subjugation by armed minorities or by outside pressures."   It is too simple—and simplistic—to suggest that nothing else animated the nation's approach toward world affairs, but no principle has been more important in explaining American foreign policy conduct for a half century.   Containing communism and the threat of Soviet expansionism whenever and wherever they might appear were the overriding objectives.   Thus, globalism, anticommunism, and containment were inextricably intertwined as defining elements of America's post–World War II grand strategy.

What should America's grand strategy in the post–Cold War world be?

We begin our search for an answer with an essay by the eminent diplomatic historian John Lewis Gaddis, "Toward the Post–Cold War World."

Gaddis provides a panoramic view of the environment confronting the United States now that the Cold War has ended. Arguing that the geopolitical map that provided a lens for viewing world politics during the Cold War— framed as a contest between democracy and totalitarianism—may no longer be usable, Gaddis describes the new cartography as a contest between the forces of integration and disintegration. Each force subsumes a number of prevailing global trends with which the United States must grapple as it seeks to protect American national interests in a changed and changing world. These forces range from the emergence of a potential new superpower in the form of a consolidated European Community and an ascendant Germany, to the revival of nationalism and the protectionist policies it rationalizes, the resurgence of fundamentalist religious movements, and the emergence of ecological threats in the form of global warming and excessive population pressures. The new geopolitical landscape can be encapsulated as a com- petition between the forces of integration and disintegration. As Gaddis argues the end . . . of the Cold War brings not an end to threats, but rather a diffusion of them, as "one can no longer plausibly point to a single source of danger, as one could throughout most of [the Cold War]."

How might the United States best safeguard its interests in this emergent post–Cold War world? Gaddis examines alternatives for enhancing the bases on which American security rests with respect to several specific issues: the reconstruction of the Soviet Union and Eastern Europe; the creation of new security and economic structures for Europe; the deterrence of aggression of the sort symbolized by Saddam Hussein's attack on Kuwait; the costs and benefits of economic and political integration; and the resuscitation of do- mestic financial solvency.

As Gaddis takes care to explain, the post–Cold War environment defies easy characterization, which explains why the debate over the future of Amer- ican foreign policy often leads to widely divergent prescriptions. The basis for these divergent viewpoints is the primary concern of the second essay. In "Entangled Forever," Josef Joffe examines the commonly held view that the West's victory over communism will lay to rest the U.S. obsession with the spearhead of the so-called communist challenge, the Soviet Union. Many observers, adhering to the view that the Cold War was rooted primarily in ideological incompatibilities, assume that the repudiation of communism in the Soviet Union and Eastern Europe simultaneously removed the sources of animosity toward the Soviet Union and policymakers' obsession with Amer- ica's ideological foe. Not necessarily so, Joffe argues. Communism may be dead, but the logic of *realpolitik* continues. In Joffe's words, "The death of communism spells neither the birth of a new order nor the end of conflict." The Soviet Union remains formidable, new centers of power are emerging, and new conflicts are coming to the fore as the Cold War conflict recedes. Thus, the United States cannot return to isolationism, despite the Soviet

Union's rejection of communism and its withdrawal from competition for global influence. Instead, the United States must continue to bear the burden and exercise the responsibility of power, for it remains "entangled forever."

Whether the United States will follow Joffe's prescription depends on the outcome of the third debate on the role of the United States in world affairs. Robert W. Tucker examines two competing viewpoints in this debate in his essay, "1989 and All That." One is reflected in the view of those who believe the United States "should once again play a more modest role in the world," the other in the view of those who believe that its "post–World War II role must be held up as a model for the future." The case for each view is compelling, and Tucker's tightly constructed logic makes it difficult to determine which is likely to prevail. Events such as the Persian Gulf War and changes in the behavior of the Soviet Union may ultimately prove decisive in tipping the balance in favor of one or the other.

PREPARING FOR A MULTIPOLAR WORLD

The United States emerged from World War II as the single most powerful nation in the world. Eventually, the Soviet Union would rival the United States militarily, thus giving rise to a bipolar power configuration, but for a brief time the United States was the sole pole of power.

As noted previously, the end of the Cold War may signal that the United States has once more emerged as the world's single dominant actor. It is the hegemonic power to which other nations in the Northern Hemisphere will turn for leadership, according to this viewpoint, as they did in the case of the crisis over Kuwait and the Persian Gulf War. "The unipolar moment means that with the close of the century's three great Northern civil wars (World War I, World War II and the Cold War) an ideologically pacified North seeks security and order by aligning its foreign policy behind that of the United States," argues Krauthammer. "That is what is taking shape . . . in the Persian Gulf. And for the future, it is the shape of things to come."[12]

An emergent multipolarity is more commonly anticipated. In this world, as power comes to be distributed relatively equally among four or five great powers, new centers of power—for example, Germany, Japan, China, and a united Europe—will emerge to challenge the dominance of the United States.

Historical experience suggests that when power is distributed equally, political relationships are typically fluid and subject to change. Each player in the game is assertive, independent, and distrustful of the motives of the others; diplomacy displays a rational, nonideological, chesslike character; alliances and alignments are unstable and of short duration; and conflict is intense as each contender for predominance nervously fears the power accumulation of the other challengers and seeks to protect itself from their domination by struggling for its own supremacy. Historically, periods of multipolar balance-of-power politics have typically ended in global war, which resolves the contest by creating a victorious new world leader, as happened after World War II.

By way of contrast, the bipolar era following World War II was remarkably peaceful. To be sure, crises were endemic, interventions in the Third World were frequent and often bloody, and the fear of widespread destruction was always present, but systemwide war among the great powers did not occur. Paradoxically, the perpetual competition and enormous destructive power in the hands of the contestants produced caution and stability rather than reck-lessness and war. Thus, the half century following World War II is appro-priately characterized as the era of the long peace.[13]

The apparent advantages of bipolarity over multipolarity lead John J. Mearsheimer to examine "Why We Will Soon Miss the Cold War." His attention is on Europe, where the Cold War began and ended but whose fate is now uncertain. Mearsheimer's examination of the reasons for prolonged peace in Europe reinforces the conclusions that bipolar systems tend to be stable and that nuclear weapons breed caution. If these restraints are lifted and Europe reverts to multipolarity, he warns, a new era of major crises and wars will follow.

Some maintain that European economic interdependence may anchor sta-bility and that peace will be strengthened further because Europe's liberal democracies are unlikely to wage war against one another. Mearsheimer suggests, however, that these theories, too, are inapplicable to an emergent multipolar world. He also predicts that more European countries, including possibly the united Germany, will seek nuclear arsenals if the superpowers reduce their presence on the Continent. Mearsheimer shows that under conditions in which nuclear weapons are removed from Europe and a nuclear-free zone is created, or such weapons proliferate on the Continent, the prob-able outcome will be the same: war will eventually erupt. By implication, the United States should prepare itself to preserve the conditions that gave rise to the long peace. This speaks to a continuing American presence in the European theater and a renewed commitment to manage it.

Earl C. Ravenal also examines the implications of the changing structure of the international system in his essay, "The Case for Adjustment." Ravenal depicts the future that policymakers face as "not merely a choice among foreign policy alternatives, but literally a choice of worlds—alternative states of the international system." In his view, the choice is nothing less than giving up America's post–World War II penchant to seek to control its adversary (the Soviet Union) and the global system writ large. Acting as a global gendarme, American policymakers are alleged to have indulged "in the conceit that they were immune . . . from the constraints of the interna-tional system." The time has now come to jettison that illusion of autonomy and power, Ravenal argues, and adjust American policy to the basic reality that "the shape of the entire system—as well as the conduct of the individual members—is moving beyond the determinative reach of either the United

States or the Soviet Union." Contrary to Joffe, Ravenal argues that America is not preordained to remain "entangled forever" in the affairs of others or in the quest for world leadership because "the age of the superpowers is passing." Ravenal recommends a new course that accommodates the United States to the diffusion of power based on a set of noninterventionist principles for a post–Cold War system that seeks to close the perceived gap between the nation's resources and its commitments.

NEW AGENDAS IN A CHANGING WORLD

To those persuaded by the logic of *realpolitik*, the end of the Cold War requires no fundamental redefinition of American interests and policies—the search for power, prestige, and position should continue in much the same way it has been pursued since the post–World War II grand strategy was put into place in the late 1940s. "I know of no change in policy, only of circumstances" was the way Secretary of State John Quincy Adams in 1823 extolled the primacy of power as a principle of statecraft.

To others, the passing of the Cold War permits problems other than the containment of communism and Soviet expansionism to now receive greater attention. As William G. Hyland put it in 1990, "Now, for the first time in half a century, the United States has the opportunity to reconstruct its foreign policy free of most of the constraints and pressures of the Cold War."[14] Under such circumstances, Hyland continues, the main questions are these: "For what purpose and to what end should America commit its awesome power and resources? What will be the new priorities for a post-containment foreign policy, and which instruments will be most effective?"[15]

Opinions about the purposes most advantageous to the United States in the post–Cold War world diverge widely. In "Rethinking National Security: Democracy and Economic Independence," Theodore C. Sorensen argues for a thorough rethinking of the concept of national security. Perceiving a "conceptual vacuum" to be present in Washington policy-making circles, Sorensen urges that a prudent redefinition of America's national interests calls for "the preservation of this nation's economic effectiveness and independence in the global marketplace, and the peaceful enhancement of democracy around the world." Neither requires retrenchment nor withdrawal from the world scene; on the contrary, both necessitate global activism but are much less costly than the defense-oriented anti-Soviet policies of the Cold War era. Sorensen assesses the reasons behind these prescriptions and the conditions that make them compelling roads to the enhancement of U.S. national security.

Economic revitalization has commanded widespread attention in recent years, and until the outbreak of the Persian Gulf War, the Bush administration often extolled the need to promote democracy abroad, facts that suggest Sorensen's prescriptions are views widely shared among policymakers and other elites concerned with the objectives of American foreign policy in the post–Cold War world. Still, other potential goals contend for prominence and position on the new foreign policy agenda. The world beyond U.S. borders is fraught with many pressing problems that arguably demand attention along with the quest for economic revitalization and the promotion of democratic institutions. For example, American welfare and security are threatened not merely by the weapons of adversaries such as Iraq's Saddam Hussein, but by international debt, drug trafficking, population growth, resource scarcities, and the widening gap between the world's rich and poor (and the suffering, injustice, and external aggression those deprivations often create).

Especially ominous in the eyes of many observers are the host of ecological problems associated with worldwide environmental degradation and global warming. In "Preserving the Global Environment: Implications for U.S. Policy," Jessica Tuchman Mathews describes two broad political strategies for promoting collective environmental problem solving at the international level. One, the "quantum leap approach," "emphasizes the immensity of the problems, and . . . urges vast, bold policy leaps . . . to capture attention and to galvanize support for action." The other, "ambitious incrementalism," "emphasizes the relatively modest steps needed to weave environmental concerns into the fabric of mainstream economic and foreign policy." Mathews concludes that the latter strategy "is more likely to permanently change the policy context" and proceeds to catalog the steps the United States must take to exercise a leadership role on the emerging environmental agenda of the future. Many steps will require rethinking the nation's foreign policy priorities at home as well as abroad.

NEW AGENDAS IN DOMESTIC POLITICS

Part of the answer to the puzzle surrounding how American leaders are likely to set the nation's foreign policy priorities in the wake of the Cold War— that is, where the clues reside to predict if and how the United States will adjust its foreign policies to the emergent post–Cold War international system—can be found in domestic policies: the ways in which the United States organizes itself for making foreign policy choices, and the internal political and institutional pressures that influence its decision-making procedures and outcomes. In an interdependent world, foreign policy is an extension of domestic policy, and the two realms are inextricably intertwined. How the United States chooses to respond to the advent of a new geopolitical environment will therefore be fundamentally affected not just by the characteristics of that emergent system but also by domestic priorities.

In "Is the United States Capable of Acting Strategically? Congress and the President," Aaron L. Friedberg asks how recent changes and continuities in both America's external and internal political environments will affect the ability of the United States to make adaptive adjustments to new global realities. He is concerned that the diffusion of foreign policy responsibility between Congress and the president poses barriers to effective policy planning and implementation in three broad issue areas—trade, defense, and diplomacy—that increasingly require "strategic action" on the part of the United States if it is to promote its foreign policy interests and objectives effectively. Friedberg concludes by prescribing three "cures" or approaches with which "the United States can cope with the limitations imposed by the dispersal of domestic authority over its foreign policy."

America's future foreign policy objectives, and possible redirections in them, will be influenced not only by interactions between Congress and the president but also by developments in the larger domestic political system. In "Post–Cold War Politics," Norman J. Ornstein and Mark Schmitt evaluate how the end of the Cold War is likely to impact American politics and the issues regarded as salient on the domestic political agenda. "How will the U.S. political system operate without anticommunism as its central organizing principle?" they ask. The question is especially pertinent to the Republican party, for which anticommunism has been a foreign policy staple since early in the post–World War II era.

Ornstein and Schmitt's far-reaching survey explores probable outcomes for partisan politics as anticommunism recedes and alternative foreign policy issues vie for prominence in the thinking of party elites and their followers. Particularly inviting as they survey the issues and positions likely to dominate the domestic debate is the possibility that the two political parties could play a role in framing new policy objectives. They postulate, for example, that "the domestic political message of extending democracy's reach could be linked to economic nationalism in a way that could give it a more positive gloss." Also treated is a possible return to isolationism and the equally compelling counter-thesis that the American people crave a "big ambition" that could reorient "American political life toward a new global purpose."

Of similar importance in determining how various scenarios regarding the objectives of American foreign policy might unfold will be changes in the thinking and opinions of the American public. How critical a role public opinion plays in the policy process has long been disputed, but the ubiquity of polling in contemporary America is testimony to the importance American policymakers attach to what American people think and what they are thinking about. And some of what they have been learning has been startling indeed, including, for example, the finding that the American people had come—even before the Berlin Wall fell—to see Japan, not the Soviet Union, and nonmilitary issues, not military ones, as the principal threats to American national security.[16]

In our final selection in Part I, "Public Opinion: The Pulse of the '90s," John E. Rielly discusses recent trends in Americans' foreign policy attitudes. Basing his discussion on late 1990 surveys of opinion leaders and the mass public that extend a series of well-known and widely followed polls, Rielly documents important shifts in attitudes since the collapse of communism and the demise of Soviet power. The results reinforced earlier findings from other surveys that demonstrated the American people no longer saw the Soviet Union as the principal threat; instead, a majority believed that the former adversary is one of the three leading countries in which the United States has a vital interest. Equally revealing, both the public and American leaders believed that despite the Persian Gulf crisis—in its fourth month at the time the surveys were completed—domestic problems still posed a grave threat to the United States. These opinions can be expected to shape the proposals politicians make to the people they lead and on whom they depend for election. Hence, the end of the Cold War will change not only America's posture toward the world beyond its borders but also the setting of domestic priorities.

NOTES

1. Cited in Walter LeFeber, *The American Age: United States Foreign Policy at Home and Abroad since 1750* (New York: Norton, 1989), p. 380.

2. Cited in Michael T. Klare, "The New World War," *Progressive* 54 (November 1990), p. 16.

3. Charles Krauthammer, "The Unipolar Moment," *Foreign Affairs* 70 (No. 1, 1991), pp. 23, 24. See also Charles Krauthammer, "Universal Dominion: Toward a Unipolar World," *National Interest* 18 (Winter 1989–90), pp. 46–49.

4. The theme of "democracy on the march" has been applied by American policy-makers not only to the Soviet Union and its allies but to a number of other world regions as well. The trend toward democracy worldwide and strategies for propelling it forward are discussed in Larry Diamond, "Beyond Authoritarianism and Totalitarianism: Strategies for Democratization," *Washington Quarterly* 12 (Winter 1989), pp. 141–63.

5. Francis Fukuyama, "The End of History?" *National Interest* 16 (Summer 1989), p. 4.

6. Walter Lippmann, *U.S. Foreign Policy: Shield of the Republic* (Boston: Little, Brown, 1943), p. 9.

7. Samuel P. Huntington, "Coping with the Lippmann Gap," *Foreign Affairs* 66 (No. 3, 1988), pp. 453–477.

8. James Chace, "A New Grand Strategy," *Foreign Policy* 70 (Spring 1988), p. 3.

9. Paul Kennedy, *The Rise and Fall of the Great Powers: Economic Change and Military Conflict from 1500 to 2000* (New York: Random House, 1987), pp. 514–15.

10. Kennedy, p. 515.

11. Krauthammer, "The Unipolar Moment," pp. 26–27.

12. Krauthammer, "The Unipolar Moment," p. 25.

13. See, among others, John Lewis Gaddis, *The Long Peace: Inquiries into the History of the Cold War* (New York: Oxford University Press, 1987); and Charles W. Kegley, Jr. (ed.), *The Long Postwar Peace* (New York: HarperCollins, 1991).

14. William G. Hyland, "America's New Course," *Foreign Affairs* 69 (Spring 1990), p. 1.

15. Hyland, p. 2.

16. See Americans Talk Security, *Compendium: Results from Twelve National Surveys on National Security Issues Conducted from October 1987 to December 1988* (Boston: Americans Talk Security, n.d.), pp. 287, 9.

1 TOWARD THE POST–COLD WAR WORLD

John Lewis Gaddis

I

For the first time in over half a century, no single great power, or coalition of powers, poses a "clear and present danger" to the national security of the United States. The end of the Cold War has left Americans in the fortunate position of being without an obvious major adversary. Given the costs of confronting adversaries who have been all too obvious since the beginning of World War II, that is a condition worthy of greater appreciation than it has so far received.

It would be foolish to claim, though, that the United States after 1991 can return to the role it played in world affairs before 1941. For as the history of the 1930s suggests, the absence of imminent threat is no guarantee that threats do not exist. Nor will the isolationism of that era be possible in the 1990s. Advances in military technology and the progress of economic integration have long since removed the insulation from the rest of the world that geographical distance used to provide. The passing of the Cold War world by no means implies an end to American involvement in whatever world is to follow; it only means that the nature and the extent of that involvement are not yet clear.

Finding one's way through unfamiliar terrain generally requires a map of some sort. Cartography, like cognition itself, is a necessary simplification that allows us to see where we are, and where we may be going. The assertion that the world was divided between the forces of democracy and those of totalitarianism—to use the precise distinction made in President Harry S Truman's announcement of the Truman Doctrine—was of course a vast simplification of what was actually happening in 1947. But it was probably a necessary one: it was an exercise in geopolitical cartography that depicted

16

the international landscape in terms everyone could understand, and so doing prepared the way for the more sophisticated strategy of containment that was soon to follow.

The end of the Cold War was too sweeping a defeat for totalitarianism— and too sweeping a victory for democracy—for this old geopolitical map to be of use any longer.   But another form of competition has been emerging that could be just as stark and just as pervasive as was the rivalry between democracy and totalitarianism at the height of the Cold War: it is the contest between forces of integration and fragmentation in the contemporary international environment.   The search for a new geopolitical cartography might well begin here.

II

I use the term "integration" in its most general sense, which is the act of bringing things together to constitute something that is whole.   It involves breaking down barriers that have historically separated nations and peoples in such diverse areas as politics, economics, religion, technology and culture. It means, quite literally, the approach to what we might call—echoing some of the most visionary language of World War II—one world.

Integration is happening in a variety of ways.   Consider, first, the communications revolution, which has made it impossible for any nation to deny its citizens knowledge of what is going on elsewhere.   This is a new condition in international politics, the importance of which became clear as revolution swept through eastern Europe in the fall of 1989.   A new kind of domino theory has emerged, in which the achievement of liberty in one country causes repressive regimes to topple, or at least to wobble, in others.   Integration through communications has largely brought this about.

Consider, next, economics.   These days, no nation—not even the Soviet Union, or China, or South Africa or Iraq—can maintain itself apart from the rest of the world for very long.   That is because individual nations depend, for their own prosperity, upon the prosperity of others to a far greater extent than in the past.   Integration also means that transnational actors like multinational corporations and economic cartels can have a powerful influence on what happens to national states.   And in Europe, integration has led to the creation of a potential new superpower in the form of the European Community (EC).   Europe as a whole, not just Britain, France or Germany, is already a major player in the world economy, and it may soon become one in world politics as well.

Consider, as a third manifestation of integration, security.   It used to be the case that nations relied exclusively upon their own strength to ensure their safety, and that is still primarily the case.   But Woodrow Wilson began the movement toward collective security after World War I with his proposal for a League of Nations, and although that organization proved ineffective, it did give rise to a United Nations that in recent years has become a major force in international diplomacy. It is significant that the United States waited to gain U.N. approval before using force in the Persian Gulf. Washington has not always been so solicitous in the past, and the fact that the Bush administration proceeded in this way suggests that is has come to see important advantages in the collective approach, which is to say the integrative approach, to security.

Then consider the integration of ideas. The combination of easy communications, unprecedented prosperity and freedom from war—which is, after all, the combination the Cold War gave us—made possible yet another integrationist phenomenon: ideas now flow more freely throughout the world than ever before. This trend has had a revolutionary effect in certain authoritarian countries, where governments found they had to educate their populations in order to continue to compete in a global economy, only to discover that the act of educating them exposed their minds to the realm of ideas and ultimately worked to undermine the legitimacy of authoritarianism itself.[1] The consequences can be seen in Chinese students who prefer statues of liberty to statues of Mao, in Soviet parliamentarians who routinely harangue their own leaders on national television and in the remarkable sight of the ... president of Czechoslovakia [Václav Havel]—himself a living symbol of the power of ideas—lecturing the Congress of the United States on the virtues of Jeffersonian democracy.

Finally, consider peace. It has long been a central assumption of liberal political philosophers that if only one could maximize the flow of ideas, commodities, capital and people across international boundaries, then the causes of war would drop away. It was for a long time an idea based more on faith than on reality. But there is some reason to think that a by-product of integration since 1945 has indeed been peace, at least among the great powers. The prosperity associated with market economics tends to encourage the growth of liberal democracies; and one of the few patterns that holds up throughout modern history is that liberal democracies do not go to war with one another.[2] From this perspective, then, the old nineteenth-century liberal vision of a peaceful, integrated, interdependent and capitalist world may at last be coming true.

III

Would that it were so. Unfortunately, the forces of integration are not the only ones active in the world today. There are also forces of fragmentation at work that are resurrecting old barriers between nations and peoples—and creating new ones—even as others are tumbling. Some of these forces have begun to manifest themselves with unexpected strength, just when it looked as though integration was about to prevail. The most important of them is nationalism.

There is, to be sure, nothing new about nationalism. Given that the past half century has seen the number of sovereign states more than triple, it can hardly be said that nationalism was in a state of suspended animation during the Cold War. Still, many observers did have the sense that, among the great powers at least, nationalism after World War II had been on the wane.

The very existence of two rival superpowers, which is really to say, two supranational powers, created this impression. We rarely thought of the Cold War as a conflict between competing Soviet and American nationalism: we saw it, rather, as a contest between two great international ideologies, or between two antagonistic military blocs, or between two geographical regions we imprecisely labeled "East" and "West." One could even argue that the Cold War discouraged nationalism, particularly in western Europe and the Mediterranean, where the mutual need to contain the Soviet Union moderated old animosities like those between the French and the Germans, or the Greeks and the Turks, or the British and everybody else. Much the same thing happened, although by different and more brutal means, in eastern Europe, where Moscow used the Warsaw Pact to suppress long-simmering feuds between the Hungarians and the Romanians, or the Czechs and the Poles, or the (East) Germans and everybody else. Nationalism might still exist in other parts of the world, we used to tell each other, but it had become a historical curiosity in Europe. There were even those who argued, until quite recently, that the Germans had become such good Europeans that they were now virtually immune to nationalist appeals and so had lost whatever interest they might once have had in reunification.

Today the situation looks very different. Germany has reunified, and no one—particularly no one living alongside that new state—is quite sure of the consequences. Romanians and Hungarians threaten each other regularly now that the Warsaw Pact is defunct, and nationalist sentiments are manifesting themselves elsewhere in eastern and southeastern Europe, particularly in Yugoslavia, which appears to be on the verge of breaking up.

The same thing could even happen to the Soviet Union itself: nationalist pressures the regime thought it had smothered as far back as seven decades ago are coming to the forefront once again, to such an extent that we can no longer take for granted the continued existence of that country in the form that we have known it.

Nor should we assume that the West is immune from the fragmenting effects of nationalism. The Irish question ought to be a perpetual reminder of their durability; there is also the Basque problem in Spain, and the rivalry between the Flemings and the Walloons in Belgium. The American presence in the Philippines is becoming increasingly tenuous in the face of growing nationalism, and similar pressures are building in South Korea. Nationalism is even becoming an issue in Japan, what with recent controversies over the treatment of World War II in Japanese history textbooks and the Shinto ceremonies that officially began the reign of the Emperor Akihito. It is worth recalling as well how close the Canadian confederation came in 1990 to breaking up—as it yet may—over the separatist aspirations of Quebec. There was even a point [in 1990] when the Mohawk Indians were demanding, from Quebec no less, recognition of their own rights as a sovereign state.

But the forces of fragmentation do not just take the form of pressures for self-determination, formidable though those may be. They also show up in the field of economics, where they manifest themselves as protectionism: the effort, by various means, to insulate individual economies from the workings of world market forces. They show up in the racial tension that can develop, both among states and within them: the recent killings of blacks by blacks in South Africa, after the release of Nelson Mandela, illustrates the problem clearly.

They certainly show up in the area of religion. The resurgence of Islam might be seen by some as an integrationist force in the Middle East. But it is surely fragmentationist to the extent that it seeks to set that particular region off from the rest of the world by reviving ancient and not-so-ancient grievances against the West, both real and imagined. Forces of fragmentation can even show up as a simple drive for power, which is the only way I can make sense out of the fiendishly complex events that have torn Lebanon apart since the civil war began there in 1975. One can look at Beirut as it has been for the past decade and a half and get a good sense of what the world would look like if the forces of fragmentation should ultimately have their way.

Fragmenting tendencies are also on the rise—they have never been wholly absent—within American society itself. It would be difficult to underestimate the disintegrative effects of the drug crisis in this country, or of the breakdown of our system for elementary and secondary education, or of the emergence of what appears to be a permanent social and economic "underclass." Well-intentioned efforts to decrease racial and sexual discrimination have increased racial and sexual—as well as constitutional—tensions.[3] Linguistic anxieties lurk just beneath the surface, as the movement to make English the official language of the United States suggests. Immigration may well be increasing at a faster rate than cultural assimilation, which in itself has been a less than perfect process. Regional rivalries are developing over such issues as energy costs, pollution control and the bailout of the savings and loan industry. And the rise of special interest groups, together with their ability to apply instant pressure through instant communications, has thrown American politics into such disarray that elections are reduced to the unleashing of attack videos, and the preparation of the budget has come to resemble the endless haggling of rug merchants in some Oriental bazaar. When the leading light of American conservatism has to call for a return to a sense of *collective* interest, then the forces of fragmentation have proceeded very far indeed.[4]

All of this suggests that the problems we will confront in the post–Cold War world are more likely to arise from competing processes—integration versus fragmentation—than from the kinds of competing ideological visions that dominated the Cold War. Unlike the old rivalry between democracy and totalitarianism, though, the new geopolitical cartography provides no immediately obvious answer to the question of which of these processes might most threaten the future security interests of the United States.

IV

It would appear, at first glance, that the forces of integration ought to be the more benign. Those forces brought the Cold War to an end. They provided the basis for the relative prosperity that most of the developed world enjoyed during that conflict, and they offer the most plausible method of extending that prosperity into the post–Cold War era. They combine materialism and idealism in a way that seems natural to Americans, who tend to combine these traits in their own national character. And they hold out the promise of an international order in which collective, not unilateral, security becomes the norm.

But is the trend toward integration consistent with the traditional American interest, dating back to the Founding Fathers, in the balancing of power? Has that interest become obsolete in the new world that we now confront? The longstanding American commitment to the balance of power was based on the assumption that the nation would survive most comfortably in a world of diversity, not uniformity: in a homogeneous world, presumably, one would not need to balance power at all. No one would claim that the progress of integration has brought us anywhere close to such a world. Still, the contradiction that exists between the acts of balancing and integrating power ought to make us look carefully at the post–Cold War geopolitical map. Jumping to conclusions—in favor of either integrationist or fragmentationist alternatives—could be a mistake.

Consider the long-term ecological problems we are likely to face. The prospect of global warming looms as a constraint upon future economic development conducted in traditional—which is to say, polluting—ways. Integration here, in the form of expanding industrialization and enhanced agricultural productivity, has created a new kind of danger. The worldwide AIDS epidemic illustrates how one integrative force, the increasing flow of people across international boundaries, can undermine the effects of another, which is the progress made toward the conquest of disease. Population pressure, itself the result of progress in agricultural productivity and in conquering disease, is in turn magnifying disparities in living standards that already exist in certain parts of the world, with potentially disintegrative results. The forces of integration, therefore, provide no automatic protection against ecological threats: indeed, they are part of the problem. Despite classical liberal assumptions, we would be unwise in assuming that an ever-increasing flow of people, commodities and technology across international borders will necessarily, at least from the ecological standpoint, make the world a safer place.

Consider, next, the future of Europe. The reunification of Germany, together with the enfeeblement and possible breakup of the Soviet Union, is one of the most abrupt realignments of political, military and economic power in modern history.   It has come about largely as a result of those integrative forces that ended the Cold War: the much-celebrated triumph of democratic politics and market economics.[5]   And yet, this victory for liberalism in Europe is producing both integrative and disintegrative consequences.   In Germany, demands for self-determination have brought political integration, to be sure, but the economic effects could be disintegrative.   There are concerns now over whether the progress the EC has made toward removing trade and immigration barriers will be sufficient to tie the newly unified Germany firmly to the West; or whether the new Germany will build its own center of power further to the east, with the risk that this might undo the anticipated benefits of 1992.

In the Soviet Union, the triumph of liberalism has had profoundly disintegrative consequences.   The central government faces the possibility of becoming irrelevant as power diffuses down to the level of the republics, and even below.   No one knows what the future political configuration, to say nothing of ideological orientation, of the potential successor states might be. Civil war, and even international war growing out of civil war, are by no means unrealistic prospects; such disruptions would be all the more dangerous because the Soviet Union's massive arsenal of nuclear and conventional weapons will not disappear, even if the Soviet Union itself does.[6]   The future of Europe, in short, is not at all clear, and it is the increasing tension between processes of integration and fragmentation that has suddenly made the picture there so cloudy.

Then consider the Middle East and Africa.   The combination of German reunification with Soviet collapse, if it occurs, will involve the most dramatic changes in international boundaries since the end of World War II.   And yet no one seems to be thinking about what precedents this might set for other parts of the world where boundaries inherited from the colonial era do not even come close to coinciding with patterns of ethnicity, nationality or religion.   If the Lithuanians are to get their own state, it will not be easy to explain to the Palestinians or the Kurds or the Eritreans why they should not have theirs also.   If the boundaries of the dying Soviet empire are to be revised, then why should boundaries established by empires long since dead be preserved?

Finally, consider the Iraqi invasion of Kuwait.   It was Iraq's integration into the international market in sophisticated military technology that made it possible for Saddam Hussein to perform this act of aggression.   His arsenal of chemical and biological weapons, to say nothing of his surface-to-air-missiles, Scuds, Mirages, the nuclear weapons he probably would have had if the Israelis had not bombed his reactor in 1981 and the long-range artillery he certainly would have had if the British had not become suspicious of his orders for very thick "oil pipes" early in 1990—all of this hardware was not forged by ingenious and self-reliant Iraqi craftsmen, working tirelessly along the banks of the Euphrates. Saddam obtained it, rather, by exploiting an important consequence of integration, which is the inability or unwillingness of highly industrialized states to control what their own entrepreneurs, even those involved in the sale of lethal commodities, do to turn a profit.

The global energy market—another integrationist phenomenon—created the riches that made Kuwait such a tempting target in the first place; it also brought about the dependence on Middle Eastern oil that caused so rapid a military response on the part of the United States, its allies and even some of their former adversaries. The eagerness of this improbable coalition to defend the principle of collective security would hardly have been as great if Benin had attacked Burkina Faso, or vice versa.

There is, of course, no assurance that Saddam Hussein would have refrained from invading Kuwait if the Cold War had been at its height. But there is a fair chance that either the United States or the Soviet Union—depending upon which superpower Iraq was aligned with at the time—would have sought to exert a restraining influence, if only to keep its principal rival from exploiting the situation to its own advantage. Certainly distractions associated with the end of the Cold War in Europe during the first half of 1990 prevented both Washington and Moscow from giving the attention they should have to Persian Gulf affairs.

It is also worth remembering that the first post—Cold War year [1990] saw, in addition to the Iraqi occupation of Kuwait, the near-outbreak of war between India and Pakistan, an intensification of tension between Israel and its Arab neighbors, a renewed Syrian drive to impose control over Lebanon and a violent civil war in Liberia. Conflict in the Third World, it appears, is not going to go away just because the Cold War has; indeed it may well intensify.

Finally, consider one other form of regional conflict that is likely to affect the post—Cold War era: it is what we might call the "post-Marxist revolution" crisis. The most potent revolutionary force in the Third World these days may well be democracy. But it is no clearer there than it is in Europe that this supposedly integrative "triumph of liberalism" will necessarily promote peace. For just as the United States used to justify its intervention in Third World countries as a means of "inoculating" them against the "bacillus" of communism, so the post—Cold War era could see military interventions by the old democracies for the purpose of confirming in power—or restoring to power—new democracies. The violent, but overwhelmingly popular, American military operation to apprehend General Manuel Antonio Noriega in Panama could well portend things to come.

Threats can arise, though, not only from external sources; for the way in which a nation chooses to respond to threats can, under certain circumstances, pose as much of a danger to its long-term interests as do developments beyond its borders. The United States did not *have* to involve itself, to the extent that it did, in the Vietnam War. It did not *have* to become as dependent as it has on foreign oil. It did not *have* to accumulate such massive budget deficits that the government will have no choice but to allocate a significant percentage of its revenues, well into the twenty-first century, to paying off the accumulated debt. All of these were decisions Americans made, not their adversaries; yet their consequences have constrained, and in the case of energy dependency and the national debt, will continue to constrain, American freedom of action in the world for years to come.

These problems evolved from a curious unevenness that exists within the United States these days in the willingness to bear pain. Americans have readily accepted pain in connection with their integrative role as a global peacekeeper. They have repeatedly sent troops and resources overseas for the purpose of resisting aggression, even in situations where the probability of an attack was remote and where the states they were defending did not always see fit to contribute proportionately to their own defense. The United States has been unwilling to accept even moderate pain, though, when it comes either to raising the taxes necessary to support the government expenditures its citizens demand, or to cutting back on those expenditures to bring them into line with the taxes its citizens are willing to pay. The United States is generous, even profligate, with its military manpower and hardware, but it is selfish to the point of irresponsibility when it comes to issues of lifestyle and pocketbook.[7] As a result, a kind of division of labor has developed within the international community, in which the United States contributes the troops and the weaponry needed to sustain the balance of power, while its allies finance the budgetary, energy and trade deficits Americans incur through their unwillingness to make even minimal sacrifices in living standards.

Whatever the causes of this situation, the long-term effects cannot be healthy ones. Americans will not indefinitely serve as "mercenaries" overseas, especially when the troops recruited in that capacity come, as they disproportionately do, from the less fortunate social, economic and educational classes. Resentment over this pattern—when it develops—is likely to undermine whatever foreign policy consensus may yet remain. Pressures will eventually build for *all* Americans to bear their fair share of *all* the burdens that are involved in being a world power, and that may considerably diminish the attractions of continuing to be one.

The end of the Cold War, therefore, brings not an end to threats, but rather a diffusion of them: one can no longer plausibly point to a single source of danger, as one could throughout most of that conflict, but dangers there still will be. The architects of containment, when they confronted the struggle between democracy and totalitarianism in 1947, knew which side they were on; the post—Cold War geopolitical cartography, however, provides no comparable clarity. In one sense, this represents progress. The very absence of clear and present danger testifies to American success in so balancing power during the past four and a half decades that totalitarianism, at least in the forms we have considered threatening throughout most of this century, is now defunct. But, in another sense, the new competition between the forces of integration and fragmentation presents us with difficult choices, precisely because it is by no means as clear as it was during the Cold War which tendency we should want to see prevail.

V

Examine, first, the most extreme alternatives. A fully integrated world would be one in which individual countries would lose control of their borders and would be dependent on others for critical resources, capital and markets. It would mean, therefore, a progressive loss of national sovereignty, and ultimately the loss of whatever remained of national identity. A fully fragmented world would approximate the Hobbesian state of anarchy that theorists of international relations assume exists but that, in practice, never has: the world would be reduced to a gaggle of quarreling principalities, with war or the threat of war as the only means of settling disputes among them. Both of these extremes—for these are obviously caricatures—would undermine the international state system as we now know it: the first by submerging the autonomy of states within a supranational economic order; the second by so shattering state authority as to render it impotent.

No one seriously claims that, with the end of the Cold War, we can abandon the international state system or relinquish national sovereignty: not even our most visionary visionaries are prepared to go that far. This suggests, therefore, that the United States and its allies retain the interest they have always had in the balancing of power, but that this time the power to be balanced is less that of states or ideologies than of the processes—transcending states and ideologies—that are tending toward integrationist and fragmentationist extremes. Instead of balancing the forces of democracy against those of totalitarianism, the new task may well be to balance the forces of integration and fragmentation against each other.

What would this mean in practical terms? In the best of all possible worlds, of course, it would require taking no action at all, because integrationist and fragmentationist forces would balance themselves. Unfortunately, though, in the imperfect world in which we live things rarely work out this neatly. Gaps generally exist between what one wants to have happen and what seems likely to happen; it is here that the choices of states—and of the leaders who govern them—make a difference.

These choices in the post–Cold War world are likely to center on those areas in which integrationist and fragmentationist forces are not now balanced; where the triumph of one over the other could upset the international stability upon which rest the security interests of the United States, its allies, and other like-minded states; and where action is therefore needed to restore equilibrium. They are likely to include the following:

The Soviet Union and Eastern Europe

Over the next decade, the most serious source of instability in world politics will probably be the political, economic and social fragmentation that is already developing where communism has collapsed. Marxism-Leninism could hardly have suffered a more resounding defeat if World War III had been fought to the point of total victory for the West. Fortunately victory, this time, did not require a war. The trouble with victory, though, is that it tends to produce power imbalances. It was precisely to avoid this danger that the peacemakers of 1815 and 1945, who designed the two most durable peace settlements of modern times, moved quickly after their respective triumphs to rehabilitate defeated adversaries and to invite them back into the inter-national state system. Perhaps because the communist regimes of the Soviet Union and eastern Europe have not actually suffered a military defeat—and also because of recent distractions in the Persian Gulf—we in the West are not focusing as carefully as we should on the problems of reconstruction and reintegration in that part of the world. But should fragmentationist forces prevail there, the resulting anarchy—and mass emigration away from an-archy—could destabilize any number of power balances. The situation then would certainly command our attention, even if it does not now.

The peoples of the Soviet Union and eastern Europe will of course have to bear the principal burdens of reconstruction. But they will not be able to accomplish this task alone, and already discouragement and demoralization have set in among them. It is in dealing with this kind of despair that aid from the "West"—including Japan—can have its greatest impact. A mul-tinational Marshall Plan for former communist states sounds impractical given the extent of the problem and the existence of competing priorities at home, but the "highly leveraged" character of that earlier and highly suc-cessful enterprise ought not to be forgotten. The Marshall Plan worked by employing small amounts of economic assistance to produce large psycho-logical effects. It restored self-confidence in Europe just at the point, some two to three years after the end of the war, at which it was sagging. What was critical was not so much the extent of the aid provided as its timing, its targeting and its publicity: its main purpose was to shift the expectations of its recipients from the belief that things could only get worse to the conviction that they would eventually get better.

It will serve no one's interests in the West now, anymore than it would have served the interests of the victorious allies after World War II, to allow despair, demoralization and disintegration to prevail in the territories of defeated Cold War adversaries. What happened in Germany after World War I ought to provide a sufficiently clear warning of the consequences that can follow when victors neglect the interests of those they have vanquished, and thereby, in the long run, neglect their own.

New Security and Economic Structures for Europe

Glaciers, when they invade a continent, not only obscure its topography but, through the weight of the accumulated ice, literally press its surface down into the earth's mantle. Retreats of glaciers cause old features of the landscape slowly to rise up again, sometimes altered, sometimes not. The expansion of Soviet and American influence over Europe at the end of World War II had something of the effect of such a glacier. It froze things in place, thereby obscuring old rivalries and bringing peace—even if a "cold" peace—to a continent that had known little of it throughout its history.

But now that the Cold War is over, geopolitical glaciers are retreating, the situation is becoming fluid once again, and certain familiar features of the European landscape—a single strong German state, together with ethnic and religious antagonisms among Germany's neighbors to the east—are once more coming into view. The critical question for the future stability of Europe is the extent to which the Cold War glacier permanently altered the terrain it covered for so long. Integrationist structures like the EC and NATO [the North Atlantic Treaty Organization] suggest such alteration; but they could also have been artifacts of the glaciation itself. If so, these organizations will become increasingly vulnerable as the forces of fragmentation revive.

No economic or security structure for Europe can hope to be viable over the long term unless it incorporates and benefits all of the major states on that continent: the classic lesson is the Versailles Treaty of 1919, which sought to build a peace that treated Germany as a pariah and excluded Soviet Russia altogether. But neither the EC nor NATO has given sufficient attention to how each might restructure itself to accommodate the interests of the former Warsaw Pact states, including whatever is left of the Soviet Union. Few efforts have been made to think through how these integrative organizations might expand the scope of their activities to counter the fragmentationist challenges—coming from the reunification of Germany, the liberation of eastern Europe and the possible collapse of the U.S.S.R.—that are already evident.[8]

The United States has used its influence, over the years, to favor integration over fragmentation in Europe; indeed without that influence, it is difficult to see how integration could have proceeded as far as it has. But Americans cannot expect to maintain the authority the Cold War gave them on the continent for very much longer, especially now that the Soviet "glacier" is so obviously retreating. We would do well, then, to consider what new or modified integrative structures might replace the role that the United States—and, by very different means, its former adversaries—played in "freezing" disintegrative forces in Europe during the Cold War. Otherwise, serious imbalances could develop in that part of the world as well.

Deterring Aggression

One thing the Cold War did was to make the use of force by the great powers against one another virtually unthinkable. It created inducements that caused states to seek to resolve peacefully—or even to learn to live with—accumulated grievances that could easily, prior to 1945, have provoked major wars. It did this by appealing more to fear than to logic, but patterns of behavior that arise out of fear can, in time, come to seem quite logical. Few today would question the desirability of perpetuating, and if necessary reinforcing, the inhibitions that arose, during the postwar decades, against once violent patterns of great power behavior.

The unprecedented multinational response to Saddam Hussein's aggression against Kuwait suggests that an opportunity now exists to extend disincentives to war beyond the realm of the great powers. The need to do this is urgent because the end of the Cold War is likely to end the informal crisis-management regime the United States and the Soviet Union have relied upon in the past to keep such regional conflicts limited.

Woodrow Wilson's vision of collective international action to deter aggression failed to materialize after 1919 because of European appeasement and American isolationism, and after 1945 because of the great power rivalries that produced the Cold War. None of these difficulties exist today. The world has a third chance to give Wilson's plan the fair test it has never received, and fate has even provided an appropriate occasion: successful U.N. action to restore Kuwaiti independence sets a powerful example that could advance us some distance toward bringing the conduct of international relations within the framework of international law that has long existed alongside it, but too often apart from it.[9]

Can such a legalistic vision sustain the realistic security interests of the United States? Whether rightly or wrongly, the answer was negative after World Wars I and II; but Americans have reasons, this time, for giving a more positive reply. The "long peace" that was the Cold War has already created in the practice of the great powers mechanisms for deterring aggression that have worked remarkably well: these did not exist prior to 1945. There could be real advantages now in codifying and extending this behavior as widely as possible. The evolution of a new world order designed to deter aggression could ensure that the most important benefits of the "long peace" survive the demise of the Cold War. It could also counteract the dangerous conviction, which American leaders still at times appear to hold, that only the United States has the will and the capacity to take the lead in policing (or nannying) the world.

Finding Appropriate Limits of Interdependence

The Iraqi invasion of Kuwait raises another issue, though, that will involve more difficult choices: it has to do with just how far we want economic integration to proceed. The purpose of having global markets is to ensure prosperity, not to compromise national sovereignty.   And yet, it was the international market in oil and armaments that made it possible for Saddam Hussein to violate Kuwaiti sovereignty.   Economic integration, in this instance, produced literal political fragmentation.   This unexpected and dangerous juxtaposition suggests strongly the need to think, more seriously than we have to this point, about how the economic and political forces that are shaping our world intersect with one another, and about where our own security interests with respect to these lie.

Certainly there is much to be said, from a strictly economic perspective, in favor of reducing barriers to trade, investment and even labor flows across international boundaries if the result is to maximize production, minimize prices and ensure that consumer needs are satisfied.   But what if the result is also to allow despots easy access to sophisticated military technology, or to increase the West's reliance on energy resources it does not control?   Do market principles require that we welcome on a continuing basis the dispatch of troops to safeguard critical supplies halfway around the world?   There are political costs to be paid for economic integration, and we are only now beginning to realize what they are.

These issues are only part of the much larger problem of how one balances the advantages of economic integration against its political and social disadvantages.   Are Americans really sure, for example, that they want to integrate their own economy into the world market if the result of doing that is to shut down industries they have historically relied upon for both jobs and national defense?   When the effects of integration are to transform once-diversified industrial complexes into strings of fast-food outlets and shopping malls, with the reduction in wages that kind of employment normally brings, one can hardly expect people to be out in the streets cheering for them, however ingenious the rationalizations of our professional economists.

Increasing labor mobility, together with the liberalized immigration policies that facilitate it, provides yet another example of how economic integration could produce political fragmentation.   There are undeniable advantages in allowing immigration, not just because it provides cheap labor but also because in some instances the host nation can gain a diverse array of sophisticated skills as a result.   But immigration also risks altering national identity, and the forces of integration have by no means advanced to the point at which one can dismiss concerns over that issue as anachronistic.[10]   As a nation of immigrants, the United States handles problems of cultural assimilation more easily than most nations.   Still, they are real problems, and they exist on a world-wide scale.   Attempts to write them off as reflections of an antiquated "nationalism," or even "racism," are not likely to make them go away.

What all of this suggests, therefore, is that we need better mechanisms for balancing the processes of integration and fragmentation at those points at which economic forces intersect those of politics and culture.   The increasing permeability of boundaries is going to be an important characteristic of the post—Cold War world, and it would be a great mistake to assume—as market principles encourage us to assume—that in such an environment an "invisible hand" will always produce the greatest benefits for the greatest number. As in most other areas, an equilibrium will be necessary: if imbalances of power are not to develop, then a certain amount of protectionism, within prudent limits, may be required.

Regaining Solvency

The principle of balancing power also requires that ends be balanced against means. National security, even in the most auspicious of circumstances, does not come cheap. This country's reluctance to bring the costs of providing for its security into line with what it is willing to pay suggests that integrative and disintegrative mechanisms are imperfectly balanced within the United States as well as beyond its borders.

The last American president to preoccupy himself with solvency, Dwight D. Eisenhower, regularly insisted that the National Security Council specify as "the basic objective of our national security policies: maintaining the security of the United States and the vitality of its fundamental values and institutions." To achieve the former without securing the latter, he warned, would be to "destroy what we are attempting to defend."[11]

Too often during the years that have followed Eisenhower's presidency the quest for security has overwhelmed concern for the vitality of fundamental values and institutions. The Vietnam War, which came close to tearing this country apart, was fought for geopolitical reasons that remain obscure to this day. The Watergate and Iran-contra scandals revealed how excesses committed in the name of national security can subvert constitutional processes. And no one would be more appalled than Eisenhower himself to see the extent to which Americans now finance the costs of defense—as well as everything else—on credit extended by the unborn (who cannot object to the process) and by foreigners (who someday may).

A return to solvency in its broadest sense—by which I mean not just balanced budgets but bearing the full pain of what one is doing at the time one is doing it—might discipline our conception of the national interest in the way that it should be disciplined: through the constantly annoying, but also intellectually bracing, demands of stringency. The result might well be less grandiose visions, but more sustainable policies.

VI

Which is going to win—integration or fragmentation? At first glance, it would seem that the forces of integration will almost certainly prevail. One cannot run a modern postindustrial economy without such forces, and that, many people would say, is the most important thing in the world. But that is also a parochial view.   Running a postindustrial economy may not be the most important thing to the peasant in the Sudan, or to the young urban black in the United States or to the Palestinian who has spent his entire life in a refugee camp.   For those people, forces that might appear to us to be fragmentationist can be profoundly integrationist, in that they give meaning to otherwise meaningless lives.

We should also recognize that the forces of integration may not be as deeply rooted as we like to think.   It comes as something of a shock when one realizes that the most important of them—the global market, collective security, the "long peace" itself—were products of the Cold War.   Their survival is by no means guaranteed into the post–Cold War era.   Fragmentationist forces have been around much longer than integrationist forces, and now that the Cold War is over, they may grow stronger than at any point in the last half century.

We should not necessarily conclude from this, though, that it will always be in our interest to try to ensure that the forces of integration come out on top.   Surely, in light of the Persian Gulf War, the international community will want to restrict future sales of arms across boundaries, and it would not be a bad idea to develop alternatives to dependency on Middle East oil as well.   The increasing permeability of borders—the very thing most of the world welcomes when it comes to the free flow of ideas—will by no means be as welcome when commodities, capital and labor begin flowing with equal freedom.   And Americans are already beginning to move away from the view that they can leave everything—international trade, energy resources and especially the regulation of the savings and loan industry—to the "invisible hand" of market forces that the integrationist model in principle recommends.

But swinging toward autarchy, nationalism or isolationism will not do either.   The forces of fragmentation lurk just beneath the surface, and it would take little encouragement for them to reassert themselves, with all the dangers historical experience suggests would accompany such a development. We need to maintain a healthy skepticism about integration: there is no reason to turn it into some kind of sacred cow.   But we also need to balance that skepticism with a keen sense of how unhealthy fragmentationist forces can be if allowed free rein.

So we are left, as usual, groping for the middle ground, for that rejection of extremes, that judicious balancing of pluses and minuses, that is typical of how [essays] like this are supposed to end.   This one will be no exception to that rule.   I would point out, though, that practical statecraft boils down, most of the time, to just this task of attempting to navigate the middle course, while avoiding the rocks and shoals that lie on either side.   Certainly Americans, of all peoples, should find this a familiar procedure, for what is our own Constitution if not the most elegant political text ever composed on how to balance the forces of integration against those of fragmentation?   It had been necessary, Madison wrote in *The Federalist*, no. 51, so to contrive "the interior structure of the government as that its several constituent parts may, by their mutual relations, be the means of keeping each other in their proper places."[12]   That would not be a bad design to follow with regard to the external world as all of us think about how we might come to grips—as the Founding Fathers had to—with the centripetal and centrifugal forces that are already shaping our lives.

Notes

1. See Theodore S. Hamerow, *From the Finland Station: The Graying of Revolution in the Twentieth Century*, New York: Basic Books, 1990, pp. 210–25, 300–9.

2. Michael Doyle, "Kant, Liberal Legacies, and Foreign Affairs," *Philosophy and Public Affairs*, Summer/Fall 1983, pp. 205–35, 323–35; also Doyle, "Liberalism and World Politics," *American Political Science Review*, December 1986, pp. 1151–69.

3. See "Race on Campus," *The New Republic*, Feb. 18, 1991; also Dinesh D'Souza, "Illiberal Education," *The Atlantic*, March 1991, pp. 51–79.

4. William F. Buckley, Jr., *Gratitude: Reflections On What We Owe To Our Country*, New York: Random House, 1990.

5. An extreme, but prominent, example of such celebration is Francis Fukuyama, "The End of History?" *The National Interest*, Summer 1989, pp. 3–18.

6. The depressing possibilities are well summarized in George F. Kennan, "Communism in Russian History," *Foreign Affairs*, Winter 1990/91, pp. 182–84.

7. James Chace has suggested, persuasively in my view, that this attitude goes back to Lyndon Johnson's attempt to fight the Vietnam War without asking for sacrifices on the home front.   See his *Solvency: The Price of Survival*, New York: Random House, 1981, p. 15.

8. The Conference on Security and Cooperation in Europe, now little more than a framework for negotiations, suffers from a deficiency opposite to that of NATO and the European Community: with the single exception of Albania, it includes all of the states of Europe, from the largest to the most microscopic, and it requires unanimity in order to act, which in most cases ensures that it will not.

9. For an eloquent discussion of the advantages adherence to international law can offer, see Daniel Patrick Moynihan, *On the Law of Nations*. Cambridge: Harvard University Press, 1990.

10. William H. McNeill sets this problem within a long-term historical context in "Winds of Change," in Nicholas X. Rizopoulos, ed., *Sea-Changes: American Foreign Policy in a World Transformed*, New York: Council on Foreign Relations Press, 1990, pp. 184–87.

11. John Lewis Gaddis, *Strategies of Containment: A Critical Appraisal of Postwar American National Security Policy*, New York: Oxford University Press, 1982, pp. 135–36.

12. *The Federalist Papers*, New York: New American Library, 1961, p. 320.

2 ENTANGLED FOREVER

Josef Joffe

"If communism is dead," Irving Kristol pointed out to the 1990 gathering of the Committee for the Free World, "then anticommunism is dead, too." This is true in a way of a tautology—*per definitionem*. Alas, there is more than a vacuous truism to this proposition. For it puts the axe to the roots of almost half a century of American foreign policy.

Or does it?

Realpolitikers would fiercely deny such a lapidary DOA pronouncement. They would insist that anticommunism was but the icing on the cake, rich as it was. American foreign policy since 1945 has followed interest rather than ideology, and so the former will outlive the latter. Cut through the anticommunist clamor, they would contend, and you discern the classic behavior of a normal great power.

Their rebuttal might continue along these lines: The end of American innocence came as early as 1947—when Britain abdicated responsibility for embattled Greece. With Stalin set on expansion, and Britain and France—both exhausted—out of the equation, the United States had to assume the burden of the balance for good. No longer could the U.S. withdraw behind the cozy barrier of the Atlantic (and the fog of idealist *pronunciamento*). Like the great powers of yore, America was now irrevocably stuck in the self-help system that is the essence of world politics, and so it had to obey the system's eternal rules.

Which it did—consciously or not. True, the Truman Doctrine, the founding document, was enveloped in the grandiloquent oratory of antitotalitarianism. So were NATO [the North Atlantic Treaty Organization], SEATO [the Southeast Asian Treaty Organization], et al., those Cold War alliances thrown up around the Soviet Union. But in essence, these were the time-honored tools of power politics—coalitions sponsored by the U.S. in order to constrain the one and only rival who threatened America's physical security.

Move and countermove, thrust and parry, became the choreography of a stylized, sometimes bloody "grand strategy" Americans had always learned to despise as the game of princes and despots.   But "containment" was the same game nonetheless.   Whether it came to coalition-building (as in NATO) or coalition war (as in Korea), whether the crisis was over Berlin or Cuba— all the way down to the Euromissile Battle of the 1980s—the U.S. acted as great powers have always done: so as to balance or best its existential foe.

By way of Q.E.D., our *realpolitiker* would conclude: The power of Soviet Russia and not the threat of communism was the motivating force of postwar American foreign policy.   How else would we explain our long-term love affair with the communist despots of China, which even the Tiananmen Massacre could not interrupt?   How else would we explain our "policy of differentiation" in communist Eastern Europe which ranged us along such sterling characters as Nicolae Ceausescu?   Indeed, if the real game was value rather than balance, why did America fall into bed with a long succession of nasties from Chiang Kai-shek to Manuel Noriega (before he was fingered as drug lord)?

If the *realpolitikers* are right, then all is not lost now that "communism is dead" and Mikhail Gorbachev is dragging his country into democracy and the free market.   If Russian power rather than Soviet ideology is the problem, then America's purpose must still address itself to the great existential threat embodied by Moscow.   Communism might disappear, but thermonuclear weapons and vast conventional forces will not.   (Precisely for this reason, even a disintegrating Muscovite empire will pose the single most important danger for world stability and American security.)   Russian democracy would change hardball into softball, but not the rules themselves (which, at any rate, must always take into account a reversion to yesterday's pitching and slugging).   Alas, in spinning this tale, the *realpolitiker* has left out a critical part.   Democracies do not like *realpolitik*, and none has disliked it more than America, the oldest democracy which was founded in revulsion against the "corrupt game of princes" that was Europe's bloody lot.

In their own minds, Americans never went to war to uphold the balance of power, let alone for glory or booty.   What really riled them in their first war was the "Cruelty & Perfidy" of George III—above and beyond his "plundering our seas [and] ravaging our Coasts."   When America at last entered the war against Germany in 1917 and 1941, the nation did not think about the European balance but about the sheer evil of Kaiser Bill and Adolf Hitler.   Nor was Russian power the problem that galvanized American society during the Cold War; it was the *ideological* enemy as embodied in the persons of Stalin and his successors.

Writing [in 1835] about "Democracy in America," Tocqueville reminds us of the basic reason: "There are two things that a democratic people always will find very difficult—to begin a war and to end it."   In other words: Democracies do worst in the twilight zone between war and peace.   Unless they are roused by great passions or great ideologies, they turn their backs on "reason of state."   Yet once they are so roused, they similarly ignore the subtle intricacies of diplomacy.   Instead, they will fight to the bloody finish when the foe is at last crushed as prelude to his moral-political reform.

Indeed, reason of state or the "primacy of foreign policy" are fundamentally alien to the democratic spirit.   They imply a realm of policy that is above and beyond the fray of democratic politics.   If the people are the sovereign, *no* issue must be excluded from the public debate.   The very idea of the "primacy of foreign policy" is antidemocratic because it presumes a "national interest" defined and guarded by an elite not beholden to the normal democratic contest.

Finally, the principles of democracy do not mesh too well with those of diplomacy.   Diplomacy must be subtle; democracy lives by the rough and tumble of domestic politics.   Democratic politics is to choose between stark alternatives, either ideological or personal; diplomacy is a game of ambiguous rules and stark dilemmas that are not so much resolved as muted or suspended.   Democracy obeys the rule of law; diplomacy is the art of ruse and reinsurance.   Democratic politics thrives on publicity and public discourse. Diplomacy must act with circumspection and secrecy, frequently pretending one objective (portrayed as lofty) even as it pursues another (which happens to be quite self-serving).

In short, democracies do not like Clausewitz.   It is either total peace or total war, be it hot or cold.   If suitably galvanized by an ideological threat and moral purpose, they will "pay any price" and "bear any burden," as John F. Kennedy put it, but they will not move smoothly along the "Clausewitzian continuum" where ideology means little and power everything, where diplomacy and force are but shades of one and the same spectrum of choices.

Yet if the Cold War ([also known as] ideological threat) is over, then we have a problem.   Neo-isolationists could point to the collapse of Soviet power, declare victory, and go home.   Internationalists could point to the collapse of communism, declare the "end of history," and also join the homeward trek.   Both sides would unite in the conviction that America no longer needs to sustain the struggle—indeed, remain chained to the world—because the threat had vanished.   Isolationists would feel safe in physical insulation; internationalists would conclude that the vision of the Enlightenment had at last come true.   Since only despots make war, while democracies are inherently pacific, international politics henceforth will be reduced to global domestic policy.   Welfare, not warfare, will shape its rules; global threats like ozone holes and pollution will dictate the agenda—and cooperation, to boot.

Realpolitikers ignore the domestic side of democratic foreign policy and pooh-pooh change.   *Idealpolitikers* fall for the opposite temptation.   Believing, as had Jefferson, that there is "but one system of ethics for men and for nations," they are always quick to spot a new "paradigm" in the making while ignoring that states, no matter what their constitution, remain chained to the self-help system.   Whereas the citizen can *assume* security, the state cannot.   In the self-help system, great conflicts like the Cold War may abate, even vanish—but not so the necessity to worry about security, status, and position.   Old conflicts might return, new conflicts might supersede them. Even in peace, nations cannot take tranquility for granted as long as they live in a "state of nature" lacking both an arbiter of conflict and enforcer of peace.

The existence of *states* defines the essence of the game.   Whence it follows that only their disappearance could usher in a new paradigm of global politics. Yet despite the onslaught of trans-, sub-, and supranational forces, the nation-state is alive and well.   And so, the old rules of the self-help system will survive, too.   Nor do the retraction of Soviet power and the collapse of Soviet ideology change the fundamentals.   Even without its far-flung empire, Russia will still be the largest country on earth.   Even with a democratic political culture, nuclear-armed Russia will still be the only country that can annihilate the United States.

Has nothing changed then?   This is not the real issue.   If completed, the democratization of the Soviet Union certainly would remove the peculiar intensity that attended the conflict in decades past.   If continued, the re-traction of Soviet power will remove many sources of the struggle—above all in Europe, the original and foremost arena of the Cold War, where the forward-projection of Soviet power was the *casus belli*.   Yet waning stridency and diminishing stakes do not signify the end of conflict, let alone the end of the self-help system.   And so, there is no exit for the United States.

First, take the Soviet Union.   Though lily-white democrats they might yet become, the heirs of Lenin and Stalin will still preside over the greatest military power apart from the United States.   Though the competition will be muted and encased by cooperation, one thing will and cannot change: Unless the USSR self-destructs or another superpower arises, only America and Russia can extinguish one another.   That is an existential fact with consequences. It limits both trust and cooperation, and it will keep the game of containment and counter-containment going.   Each must still keep a wary eye on the other, and each must take care that his competitor-partner does not accu-mulate too many assets that might yet be turned to malign uses.   And so, American policy must still harken the commands of the self-help system, cooperating where it can and competing where it must.

Second, take the international system.   Twenty years after the first wave of "multipolarism," whose proponents declared the death of bipolarity and the birth of a tri- or quintapolar world, there is now the sequel with the subtitle "The Decline of American Power."   The obvious need not be gainsaid. The U.S. is good merely for a quarter of the gross global product, and no longer for one-half.   Germany (plus the EC [European Community]) and Japan are serious, though still much smaller, commercial competitors, and there are at least five nuclear powers.   As force has become less fungible, other "currencies" of influence have moved to the fore; power in general has become more diffused.   Yet in a critical respect, the world is more "unipolar" than ever.

As was true twenty years ago, the U.S. is the only nation present at each gaming table—the strategic, the conventional-military, the diplomatic, economic, and ideological-cultural one.   And at each table, it is the dominant player to boot.   The Soviet Union was always a developing country with thermonuclear weapons; today, it is an economic basket case which has lost even its ideological trump card.   To make this case is not to crow but to stress the special responsibility that has devolved upon America as its existential rival is deflating.

Nor are the new centers of power—Germany, Japan, China—ready to assume the burden of global management.   China is a societal earthquake waiting to happen.   Germany has its hands full with reunification and thereafter will be busy with its many conflicting obligations between EC integration and *Mitteleuropa*, between pacifying and containing Russia.   Japan will have to come to grips with the sharpening tensions between consumerism and mega-mercantilism before even beginning to contemplate an autonomous strategic role in East Asia.   The mighty yen and deutschemark can always bring down the American dollar, beholden as it is to the German interest rate and to Japanese bond hoarders.   But neither MITI [the Japanese Ministry of International Trade and Industry] nor the Bundesbank can deal with Soviet SS−24 missiles, Lithuanian separatists, or Iraqi poison gas.

Which brings us to the third reason why there is no exit for the United States.   As the previous dominant conflict (a.k.a. Cold War) is declining, many lesser ones (with a heavy growth potential) are jostling to take the Cold War's place.   Here is an abbreviated checklist: the disintegration of the Soviet Union, Iraqi ambitions, Libyan mischief, economic catastrophe in Eastern Europe, Yugoslavia's explosion, Arab-Israeli war, nuclear and poison gas proliferation, Islamic fundamentalism, the collapse of the marvelous Western economy that stretches from Frankfurt via New York to Tokyo.   Take your pick and try to imagine any crisis management minus the United States.

To all of this, a neo-isolationist might rightfully reply: "You have made the *world's* case for America's entanglement.   But what's in it for the *United States?*"   The point is well taken.   To shoulder the burden would require a sense of responsibility that is (a) costly and (b) not self-evident to a society unwilling to sustain *les vastes entreprises* (as de Gaulle put it) in the absence of an overweening ideological threat.   Moreover, many items on the checklist of conflict do not undermine the isolationist creed because such crises do not necessarily affect American physical security.   Let the Europeans take care of Qaddafi.   Yugoslavia '90 is not Sarajevo '14; today, no great power will start World War III because of Serbian nationalism.

The counter-reply is an old one.   If you don't believe that power is destiny, then how about: "What is good for the world, is good for America?"   While it is true that a nuclear-armed United States can assure its own security (as it always could), great powers have interests which transcend their national space, requiring order beyond borders. Conflict in Yugoslavia may not spill over; conflict in the Middle East, a strategic locale harboring a strategic resource (oil), has a nasty habit of attracting outsiders. Europe may be on the road to pacification, but it is not foreordained that the Continent can take care of itself.

The underlying problem has hardly vanished. There is Russia, larger and militarily more potent than anybody else, and there is Germany, the biggest economic player at the fulcrum of the European balance which is now being liberated from the fetters of dependence the Cold War has wrought. On the other hand, there is an abiding American interest in European order for reasons both strategic and economic (which this analysis assumes to be self-evident). If the past 120 years are a guide, Germany and Russia are not the ideal co-managers. When they have not been at each other's throat, they have conspired against the rest while simultaneously trying to weaken each other. By contrast, Europe has flourished, as after 1945, when a power stronger than both was ensconced in the system. That power was, and remains, America.

The U.S. need not be there with 300,000 troops once force levels come down everywhere. But given America's stake in a prosperous and peaceful Europe, the U.S. ought to play the same role tomorrow as it did yesterday: as protector and pacifier from within. America on the inside would hold the balance against a diminished, but still potent Soviet Union. And in so doing, the U.S. would pull the sting of German power, thus allowing the entire Continent to acquire the cooperative habits that came to bless Western Europe in the past forty years. It should not be assumed that an autochthonous order will arise, just because the Cold War structures are crumbling. Renationalization and the return to pre–1945 modes of behavior are just as likely in the absence of an Atlantic anchor.

But what if there is a "new paradigm" in the making—with welfare shouldering aside warfare? That would add, rather than subtract, reasons for America living up to its Number One role. Twenty years ago, exports came to 4 percent of American GNP; today, that proportion has more than doubled. At the same time, America's vulnerability to global economic forces (interest rates, capital movements, protectionism) has soared. While the U.S. can no longer dominate the world economy, its two closest competitors (Germany-EC and Japan) are neither willing nor able to assume the burden of global management that underlies the marvelous resilience of the Western economy. By virtue of size and position, the U.S. remains the hub. That role and new vulnerabilities hardly counsel self-sufficiency because the United States will suffer more than most if free trade and monetary stability collapse. But there is more: Precisely because the U.S. has accumulated new economic handicaps in the 1970s and 1980s, it must not abandon its politico-strategic assets. Being present in Europe, for instance, gives the U.S. a more audible say in economic decision-making than from a solitary perch across the Atlantic.

Granted, but why should Washington bomb Qaddafi, stop Iraqi nuclear ambitions, fiddle with Messrs. Shamir and Arafat, "resocialize" Iran, democratize Nicaragua, and seek a settlement in Cambodia? The answer is twofold. First, while peace and the "new paradigm" might yet rule over the "northern" world that stretches eastward from San Francisco to Vladivostok, the "old paradigm"— ambition, fear, and violence—is alive and well everywhere else. Second, these conflicts have a way of impinging on the United States. Iraqi nuclear weapons may pose threats at one step removed, but when Pan Am 103 explodes over Lockerbie, the challenge is direct, brutal, and bloody.

Wherever the "old paradigm" persists, American interests will be affected. Nor could American interests be scaled down like those, say, of Canada, in order to get out of harm's way. The United States is too big, too visible, and too much of a weight in the balance to revert to the role Tocqueville had described thus: "The country is as much removed from the passions of the Old World by its position as by its wishes, and it is called upon neither to repudiate nor to espouse them"; hence "the foreign policy of the United States ... consists more in abstaining than in acting." Yet today, even abstention will have consequences for the world and then for America itself, and so there is no exit.

Finally, there is also *pleasure* in being Number One. To exert power is better than suffering it; to be at the helm is better than hunkering down in the hold. With the Soviet Union (temporarily) receding from the world scene, the U.S. need not respond to each and every change by treating it as harbinger of bigger and worse things to come. There will be some safety in indifference, and not every crisis need be approached as if it were a wholly-owned subsidiary of American diplomacy. But the death of communism spells neither the birth of a new order nor the end of conflict. It is the great powers that build and maintain international order, and those who shape it most also gain most. With the decline of the Soviet Union, there is only one truly great power left in the system. Therein lies the purpose and the profit of American power at the threshold of the twenty-first century.

3 1989 AND ALL THAT

Robert W. Tucker

I

The events of 1989 not only brought to an end the division of Europe, they also brought to an end the postwar role of the Soviet Union in Europe, for that role depended above all on the once clearly recognized division of the continent and, of course, the political-military consequences acknowledged to follow from that division. These consequences no longer obtain, however. . . . The view that they still do obtain, if admittedly in attenuated form, must depend on the possibility that the Soviet government—whether that of Mikhail Gorbachev or of a successor—may yet employ military power to prevent unwanted developments. If that prospect cannot be entirely ruled out, it nevertheless now remains so small that it may be all but discounted, for the military power needed to stay the developments that have now been set firmly in train . . . would have to be very considerable. To succeed, the effort required would greatly tax the Soviet Union's resources and, by doing so, place in further jeopardy, if not simply put an end to, efforts of domestic economic reform. The suppression once again of popular aspirations to freedom and self-determination in Eastern Europe would be seen as vindicating those opposed from the outset to liberalization in the Soviet Union. At best, such suppression would set the clock back 30 years in Soviet relations with the West. At worst, it would directly threaten a general war in Europe, if only because those circumstances that formerly assured the Soviet Union that military intervention could be undertaken in reasonable safety no longer exist. The division once clearly recognized, if not legitimized, is no longer so. The once acknowledged power, if not the right, to intervene is no longer acknowledged and would now be very dangerous to exercise.

The end of Europe's division signals as well the end of the great conflict that has dominated world politics since World War II. It does so not because, as the conventional view has it, the Cold War arose out of the division of Europe and will therefore end when this division is ended, but because the

Note: Section headings have been renumbered.

abandonment by the Soviet Union of its core external interest marks the onset of the long-term decline of Soviet global power and influence. The principal cause of the Cold War was the essential duopoly of power left by World War II, a duopoly that quite naturally resulted in the filling of a vacuum (Europe) that had once been the center of the international system and the control of which would have conferred great, and perhaps decisive, power advantage to its possessor. What gave the resulting conflict its particular intensity, of course, was the profound ideological gulf that separated the Soviet Union and the United States. But the root cause of the conflict was to be found in the structural circumstances that characterized the international system at the close of World War II.

Although not the principal cause, Europe has unquestionably been the principal symptom and stake of the conflict. For this reason, as long as a divided Europe persisted, the Cold War could have been expected to persist. Even if that division had earlier been brought to an end, although in circumstances other than those that in fact have marked its end, the Cold War could have been expected to persist in some form. For it is very difficult to imagine even a reformed, though still vibrant and powerful, Soviet Union's long resisting the temptation to gain ascendant influence over a Europe that, whatever the extent of its economic integration, continued to lack political unity. Barring a radical change in America's outlook and policy, this nation could be expected to counter such Soviet aspirations.

It is not so much, then, the end of Europe's division that signals an end of the Cold War as it is the circumstance that above all led to this end: the decline of Soviet power. Nor does it matter here that this decline did not occur overnight, that its root causes are profound, and that its consequences might well have been put off for a number of years and remained unacknowledged by a different Soviet leadership. What does matter is that these consequences were acknowledged and acted upon in Europe by the present leadership. Once drawn they have become all but irreversible in the continent that gave rise to the Cold War. . . .

II

It is all but inevitable that the end of the Cold War will give rise to yet another debate over American foreign policy. The signs of such debate are already apparent in the emergent dialogue between those who believe that we should once again play a much more modest role in the world and those who believe that America's post–World War II role must be held up as the model for the future. To date, it is the supporters of continuity who clearly appear to enjoy a position of advantage. But this is to be accounted for in part by the persisting view that their position responds, after all, to the natural order of things. Once it becomes clear that this order, the postwar dispensation, is no more and that we now live in a very different world, the advantage that is conferred by the force of the habitual will erode.   The advocates of change will then have their day.

The case for having the United States play a far more modest role in the post–Cold War world is rooted in the history of the past fifty years and the vast changes that have occurred during this period.   America abandoned a policy of isolation and intervened in World War II because a fascist victory would have threatened the nation's physical security and material well-being. This threat apart, a fascist victory also held out the prospect of a world in which America's political and economic frontiers would have to become coterminous with its territorial frontiers, a world in which societies that shared our institutions and values might very possibly disappear—in sum, a world in which the American example and American influence would become irrelevant.   In such a world, it was believed, America would find it difficult, and perhaps impossible, to realize its promise, since a hostile world from which America was shut out would inevitably affect the integrity of the nation's institutions and the quality of its domestic life.   The issues of physical security and economic well-being apart, it was to prevent this prospect from materializing that the United States abandoned its interwar isolationism and intervened in World War II.

It was for roughly the same reasons that, in the years following the war, this country adopted a policy of containing Soviet power.   The initial measures of containment, the Marshall Plan and the Atlantic alliance, formally expressed and thereby made unmistakable the vital American interest in preserving the security and independence of the nations of Western Europe. In the context of Soviet-American rivalry, they formed a clear acknowledgment that the domination of Western Europe by the Soviet Union might well shift the balance of power decisively against the United States and that, at the very least, such domination would result in a security problem that would severely strain the nation's resources and jeopardize its institutions.

Although the circumstances of the late 1940s made the application of containment roughly identical with a conventional balance of power policy, from the outset containment also expressed an interest that went beyond security, narrowly conceived.   From the outset, a conventional security interest was joined with a broader interest in preserving and extending the institutions of freedom.   The Truman Doctrine expressed these two aspects of containment, that of organizing power and that of vindicating purpose. In its refusal to distinguish clearly between the two aspects, the Truman Doctrine foreshadowed the subsequent history of containment and the refusal to distinguish clearly between the interest in securing a balance of power and the interest in extending freedom.   That refusal, in turn, has reflected the conviction, deeply rooted in the American consciousness, that the successful pursuit of the American purpose is, in the long term, the only truly reliable method of achieving both peace and security.

The outcome of the Cold War has at last put an end to the circumstances that required America's intervention, first in a global conflict and then in a protracted contest that came to encompass most of the world. In the fifty years that have elapsed since the abandonment of isolation, the structure of American security, both in its narrower and in its broader dimensions, has changed radically. It has changed radically by virtue of the military defeat (or, in the case of the Soviet Union, the functional equivalent of military defeat) of those powers that threatened the nation's physical security. And it has changed radically by virtue of the progressive triumph of those institutions and values the extension of which has long formed the American purpose—a purpose that has in turn been equated with the nation's greater-than-physical security. The prospect of a world in which the American example and the influence of American institutions and values might decline, let alone become irrelevant, has never seemed more remote.

It is quite true that as a result of nuclear-missile weapons, the United States is physically vulnerable today in a way it was not vulnerable in the interwar period. But this ultimate vulnerability cannot be significantly reduced—let alone removed—by the attempt to retain our postwar role. Against the possibility of attack by nuclear-missile weapons, a possibility that will exist as long as nuclear weapons exist, our present alliances afford little, if any, protection. In any event, that possibility must be considered virtually negligible today not only because our once great adversary no longer lays claim to interests and harbors ambitions that could lead to situations in which nuclear weapons might be threatened, but also because experience has shown how limited the utility of these weapons is, save for defensive purposes.

These are the general considerations in support of having the United States play a far more modest world role in the post–Cold War period. The conclusions they suggest are apparent. The reasons that prompted this country to play the great role it did for half a century are no longer valid. A new world has come into being, one in which America's security in both its narrower and its broader dimensions is no longer at serious risk. This being the case, it must be asked, why should this country persist in efforts that respond to circumstances now past? Why should it continue to maintain substantial forces in Europe and in the western Pacific? Whose interests are served by its doing so?

There are, of course, the constraints imposed by a period of transition. But these constraints apart, the case for maintaining a continuity of role rests essentially on the propositions that the world will have a continuing need for a power able to maintain peace and stability and that only this country can fill that need. The United States must preserve a peace that remains fragile. It must do so because it is not only the world's greatest power but the most trusted one. The argument for preserving a continuity of role thus increasingly resembles today the rationale for collective security rather than for alliances. The peacekeeping role we are now urged to pursue is one that is directed no longer against a particular state or states, but against disturbers of the peace regardless of their identity. Accordingly, the interests that are served by accepting this peacekeeping role are those of the international community as a whole.

Although the principal sources of instability are usually described in general terms, it is apparent that they are now considered to be our major postwar allies, Germany and Japan. The need of retaining a substantial American military presence in Europe and in Asia is primarily to reassure the neighbors of these states. To reassure them against what, however? If the answer is to reassure them against the threat of military expansion, the political reality will be that of tacit alliances between the United States and the neighbors of Germany and Japan that have as their object the containment of these two states. In time, such arrangements are bound to generate resentment on the part of those who have been made the objects of these alliances—and this despite their initial approval and even support of them—for the continued presence of American forces will be a constant reminder to both states that they remain less than trusted by others.

On the other hand, if the purpose of maintaining a substantial American presence in Europe and Asia is to safeguard against an economic preponderance that in time may be transformed into political influence as well, the means for doing so seem quite inadequate to the end. There is no apparent way by which an American military presence, whatever its size, can contain the expansion of German and Japanese economic power. In time, this is bound to become clear to those who may have initially experienced a measure of reassurance from the continuation of this presence. When it does, the American presence may retrospectively be viewed not as having impeded but as having facilitated an expansion the consequences of which are viewed with increasing apprehension and even resentment by those who have come to believe they were lulled into a false sense of security.

At the heart of the position favoring a continuity of role is, more often than not, the unspoken assumption that even though the Cold War may have come to an end, all else will go on largely as before. We will remain the leader even though we can no longer lead quite in the manner of yesterday. Our major allies will continue to need us even though we are no longer needed quite as much as before. The satisfactions of our position will persist even though they may no longer be quite as apparent as they once were. Unfortunately, we are due for a rude awakening. The leadership role that persisted as long as the Cold War persisted is very unlikely to survive the end of that conflict. It is unlikely to do so simply because we will not be needed as before. And although the change in role will almost at once be apparent in the case of Germany, it will in a less dramatic manner eventually become apparent in the case of Japan as well.

In principle, it is of course possible that this country might retain a leadership role though the functions and frustrations of that role change. This is evidently what many supporters of continuity have in mind. With the ending of the Cold War, the United States will presumably change from leader of an alliance formed to counter the threat of Soviet power to leader of a community of nations that needs the American presence in order to maintain a still fragile peace and stability.   In practice, this change in function from that of defending freedom to that of ensuring order is apt to prove critical. Not only is the latter function a considerably more complicated one, it is also a much less appealing one.   Certainly it must prove far less appealing to this nation.   The American purpose was never seen to imply that we should play the role of policeman to the world.   It did imply that we might one day have to free the world, though not to police it.   One polices the world because men and nations are recalcitrant, because they often have deeply conflicting aspirations, and because they are usually influenced more by precept than by example—even the best of examples.   These are the convictions of a traditional outlook on statecraft; they are not the convictions that have moved this nation.

Even if the neutral role of policeman were more congenial to this nation, the question that it holds out for us would insistently arise.   It must not be assumed that the rewards for being policeman to the world will be the same as were the rewards for being defender of the free world.   They will not be the same.   The deference, such as it was, shown in the past to American interests and wishes is unlikely to be shown in the future, since the principal incentive for according such deference will no longer be apparent.   In the past, the security America provided its allies was security against a quite specific threat—a threat, moreover, that the protected could not begin to counter effectively with their own unaided resources.   In the future, this will no longer be the case.   The function of preserving order may, of course, be considered a security-conferring function as well, but it is not one that is directed against a particular party.   Instead, it is directed against a general threat, a threat to peace and stability, regardless of the identity of the party responsible for the threat.   This being so, the utility of America to its major Cold War allies will of necessity become ambiguous in the new dispensation. Circumstances may even arise in which the policeman's role will require that we place ourselves in opposition to our former allies.

At best, then, the expectation must be that the American role will be viewed in the future with more diffidence by others than it was in the past.   It will be exercised on behalf of those who will find much less need for it than they once did.   Even when its exercise appears clearly to respond to need—for example, in the event of a renewed threat of access to the oil of the Persian Gulf—it may elicit little cooperation from those we regard as among the principal beneficiaries.   These states will constitute our principle trading partners, states with which we may then, as now, run a deficit.   With the Cold War a receding memory, but with financial stringency a persisting reality, how long can we be expected to maintain a role that, while no longer required for our security, is viewed by others with the mixture of ingratitude and resentment that has always been the lot of the policeman?

This, in brief, is the case for why the United States should play a much more modest role in the post–Cold War world.   Persuasive though this case is in many respects, doubt must nevertheless persist that it foreshadows the future.   Great powers are not in the habit of voluntarily relinquishing the role to which they have become accustomed, and this despite the fact that the circumstances initially prompting the assumption of the role have changed. It may be argued that when the attainment of great power was relatively easy, as it was for this country, the relinquishing of power should prove correspondingly easy, and particularly so given America's historic traditions. But against this view of easy come, easy go, must be set the consideration that the American experience in world leadership has been, on the whole, a remarkably successful one.   In statecraft, as elsewhere, success normally leads not to withdrawal but to reengagement.

Still more important than these considerations, it would seem, is the process whereby over time, a role becomes invested with a force and sentiment that render it increasingly invulnerable to criticism and change.   Then, too, there is seldom a lack of plausible justification for maintaining a role that has come to be seen as part of the accepted order of things and that has been attended by success.   America's postwar role has been so important and pervasive, it is difficult to imagine a world in which that role is substantially diminished. At the same time, it is not difficult for many to imagine the dangers a marked diminution of the American presence would bring in its wake.   Although the threat of Soviet arms has receded, the threat of global instability has taken its place.   In Europe and, even more, in Asia, this threat of renewed competitions in arms and of heightened tensions can supposedly be kept down only by maintaining the American commitment and presence.

This justification for preserving a continuity of role cannot be effectively turned aside by pointing out that it is quite likely mistaken in its assumptions about the role of force in the international system now emerging, just as it is quite likely mistaken in its assumptions about the principal threat to global stability in the period ahead.   Even if it can be shown that these assumptions are probably misplaced, and that the emerging system will be both peaceful and stable, and almost surely in the mutual relations of the great powers, events might always turn out otherwise.   There is no way of *knowing*, for example, what the effect would be of withdrawing American forces from Japan.   That such withdrawal would lead Japan's neighbors to arm themselves as they have not done in the postwar period and that this response would in turn prompt Japan to new arms efforts seems unlikely.   Yet this result cannot simply be precluded.   It is even possible that a withdrawal of American forces might in time cause Japan to seriously consider acquiring nuclear arms, and this despite America's continued willingness to guarantee Japan's security.

These considerations reflect the innate caution and conservatism that normally mark the conduct of foreign policy.   What may well give them a special persuasiveness is the prospect that the substance of the role may be maintained, though at markedly diminished costs.   Whether calculated in blood or in treasure, this prospect does appear increasingly likely.   To the extent that force is actively employed as a means of policy, the expectation must be that it will be limited to demonstrative uses (Grenada, Libya, Panama, etc.).   In time, limitations on the use of military power will be reflected in the size of the nation's military forces.   Even if the ancient game itself has not at last changed, it holds out the promise today of having moderated to a degree altogether unexpected only yesterday.   This moderation may prove to be the essential condition for maintaining a role that was taken on for reasons and in circumstances that are now a matter of the past.

4 WHY WE WILL SOON MISS THE COLD WAR

John J. Mearsheimer

... We may ... wake up one day lamenting the loss of the order that the Cold War gave to the anarchy of international relations. For untamed anarchy is what Europe knew in the forty-five years of this century before the Cold War, and untamed anarchy—Hobbes's war of all against all—is a prime cause of armed conflict. Those who think that armed conflicts among the European states are now out of the question, that the two world wars burned all the war out of Europe, are projecting unwarranted optimism onto the future. ... The prospect of major crises, even wars, in Europe is likely to increase dramatically now that the Cold War is receding into history. The next forty-five years in Europe ... are likely to be substantially more violent than the past forty-five years, the era that we may someday look back upon not as the Cold War but as the Long Peace, in John Lewis Gaddis's phrase.

This pessimistic conclusion rests on the general argument that the distribution and character of military power among states are the root causes of war and peace. Specifically, the peace in Europe since 1945—precarious at first, but increasingly robust over time—has flowed from three factors: the bipolar distribution of military power on the Continent; the rough military equality between the polar powers, the United States and the Soviet Union; and the ritualistically deplored fact that each of these superpowers is armed with a large nuclear arsenal. ...

A "HARD" THEORY OF PEACE

What caused the era of violence in Europe before 1945, and why has the postwar era, the period of the Cold War, been so much more peaceful? The two world wars before 1945 had myriad particular and unrepeatable causes, but to the student of international relations seeking to establish generalizations about the behavior of states in the past which might illuminate their behavior in the future, two fundamental causes stand out. These are the multipolar distribution of power in Europe, and the imbalances of strength that often developed among the great powers as they jostled for supremacy or advantage.

There is something elementary about the geometry of power in international relations, and so its importance is easy to overlook. "Bipolarity" and "multipolarity" are ungainly but necessary coinages. The Cold War, with two superpowers serving to anchor rival alliances of clearly inferior powers, is our model of bipolarity. Europe in 1914, with France, Germany, Great Britain, Austria-Hungary, and Russia positioned as great powers, is our model of multipolarity.

If the example of 1914 is convincing enough evidence that multipolar systems are the more dangerous geometry of power, then perhaps I should rest my case. Alas for theoretical elegance, there are no empirical studies providing conclusive support for this proposition. From its beginnings until 1945 the European state system was multipolar, so this history is barren of comparisons that would reveal the differing effects of the two systems. Earlier history, to be sure, does furnish scattered examples of bipolar systems, including some—Athens and Sparta, Rome and Carthage—that were warlike. But this history is inconclusive, because it is incomplete. Lacking a comprehensive survey of history, we can't do much more than offer examples—now on this, now on that side of the debate. As a result, the case made here rests chiefly on deduction.

Deductively, a bipolar system is more peaceful for the simple reason that under it only two major powers are in contention. Moreover, those great powers generally demand allegiance from minor powers in the system, which is likely to produce rigid alliance structures. The smaller states are then secure from each other as well as from attack by the rival great power. Consequently (to make a Dick-and-Jane point with a well-worn social-science term), a bipolar system has only one dyad across which war might break out. A multipolar system is much more fluid and has many such dyads. Therefore, other things being equal, war is statistically more likely in a multipolar system than it is in a bipolar one. Admittedly, wars in a multipolar world that involve only minor powers or only one major power are not likely to be as devastating as a conflict between two major powers. But small wars always have the potential to widen into big wars.

Also, deterrence is difficult to maintain in a multipolar state system, because power imbalances are commonplace, and when power asymmetries develop, the strong become hard to deter. Two great powers can join together to attack a third state, as Germany and the Soviet Union did in 1939, when they ganged up on Poland. Furthermore, a major power might simply bully a weaker power in a one-on-one encounter, using its superior strength to coerce or defeat the minor state. Germany's actions against Czechoslovakia in the late 1930s provide a good example of this sort of behavior. Ganging up and bullying are largely unknown in a bipolar system, since with only two great powers dominating center stage, it is impossible to produce the power asymmetries that result in ganging up and bullying.

There is a second reason that deterrence is more problematic under multipolarity. The resolve of opposing states and also the size and strength of opposing coalitions are hard to calculate in this geometry of power, because the shape of the international order tends to remain in flux, owing to the tendency of coalitions to gain and lose partners. This can lead aggressors to conclude falsely that they can coerce others by bluffing war, or even achieve outright victory on the battlefield. For example, Germany was not certain before 1914 that Britain would oppose it if it reached for Continental hegemony, and Germany completely failed to foresee that the United States would eventually move to contain it. In 1939 Germany hoped that France and Britain would stand aside as it conquered Poland, and again failed to foresee the eventual American entry into the war. As a result, Germany exaggerated its prospects for success, which undermined deterrence by encouraging German adventurism.

The prospects for peace, however, are not simply a function of the number of great powers in the system. They are also affected by the relative military strength of those major states. Bipolar and multipolar systems both are likely to be more peaceful when power is distributed equally in them. Power inequalities invite war, because they increase an aggressor's prospects for victory on the battlefield. Most of the general wars that have tormented Europe over the past five centuries have involved one particularly powerful state against the other major powers in the system. This pattern characterized the wars that grew from the attempts at hegemony by Charles V, Philip II, Louis XIV, Revolutionary and Napoleonic France, Wilhelmine Germany, and Nazi Germany. Hence the size of the gap in military power between the two leading states in the system is a key determinant of stability. Small gaps foster peace; larger gaps promote war.

Nuclear weapons seem to be in almost everybody's bad book, but the fact is that they are a powerful force for peace. Deterrence is most likely to hold when the costs and risks of going to war are unambiguously stark. The more horrible the prospect of war, the less likely war is. Deterrence is also more robust when conquest is more difficult. Potential aggressor states are given pause by the patent futility of attempts at expansion.

Nuclear weapons favor peace on both counts. They are weapons of mass destruction, and would produce horrendous devastation if used in any numbers. Moreover, they are more useful for self-defense than for aggression. If both sides' nuclear arsenals are secure from attack, creating an arrangement of mutual assured destruction, neither side can employ these weapons to gain a meaningful military advantage. International conflicts then become tests of pure will. Who would dare to use these weapons of unimaginable destructive power?   Defenders have the advantage here, because defenders usually value their freedom more than aggressors value new conquests.

Nuclear weapons further bolster peace by moving power relations among states toward equality.   States that possess nuclear deterrents can stand up to one another, even if their nuclear arsenals vary greatly in size, as long as both sides have an assured destruction capability.   In addition, mutual assured destruction helps alleviate the vexed problem of miscalculation by leaving little doubt about the relative power of states.

No discussion of the causes of peace in the twentieth century would be complete without a word on nationalism.   With "nationalism" as a synonym for "love of country" I have no quarrel.   But hypernationalism, the belief that other nations or nation-states are both inferior and threatening, is perhaps the single greatest domestic threat to peace, although it is still not a leading force in world politics.   Hypernationalism arose in the past among European states because most of them were nation-states—states composed mainly of people from a single ethnic group—that existed in an anarchic world, under constant threat from other states.   In such a system people who love their own nation can easily come to be contemptuous of the nationalities inhabiting opposing states.   The problem is worsened when domestic elites demonize a rival nation to drum up support for national-security policy.

Hypernationalism finds its most fertile soil under military systems relying on mass armies.   These require sacrifices to sustain, and the state is tempted to appeal to nationalist sentiments to mobilize its citizens to make them. The quickening of hypernationalism is least likely when states can rely on small professional armies, or on complex high-technology military organizations that operate without vast manpower.   For this reason, nuclear weapons work to dampen nationalism, because they shift the basis of military power away from mass armies and toward smaller, high-technology organizations.

Hypernationalism declined sharply in Europe after 1945, not only because of the nuclear revolution but also because the postwar occupation forces kept it down.   Moreover, the European states, no longer providing their own security, lacked an incentive to whip up nationalism to bolster public support for national defense.   But the decisive change came in the shift of the prime locus of European politics to the United States and the Soviet Union—two states made up of peoples of many different ethnic origins which had not exhibited nationalism of the virulent type found in Europe.   This welcome absence of hypernationalism has been further helped by the greater stability of the postwar order.   With less expectation of war, neither superpower felt compelled to mobilize its citizens for war.

Bipolarity, an equal balance of military power, and nuclear weapons—these, then, are the key elements of my explanation for the Long Peace.

Many thoughtful people have found the bipolar system in Europe odious and have sought to end it by dismantling the Soviet empire in Eastern Europe and diminishing Soviet military power. Many have also lamented the military equality obtaining between the superpowers; some have decried the indecisive stalemate it produced, recommending instead a search for military superiority; others have lamented the investment of hundreds of billions of dollars to deter a war that never happened, proving not that the investment, though expensive, paid off, but rather that it was wasted. As for nuclear weapons, well, they are a certifiable Bad Thing. The odium attached to these props of the postwar order has kept many in the West from recognizing a hard truth: they have kept the peace.

But so much for the past. What will keep the peace in the future? Specifically, what new order is likely to emerge if NATO [North Atlantic Treaty Organization] and the Warsaw Pact dissolve, which they will do if the Cold War is really over, and the Soviets withdraw from Eastern Europe and the Americans quit Western Europe, taking their nuclear weapons with them— and should we welcome or fear it?

One dimension of the new European order is certain: it will be multipolar. Germany, France, Britain, and perhaps Italy will assume major-power status. The Soviet Union will decline from superpower status, not only because its military is sure to shrink in size but also because moving forces out of Eastern Europe will make it more difficult for the Soviets to project power onto the Continent. They will, of course, remain a major European power. The resulting four- or five-power system will suffer the problems endemic to multipolar systems—and will therefore be prone to instability. The other two dimensions—the distribution of power among the major states and the distribution of nuclear weapons—are less certain. Indeed, who gets nuclear weapons is likely to be the most problematic question facing the new Europe. Three scenarios of the nuclear future in Europe are possible.

THE "EUROPE WITHOUT NUCLEAR WEAPONS" SCENARIO

Many Europeans (and some Americans) seek to eliminate nuclear weapons from Europe altogether. Fashioning this nuclear-free Europe would require that Britain, France, and the Soviet Union rid themselves of these talismans of their sovereignty—an improbable eventuality, to say the least. Those who wish for it nevertheless believe that it would be the most peaceful arrangement possible. In fact a nuclear-free Europe has the distinction of being the most dangerous among the envisionable post–Cold War orders. The pacifying effects of nuclear weapons—the caution they generate, the security they provide, the rough equality they impose, and the clarity of the relative power they create—would be lost. Peace would then depend on the other dimensions of the new order—the number of poles and the distribution of power among them. The geometry of power in Europe would look much as it did between the world wars—a design for tension, crisis, and possibly even war.

The Soviet Union and [the] unified Germany would likely be the most powerful states in a nuclear-free Europe. A band of small independent states in Eastern Europe would lie between them. These minor Eastern European powers would be likely to fear the Soviets as much as the Germans, and thus would probably not be disposed to cooperate with the Soviets to deter possible German aggression. In fact, this very problem arose in the 1930s, and the past forty-five years of Soviet occupation have surely done little to mitigate Eastern European fears of a Soviet military presence. Thus scenarios in which Germany uses force against Poland, Czechoslovakia, or even Austria enter the realm of the possible in a nuclear-free Europe.

Then, too, the Soviet withdrawal from Eastern Europe hardly guarantees a permanent exit. Indeed, the Russian presence in Eastern Europe has surged and ebbed repeatedly over the past few centuries. In a grave warning, a member of President Mikhail Gorbachev's negotiating team at the [1990] Washington summit said, "You have the same explosive mixture you had in Germany in the 1930s. The humiliation of a great power. Economic troubles. The rise of nationalism. You should not underestimate the danger."

Conflicts between Eastern European states might also threaten the stability of the new European order. . . .

Warfare in Eastern Europe . . . might widen to include the major powers, especially if disorder created fluid politics that offered opportunities for expanded influence, or threatened defeat for states friendly to one or another of the major powers. During the Cold War both superpowers were drawn into Third World conflicts across the globe, often in distant areas of little strategic importance. Eastern Europe is directly adjacent to both the Soviet Union and Germany, and it has considerable economic and strategic importance. Thus trouble in Eastern Europe would offer even greater temptations to these powers than past conflicts in the Third World offered to the superpowers. Furthermore, Eastern European states would have a strong incentive to drag the major powers into their local conflicts, because the results of such conflicts would be largely determined by the relative success of each party in finding external allies.

It is difficult to predict the precise balance of conventional military power that will emerge in post–Cold War Europe. The Soviet Union might recover its strength soon after withdrawing from Eastern Europe. In that case Soviet power would outmatch German power. But centrifugal national forces might pull the Soviet Union apart, leaving no remnant state that is the equal of [the] unified Germany. Finally, and probably most likely, Germany and the Soviet Union might emerge as powers of roughly equal strength. The first two geometries of power, with their marked military inequality between the two leading countries, would be especially worrisome, although there would be cause for concern even if Soviet and German power were balanced.

A non-nuclear Europe, to round out this catalogue of dangers, would likely be especially disturbed by hypernationalism, since security in such an order would rest on mass armies, which, as we have seen, often cannot be maintained without a mobilized public. The problem would probably be most acute in Eastern Europe, with its uncertain borders and irredentist minority groups. But there is also potential for trouble in Germany. The Germans have generally done an admirable job of combating hypernationalism over the past forty-five years, and of confounding the dark side of their past. Nevertheless, a portent like the recent call of some prominent Germanys for a return to greater nationalism in historical education is disquieting.

For all these reasons, it is perhaps just as well that a nuclear-free Europe, much as it may be longed for by so many Europeans, does not appear to be in the cards.

THE "CURRENT OWNERSHIP" SCENARIO

Under this scenario Britain, France, and the Soviet Union retain their nuclear weapons, but no new nuclear powers emerge in Europe. This vision of a nuclear-free zone in Central Europe, with nuclear weapons remaining on the flanks of the Continent, is also popular in Europe, but it, too, has doubtful prospects.

Germany will prevent it over the long run. The Germans are not likely to be willing to rely on the Poles or the Czechs to provide their forward defense against a possible direct Soviet conventional attack on their homeland. Nor are the Germans likely to trust the Soviet Union to refrain for all time from nuclear blackmail against a non-nuclear Germany. Hence they will eventually look to a nuclear weapons as the surest means of security, just as NATO has done.

The small states of Eastern Europe will also have strong incentives to acquire nuclear weapons. Without them they would be open to nuclear blackmail by the Soviet Union, or by Germany if proliferation stopped there. Even if those major powers did not have nuclear arsenals, no Eastern European state could match German or Soviet conventional strength.

Clearly, then, a scenario in which current ownership continues, without proliferation, seems very unlikely.

THE "NUCLEAR PROLIFERATION" SCENARIO

The most probable scenario in the wake of the Cold War is further nuclear proliferation in Europe. This outcome is laden with dangers, but it also might just provide the best hope for maintaining stability on the Continent. Everything depends on how proliferation is managed. Mismanaged proliferation could produce disaster; well-managed proliferation could produce an order nearly as stable as that of the Long Peace. . . .

. . . I am pessimistic that proliferation can be well managed. The members of the nuclear club are likely to resist proliferation, but they cannot easily manage this tricky process while at the same time resisting it—and they will several motives to resist.   The established nuclear powers will be exceedingly chary of helping the new nuclear powers build secure deterrents, simply because it goes against the grain of state behavior to share military secrets with other states.   After all, knowledge of sensitive military technology could be turned against the donor state if that technology were passed on to adversaries.   Furthermore, proliferation in Europe will undermine the legitimacy of the 1968 Nuclear Non-Proliferation Treaty, and this could open the floodgates of proliferation worldwide.   The current nuclear powers will not want that to happen, and so they will probably spend their energy trying to thwart proliferation, rather than seeking to manage it.

The best time for proliferation to occur would be during a period of relative international calm.   Proliferation in the midst of a crisis would obviously be dangerous, since states in conflict with an emerging nuclear power would then have a powerful incentive to interrupt the process by force.   However, the opposition to proliferation by citizens of the potential nuclear powers would be so vociferous, and the external resistance from the nuclear club would be so great, that it might take a crisis to make those powers willing to pay the domestic and international costs of building a nuclear force.   All of which means that proliferation is likely to occur under international conditions that virtually ensure it will be mismanaged.

IS WAR OBSOLETE?

Many students of European politics will reject my pessimistic analysis of post–Cold War Europe.   They will say that a multipolar Europe, with or without nuclear weapons, will be no less peaceful than the present order. Three specific scenarios for a peaceful future have been advanced, each of which rests on a well-known theory of international relations.   However, each of these "soft" theories of peace is flawed.

Under the first optimistic scenario, a non-nuclear Europe would remain peaceful because Europeans recognize that even a conventional war would be horrific.   Sobered by history, national leaders will take care to avoid war. This scenario rests on the "obsolescence of war" theory, which posits that modern conventional war had become so deadly by 1945 as to be unthinkable as an instrument of statecraft.   War is yesterday's nightmare.

The fact that the Second World War occurred casts doubt on this theory: if any war could have persuaded Europeans to forswear conventional war, it should have been the First World War, with its vast casualties.   The key flaw in this theory is the assumption that all conventional wars will be long and bloody wars of attrition.   Proponents ignore the evidence of several wars since 1945, as well as several campaign-ending battles of the Second World War, that it is still possible to gain a quick and decisive victory on the conventional battlefield and avoid the devastation of a protracted conflict.

Conventional wars can be won rather cheaply; nuclear war cannot be, because neither side can escape devastation by the other, regardless of what happens on the battlefield.   Thus the incentives to avoid war are of another order of intensity in a nuclear world than they are in a conventional world.

There are several other flaws in this scenario.   There is no systematic evidence demonstrating that Europeans believe war is obsolete.   The Romanians and the Hungarians don't seem to have gotten the message.   However, even if it were widely believed in Europe that war is no longer thinkable, attitudes could change.   Public opinion on national-security issues is notoriously fickle and responsive to manipulation by elites as well as to changes in the international environment.   An end to the Cold War, as we have seen, will be accompanied by a sea change in the geometry of power in Europe, which will surely alter European thinking about questions of war and peace. Is it not possible, for example, that German thinking about the benefits of controlling Eastern Europe will change markedly once American forces are withdrawn from Central Europe and the Germans are left to provide for their own security?   Is it not possible that they would countenance a conventional war against a substantially weaker Eastern European state to enhance their position vis-à-vis the Soviet Union? Finally, only one country need decide that war is thinkable to make war possible.

IS PROSPERITY THE PATH TO PEACE?

Proponents of the second optimistic scenario base their optimism about the future of Europe on the unified European market coming in 1992—the realization of the dream of the European Community.   A strong EC, they argue, ensures that the European economy will remain open and prosperous, which will keep the European states cooperating with one another.   Prosperity will make for peace.   The threat of an aggressive Germany will be removed by enclosing the newly unified German state in the benign embrace of the EC.   Even Eastern Europe and the Soviet Union can eventually be brought into the EC.   Peace and prosperity will then extend their sway from the Atlantic to the Urals.

This scenario is based on the theory of economic liberalism, which assumes that states are primarily motivated by the desire to achieve prosperity and that leaders place the material welfare of their publics above all other considerations, including security.   Stability flows not from military power but from the creation of a liberal economic order.

A liberal economic order works in several ways to enhance peace and dampen conflict.   In the first place, it requires significant political cooperation to make the trading system work—make states richer.   The more prosperous states grow, the greater their incentive for further political cooperation.   A benevolent spiral relationship sets in between political cooperation and prosperity.   Second, a liberal economic order fosters economic interdependence, a situation in which states are mutually vulnerable in the economic realm. When interdependence is high, the theory holds, there is less temptation to cheat or behave aggressively toward other states, because all states can retaliate economically.   Finally, some theorists argue, an international institution like the EC will, with ever-increasing political cooperation, become so powerful that it will take on a life of its own, eventually evolving into a superstate. . . .

This theory has one grave flaw: the main assumption underpinning it is wrong.   States are not primarily motivated by the desire to achieve prosperity. Although economic calculations are hardly trivial to them, states operate in both an international political and an international economic environment, and the former dominates the latter when the two systems come into conflict. Survival in an anarchic international political system is the highest goal a state can have.

Proponents of economic liberalism largely ignore the effects of anarchy on state behavior and concentrate instead on economic motives.   When this omission is corrected, however, their arguments collapse for two reasons.

Competition for security makes it difficult for states to cooperate, which, according to the theory of economic liberalism, they must do.   When security is scarce, states become more concerned about relative than about absolute gains.   They ask of an exchange not "Will both of us gain?" but "Who will gain more?"   They reject even cooperation that will yield an absolute economic gain if the other state will gain more, from fear that the other might convert its gain to military strength, and then use this strength to win by coercion in later rounds.   Cooperation is much easier to achieve if states worry only about absolute gains.   The goal, then, is simply to ensure that the overall economic pie is expanding and that each state is getting at least some part of the increase.   However, anarchy guarantees that security will often be scarce; this heightens states' concerns about relative gains, which makes cooperation difficult unless the pie can be finely sliced to reflect, and thus not disturb, the current balance of power.

Interdependence, moreover, is as likely to lead to conflict as to cooperation, because states will struggle to escape the vulnerability that interdependence creates, in order to bolster their national security.   In time of crisis or war, states that depend on others for critical economic supplies will fear cutoff or blackmail; they may well respond by trying to seize the source of supply by force of arms.   There are numerous historical examples of states' pursuing aggressive military policies for the purpose of achieving economic autarky. One thinks of both Japan and Germany during the interwar period.   And one recalls that during the Arab oil embargo of the early 1970s there was much talk in America about using military force to seize Arab oil fields. . . .

We certainly see a correlation [during the Cold War] between interdependence and stability, but that does not mean that interdependence has caused cooperation among the Western democracies.   More likely the Cold

War was the prime cause of cooperation among the Western democracies, and the main reason that intra-EC relations have flourished.

A powerful and potentially dangerous Soviet Union forced the Western democracies to band together to meet a common threat. This threat muted concerns about relative gains arising from economic cooperation among the EC states by giving each Western democracy a vested interest in seeing its alliance partners grow powerful. Each increment of power helped deter the Soviets. Moreover, they all had a powerful incentive to avoid conflict with one another while the Soviet Union loomed to the East, ready to harvest the grain of Western quarrels.

In addition, America's hegemonic position in NATO, the military counterpart to the EC, mitigated the effects of anarchy on the Western democracies and induced cooperation among them. America not only provided protection against the Soviet threat; it also guaranteed that no EC state would aggress against another. . . .

Take away the present Soviet threat to Western Europe, send the American forces home, and relations among the EC states will be fundamentally altered. Without a common Soviet threat or an American night watchman, Western European states will do what they did for centuries before the onset of the Cold War—look upon one another with abiding suspicion. Consequently, they will worry about imbalances in gains and about the loss of autonomy that results from cooperation. Cooperation in this new order will be more difficult than it was during the Cold War. Conflict will be more likely.

In sum, there are good reasons for being skeptical about the claim that a more powerful EC can provide the basis for peace in a multipolar Europe.

DO DEMOCRACIES REALLY LOVE PEACE?

Under the third scenario war is avoided because many European states have become democratic since the early twentieth century, and liberal democracies simply do not fight one another. At a minimum, the presence of liberal democracies in Western Europe renders that half of Europe free from armed conflict. At a maximum, democracy spreads to Eastern Europe and the Soviet Union, bolstering peace. The idea that peace is cognate with democracy is a vision of international relations shared by both liberals and neoconservatives.

This scenario rests on the "peace-loving democracies" theory. Two arguments are made for it.

First, some claim that authoritarian leaders are more likely to go to war than leaders of democracies, because authoritarian leaders are not accountable to their publics, which carry the main burdens of war. In a democracy the citizenry, which pays the price of war, has a greater say in what the government does. The people, so the argument goes, are more hesitant to start trouble, because it is they who must pay the bloody price; hence the greater their power, the fewer wars.

The second argument rests on the claim that the citizens of liberal democracies respect popular democratic rights—those of their countrymen, and those of people in other states. They view democratic governments as more legitimate than others, and so are loath to impose a foreign regime on a democratic state by force. Thus an inhibition on war missing from other international relationships is introduced when two democracies face each other.

The first of these arguments is flawed because it is not possible to sustain the claim that the people in a democracy are especially sensitive to the costs of war and therefore less willing than authoritarian leaders to fight wars. In fact the historical record shows that democracies are every bit as likely to fight wars as are authoritarian states, though admittedly, thus far, not with other democracies.

Furthermore, mass publics, whether in a democracy or not, can become deeply imbued with nationalistic or religious fervor, making them prone to support aggression and quite indifferent to costs. The widespread public support in post-Revolutionary France for Napoleon's wars is just one example of this phenomenon. At the same time, authoritarian leaders are often fearful of going to war, because war tends to unleash democratic forces that can undermine the regime. In short, war can impose high costs on authoritarian leaders as well as on their citizenry.

The second argument, which emphasizes the transnational respect for democratic rights among democracies, rests on a secondary factor that is generally overridden by other factors such as nationalism and religious fundamentalism. Moreover, there is another problem with the argument. The possibility always exists that a democracy, especially the kind of fledgling democracy emerging in Eastern Europe, will revert to an authoritarian state. This threat of backsliding means that one democratic state can never be sure that another democratic state will not turn on it sometime in the future. Liberal democracies must therefore worry about relative power among themselves, which is tantamount to saying that each has an incentive to consider aggression against another to forestall trouble. Lamentably, it is not possible for even liberal democracies to transcend anarchy. . . .

While the spread of democracy across Europe has great potential benefits for human rights, it will not guarantee peaceful relations among the states of post–Cold War Europe. Most Americans will find this argument counterintuitive. They see the United States as fundamentally peace-loving, and they ascribe this peacefulness to its democratic character. From this they generalize that democracies are more peaceful than authoritarian states, which leads them to conclude that the complete democratization of Europe would largely eliminate the threat of war. This view of international politics is likely to be repudiated by the events of coming years.

MISSING THE COLD WAR

The implications of my analysis are straightforward, if paradoxical. De-velopments that threaten to end the Cold War are dangerous. The West has an interest in maintaining peace in Europe. It therefore has an interest in maintaining the Cold War order, and hence has an interest in continuing the Cold War confrontation. The Cold War antagonism could be continued at lower levels of East-West tension than have prevailed in the past, but a complete end to the Cold War would create more problems than it would solve.

The fate of the Cold War is mainly in the hands of the Soviet Union. The Soviet Union is the only superpower that can seriously threaten to overrun Europe, and the Soviet threat provides the glue that holds NATO together. Take away that offensive threat and the United States is likely to abandon the Continent; the defensive alliance it has headed for forty years may well then disintegrate, bringing an end to the bipolar order that has kept the peace of Europe for the past forty-five years.

There is little the Americans or the West Europeans can do to perpetuate the Cold War.

For one thing, domestic politics preclude it. Western leaders obviously cannot base national-security policy on the need to maintain forces in Central Europe simply to keep the Soviets there. The idea of deploying large numbers of troops in order to bait the Soviets into an order-keeping competition would be dismissed as bizarre, and contrary to the general belief that ending the Cold War and removing the Soviet yoke from Eastern Europe would make the world safer and better.

For another, the idea of propping up a declining rival runs counter to the basic behavior of states. States are principally concerned about their relative power in the system—hence they look for opportunities to take advantage of one another. If anything, they prefer to see adversaries decline, and invariably do whatever they can to speed up the process and maximize the distance of the fall. States, in other words, do not ask which distribution of power best facilitates stability and then do everything possible to build or maintain such an order. Instead, each pursues the narrower aim of maxi-mizing its power advantage over potential adversaries. The particular in-ternational order that results is simply a by-product of that competition.

Consider, for example, the origins of the Cold War order in Europe. No state intended to create it. In fact the United States and the Soviet Union each worked hard in the early years of the Cold War to undermine the other's position in Europe, which would have ended the bipolar order on the Con-tinent. The remarkably stable system that emerged in Europe in the late 1940s was the unintended consequence of an intense competition between the superpowers.

Moreover, even if the Americans and the West Europeans wanted to help the Soviets maintain their status as a superpower, it is not apparent that they could do so. The Soviet Union is leaving Eastern Europe and cutting its military forces largely because its economy is floundering badly. The Soviets don't know how to fix their economy themselves, and there is little that Western governments can do to help them. The West can and should avoid doing malicious mischief to the Soviet economy, but at this juncture it is difficult to see how the West can have a significant positive influence.

The fact that the West cannot sustain the Cold War does not mean that the United States should make no attempt to preserve the current order. It should do what it can to avert a complete mutual withdrawal from Europe. For instance, the American negotiating position at the conventional-arms-control talks should aim toward large mutual force reductions but should not contemplate complete mutual withdrawal. The Soviets may opt to withdraw all their forces unilaterally anyway; if so, there is little the United States can do to stop them.

Should complete Soviet withdrawal from Eastern Europe prove unavoidable, the West would confront the question of how to maintain peace in a multipolar Europe. Three policy prescriptions are in order.

First, the United States should encourage the limited and carefully managed proliferation of nuclear weapons in Europe. The best hope for avoiding war in post–Cold War Europe is nuclear deterrence; hence some nuclear proliferation is necessary, to compensate for the withdrawal of the Soviet and American nuclear arsenals from Central Europe. Ideally, as I have argued, nuclear weapons would spread to Germany but to no other state.

Second, Britain and the United States, as well as the Continental states, will have to counter any emerging aggressor actively and efficiently, in order to offset the ganging up and bullying that are sure to arise in post–Cold War Europe. Balancing in a multipolar system, however, is usually a problem-ridden enterprise, because of either geography or the problems of coordination. Britain and the United States, physically separated from the Continent, may conclude that they have little interest in what happens there. That would be abandoning their responsibilities and, more important, their interests. Both states failed to counter Germany before the two world wars, making war more likely. It is essential for peace in Europe that they not repeat their past mistakes.

Both states must maintain military forces that can be deployed against Continental states that threaten to start a war. To do this they must persuade their citizens to support a policy of continued Continental commitment. This will be more difficult than it once was, because its principal purpose will be to preserve peace, rather than to prevent an imminent hegemony, and the prevention of hegemony is a simpler goal to explain publicly. Furthermore, this prescription asks both countries to take on an unaccustomed task, given that it is the basic nature of states to focus on maximizing relative power, not on bolstering stability. Nevertheless, the British and the Americans have a real stake in peace, especially since there is the risk that a European war might involve the large-scale use of nuclear weapons. Therefore, it should be possible for their governments to lead their publics to recognize this interest and support policies that protect it.

The Soviet Union may eventually return to its past expansionism and threaten to upset the status quo. If so, we are back to the Cold War. However, if the Soviets adhere to status-quo policies, Soviet power could play a key role in countering Germany and in maintaining order in Eastern Europe. It is important in those cases where the Soviets are acting in a balancing capacity that the United States cooperate with its former adversary and not let residual distrust from the Cold War obtrude.

Third, a concerted effort should be made to keep hypernationalism at bay, especially in Eastern Europe. Nationalism has been contained during the Cold War, but it is likely to re-emerge once Soviet and American forces leave the heart of Europe. It will be a force for trouble unless curbed. The teaching of honest national history is especially important, since the teaching of false, chauvinist history is the main vehicle for spreading hypernationalism. States that teach a dishonestly self-exculpating or self-glorifying history should be publicly criticized and sanctioned.

None of these tasks will be easy. In fact, I expect that the bulk of my prescriptions will not be followed; most run contrary to important strains of domestic American and European opinion, and to the basic nature of state behavior. And even if they are followed, peace in Europe will not be guaranteed. If the Cold War is truly behind us, therefore, the stability of the past forty-five years is not likely to be seen again in the coming decades.

5 THE CASE FOR ADJUSTMENT

Earl C. Ravenal

For the first time in almost half a century, both the United States and the Soviet Union have a chance to plan their strategies and military forces without exclusive and obsessive reference to one another. Presented to the United States—indeed to both waning superpowers—is not merely a choice among foreign policy alternatives, but literally a choice of worlds—alternative states of the international system. But the two powers must realize that the international system, as the environment in which foreign and military policy is made, also operates as a set of constraints, especially because it is increasingly outside the control of the nations themselves. Thus, it is important for each side to understand where that system is going, not next week, but over the broad span of the future—say, the next 15 to 30 years—and to view it with sufficient perspective, even abstraction, to discern its emerging structural outlines. At stake is common security for these two great nations.

For the past 45 years, the two superpowers enjoyed substantial autonomy from the pressures of lesser countries; and they could indulge themselves in the conceit that they were immune also from the constraints of the international system in the large—indeed, that their actions, together certainly but even singly, altered and shaped that system. (But that, of course, is the definition of a superpower.) Now Moscow and Washington face a basic decision: either to renew their attempt at control, or to make a serious adjustment to the workings of the international system. The judgment here is that both of the superpowers will increasingly have to take the international system as they find it. The shape of the entire system—as well as the conduct of the individual members—is moving beyond the determinative reach of either the United States or the Soviet Union. The age of the superpowers is passing.

History is properly seen as the unfolding and shifting of the parameters of the international system, which is mostly a political-military universe. Although the phenomenon went unnoticed in the flurry of renewed Cold War

Note: Footnotes have been deleted.

preparations, a shift of parametric conditions of the system in the early 1980s caused the superpowers to realize that competitive intervention in the so-called Third World was not only increasingly inhibited and frustrated, but unnecessary.   By 1985 Soviet leaders seem to have come to a dual recognition: that there was no profit in winning the Third World, and that the United States was not the inevitable enemy or even competitor.   With that knowledge, Gorbachev began to explore accommodation with the United States.

A parallel recognition on the American side probably took place earlier than commonly realized.   The essential failure of the Reagan Doctrine played its part in this.   The Reagan Doctrine was articulated—or, more characteristically, unarticulated—in 1985, but in effect this effort was policy from the inception of the Reagan administration and formed part of its attempt to restore American dominance in the world, more or less the way it had existed, in reality or in nostalgia, 25 or 30 years before.   Even this cheap and wishful policy of revanchism at the periphery of the communist empire proved to be ephemeral, because it was unmanageable and politically unsustainable. Meanwhile, Reagan's defense policy, a central part of the policy of restoration, also proved unmanageable.   It raised defense spending in constant 1991 dollars to nearly $351 billion a year at its peak in fiscal year 1985, but that budget reflected plans made as early as 1983.   In other words, the momentum of American restoration had crested well before the end of Ronald Reagan's first term.

The efforts of the Reagan administration are now being hailed, in some circles, as the burst of demonstrable strength that brought about the final capitulation of the communist world.   On the contrary, they should be seen as the most recent "bend point" in post–World War II American foreign policy.   An earlier important point of deflection was the Nixon Doctrine (writ large), which attempted to move the international system from unsupportable bipolar confrontation to the more subtle and efficient multipolar balance of power.   Ironically, precisely because the Reagan administration tried so ambitiously and still failed, it provided, despite itself, another piece of evidence that the age of the superpowers was passing.

Early in the 1980s, one could identify three large areas in which mutual accommodation would have to be made between the United States and the Soviet Union if relations were to be placed on a firmer foundation.   The first was arms control.   The second was some kind of disengagement from Central Europe—a truce between the alliances, a settlement of the German question, a putting back together of Europe.   Third was a modus vivendi regarding intervention in the Third World, that playground of the displaced ambitions of the two Cold War contestants.

The first area was an easy target, even in the early 1980s.   The requisite formulas of a successful arms control agreement were straightforward, the area was subject to the exercise of rationality, and the essential interest of the two parties was demonstrably common: Each side should have wanted to eliminate those combinations of arms that created crisis instability, the only avenue to a possible nuclear war involving the homelands of the two powers.

The second area has now been resolved, in its essential direction, by history and by the will of the peoples of Eastern Europe, though the institutional arrangements of Europe still do not reflect the changes.   The Soviet side deserves credit for intelligent initiatives permitting the sweeping retrenchment of its power in Central and Eastern Europe, but these were essentially accommodations of reality—a fact that does not render the initiatives any less constructive or imaginative.   What is less evident, but now in train, is that under the cover of Soviet acquiescence in German participation in NATO [the North Atlantic Treaty Organization], the United States, too, is being pried out of its geopolitical position in Europe.

Superpower competition in the Third World has been the most intractable of the three areas.   Yet, there too, both parties have been responding to the (imperfectly learned) lessons of Vietnam and Afghanistan: the shifting and unsound basis for political allegiance; the transience of any gains, political or military; the exemplary ingratitude of clients; the grossly unfavorable cost-benefit ratio of intervention; the bottomless pit of economic aid; and finally the rise of self-sufficient and powerful regional hegemonic powers, suspicious and resentful of extraregional penetration.

CONDOMINIUM OR DISENGAGEMENT

The large options afforded each of the waning superpowers are two: The first is to attempt to achieve condominium.   Leonid Brezhnev and Richard Nixon played with this approach in 1972 and 1973, and Mikhail Gorbachev has been offering it to his American counterparts since the summit meeting at Reykjavík in 1986.   Condominium would represent a collusion by Moscow and Washington to rescue the declining domestic fortunes and international status of each.   It is an intelligent response and a real option, but it is not the main current of history.

The other alternative is mutual disengagement.   It is a course more likely to be taken, precisely because it is more the product of the objective realities of the unfolding international system, namely the fragmentation and the regionalization of power.   Each is making extraregional intervention by the great powers unproductive, on the one hand, and unnecessary, on the other.

President George Bush's mobilization of America and the world to intervene in the Persian Gulf may seem to invalidate this categorization of alternatives. But his actions are subject to two divergent interpretations, and neither is promising.   One is that America is attempting true multilateral "collective security," involving a genuine coalition of nations (though somewhat hectored by American diplomacy) to secure order in every region of the world.   The other interpretation—and, in my view, the "inner meaning" and objective intent of the move—is that America has embarked on an aggressive assertion of strategic independence; the deployments in the Persian Gulf represent a new birth of ambitious American unilateralism, appropriate to the status of the "sole remaining superpower," as is heard repeatedly these days. Of course, if this action expresses a "Bush Doctrine," its nature and goals remain as yet unarticulated—perhaps a metaphor for the entire Bush administration. Nevertheless, the content of such a doctrine would be that the United States, as the lone superpower survivor of the Cold War, can afford to retrench somewhat in its tangible military power and defense budgets but still needs to keep a good deal of force in order to wield decisive world influence. This second interpretation harbors an actual disdain by the United States for allies and for the processes of international organization, but it masks such attitudes in the rhetoric and institutions of collective security.

Whether the U.S. initiative in the Persian Gulf conforms to the first or second interpretation, it will be the last gasp of either idealistic American support for collective security or the impulse of American unilateralism. The events since the Iraqi invasion of Kuwait in August 1990 only *seem* to confirm the common wisdom about American national strategy in the post–Cold War era: namely, that with the waning of bipolar competition with the Soviet Union, particularly in the European theater, U.S. strategy can now be directed to active intervention to resolve conflicts in other regions on terms favorable to American interests; and that those interests themselves are to be defined broadly as the maintenance of stability and order in any and every region of the world.

In fact, the lessons being drawn from the Persian Gulf crisis are both overdrawn and misleading. Disturbances in the international system will take place. They may even be severe, and they often will be of a political-military, not merely an economic or cultural, nature. Such disturbances will take place in most regions and for the foreseeable future. But these will not threaten the core values of American society nor will they, in most cases, respond favorably and durably to American military intervention. They will reflect the regionalization of power—the fragmentation of power both among and within the regions of the world; and therefore, they will contain the potential of self-limitation. Far from compounding "the threat" to the United States, multiple international or intersocietal rivalries, and even death struggles, will fracture and waste and deflect otherwise possible aggregations of potent and hostile force. In short, these disturbances do not require an American political-military response.

American policy should be to quarantine regional violence and compartmentalize regional instability, but not by active intervention. Compartmentalization can be accomplished, almost by definition, better through nonintervention than through automatically universalizing the quarrel, which has been the American response in the Gulf crisis. Indeed, U.S. intervention in other-regional antagonisms and conflicts—whether unilaterally or collectively—is the only way that such violence can reach America's shores and heartland or impair the core values and true interests of American society.

At most, American policy should encourage regional balances of power, whether bipolar or multipolar. The balances do not even have to be neat and precisely calibrated: Rough and messy ones will do. In the Persian Gulf and Southwest Asia, incessant and feckless American intervention not only has, over the years, antagonized and neutralized potentially effective power balancers—Iran is still the obvious hegemon in the area—but has also, in the present instance, largely preempted the power-balancing role that intraregional countries should be performing. American intervention encourages regional countries to hang back, perhaps placating urgent and personal American presidential appeals with small or even token gestures of cooperation, and watch the Americans do the geopolitical work they should be doing for themselves.

What goes for the United States goes also, *mutatis mutandis*, for the other erstwhile superpower. Instead of aspiring to condominial intervention with the United States, the Soviet Union should join the United States merely in a bargain not to intervene—a mutual nonintervention pact, but tacit and fortified only by cumulative example. Mutual nonintervention would remove the suspicion that one or the other was deliberately trying to profit by intervening in some regional situation, whether by taking sides or just by interposing its arbitration or good offices.

More conflict and less determinacy within other regions of the world would not—contrary to prevalent perceptions—create more danger and less stability in the entire international system, or in the immediate precincts of the United States (the latter judgment applies less comfortably to the Soviet Union). Quite the contrary, isolation of conflicts within other regions— regardless of how those conflicts were resolved, or not resolved—would contribute to a kind of "metastability" of the entire international system, that is, a situation where even extreme political fluidity and violent and abrupt change could occur within regions, yet the structure of the entire system would not be undermined. Nations such as the United States could remain neutral and substantially unaffected by disturbances in other regions.

True, serious indirect effects could ensue from such other-regional quarrels, such as resource denials and excessive price fluctuations of certain commodities. These effects could be envisaged and in some way provided for, but military intervention is unlikely to be a rewarding option. The American intervention in the Persian Gulf is pertinent here: Ostensibly to protect the oil flowing to the United States from this region, U.S. military preparations are costing between \$180 and \$280 a barrel (depending on the comprehensiveness of the accounting of costs). [These figures do not include the costs of the Persian Gulf War, which began after this essay was written—Eds.] Instead, Washington should permit the market, acting in anticipation and fear of resource denial, to discount risks and to provide incentives to hedge against such denial, through diversification and substitution of energy sources and other contingent arrangements.

As the real and hard lessons of the Gulf seep in, the U.S. intervention will be seen, not as a harbinger of renewed order and control, but merely as another piece of evidence that power in the international system is disintegrating.   Then America's choices will be narrowed again and will converge on the acceptance of mutual disengagement.   At that point mutual disengagement will become the course of security for both of the superpowers, not through their predilection or willful selection, but because it is dictated, or at least strongly indicated, by the entire course and structure of the international system.

GENERAL UNALIGNMENT

What is the future shape of that international system likely to be? Several types of international systems can be differentiated and are ideally possible: unitary state or universal empire; collective security, including the variant of condominium; bipolar confrontation of blocs; multipolar balance of power; or general unalignment.   The system that appears to be most probable, in the mid-range of 15 to 30 years, is what might be called general unalignment. This is a system, beyond the present controlled multipolar balance of power of four, five, or six nations, that has the following characteristics: a more extensive fragmentation of power and political-military initiative; a variety of power configurations in regions of the world, from hegemony to blocked hegemony and a more even balance of nations; and somewhat wider nuclear proliferation.   It is a system that can occur either if several important nations pursue minimal involvement, or if the diffusion of power becomes sufficient to allow autonomous political-military behavior by more than perhaps eight to ten states. . . .

What will be the characteristics of the emerging international system, within which, much more than upon which, the foreign policy of the important nations will have to operate?   There are six:

The first is the high probability of troubles, such as embargoes, expropriations, coups, revolutions, externally supported subversions, and thrusts by impatient irredentist states.

The second is increasing interdependence, a tendency that has a different implication from the one its proponents usually assert.   Interdependence is a set of functional linkages of nations: resources, access routes, economic activities and organizations, emigrating populations, and the physical environment.   These ties harbor problems that could be aggravated to the point that they become threats to the security of nations, demanding—but not offering—solutions.

The third element of the future international system is the probable absence of an ultimate adjustment mechanism in the form of any supranational institution or arrangements that can authoritatively police the system, dispensing justice and granting relief.   Of course, some organized cooperation among states will occur, but the situation described here is expressive of the structural fact that the future international system will lack hierarchy.

A fourth factor is an interim conclusion of the first three. Action of states to bring about conditions in the external system that enhance their security will take the form of unilateral interventions rather than collaborative world order. This is not to say that such interventions will be advisable or effective, or that the current superpowers have not begun to learn from the frustration or the disproportionate expense of such ventures.

The fifth characteristic of the future—the heart of this analysis—is the diffusion of power beyond some ideal geometry of powerful but "responsible" states. By all measures of power—military, whether nuclear or conventional, actual or potential; economic, whether in total wealth or commercial weight; or political—there may be a dozen and a half or more salient states. They will not necessarily be equal, and they may not necessarily be armed with nuclear weapons, but they will be potent to the point of enjoying the possibility of significant independent action.

For a time frame of the next 15 to 30 years, hegemonic powers (not in order and not all unopposed, of course) will include China, Japan, the United States, and the USSR; another tier consisting of the rising regional countries Brazil, India, Indonesia, Iran, and Nigeria; and a list of ponderable though doubtful contenders: Egypt, Germany, South Africa, and Vietnam. Counterhegemonic powers will be the more obvious ones: Argentina, France, Israel, and Pakistan; and perhaps a few of the less obvious or more doubtful ones: Australia, Bangladesh, Britain, Canada, Iraq, Mexico, Saudi Arabia, South Korea, Sweden, Syria, and Yugoslavia. This list, though derived from orderly criteria, is more indicative than definitive of the actual individual nations; yet it is definitive of the structure of the whole future international system.

The diffusion of power has several consequences. One is that cracks appear in military alliances and limits become evident in political unions. Another aspect of diffusion is the growing impracticality of using military power, whether nuclear, conventional, or subconventional, for political purposes. (This is not, however, to assert either the absolute or the relative uselessness of military force.)

The sixth condition that will complicate enforcement of international order, collectively or unilaterally, is the absence of domestic support for military intervention, not just in America but to a certain extent in most countries. The lack of public support might not prevent interventions, but it might critically inhibit their prosecution. This may be America's enduring lesson from Vietnam, and the Soviet Union's from Afghanistan.

Nowadays, with the disintegration of the communist world, it is frequently suggested that new kinds of threats—arising from a matrix of economic causes, environmental factors, population-based problems such as emigration, and social phenomena such as terrorism and narcotics—will be peculiarly virulent and dangerous to the security of the United States. Such new disturbances will certainly be vexing and frustrating. But those that are not elevated to the strategic level (and this, pointedly, should include narcotics) are not prime candidates for the use of, or the preparation of, military force.

Even those that do get elevated to strategic significance (such as politically directed embargoes or terrorism orchestrated for real military effect) are not such that they require the types and magnitudes of military preparation that the world has grown accustomed to over the past four decades. Perhaps at a low, constant level some more-vigilant passive defenses could be considered, but that is all. In other words, despite the salience of the new functional issues, they would remain, on the scale of grand strategy, nuisances—reminders of the increasingly stultified police role of the erstwhile superpowers. The situation may be nasty and brutish, but it will not be short.

PRINCIPLES FOR NATIONAL STRATEGY

Thus, the United States and the Soviet Union should be seeking principles—general yet practical—for national security in an era in which the traditional precise defense planning algorithms are irrelevant because the array of threats has become diffuse to the point of being conjectural. The criteria of defense objectives and military missions will be their appropriateness to the international system and the situation and status of the nation.

The values that the American defense program is designed to protect should be the core values of society: the lives and domestic property of citizens, the integrity of national territory, and the autonomy of political processes. They would not include "milieu goals," that is, the shape of the international system according to some abstract principle or ideological tenet. The values to be protected also would not include the propagation of human rights or political and economic principles beyond U.S. borders.

The functions of military forces would be threefold. First, they would perform the real mission—though it happens to be the least likely to be required—of defending the approaches to U.S. territory by land, sea, air, and space. This criterion is not to be translated rigidly into some geographical security frontier—say, down the middle of the Pacific or the Atlantic or somewhere in Central America. The extent to which the United States would reach beyond its political boundaries and engage an aggressor would depend, rather, on judgments that the threat was directed against the United States, massive, cumulative, and irreversible (but for timely intervention). Those constitute more a set of functional criteria.

Second, U.S. forces would be designed as "second-chance" forces. This criterion has somewhat different meanings for strategic nuclear forces as opposed to general purpose forces. As for strategic nuclear forces, regardless of a dramatic attenuation of international threats, the United States must always keep forces capable of deterring both direct nuclear attacks on its homeland and nuclear pressures directed by organized forces in the world. Deterrence must extend to regional powers that might pose direct threats of mass destruction through nuclear, or also chemical and biological, weapons. Of course, that requisite is far less demanding than the large capabilities demanded by extended deterrence, which involves the attempt to spread the U.S. nuclear mantle over other nations and less-than-vital interests. The United States would have to retain strategic deterrence in the form of offensive nuclear forces, though not necessarily the traditional ones; these weapons would be reserved for a second strike at military targets. Washington might also have to maintain a strong research program in strategic defense, though not building or deploying systems prematurely.

In the case of general purpose forces, it is important, especially when prescribing a severely low force structure in the first place, not to go below the level or types of forces upon which the United States would have to rebuild in the event that current benign threat assumptions were wrong, in some massive and potentially irreversible way, and the international system became directly and tangibly menacing. In that event, the United States would want to have maintained a diverse cadre of defensive units and a core of diverse defensive activities to hold vital positions and form the basis on which to rebuild American strength with sufficient speed. This argues against tailoring too radically or specifically for precise missions, which may prove illusory.

In a radically smaller defense program, research and development would rise as a proportion of the whole. This is part of a second-chance approach. Readiness categories (operations and maintenance) could slip a bit. After all, readiness for what? But the qualitative technological edge must be maintained, since to maintain it, longer lead-times are required. It is important to keep burnished the potential to fight effectively on the battlefields of the future, even if present invitations to war are declined.

The third function of military forces would be deterrence—but only of attacks or pressures against U.S. territory, society, political processes, property, and military forces. That mission can be labeled "finite essential deterrence." Abjuring extended deterrence would obviate the need for counterforce targeting in the strict sense—i.e., the use of some fraction of the strategic nuclear force to attack the enemy's missiles in their silos—for it can be demonstrated that this targeting proceeds from the requisites of alliance commitment and guarantee. Abandoning counterforce targeting will, logically, remove the incentive to strike first, and thus specifically contribute to crisis stability, which will become more prevalent generally as the superpowers—up to now serving as guarantors for their alliance partners—reserve their weapons for their own essential deterrence and thus forestall the escalation of regional conflicts.

It remains to translate the principles of foreign policy and national strategy into a defense program. The point of departure and comparison is the defense program that the Bush administration requested after its first few months in office; it would have required, for fiscal year 1991, $311 billion in budgetary authority; 2,120,000 military personnel; a general purpose force structure that includes twenty and two-thirds land divisions (seventeen and two-thirds army and three marine), twenty-five air force tactical air wing equivalents, fourteen aircraft carrier battle groups with thirteen navy tactical air wings; and the standard triad of strategic nuclear forces. Over the five years to 1995, this program would have produced cumulative defense costs of $1.684 trillion.

Now, a conservative projection of where the executive and legislative branches, assuming current trends, will move the defense program in five years is $250 billion (in 1991 dollars); 1.73 million military personnel; and a force structure of sixteen and one-third land divisions (fourteen army and two and one-third marine), eighteen air force tactical air wings, and twelve aircraft carriers with eleven navy air wings, in addition to a nuclear triad reduced by the Strategic Arms Reduction Treaty. This program will come to a five-year bill of $1.457 trillion. Thus, this administration will have predictably delivered, over the next five years, comparative savings of $227 billion. [Again it should be noted that these data do not include the cost of the Persian Gulf War—Eds.]

The predicted Bush administration defense program for 1995 opportunistically takes advantage of the decreased threat of major war—particularly of the now practical absurdity of the previously feared short-warning Soviet attack on Western Europe. Nevertheless, it still provides a global interventionary force structure and still harbors an expensively implemented commitment to NATO.

In contrast, a noninterventionist defense program, after a five-year sequence of cuts, would cost (in 1991 dollars) $150 billion; require 1.125 million military personnel; and provide six army divisions and two marine divisions, eleven air force tactical air wings, and six carriers with five air wings, in addition to a dyad of strategic nuclear forces consisting of submarine-launched ballistic missiles and bombers with medium-range cruise missiles. These forces, no longer committed to overseas defense, would be based in the United States. This program would produce, over a half a decade, a further cumulative peace dividend, beyond the $227 billion already predictable, of $333 billion (or a total of $560 billion).

LEAVING HISTORY BEHIND?

The structure of the international system has not finished its evolution from its Cold War forms. To be sure, it has moved well beyond the predominant bipolar confrontation of alliances that furnished the principal characteristic of the international system in the 1950s and 1960s. But it has only begun to emerge from the multipolar balance of power phase, what historians might label the "Nixon-Kissinger" phase: This involved the effort by Washington to control the international behavior of the Soviet Union and contain associated revolutionary thrusts in the world by mobilizing and manipulating a few key powers. Now two beleaguered and exhausted nations are looking for a semblance of civility in their relations, and even entertaining some aspects of cordiality and mutual assistance. . . .

... What is lost in the self-congratulation of many Americans over the collapse of communism is the awareness that the time of the American empire has also run out.   What we are experiencing as we approach the third millennium is a transformation of the international system.   There have been many calls to adapt American foreign policy to the new agenda of the impending era, with its special economic, environmental, and social challenges. There have not been so many suggestions that the United States adapt to the impending structure of the international system.   The large task for the foreign policy of the United States—indeed, the foreign policy of the two great postwar empires—will be precisely to adjust to a world beyond order and control.

6 RETHINKING NATIONAL SECURITY: DEMOCRACY AND ECONOMIC INDEPENDENCE

Theodore C. Sorensen

I

The touchstone for our nation's security concept—the containment of Soviet military and ideological power—is gone. The primary threat cited over forty years in justification for most of our military budget, bases and overseas assistance is gone. The principal prism through which we viewed most of our worldwide diplomatic activities and alliances is gone. That they are gone is cause for rejoicing in celebration of peace and freedom. The search for a new national security focus has begun, but if the president cannot soon lead the way to a consensus among our national security decision-makers on credible new goals to guide our basic foreign policy and military planning for the long term, the current strategic vacuum is likely to be filled not only haphazardly but unwisely as well. . . .

II

. . . To be sure, it takes time for a superpower, like a supertanker, to change direction, particularly now that such a turn in this country's foreign policies requires far broader agreement within the executive branch, Congress and the nation than it did forty years ago. It takes time as well to adjust in an orderly way a huge military structure still targeted largely on the threat of a Soviet attack (as symbolized by the aerial command post still flown round

Note: Section headings have been renumbered.

74

the clock in preparation for a sudden, devastating nuclear strike).   Time should be taken.   So many developments . . . have come our way, and so few of them were foreseen in advance, that any blind rush to new long-term commitments now would be folly.

But in the absence of an early executive-legislative leadership consensus on a conceptual framework defining our national security in the post–Cold War era, that vacuum is likely to be filled by a mishmash of political considerations. Military budget reductions will reflect not actual needs but log-rolling among the services as well as pressures on the Congress from local defense plants and bases.   New or continued foreign alliances, commitments and economic and military assistance appropriations will reflect not new strategic priorities but the relative strength and influence of domestic ethnic organizations and foreign government leaders and lobbyists.   New policies on international trade and finance will reflect not our long-term objectives but turf battles in Washington and constituent interest groups back home.

Worst of all, the lack of a clear national direction in world affairs could open the way for a resurgent isolationism in both major political parties. Instinctively doubtful about "foreign entanglements," or too young to re-member any foreign policy before the Cold War, many Americans have only reluctantly gone along while this nation put up with complaining allies, poured money into ungrateful or undemocratic governments, opened our markets to disagreeable competitors, involved ourselves in other countries' internal matters, and contributed funds to multilateral organizations in which we were consistently outvoted, all in the interest of winning friends against the Soviet empire and keeping others out of the Soviet orbit.   Now there is no Soviet empire and no Soviet orbit.   Nor do these recalcitrants see any other "visible" enemy to defeat or wars to be fought.   Without a clear presidential trumpet to summon their support, their indifference or opposi-tion could handicap any effective global role for this country in the next decade. . . .

Too often in the past the mystique of national security has been invoked by the executive branch to justify or cloak excessive or unauthorized conduct, undeclared wars, unconventional covert operations, unaccountable secret de-cisions and unprecedented limitations on citizens' rights. This time a narrow definition of the term is in order. . . .

In my view, a bipartisan national consensus—essentially fixing the new terms of reference while leaving ample room for partisan disagreement on their application—could be formed around two basic national security goals for the new multipolar era, two long-term objectives deserving the kind of presidential, congressional and budgetary priority we have heretofore given to the containment of communism: the preservation of this nation's economic effectiveness and independence in the global marketplace, and the peaceful enhancement of democracy around the world.

Unlike our focus for the last forty years, these two goals—economic in-dependence and democratic enhancement—are not primarily defense-ori-ented, although our defense forces will continue to have important responsibilities; nor are they primarily Soviet-oriented, although we must, as noted, remain alert to risks in that region; nor are they as predominantly Europe-oriented as our foreign policy has traditionally been. They are not as negative in nature as containment and defense, nor as costly in tax dollars, nor as easy to simplify for political purposes. But they are equally global in scope, recognizing our continuing capacity and responsibility for world leadership.

Like containment, both of the broad phrases stated above are in need of further explication and in danger of being invoked as justification for a multitude of sins. Either, if misapplied in an aggressively nationalistic fashion, could revive American failings of long ago—specifically, protectionism and imperialism—bringing resentment and retaliation from other nations and doing great harm to our own interests. Both goals, however, if pursued constructively, creatively and in cooperation with other like-minded nations, could achieve for the United States a level of security far exceeding that we have already achieved as the Cold War draws to a close.

III

The once powerful beacon of this nation's economic strength, particularly in relative terms—relative not only to an economically ascendant Japan, a newly united Germany and Western Europe and other nations in general, but relative as well to the worldwide ranking we once enjoyed and could enjoy again—no longer shines so brightly in the global marketplace of today. We have the world's largest trade deficit. We are losing our competitive position, our market share in both domestic and export markets, in one after another of the industries in which our leadership was once vaunted: consumer electronics, machine tools, automobiles, steel, advanced computers, semiconductor chips, laser printers, and design and manufacturing technology. We have become dangerously dependent upon foreign sources for the advanced computer and semiconductor technologies that underlie modern information industries, and dangerously dependent upon foreign sources (once again) for the energy that we consume at a higher rate than any other nation to fuel our factories, homes and transportation systems. We have the largest gap between earnings and savings, the highest budget deficit (in absolute terms) and one of the lowest rates of productivity growth of any nation in the industrialized world. We have become—thanks to our trade deficit and the enormous foreign borrowings required in light of our low savings rate and large federal budget deficits—the world's largest debtor.

Does all this affect our national security? Economic strength is not a zero-sum game. America need not be number one in every category for its citizens to live comfortably and productively in freedom and safety. Contrary to the alarm often sounded, our $5.5 trillion economy [in 1990] still leads the world in total economic power, manufacturing worker productivity and scientific genius. Foreign bankers and businessmen recognize the harm to their own interests that would accompany any sudden withdrawal of their capital from this country. Absolute economic independence is no longer possible in our interdependent world.

But if these trends of deficit, debt and relative decline are permitted to persist and harden into fixed patterns, this nation's economic effectiveness and independence—meaning the flexibility to make decisions and the ability to fend for oneself, which are indispensable parts of any country's national security—would indeed be endangered. The sense of well-being that has generally characterized our way of life since emerging from the Great Depression would become increasingly dependent upon investments, deposits, credits—and thus decisions—from other countries, whose objectives and values are not inevitably the same as our own, and whose decisions will be dependent at least in part upon their appraisal of our national policies. The rise and fall of our currency and our stock markets, the prospects for inflation, recession and long-term growth in our economy, the price we pay for our gasoline and the price we charge for our grain exports—all would become more subject to the attitudes and actions of others.

Our traditional sense of flexibility in foreign affairs—the ability to mount, when needed, a Marshall Plan or Manhattan Project, whatever the cost— would be severely limited. Like the United Kingdom before us, our loss of economic influence would diminish our diplomatic and strategic influence, making us more dependent on others to take the initiative on international economic problems, less of a model for others to emulate, less able than others to provide assistance to struggling democracies, and less able to decide for ourselves the fiscal, monetary and trade measures with which we promote our values and interests both at home and abroad.

Even our national pride and will, the certainty that our children will live at least as well as their parents, the belief that we inhabit a land of plenty in which no group need be denied, the self-confidence and unity essential to the successful conduct of an affirmative foreign policy, all would suffer from the realization that we have become more vulnerable economically, that a substantial portion of our long-term assets were no longer under American ownership and control, that we were no longer among the world's top five countries in living standards, no longer the central player on a world stage where superconductors are becoming more important to the balance of power than supercarriers.

In short, unless we reverse these trends, our ability to control and protect our own destiny and daily lives—even the wages, prices, jobs, profits, home ownership and higher education opportunities of our citizens—would be threatened. Were our independence and way of life ever militarily threatened to that extent, we would prepare for war with the enemy. But the struggle and threat now are economic, not military; moreover, declaring war—a trade war—would represent a resounding defeat for our country, dependent as it is on an open trading system. Even to name and blame a supposed "enemy" would only handicap our effort to keep that system open.

That will not prevent many American politicians from discussing the trade issue in Cold War terms: singling out and verbally bashing an enemy in order to mobilize public opinion at home; dividing the world into two or three blocs in order to "contain" the other side; matching that other side move for move (in this case, meeting their closed markets with our closed markets); and focusing on the "enemy's" misconduct in order to avoid attention to our own contributions to the gulf between us. But no war, hot or cold, is in fact a useful model to meet the challenge of world trade competition.

Nevertheless two concepts from our Cold War days may be transferable. The concept of burden-sharing with Western Europe and Japan—both of whom have enjoyed chronic external balance-of-payments surpluses while we remained deep in deficit—is as fair and indispensable in avoiding a trade war as it was in avoiding a shooting war, and should be more consistently pursued. Each of the three economic superpowers—the United States, Japan and the European Community—must recognize its obligation to accept voluntarily a fair share of each other's exports (as well as those from developing nations), regardless of allegedly inherent structural impediments and differences in marketing skills and networks. Perhaps a new nonpolitical international trade equivalent of the International Monetary Fund could nudge surplus and deficit countries into balance over the long term, conditioning external help on internal reform, without the bilateral hectoring that so often merely stiffens intransigence.

In addition, the concept of mutual deterrence, under which the two nuclear superpowers have fulfilled for so long their wider obligation to the world community not to make reckless use of those ultimate weapons, could be matched by a similar undertaking now by the three economic superpowers not to engage in any firing of those ultimate economic "weapons" that could escalate into a shutdown of the world trading system. Instead they must collaborate in strengthening and enforcing the General Agreement of Tariffs and Trade rules to halt collusive arrangements, nontariff barriers and other unfair trade practices.

But this country, while dispelling any impression that its efforts to open foreign markets on a reciprocal basis to American exporters can be endlessly delayed, must also attack the domestic roots of our problem: our high budget deficits, low rate of domestic savings and investment, high cost of capital, lag in technological development, inadequate educational and job-training systems, even our frequently improvident attitudes as individuals toward quality performance and products.

We have not permanently lost the technology race, for example. The same kind of effort that we mounted to achieve technological superiority in the military arena must now be mounted to integrate our military technology with commercial activities, to translate our edge in basic research and innovation into competitive and marketable high-tech products, to become more adept at improving existing industrial technologies, and to move those improvements more quickly to market with firm control of both cost and quality. But any significant U.S. expansion of investment in new product research, development and industrial facilities will require, among other things, a recognition of their importance to our national security and thus the folly of continuing to devote federal funds for research and development almost exclusively to military and space uses.

Winning the competitiveness struggle will also require the application of more funds and talent to our educational system. This country will soon face a serious shortage of experts with engineering Ph.D.s, which are increasingly pursued in our own universities by foreign instead of American students. Our secondary school students, compared to those in other trading powers today, receive less training in math, science and foreign languages during a shorter school day in a shorter school year in an inadequately supported public school system. We have long recognized the importance of improved education to individual and family security. Now, more clearly than ever, it has become a matter of national security.

IV

The second priority that I urge, the peaceful enhancement of democracy around the world, is consistent not merely with the moral impulse traditionally underlying American foreign policy but with our long-term national security requirements as well. A global community of free nations adhering to the democratic principles of pluralism, human rights and equal opportunity under law would be a far safer and friendlier world for the United States. History tells us that governments that respect the rights of their citizens are more likely to respect the rights of their neighbors. They are less likely to generate the kind of regional, racial and religious conflicts, terrorist tactics and conventional, chemical or nuclear arms buildups that threaten the peace and unity of the world, on which our own long-range security rests.

Facilitating democracy in those countries that wish it is a role for which the United States has some preparation. From Wilson's Fourteen Points to Kennedy's Peace Corps, we have been less imperialistic and more generous toward weaker nations than any other major power in history. Several U.S. agencies have experience in democratization, much of it positive. The fortunes of war imposed upon us unique responsibilities to lay foundations of freedom in the Federal Republic of Germany and in Japan; on the whole we met both responsibilities ably. President Truman was intent on furthering the construction and reconstruction of democratic institutions around the world before Stalin's increasingly aggressive posture began to dominate American thinking.

Since then our record in peacefully encouraging other nations to move toward democracy has been mixed. President Kennedy's Alliance for Progress had some successes and some failures before it was abandoned by his successor. President Carter's emphasis on human rights still reverberates.

Today we are hopeful about Namibia, South Korea and the Philippines, and less so about South Africa and Haiti, but a final judgment on any of them would be premature. The relatively new National Endowment for Democracy (NED) clearly helped the democratic process in Chile and elsewhere; but thus far, compared to other industrialized nations, we have been largely onlookers in the democracy movements of Eastern and central Europe and southern Asia.

Where we have most clearly failed has been in our recurrent attempts to impose democracy on others by force of arms or covert operations. Democracy by definition depends upon the voluntary support and sense of responsibility of the indigenous population. Local officials who govern with the consent of U.S. military or intelligence advisers are not governing with the consent of the people. We have no wish or right to engage in what Dean Acheson once called "messianic globaloney" to direct the destiny of peaceful peoples; and we do not wish other powers to do so either. The "enhancement of democracy" must not become an excuse for U.S. military action or uninvited internal meddling in nations that fail to meet our standards but pose no viable threat to others.

Those standards must be set with tough-minded care, consistency and flexibility. We should look not for pawns or clones of the United States, not to our list of current arms and aid recipients, not even for loyal allies alone, but for authentic democracies. Inevitably we will have preferences, including those democracies with whom we have historical ties and those whose economies have been damaged by wars we urged or fueled. But not every self-proclaimed democracy deserves either that label or our support. Not every mistreated regional, tribal or ethnic minority proclaiming the right of self-determination deserves our embrace, if the community of nations is not to splinter into a welter of politically unstable and economically unsustainable units. Nor will every object of our embrace be of strategic significance in traditional balance-of-power terms. Nor will all of them feature an unmixed market economy or support our every position in the United Nations or in regional conflicts. A world "made safe for diversity" must take into account historical, cultural, social and economic differences.

But our financial, military and other support for oppressive and corrupt regimes in Africa, Asia, the Middle East and Latin America should now come to an end. No longer can they play off one superpower against the other. No longer can we maintain that their willingness to speak in opposition to Soviet expansion is more important than their willingness to tolerate serious opposition parties and newspapers at home. As new democracies emerge seeking from us financial and other forms of assistance, we will have reason enough to move away from those unwilling to adopt true reforms. We do not intend to dictate self-righteously their form of government, but neither are we obligated to support dictatorial forms of government.

The passage of nations from dictatorship to freedom is inevitably slow, difficult and often impermanent. Facilitating that passage is not simply or even primarily a matter of economic assistance.   Indeed foreign aid is frequently wasted if the stagnant bureaucracies and stifled educational systems of the old regimes do not simultaneously give way to new governmental and legal structures.   Free political institutions do not spring up and succeed automatically with the first loud blast of freedom's trumpets.

Considerable concern about the export of this country's superficial political "packaging" methods attended the arrival of American campaign consultants [in 1990] in the new democracies of Eastern and central Europe.   But pragmatic hands-on advice was in fact urgently needed by those who had never been candidates, party organizers, election commissioners or opinion pollers in an open society.   Practical politics in this country, whatever its flaws, has a unique attraction for those hoping, as a result of their harsh experience under communism, to build new political parties that are less ideologically oriented, less structured and less dominated by strong leaders.

It is undisputed, however, that more than techniques and tactics are required to develop the institutions of democracy.   As Czechoslovakia's President Václav Havel pressed upon the U.S. Congress [in 1990], those who have long been lacking not only experience but also information about human rights principles and political reforms are hungry to learn more—how to build a truly free legislature, an independent judiciary, a restrained police authority, a system of responsible local governments and a civilian-controlled defense force.   Acknowledging the major role that West Europeans and others will also play, the United States—through the Agency for International Development (AID), the U.S. Information Agency (USIA), NED and others— can surely supply whatever expert consultants, lecturers, election observers, legal precedents, textbooks and instructors these nations may request from us.

In addition to free political institutions, free economic institutions must also be in place to make economic assistance meaningful.   From agriculture and banking to transportation and energy, from the establishment of new enterprises and export markets to true cooperatives and trade unions, the need for technical and practical advice from the United States and others is enormous in these nations, North and South, making their way to freedom. The process of privatization, the prevention of monopolies, the avoidance of gross economic inequalities and predatory business behavior, the proper use of economic incentives, the organization of effective joint ventures and free enterprise zones—these are but a few examples of American know-how of interest and value to these infant democracies.

Nor is economic assistance confined to transfers of funds, food, fuel and medical supplies, important as they are to nations in transition.   Food assistance should reflect their needs as well as our surpluses.   Trade preferences and credits, debt relief, commodity agreements, investment guarantees, technology transfers (including pollution controls) and access to international finance and trade organizations are also essential to economic growth in these countries.

Building a stable and enduring democracy, always difficult, is even more difficult when complicated by the kind of massive economic problems faced today by new democracies in Europe, Central America and Africa—the very problems that contributed ultimately to their rejection of a Marxist state. Our objective must be not only the short-term alleviation of hunger, human misery and poverty but, more important, the establishment of long-term practices and policies that will strike at poverty's roots and make sustainable over the long run their economic growth and independence. Sustainable economic development requires curbs on excessive population growth and the emancipation and education of women regarding their choice of family size. It also requires effective curbs on environmental degradation, on the long-term poisoning of a nation's land, water and air resources that will ultimately defeat any economic recovery. Our assistance must stress both requirements.

Foreign aid that merely increases government bureaucracy, corruption and rigidity in a recipient country is worse than none at all. Foreign aid that is quietly but consistently conditioned upon a country's promulgation of political reform, human rights and free and fair elections should become a more common practice. No nation would be required to accept either our economic aid or our political philosophy, but neither should this nation feel required in the post—Cold War era to subsidize repression.

V

As our priorities change, so must we change a federal budget that now allocates to foreign assistance less than five percent of the amount it allocates to national defense. The Congress should not again be asked, as it [was in 1990], to allocate funds for new democracies on a one-shot, country-by-country basis with no overall plan or direction. It should not again be tempted to renege on U.N. dues in order to find money for demobilization and reform in Central America; to juggle scarce funds among programs for refugee relief, defense reconversion, Namibia's transition and Panama's reconstruction; to choose between helping freedom among the nations of Eastern Europe, for which we have striven for so long, and freedom among the poor and developing nations of the southern half of the globe that are far more likely to be future sources of regional or even global warfare.

Our armed forces are not about to be confined wholly to our own shores. Whatever new "architecture" the leaders of Europe may initiate with our help, whatever new roles and new boundaries for NATO [the North Atlantic Treaty Organization], the European Community and the Conference on Security and Cooperation in Europe may evolve, a credible American presence—dramatically reduced but not vanished militarily, and substantially increased both diplomatically and economically—should remain on that continent so long as enough Europeans seeking a counterweight (but not a military antagonist) to a reformed Russia, a resurgent Germany or recurrent European rivalries wish us to remain.   The nations of the Warsaw Pact alliance will continue to require our vigilant attention, doing whatever we reasonably can do to facilitate further internal reforms, arms reductions and troop withdrawals.   Nor can we precipitously abandon our presence and commitments in the Far East, where a substitution of Japanese for American protection would not be welcomed by all.

Nevertheless a fundamental reexamination of our national security posture should result in an American military machine vastly reshaped and reduced, reoriented more toward the speedy projection of conventional deterrent forces to other parts of the world, toward local low-intensity conflicts and terrorist activities, toward hostile acts by undemocratic and unpredictable governments in such countries as Libya, Iraq, Iran, Cuba and North Korea, toward the defense of strategic resource supply lines and the interdiction of illicit narcotics supply lines, toward curbing the proliferation of nuclear, chemical and ballistic weapons capabilities, toward verifying the implementation of arms control agreements and even providing disaster relief, infrastructural engineering and refugee shelter and transport in the least fortunate parts of the globe.   These tasks, however important, clearly do not require the same levels or the same types of U.S. personnel, missiles, planes, ships, submarines, tanks, military bases or military spending as the threat of a Soviet attack.

Reorientation will not be limited to the Pentagon.   The National Security Council, originally intended to integrate military and nonmilitary analysis, will need to expand its capacity for the latter, relying on fewer generals and Kremlinologists and more economists and election analysts, inviting to its meetings experts rarely invited in the past: from Commerce, Agriculture, the U.S. Trade Representative's office, the Environmental Protection Agency, the Council of Economic Advisers and nongovernmental organizations as well. The State Department will need to devote more attention to its stepchildren in USIA, AID, NED, the Peace Corps and other multilateral diplomatic and financial organizations.   The CIA will need to find more experts on Germany and Japan as well as the Soviet Union, on Islamic fundamentalism as well as Marxism-Leninism, on industrial as well as military espionage, and on oil-field as well as battlefield defense.

But the most important change of all is that required in the attitude of the American people and their elected leaders in Washington.   Today, as a result of more than forty years of patient and prudent determination, we are on the threshold of securing the kind of world of which we have heretofore only dreamed, a community of democracies united by their commitment to law and peace, neither threatened by hostile armies or ideologies nor dominated by any one nation politically or economically.   Because we have the largest economy, the most wealth and one of the lightest tax burdens of any industralized nation in the world, because we are the only nation that is an economic as well as a military superpower, we have both the obligation and the ability to play a principal role in building that kind of world.   Multipolarity means that we should be only one member of the team in that effort.   But at least we will be on the field of play and not merely a cheerleader or spectator on the sidelines.

Unfortunately, with neither foreign enemies nor domestic leadership to spur the American public to new and greater efforts internationally, our political thinking in recent years on the range of issues discussed above has been characterized by caution and deadlock, focusing on limiting our public revenues but not our private consumption, on constantly polling the voters but not enlightening them.   In past years, this country, whether challenged with world war or Cold War, responded boldly and decisively.   If we continue now to think small, talk poor, preach gloom and always place our individual private interests ahead of the public good, we will gradually lose respect as well as relative strength and influence in a world that will not wait.   But if we can elect leaders with the courage and wisdom to make the difficult choices required among the many demands on our government and resources—and forge a consensus on those choices—if we can put to constructive use those additional resources that the ending of the Cold War has made available to us (provided we have the good sense to utilize them), then the prospects for maintaining this country's genuine national security in a genuinely free and peaceful world will be very bright indeed.

7 PRESERVING THE GLOBAL ENVIRONMENT: IMPLICATIONS FOR U.S. POLICY

Jessica Tuchman Mathews

The end of the cold war and the decline of the United States relative to Japan and a coalescing Europe leave the geopolitical landscape fundamentally altered. In all likelihood, international problem solving in the decades ahead will, for the first time, be achieved through collective management, not hegemony. It is to precisely this form of governance that global environmental problems will yield—if sufficient vision and political will can be mustered. The challenge is to initiate change in human activities of a scale and rate comparable to the change in global circumstances.

Two broad political strategies are possible. One might be called the quantum leap approach. It emphasizes the immensity of the problems, and the distance between present policies and those that are needed. It urges vast, bold policy leaps, attempting to make the very challenge of such an approach into a political asset: a way to capture attention and to galvanize support for action. It calls for the expenditure of large sums of money, especially in North-South transfers. Today, proposals for a system of global environmental taxes would fall into this category.

The other strategy might be called ambitious incrementalism. It urges following the path of least resistance: eliminating policies that are both environmentally and economically counterproductive; taking steps that cost little or nothing or those that have immediate economic payoffs; aggressively exploiting existing technology; using well-tested policy instruments, and avoiding the highest political hurdles. It emphasizes the relatively modest steps needed to weave environmental concerns into the fabric of mainstream economic and foreign policy.

The first approach in effect makes the global environment the most important single issue on the international horizon, with concomitant shifts in spending.   The latter concentrates on using present public and governmental concern to embed environmental values and goals in international policy, and focuses immediate action on initiatives with little or no cost.

A strong case can be made for the quantum leap strategy, given the risks that fall within the range of present uncertainty.   However, the incremental approach is more likely to permanently change the policy context, so that when the next issue captures the center stage spotlight—as it inevitably will—environmental reform and sustainable policies will move steadily forward. Globally, public concern for the environment is very high and growing rapidly.   But no matter how real the problems, if concern and political attention do not produce solutions within, perhaps, a decade, fatigue and apathy will set in.   The greatest risk lies in losing this opportunity in debate over quantum leap policies that elude consensus and do not leave permanent change in their wake.

The two approaches are not mutually exclusive, of course.   Moreover, the distinction would disappear if international change continues at the pace of the past few years.   In that case, what qualifies as a quantum leap today may seem little more than a sensible next step in a year or two.   For now, however, ambitious incrementalism offers a crowded and challenging policy agenda.   It recognizes the cash shortages many governments face and puts the most difficult policy steps first into the domestic, rather than the international, domain.   For the United States, this approach would begin with steps to put its house in order, correcting egregious failures of both substance and process that damage its credibility and weaken its capacity to exercise international leadership.

Three substantive policy changes are most important: correcting the present underpricing of gasoline; ending large government subsidies for the cutting of U.S. forests; and reducing the federal budget deficit.   The real price of gasoline in the U.S. today is lower than it has been since 1918.   The combined state and federal tax of twenty-five cents per gallon compares to a tax of double that amount in Canada and taxes of $1 to more than $2 per gallon in all of the other industrialized market economies.   The illusion that the real price of gasoline is cheap chains the U.S. to a single ground transportation option—the single-passenger automobile—and blocks Detroit from producing high-mileage automobiles like the 70–120 mpg four- and five-passenger prototypes being tested by European and Japanese manufacturers in countries where gasoline taxes are high.   Since transportation accounts for nearly two-thirds of U.S. oil consumption, the underpricing of gasoline is also a major factor in the growing U.S. dependence on imported oil (now close to 50 percent) and, therefore, in its large trade deficit.

The U.S. is in no position to urge tropical countries to take difficult steps to protect their forests while it subsidizes the cutting of its own forests and the sale of publicly owned timber at far below market prices, even in most of its few rainforests.   Through its effect on interest rates, the federal budget deficit slows Third World debt repayment and raises the costs of new borrowing, as well as weakening the domestic economy.

On the procedural side, steps should be taken to shift from a diplomacy based on the primacy of bilateral relations to one that emphasizes multilateral concerns; to restore respect for international law; and to allow the U.S. to play a stronger role in the UN and other multilateral institutions. Specifically, the U.S. should as promptly as possible pay the $350 million owing in past dues to the UN, and restore financial support for the UN Fund for Population Activities. Appointments to UN headquarters and specialized agencies, as well as to institutions outside the UN system, should go to the most talented individuals available, making this the track to success in the foreign service. The State Department should be reorganized to give greater power and prestige to the multilateral and crosscutting bureaus and relatively less to the regional desks. Coveted policy appointments at State, Treasury, and the National Security Council should go to individuals experienced in multilateral diplomacy. The U.S. should demonstrate a greater commitment to be bound by negotiated agreements in which it participates, such as the Law of the Sea. And it should either refrain from armed excursions into other countries, such as those in Grenada and Panama, or avoid making a mockery of international law in justifying them.

Beyond these corrective steps, new initiatives are needed to bridge two traditional divisions in the policy cosmos: between foreign and domestic policy, and between "environmental" issues and everything else. National security in the coming decades will rest less heavily on military strength and . . . will include a growing environmental component. Security measured against the strength of an opponent will steadily give way to the measure of global security, defined principally by environmental threats and the conditions of economic interdependence. This shift calls for a strengthening of environmental expertise and influence at the Departments of State and Treasury, especially, and in the White House. . . .

Presently, the executive branch lacks an effective mechanism for producing coherent policy on issues that are equally foreign and domestic. Integration of policy on the economy, environment, energy, drugs, and many other issues is accomplished, if at all, on an ad hoc basis, through short-lived White House offices, czarships, and special advisors, often bringing debilitating turf battles in their wake. Nor can the creation of ever more Cabinet Councils do the trick, for these are associations of equals. Proposals have been made that a new post, assistant to the president for international economic affairs, be created, comparable in rank to the assistant for national security. Down this road lies an ever-expanding White House, bulging with new assistants and their staffs. Moreover, the National Security Council's influence derives from history and from its origin in legislation and cannot be recreated by fiat or built up quickly.

The logical answer to the changing nature of national security and to the need to integrate foreign and domestic policies is to change the profile of qualifications for the assistant for national security affairs, and by extension, the background and responsibilities of his or her staff. Past appointments to this post have heavily emphasized U.S.-Soviet relations and military security. Five recent national security appointments have been career military officials. Future criteria could emphasize expertise on global issues, especially economics and environment. By the same token, nine of the thirteen presidential science advisors have been either nuclear physicists or engineers. Given the new threats to planetary security, future appointments should emphasize the natural and physical earth sciences—ecology, climatology, oceanography, and so on.

Even among the once wholly domestic issues, global trends demand new approaches. One of the most difficult of these lies in forging an integrated policy embracing clean air, energy, and transportation. Each is presently managed by a different department, under different laws, with its own library of regulations and army of lawyers. Yet they are, in reality, separate manifestations of the same activities. Energy use produces 80 percent of air pollution. Transportation accounts for more than two-thirds of oil use and 40 percent of acid rain—forming nitrogen oxides and ozone-forming organic compounds. President George Bush rightly decided that his environmental policy would be based on "pollution prevention," that is, on reducing pollution before it is produced, rather than after-the-fact regulation. Clearly, for the atmosphere, source reduction can *only* be achieved through energy policies. Ultimately, therefore, it will prove futile to try . . . to fashion a national clean air policy without a national energy policy or an integrated transportation strategy. This accounts, in large part, for the endless legislative thrashing on the Clean Air Act, and the general sense that . . . it will not produce the desired result. After more than a decade without one, the United States needs an explicit national energy policy that abandons long outdated assumptions and sets annual goals for decline in energy demand, priorities among fuel options with congruent research and development (R&D) spending, and realistic fuel pricing policies.

The most subtle process change that needs to be addressed is a reevaluation of the nature of American leadership in international affairs and, therefore, of U.S. priorities among global environmental issues. There are still calls from foreign policy experts for "America to hold firmly to the reins of global leadership. There is no substitute." Yet given economic realities, and weak U.S. energy productivity (the U.S. needs twice as much energy to produce a dollar of GNP as do the other advanced market economies . . .), these calls sound like a wistful harkening to the past rather than a clear-eyed understanding of the present and likely future.

Nations other than the two cold war superpowers are already more adept and adapted to multilateral diplomacy. This is particularly true of Western Europe, now entering the longest period of uninterrupted peace in its history. It would be no surprise, in fact, if the 1990s turn out to be the European

Decade, with the U.S. and the USSR turned inward, preoccupied with their domestic difficulties, Japan unready to offer political leadership, and Western Europe . . . invigorated by its new-found political and economic strength, pioneering mechanisms for regional governance. These include solutions to regional environmental problems through Europe's new institutional machinery and leadership on the most difficult issue of all—global climate change. In these circumstances, demands that the U.S. must be in the policy forefront on every important issue seem both unrealistic and ill-advised.

On the other hand, America has in the past provided such strong leadership in areas such as population growth that it is hard to imagine much progress being made without at least its active participation. In many other areas, especially fossil fuel consumption as it relates to climate change, the U.S. is such a global presence that it has no choice but to play a leading role. The U.S. accounts for 23 percent of global carbon dioxide (CO_2) emissions from fossil fuel use: the other six of the G-7 [Group of Seven industrialized countries] nations together account for 18 percent.

The matter is even more complicated. During this decade of transition to a still undefined future, there will be a substantial policy hangover: the widespread assumption based on long postwar experience that little can happen without U.S. leadership. We can expect to hear demands from abroad for U.S. leadership—especially from European governments—even while the same countries are themselves leading the way. A careful sorting out of priorities is therefore in order. On some issues it will be appropriate for the U.S. to pave the way, to provide an example, even perhaps a success story. In certain circumstances, as in the 1978 banning of chlorofluorocarbon (CFC) use in aerosols, unilateral action may prove beneficial. In others it may well impede an international response. The U.S. should choose those areas in which it will exercise strong leadership. At the same time it should do what it can to erase the expectation that international solutions in *every* arena depend on its leadership. It should expect and encourage others to take the lead in certain areas, but without reverting in those issues to either hostility or passivity. In short, in some cases the U.S. will have to relinquish stardom for the demanding and unfamiliar role of supporting player.

A still unanswered question is whether such a role will prove acceptable to the American public and politically feasible in practice. Historically, U.S. foreign policy has swung between the poles of isolationism and interventionism. Can a middle ground—what former Ambassador Richard Gardner calls practical internationalism—be a lasting alternative? Polling data suggest that there is a very high degree of public concern on the global environment and support for much tougher policies, including a larger role for the UN and other international agencies and greater American deference to international law. However, support for domestic policy changes stops short of new taxes, the most economically efficient response in many instances. Polls also suggest a dramatic shift in Americans' perception of threats to their national security and perhaps, therefore, in their willingness to spend public funds in these new areas. How long these views will persist, and whether they can be translated into support for a steady internationalism, remains to be seen.

A number of important substantive steps toward solving global problems should also be taken domestically. Foremost among them, U.S. policy on greenhouse warming should be based on the understanding that despite the many scientific uncertainties, the phenomenon itself is not a subject of controversy: what is important is the direction of change, not the details. The science will shift constantly over the coming years, but its central policy implication—that humankind will eventually have to stabilize greenhouse gas concentrations in the atmosphere—will almost certainly not. It is this core truth, not the newest piece in the scientific puzzle, that should guide policy.

Two considerations should shape U.S. policy. The dimensions of the planetary risks inherent in global warming demand an "insurance" policy. The uncertainties in both the science and the costs of slowing the change mean that a "no regrets" approach is called for, that is, steps we will not regret however the scientific questions are answered. Together they mean that action to reduce greenhouse gas emissions should begin now if policies can be identified that are low in cost or produce substantial non-greenhouse benefits.

The most obvious of these is a decision to eliminate CFC production and use no later than 2000. A much stronger and better funded multinational effort to slow tropical deforestation, to which the U.S. should contribute its fair share, also qualifies. Most important for the U.S. is a national energy policy based on a steady decline in energy intensity of at least 3 percent per year, approximately the rate of improvement that was achieved during the high oil price years 1973–86. This would double the efficiency of U.S. energy use in about twenty years. It is a substantial initial target, though even more may well be achievable.

In fact, comparisons of current energy use practices to best-available technologies suggest that the efficiency of the major energy-use sectors—transportation, utilities, and residential and commercial buildings—can be doubled with technologies that are currently available or now in development. There is no telling what might result from a concerted research and development effort that shifts priorities away from coal and nuclear power and toward energy efficiency, solar, hydrogen, and other advanced alternative energy technologies. The technological burst that followed the Montreal CFC treaty is a timely reminder that modern technology can reap bounteous harvests in previously unplowed fields.

Finally, the "insurance/no regret" policy should include active U.S. support for the creation of an international mechanism to coordinate global policy on climate change. A GATT-like [General Agreement on Tariffs and Trade] approach, involving more or less continuous negotiation and adjustment, or an IMF [International Monetary Fund] model in which national goals are individually negotiated by a neutral staff empowered to make binding decisions, both look more promising at this juncture than the framework agreement followed by separately ratified protocols that is being discussed by governments.

Together with drastically improving its energy productivity, the U.S. should take steps to improve its overall environmental productivity, that is, to steadily reduce the use of natural resources and the consumption of environmental services (including those of air, land, and water for waste disposal) per unit of economic output. If appropriate economic incentives are adopted and an indicator of industrial environmental productivity can be developed, the private sector will most efficiently accomplish the required changes. The U.S. should also follow . . . Germany's example and revise its system of national income accounts to include consumption of environmental capital. Unilateral action of this kind by enough countries will accelerate revision of the official international methodology by the UN statistical office.

On the international scene, needed procedural and institutional initiatives are less clear. Many proposals have been made for new institutions, mergers, upgrades, and new responsibilities for existing institutions. All seem to entail at least as many negative consequences as positive ones. One clear exception is the need for additional financial resources for the United Nations Environment Programme (UNEP), whose $40 million budget is unquestionably inadequate to its responsibilities.

However, broad guidelines for procedural progress seem clear. Following a global analogy to federal-state relations in the U.S., problem solving at the global level should be reserved for those things that cannot be done locally or regionally. The global interest is not strongly represented among existing institutions, and global organizations will likely always be more cumbersome than smaller groupings. On both counts it makes good sense to do what can be done through regional and quasi-regional organizations such as the Organization for Economic Cooperation and Development (OECD) and the Economic Commission for Europe (ECE). Many of the regional groups are far too weak for effective action, but the stronger among them enjoy shared cultural values and comparable levels of economic development, which will smooth the way for agreements on policy. Dividing responsibility among the regions also allows responses to global issues to be tailored to regional differences. For example, the causes and appropriate responses to deforestation are quite different in Latin America and Southeast Asia. Moreover, the global trends significantly overlap important regional concerns on which these organizations are already taking action. The U.S. ought to work to strengthen Western Hemisphere institutions as well as the OECD and ECE, and support others such as the Amazon Pact, of which it is not a member.

A second guideline is that, wherever possible, institutional reform or innovation should make greater use of the private sector, including both the corporate community and nongovernmental organizations (NGOs). Partnerships with governments and multinational organizations in various types of public/private hybrids are especially promising. The U.S., with the strongest, best-funded, and most diverse NGO community in the world, has a special role to play in pioneering these new models. International organizations might, for example, usefully be able to adapt the principles of regulatory negotiation, in which nongovernmental constituencies are directly involved in developing regulations, to international decision making.

The greatest threat to international cooperation on the global environment, one that already shows signs of provoking a debilitating North-South deadlock, is the question of who will pay for the necessary changes. Attention to possible new sources of funds in the developing countries could help provide a solution. This is not to suggest that additional money does not also need to flow from the industrialized countries. But it would be a fatal mistake to base ambitious global plans on the promise of large North-South transfers that are not in the offing. The result would be something like the sad outcome of the recent Plan of Action for Africa, when, despite a genuine crisis and the development of an excellent international strategy, nothing happened because no additional money was forthcoming from the developed countries.

A more successful approach will pair commitments of additional funds from the North with steps to redirect substantial funds in the South. Three large sources of money are potentially available: capital flight, debt payments, and military spending. Capital flight, by its nature, is extremely difficult to pin down. Estimates range from $10–$50 billion annually. Third World debt payments are about $125 billion each year, and military spending is just under $150 billion annually, having grown twice as fast as global military expenditures for the past thirty years. In each case, releasing some of these funds for more productive uses will require cooperative North-South action. Reforms of tax policy and banking regulations in the North will help squeeze capital flight. On debt, forgiveness for the poorest countries and greatly expanded use of debt swaps, together with a more aggressive pursuit of debt reduction negotiations and involvement of commercial banks by the U.S. and other lenders, are badly needed.

Military spending offers a largely ignored opportunity to redirect the most rapidly growing use of public funds in many developing countries. The dynamics of the arms trade also makes this an opportune moment to take action. Arms exports by developing countries are already growing rapidly, making these new suppliers increasingly interested in expanding this new source of export earnings. As arms control agreements and defense budget cuts in the North cut deeply into weapons manufacturers' incomes, these producers will also turn more aggressively to Third World markets. Arms purchases are known to reflect the intensity of sellers' efforts, so that if action is not taken soon to slow the trade, weapons spending in the Third World might well rise substantially. Despite the growth in Third World exports, about three-quarters of all arms exports to developing countries are supplied by five industrialized countries (USSR, U.S., France, United Kingdom, West Germany).   Therefore, an international initiative to slow military spending will require North-South negotiations organized on a regional basis to reflect the differences in the levels and sophistication of armaments in different parts of the world.   Some of the foundation for such an effort was laid in the U.S.-Soviet Conventional Arms Transfer Talks (CATT) in the late 1970s.

It remains to be seen whether reduced defense spending in the USSR and the NATO countries will produce a peace dividend that can be diverted to environmental or any other needs.   But the end of the cold war should mean a useful peace dividend in the intelligence sector through the adaptation of existing satellites for other needs and through the redirection of funds for spy satellites to desperately needed global scientific studies and monitoring of environmental trends.   If studies show that U.S. space intelligence assets can be used in this fashion, the U.S. could also approach the Soviet Union and the other space powers to explore a pooling of these resources in the interests of long-term common security.

The gravity of human impact on the earth also suggests the need to reappraise the nation's space program.   Scientific exploration of space remains a valid national priority, but hugely expensive manned projects ultimately aimed at colonizing other planets seem badly out of place so long as the longer-term livability of our own planet remains in such jeopardy.   Funds from those projects would be better spent on . . . global security goals. . . .

The shrinking Soviet military threat offers one other important opportunity to redirect money and scientific and technological know-how toward solving the long-term environmental dilemma.   Worldwide, one-quarter of all R&D funds are devoted to military uses.   In the U.S. the figure is much higher: in fiscal 1990, two-thirds of publicly supported R&D was allocated to military purposes.   The U.S. should shift some of that money to a significant new research and development initiative: a long-term commitment to sophisticated, high-technology research in the civilian sector.   The goal would be the development of new materials, processes, and technologies in energy, agriculture, communications, transportation, materials science, and manufacturing that will allow continued economic growth with greatly diminished environmental stress.   Research would be directed both at fundamental advances in basic science and at the applied research and engineering necessary to reverse the United States' now chronic inability to turn its scientific strength into commercial products.   The Defense Department's Advanced Research Projects Administration (DARPA) provides a highly successful model on which this new agency could be based.

The economic benefits of such an investment ought to be sufficient justification for it.   But since Americans are so distrustful of federal economic investments, its environmental motivation may provide the only convincing public argument.   Harvard economist Robert Reich points out that for the past forty-five years, Americans have had to clothe major public investments in the spurious guise of military security in order to command political support, calling the highway system the "National Defense Highway Act" and the post-Sputnik push in education the "National Defense Education Act." Without the cold war to justify such investments, Reich believes, the U.S. will be unable to act in its own economic interest.   Global environmental security could provide a compelling rationale, blending real security fears with the positive motivation of a far more attractive future.   Japan's first response to global climate change has been to launch exactly such an effort, the Institute of Industrial Technology for the Global Environment, due to start operations in 1992.

Taken together, these steps would have an enormous impact on the global environment.   Individually, many are easy, some cost nothing, and some will return a sizable economic benefit.   Others, like a gasoline tax and reducing the federal deficit, are politically very difficult, yet command broad bipartisan support.   Most would require a degree of political commitment to the environment and a readiness to exercise leadership that has been absent from the White House for the past decade.

Ambitious as it is, this agenda does not come close to including everything that needs to be done, especially through international agreement.   But the actions it proposes are largely or entirely within the power of the U.S. to adopt on its own, and as such constitute a realistic goal for U.S. policy.   If carried out, this program would change the way we think about, and act to protect, national security, the U.S. role in the international community, and the way we measure economic success and, therefore, deploy economic resources.   The results, in short, should be anything but incremental.

8 IS THE UNITED STATES CAPABLE OF ACTING STRATEGICALLY? CONGRESS AND THE PRESIDENT

Aaron L. Friedberg

In human affairs change typically takes one of two forms: it is either the product of an accumulation of incremental developments or the result of sudden, discontinuous events. We happen to be living through a period in which both forms of change are occurring simultaneously. The cumulative effects of differential national growth rates are now unmistakably transforming the global economy. At the same time, a series of unanticipated political events (essentially a chain reaction of revolutions) is altering the structure and functioning of the international political system.

Under these conditions it is hardly surprising that existing U.S. approaches to the outside world should seem suddenly inadequate and that calls should be heard for . . . a new U.S. grand strategy—a clearly identified set of national objectives and a coherent plan for their attainment.

The purpose of this [selection] is not to consider what the contents of a new U.S. grand strategy should be, nor to address the important prior question of whether such a thing is even possible, given the open and diverse character of the U.S. political system. I will not examine the difficulties involved in trying to knit together the country's economic, diplomatic, and military policies so that they form an integrated whole. My focus instead will be on the problems the United States faces in trying to act strategically in any one of these three distinct realms.

Strategic behavior as the term will be used here refers to that subset of rational or goal-seeking behavior in which one actor competes against another. . . . As one actor moves and the other responds, both will have to make more or less continuous assessments of their opponent's intentions and

Note: Some footnotes have been deleted or renumbered.

capabilities in order, where necessary, to adjust their own plan of action. Strategic behavior therefore requires both that an actor be open to feedback and that it be able to modulate its own behavior as needed to achieve its objectives.

The argument that will be made here can be briefly summarized as follows: In the years ahead, this country is likely to find itself increasingly involved in situations in which strategic behavior will be necessary. While the need for strategic action is growing, however, the ability of the U.S. domestic political system to provide it appears in recent years to have diminished significantly. This mismatch between external demands and internal capacities will have costs even if, as seems most likely, it does not result in any overt disasters. Finally, while there are undoubtedly ways in which U.S. strategic performance could be enhanced, none of them will be easy to implement.

A CHANGING WORLD

Seen from the U.S. perspective, the past 40 years have been marked above all by a diminution in the U.S. economic, military, and political preponderance that characterized the early postwar period. This relative decline in its power has been forcing the United States into an increasing array of circumstances in which it can no longer rely on the application of overwhelming superiority in material resources to achieve its objectives. The need for strategic behavior has been expanding as the margin of U.S. advantage over its rivals in various spheres shrinks.

To this long-term tendency has now been added a second sudden and unanticipated development. The apparent collapse of the Soviet Union, its . . . withdrawal from much if not all of its external empire, and its evident eagerness, at the very least, to scale back on its political and military competition with the West are creating new and unfamiliar conditions. This dramatic turn of events may alleviate some of the pressures imposed on the United States by the erosion of its relative power, but it is likely to intensify others while at the same time helping to create entirely new ones.

The best way to begin to grasp what all this may mean is to look in turn at developments in each of the three major arenas of interaction between the United States and the outside world.

The Struggle for the Global Product

Since the end of World War II, the relative predominance of the United States in the world economy has gone down at the same time as the extent of the country's engagement in international markets has been going up. Thus, to take only two of a range of possible indicators, between 1945 and 1990 the U.S. share of total world output of goods and services diminished by roughly one half, while the ratio of both imports and exports to U.S. gross national product (GNP) has more than doubled.

The comparatively rapid expansion of foreign economies, the growing importance of overseas markets to U.S. companies, and the increased success of foreign firms in penetrating domestic markets have combined to bring mounting pressure on traditional U.S. approaches to both foreign and domestic economic policy.   The extension of global economic interdependence and the intensification of international commercial competition are seen by a growing number of observers as requiring new forms of governmental action.   Such action, it is argued, is needed to respond to and, in some cases, to anticipate the policies of foreign governments as they seek to promote the welfare of their own countries.   In other words, the U.S. government is being called upon increasingly to pursue economic policies that have an important strategic dimension.

For most of the postwar period the federal government has concentrated in its internal policies on promoting stable growth and finding the right mix of fiscal and monetary measures to keep the domestic economic engine turning over fast enough to prevent undue unemployment but not permitting it to race ahead so quickly that it produced excessive inflation.   Because of the perceived importance of maintaining the technological superiority of U.S. over Soviet weapon systems, the U.S. government also devoted significant resources to encouraging scientific education and basic research and supporting more narrowly focused defense and space-related research and development work.   The primary purpose of these undertakings was to enhance the nation's physical security.   It was certainly hoped (and sometimes claimed) that spin-offs from government-funded programs would help to maintain the U.S. lead in advanced civilian technologies.   But, if this did occur, it was seen as a secondary and largely fortuitous by-product of money spent for other reasons.   In general, until the 1970s, it was widely assumed that the United States would be able to preserve its overall technological advantage indefinitely and, at least as far as the government was concerned, with a minimum of exertion.

Accompanying the policy of demand management at home was a persistent U.S. effort to reduce tariff barriers and promote freer international trade. Beginning in 1945 and continuing through successive rounds of multilateral negotiations the United States has sought to encourage the greatest possible degree of trade liberalization.   Movement in this direction was widely believed to be desirable on theoretical grounds (because freer trade would lead to greater global welfare), for reasons of national economic self-interest (because, at least in the initial postwar decades, it seemed clear that far more U.S. industries would benefit from the opportunity to expand exports than would be hurt by increased exposure to imports), and for reasons of national security (because free trade would strengthen the political ties among the industrial democracies while at the same time rendering them wealthier and better able to provide for their own defense).

In the last 15 years both the internal and the external components of U.S. economic policy have begun to be called into question.   The growing volume of imports has led to an increase in pressures for protection from an array of distressed industries.   Meanwhile, the lowering of traditional tariffs has been accompanied by a growth in new, more subtle kinds of nontariff barriers (NTBs) to trade.   Because these barriers are often difficult to identify and because they typically involve practices that are not universally recognized as unfair or illegitimate, they may well lie outside the effective reach of the large, multilateral trade negotiations that have characterized the postwar era. At the same time, however, NTBs are also widely believed to be imposing serious constraints on the expansion of U.S. exports.   For this reason, in the last several years the U.S. government has been under growing domestic pressure to engage in bilateral trade expansion'negotiations with the countries whose use of NTBs is regarded as most harmful to U.S. business.

It is in this context that the need for strategic behavior becomes evident. At the peak of its economic preeminence the United States could simply push for a universal reduction in tariffs and, most important, it could afford to overlook those instances in which its allies and principal trading partners deviated from the norms of free trade.   Increasingly, however, it may have to deal more directly and more aggressively with individual countries whose business it needs and over which it therefore no longer enjoys a decisive bargaining advantage.   In order to pry open foreign markets the United States may even have to be able selectively to threaten and, in some cases, actually to close its own.

The intensifying global economic competition and, in particular, the strug- gle for dominance in high-technology industries is also giving rise to calls for new and more active internal government policies.   At the very least there is widespread agreement that the federal government needs to renew its efforts to promote basic research and scientific education while at the same time looking for new ways to encourage more investment in research and devel- opment (R&D) by private industry.   In addition to these general measures interest has grown in policies aimed at assisting specific U.S. industries in their competition with foreign firms, some of which may have benefited from so-called strategic trade or industrial policies undertaken by their own gov- ernments.

While the ultimate utility of such steps has been questioned by many economists, some have argued that, with a carefully selected mix of measures, states may be able to assist domestically based companies in gaining a sub- stantial share of world markets for key industrial products.   Dominance in one "strategic" industry (like semiconductors) could then make it easier for a country's firms to gain a decisive advantage in another (such as supercom- puters).   Initiatives of this sort, it is claimed, require effective responses from the government if the United States is to retain some of its previous advantages in high technology.

Whatever the wisdom of these particular proposals, there can be no ques- tion that world trading patterns are increasingly shaped by interaction be- tween states as well as competition among firms.

Competitive Military Strategies

In the military realm strategic behavior is usually thought of in the classical, Clausewitzian sense as being limited to the engagement of forces on the battlefield. Except in cases where one side is so superior as to be able virtually to annihilate its opponent, each will have to take account of the strengths, weaknesses, and plans of the other side if it wants to increase its chances of victory.

Prolonged but essentially peaceful confrontations between potentially hostile states may also involve two different and somewhat more subtle forms of strategic behavior. Military threats (as compared to the actual employment of force) can be used to deter an opponent from acting or to compel him to behave in certain ways. In cases where arms competitions continue over a long period of time, it is also possible that, by experimenting with, developing, or actually procuring and deploying certain kinds of military capabilities, one country may be able to influence the development and deployment decisions of its rivals.

Thanks largely to the evident superiority of the U.S. nuclear arsenal, for much of the first half of the postwar era U.S. military planners were largely unconcerned with any of these forms of strategic interaction. In the event of war the United States planned simply to unleash the biggest, fastest, and most devastating atomic attack possible on the Soviet Union. A clear capability and an unquestionable willingness to carry out massive attacks were considered the necessary and sufficient conditions for a successful policy of deterrence. U.S. weapons development and deployment decisions were driven by technological progress, objective planning requirements, and a general desire to stay ahead of the Soviets in certain categories of capability rather than by any conscious effort to shape the future evolution of the ongoing military competition.

If the first 20 years of the Cold War were marked, in the United States, by an autism born of superiority, the last two decades have been distinguished by the erosion of that earlier edge and by an accompanying increase in U.S. sensitivity to the thinking of its major opponent and to the complex dynamics of the strategic interaction between the two sides. During the 1970s U.S. intelligence experts and planners began to pay greater attention to Soviet military doctrine and to devising means of countering Soviet strategy in the event of war. This was believed to be necessary to bolster the West's defensive chances (given the narrowing gap between U.S. and Soviet nuclear capabilities and the persistent Soviet advantage in conventional forces), but it was also seen as essential for purposes of strengthening deterrence. In an era of diminished advantage the United States would have to concentrate more closely on understanding and influencing the detailed military calculations of its likely enemy, seeking, as one Secretary of Defense [Harold Brown] explained, "to make a Soviet victory as improbable (*seen through Soviet eyes*) as we can make it" (emphasis added).

Since the mid-1980s the U.S. government has also begun to consider ways of modulating the country's defensive efforts with the deliberate intention of influencing Soviet armaments decisions and driving the superpower military competition in directions more favorable to U.S. interests. As elaborated in statements by Defense Department officials, the aim of the policy of competitive strategies is to apply what is referred to as a chess match methodology to the U.S. force planning process. Choices among weapon systems and operational concepts are now to be informed by a more deliberate and systematic assessment of the likely sequence of Soviet response and subsequent U.S. counterresponse. Initiatives that cause the Soviets to channel resources into capabilities that are relatively unthreatening or that compel them to compete on ground where the United States enjoys an enduring competitive advantage are to be preferred over those that play to Soviet strengths or are likely to provoke an especially threatening response. . . .

Having grown more closely linked on the way up, the military programs of the two superpowers are unlikely to become suddenly and completely detached from one another, even as they are reduced in scale and intensity. What seems most likely, assuming a continuation of present political trends, is that the competition will be wound down in some areas (such as conventional ground forces) while continuing in others (like strategic nuclear forces) as each side seeks to provide itself with some insurance against a future breakdown in relations or a possible breakthrough in new forms of weaponry.

. . . The armaments efforts of the two superpowers will, therefore, remain coupled for some time to come. The new U.S. interest in consciously shaping that interaction is unlikely to disappear, and it may even grow as defense dollars become more scarce. . . .

Whatever happens between the superpowers, the next two decades will see a substantial growth in the military capabilities of a number of other states. . . . The diffusion of military capabilities will create a more complex situation, one that imposes new demands for strategic behavior on the United States. In establishing requirements for forces sufficient to deter attack on the United States, defense planners may soon have to take account of the capabilities, calculations, and intentions of a wider range of significant actors. As the . . . Persian Gulf crisis . . . demonstrated so vividly, in considering the actual use of force in many parts of the world, planners will have to contemplate engagements with enemies whose capabilities are much closer to those of their U.S. counterparts than has typically been true in the past.

Multipolar Diplomacy

Diplomacy involves communication and, above all, negotiation between nation states, and successful negotiation, in turn, requires a well-developed capacity for strategic behavior. Over the course of the last 45 years the volume, scope, intensity, and importance of the external negotiations entered into by the U.S. government have all increased, a trend that shows every sign of accelerating in the years ahead.

From the 1940s to the 1960s the United States engaged in relatively little serious, overt (still less, formal) bargaining with its major foreign adversaries. U.S. refusal to recognize the People's Republic of China ruled out any direct contacts between the two countries.   The nations of Eastern Europe were regarded merely as satellites of the Soviet Union with whom separate dealings were essentially impossible.   What negotiations there were between Washington and Moscow were considered far more important for their impact on the perceptions of third parties than for any concrete results that they might produce.   Until the Soviets had been worn down by a combination of external pressure and internal weakness they could not be expected to negotiate seriously with the West.   In the meantime, in the words of one top secret planning document from the 1950s, the only real reason for the United States to have dealings with the Soviet Union was "to maintain the continued support of its allies" by seeking "to convince them of its desire to reach . . . settlements."

The trend toward greater diplomatic contact with hostile powers began in the late 1960s and has been moving forward with some notable fits and starts ever since.   The Nixon-Kissinger opening to China gave way quickly to formal relations, extensive negotiations on a wide range of issues, and, in the late 1970s, a virtual tacit alliance against the Soviet Union.   Meanwhile, U.S.–Soviet arms-control negotiations have been going on for over 20 years, with the very real possibility that they will now lead to substantial reductions in both conventional and nuclear forces and to discussion of even more far-reaching cuts in the future.   After having been pushed off the superpower agenda by the collapse of détente in the mid-1970s, trade, aid, and other economic issues are back on the table, and they seem likely to remain there for the foreseeable future.   The superpowers are also now engaged in the closing stages of negotiations over the shape of the political map in Central Europe, the very issue that first gave rise to the Cold War almost half a century ago.   Finally, the scope of U.S. dealings with the former Soviet satellites has begun to expand enormously.   Some of these countries may soon make the transition from enemies to friends and perhaps eventually even to allies of the United States.

Even at the peak of its hegemonic power the United States was never able completely to dominate its friends in Europe and the Far East.   Nevertheless, it seems fair to say that with time the ratio of dictation to genuine negotiation in relations between the United States and its allies has been going steadily downward.   This evolution is the product of two tendencies, both of which will only grow stronger in the years ahead.   As they have recovered from the effects of World War II, U.S. allies have become wealthier, stronger, and more self-confident than they were in the immediate postwar period.   At the same time, with the gradual warming in East-West relations, their anxiety over external military threats has tended to diminish, a fact that has given rise to increasingly frequent debates over burden-sharing with their senior alliance partner.

The apparent collapse of Soviet power will further loosen the ties that bind the United States to its allies and weaken the willingness of all parties to sacrifice other interests (and, in particular, economic interests) to the higher goal of maintaining alliance solidarity.   Whether this shift increases the leverage of the United States (which will be less concerned about the defection of its erstwhile charges) more than that of its allies (who will be less fearful of antagonizing their former protector) remains to be seen.   What seems clear is that, far from ushering in a period of "kinder, gentler," and more purely cooperative relations among the industrial democracies, the end of the Cold War is likely to mark the dawning of an era of tougher bargaining and greater national self-assertion.

Over the long run the disintegration of postwar blocs may represent the first decisive step in a process that will eventually transform the structure of the international system. . . . Together with China, the United States, and a weakened Soviet Union, Germany and Japan will form the core of a new international system.   The long-awaited (and often heralded) transition from bipolarity to multipolarity seems finally to be at hand.

In the past, multipolar systems have been characterized by a high degree of strategic interaction among the major powers that make them up.   As compared to a bipolar world, the array of possible diplomatic combinations and, therefore, the scope for maneuver and the degree of uncertainty are all considerably enlarged.   According to Kenneth Waltz:

> In multipolar systems there are too many powers to permit any of them to draw clear and fixed lines between allies and adversaries. . . . With three or more powers flexibility of alliances keeps relations of friendship and enmity fluid and makes everyone's estimate of the present and future relation of forces uncertain.[1]

Given the existence of nuclear weapons and the evident dangers of war, the multipolar diplomacy of the future may be somewhat more relaxed than has typically been the case in the past.   The United States might not have to fear the immediate military consequences of a renewed alliance between the Soviet Union and China, for example, or between China and Japan.   But almost any one of the possible new combinations of powers would be less favorable to U.S. interests than that which exists today.   This fact will give a new urgency and importance to negotiations with each of the major players and a new strategic dimension to U.S. diplomacy.

A CHANGED DOMESTIC SYSTEM

In the U.S. system the effective execution of foreign policy is critically dependent on some measure of coordination between the president and Congress.   This is so because the provisions of the Constitution relating to external action bestow overlapping powers on the executive and legislative branches of government. . . .

Without some measure of compromise and coordination between the branches there would be no possibility of the United States following a steady pattern in its external relations. Fear that the country might prove incapable of sustaining a consistent course (and, in particular, one that was so much at odds with its previous tendencies) was uppermost in the minds of the architects of postwar U.S. foreign policy, and it remains a central concern of many contemporary observers. As important as it is (or was), however, consistency requires only a relatively modest degree of coordination between the executive and the legislature. Flexibility, on the other hand, demands an even larger measure of communication and cooperation between the two branches. . . .

If the world is truly changing in all (or even some) of the ways that have already been described, then consistency may be the problem of the past for the United States and flexibility the challenge of the future. Without flexibility there can be no maneuver and thus no strategic behavior. If the need for such behavior is growing, therefore, the need for closer executive–legislative coordination must also be increasing. The manner in which the functioning of the U.S. political system has evolved in recent years, however, has made such closeness considerably more difficult to achieve.

For at least 20 years after 1945 the United States pursued its diplomatic, economic, and military policies with more consistency than many postwar observers had ever believed attainable. This accomplishment was the product of an arrangement under which the Congress essentially delegated a good portion of its authority over foreign policy to the president. The conditions that made this possible have been variously described, but three elements were clearly of central importance:

First, consensus. From the forties to the sixties there was general, widespread agreement on the nation's fundamental foreign policy aims and on the means that should be employed in achieving them. The depth and breadth of this consensus have sometimes been exaggerated in retrospect, but there can be no denying that most participants in the political process accepted the need for containment, deterrence, entangling overseas alliances, forward deployment of U.S. forces, and the continuing promotion of free international trade.

Second, institutional arrangements. The concentration of congressional power in the hands of a relatively small number of key figures eased the process of consultation and coordination between the branches. As long as a handful of committee chairmen were on board, the executive could count on whatever congressional support it needed to sustain its policies. Even if they had entertained dissenting views, most of the more ordinary members of the House and Senate lacked the resources to pursue an independent course in challenging the president's leadership on foreign policy.

Third, the distribution of party power. Further greasing the wheels of executive–legislative coordination was the fact that, for much of the first two postwar decades, both branches were firmly in the hands of either the Republicans or (far more often) the Democrats. For 14 of the 22 years between 1945 and 1967 the same party controlled the White House, the

Senate, and the House of Representatives. Although it did not eliminate partisan conflict over foreign policy, this fact of political life helped to limit the impact of those struggles that did occur.

Consistency was the virtue of the initial postwar system of control over foreign policy but, as has often been pointed out, it was also its major vice. The arrangements that grew up in the immediate postwar period made it easier for the United States to launch and sustain a set of policies that served its own interests and those of its allies. But they also made it easier for the country to pursue containment to its illogical extreme in Vietnam and more difficult for it to change direction once the dangers of that undertaking had begun to become apparent.

From the mid-1960s onwards each of the three factors that once combined to encourage coordination between the president and Congress and to promote consistency in U.S. foreign policy grew significantly weaker. The postwar consensus was not entirely shattered by Vietnam, as is often claimed, but portions of it did become objects of dispute and disagreement. In particular, policies aimed at maintaining high levels of defense expenditure and at extending containment from Western Europe and Northeast Asia to parts of the Third World could no longer count on near-universal elite or mass acceptance. Support for a continued U.S. commitment to the North Atlantic Treaty Organization (NATO) and for ongoing efforts to maintain a liberal world trading regime remained strong, but, beginning in the early 1970s, even these fundamental tenets of postwar foreign policy dogma were open to challenge in a way that they had never been before.

Perhaps more important than the weakening of consensus on matters of substance that began with Vietnam was its unraveling with regard to procedure. As the disaster in Southeast Asia deepened, the generally accepted notion that responsible foreign policy could only be made by a strong president unencumbered by an intrusive Congress began to be called into question. In the late 1960s congressional reformers set out first to alter the balance of power inside the House and Senate and then to overhaul fundamentally the relationship between Congress and the executive.

The internal reforms of the Vietnam period produced what [political scientist] Samuel Huntington has called "a tremendous dispersion of power" within the Congress. The overturning of the seniority system, the proliferation of subcommittees, and the expansion in staff and research resources made it easier for individual members to pursue their own paths on matters of foreign policy and more difficult for the executive branch to cooperate with (still less to control) the Congress. Instead of simply following the president's lead, Congress began to reassert its authority, establishing procedures aimed at monitoring, constraining, and sometimes blocking executive initiatives.

Although for a time the "imperial presidency" appeared to have been replaced by an "imperial Congress," during the 1980s the pendulum of power swung back some distance in the direction of the executive. While the president may have regained the initiative, however, Congress has retained a substantial and much enlarged capacity for oversight and control. . . .

The decay of consensus and the shift in institutional arrangements has made for more frequent executive–legislative disputes on an increasingly wide range of foreign policy issues. Adding to the intensity of these conflicts has been the fact that, since the late 1960s, partisan political power has come to be more sharply split between the branches of government than in preceding decades. From 1967 to 1990 the same party will have been firmly in control of both Congress and the presidency for only four years. Given this division it is hardly surprising that debates over foreign affairs have become more harsh and partisan in tone.

Over the past 20 years the degree of coordination between the executive and legislative branches of government has gone down and so, too, has the country's capacity to sustain a consistent foreign policy. While this has been occurring the external situation has been changing in ways that seem to require greater flexibility and therefore an even larger measure of inter-branch cooperation. . . .

CONSEQUENCES

The increased difficulty of executive–legislative coordination makes it less likely that the United States will be able effectively to pursue the various forms of strategic behavior described above. This point can be illustrated with reference to a single example from each of the three broad issue areas: economic, military, and diplomatic.

Trade

Efforts to force foreign countries to reduce trade barriers by controlling their access to the U.S. market may make sense, at least in the abstract. But compellent threats of the sort that would be required to achieve this end are generally quite difficult to implement effectively, even where the authority to make and execute them is relatively concentrated. Where that authority is dispersed the difficulties of doing so will be even greater.

In analyzing how the United States ought to respond to the trade policies of other countries, economist Avinash Dixit points out that, "typically compellence has to be achieved by starting to punish the other party and then relaxing if they do what we want." Thus, in confronting a country that has closed its markets to U.S. exports "we will have to close our market and offer to open it if they open theirs." Both steps in this process, initiation and relaxation, will present problems in a system with an open trade policymaking process. . . .

Dixit concludes his analysis of "aggressive reciprocity" by arguing that, if the United States were ever to want to engage in this or other forms of strategic behavior it would have to change

> its conduct of trade policy, and perhaps of economic policy more generally, in quite substantial ways. Policy mechanisms should be based on firmer and clearer rules and allow less direction after the fact. There should be less scope for continuous political input or pressure from affected interests. And, if possible, there should be greater unity of purpose and better agreed objectives.[2]

None of these changes appears especially likely in the foreseeable future and, indeed, current trends seem to point in exactly the opposite direction. I. M. Destler describes the ongoing deterioration of an arrangement under which, since the 1930s, Congress has delegated to the executive much of its constitutionally mandated power over the regulation of foreign commerce. This system permitted both branches of government to insulate themselves from protectionist pressures, and it freed the executive to pursue a policy of trade liberalization.[3]

In recent years, as a result both of external and internal developments (the increasing importance of trade to the U.S. economy, an erosion of the earlier bipartisan antiprotection consensus, and the dispersal of policymaking power in Congress), the old coordinating mechanisms have started to break down and the legislative branch has begun to reassert itself on trade issues. Agreement on ends and means has diminished, and the openness of the process to political pressures has begun to increase. Destler warns that these trends may lead eventually to a situation in which Congress (and through it an array of special interest groups) will once again control the nation's commercial policies, thereby unleashing a wave of protectionism. Whether or not this happens, the increasingly open and disputatious manner in which trade policy is now made makes it more difficult and certainly more dangerous for the United States to use compellent threats to negotiate reductions in foreign import barriers.

Defense

Central to the idea of competitive strategies is the assumption that the United States will be able to modulate its own military efforts so as to produce some deliberate impact on those of its likely opponents. If, for example, the United States wanted to force the Soviet Union to continue sinking vast sums into its air defense network, it might have to develop and deploy weapons that would place Soviet defensive systems under increasing technological stress. Once the Soviets had invested heavily in meeting the threat posed by a given U.S. weapon (cruise missiles, for example), the United States might wish to introduce a new one with different performance characteristics (perhaps a "stealthy" cruise missile). The purpose of such a carefully phased series of deployments would be to render each new generation of air defenses obsolete just as it came into service, thereby forcing the Soviets, at great cost, to start all over again.

Successful implementation of any plan of this sort would demand an especially responsive process for the development and deployment of new weapons.   Intelligence information about the vulnerabilities, plans, and likely reactions of an opponent would have to be integrated into weapons design in a timely fashion.   Research into promising new technologies would have to be sustained over considerable periods of time, and decisions on what weapons to buy and exactly when and in what numbers to deploy them would have to be made deliberately and with precision.   Finally, in order to increase the odds that a particular competitive maneuver imposed greater burdens on an opponent than on the United States, the entire process would have to be as efficient and inexpensive as possible.

In large measure the key to competitive strategies is weapons procurement, a process over which the Congress, with its power "to raise and support Armies" and "to provide and maintain a Navy," clearly has the ultimate constitutional authority.   Without a substantial measure of executive–legislative cooperation on military policy it is, therefore, difficult to see how the United States could ever engage in any of the more sophisticated forms of strategic military behavior.   Such cooperation is not impossible to imagine, but it has certainly not been much in evidence over the course of the past 15 years.

In one recent study, [political scientist] Robert Art describes how Congress has become ever more deeply involved, not in overseeing and approving the broad outlines of the annual defense budget, but in examining and modifying even its most minute details.   According to Art this tendency has been growing since the 1960s when Congress began to require annual authorizations, first for weapons procurement, and then for the other major portions of the budget.   In the 1970s "disillusionment with the 'imperial Presidency,' " the "antidefense mood of the country," and, most important of all, an explosion in the size of defense committee staffs encouraged an even higher degree of congressional scrutiny and involvement.   By the 1980s the various responsible House and Senate committees were making hundreds and even thousands of changes in each year's defense program.

Art asserts that the trend toward micromanagement has drawn the attention of the Congress, and with it the Defense Department, away from broad considerations of national military strategy and toward the neverending struggle over the coming year's budget.   The increased scope and depth of executive–legislative disputes on defense procurement has also contributed to a decline in the stability of funding for major weapons programs and this, in turn, has tended to lengthen and make more expensive the process through which new systems are developed and deployed.

With the rise in interbranch contention over defense issues, it has become increasingly difficult for the United States government to formulate and implement even a minimally coherent overall military program, let alone to fine-tune it for strategic purposes in any more subtle way.

Diplomacy

Kenneth Waltz notes in his analysis of the implications of multipolarity that "with more than two states, the politics of power turn on the diplomacy by which alliances are made, maintained and disrupted." In a situation in which there are several roughly equal states, alignments may form and re-form at a rapid pace and with considerable frequency. Under these conditions a capacity for diplomatic flexibility (the ability to negotiate and implement agreements reliably and with some dispatch) could become an important national attribute.

In this regard the United States will probably always be at a distinct disadvantage, although perhaps not as much as the recent history of executive–legislative disputes over diplomacy would seem to suggest. The design of the U.S. system was intended precisely to reduce the likelihood that the country's leaders would be able to engage in complex diplomatic dealings with foreign powers. After some debate, the Founding Fathers decided to permit the president to negotiate treaties with other governments (rather than bestowing that power exclusively on the Senate), but they went on to require that the Senate approve any such agreements by an overwhelming two-thirds majority. This high barrier was meant to make it difficult for a U.S. president to bind his country to any other and, over the years, it has been the downfall of a significant number of treaties.

For most of U.S. history the country's internal arrangements coincided well with the general direction of its external policies. As long as the United States remained largely aloof from the outside world, the difficulties it would have faced in trying to make commitments to other states made little practical difference. It was only with the post–1945 emergence of the United States as a major global power that this situation began to change considerably.

In the first chill of the Cold War, successive U.S. presidents (with the help of key congressional leaders) were able to guide the United States into a web of entangling peacetime alliances of the sort that it had always avoided in the past. Once entered upon, these agreements became substantially insulated from the ebb and flow of congressional and popular opinion regarding their utility. In addition to locking the country into a set of commitments, postwar presidents also sought to avoid the cumbersome formal treaty-making process altogether through the use of direct, unratified executive agreements with the leaders of foreign powers. This practice became increasingly common in the fifties and sixties to the point where, in contrast to the prewar era, executive agreements came to far outnumber actual treaties.

The 1970s marked the beginning of a period of expanding negotiations (especially between the United States and its Communist rivals), diminished consensus on the country's external goals, and intensified congressional efforts to regain control over U.S. diplomacy. In an attempt to close off (or at least to shrink) the executive agreements loophole, Congress passed legislation requiring that it be notified of any such arrangements and setting out guidelines defining those situations in which they could be used in place of treaties. When the president proposed formal agreements, powerful congressional minorities were able on several notable occasions to block their passage or to force costly and damaging ratification battles. These were followed in the 1980s by a series of less cataclysmic but no less destructive interbranch struggles over the nation's diplomatic direction, with the executive seeking to reassert its prerogatives (even to the point of unilaterally redefining the meaning of previously ratified agreements) and Congress trying to use the power of the purse to impose on the president its view of the proper course to follow in negotiations.

Even with a substantial degree of executive–legislative agreement, there will always be limits on the capacity of the United States to pursue diplomatic policies of great subtlety or suppleness. The less coordination there is between the branches, however, the lower the likelihood that the country will be able to behave with even a modest measure of flexibility. If the coming era of multipolarity is anything like those of the past, diplomatic flexibility, and hence domestic political cooperation, will be at a premium.

CURES

There are basically three ways in which the United States can cope with the limitations imposed by the dispersal of domestic authority over its foreign policy.

Second-Best Strategies

The first solution would simply be to avoid those forms of strategic behavior that depend inordinately on interbranch coordination. For example, the successful conduct of a policy of aggressive trade reciprocity may require the concentration of more power in the hands of the president than is politically feasible (or desirable). Without such concentration, however, attempts to raise and lower trade barriers could easily trigger the flood of protectionism that critics of reciprocity fear and warn against. Under the most likely domestic political conditions then, the pursuit of a cure to foreign trade barriers could easily turn out to be far worse than the disease. There would surely be gains to be had from pursuing a perfect strategic trade policy (including greater access to foreign markets and, presumably, a higher national income), but the requirements of such a policy may simply exceed the capacities of the U.S. political system.

Two-Level Games

Instead of trying to avoid executive–legislative conflicts over foreign policy it may be possible at times to embrace them and turn them to the strategic advantage of the United States. The most obvious way of doing this would be for the president to play "good cop" to a congressional "bad cop." With Congress threatening to take steps harmful to the interests of another country, the president might be able to extract greater concessions in negotiations than would otherwise be obtainable.

This approach will undoubtedly work in some situations, some of the time. It would be a mistake, however, to view it as a way of avoiding altogether the problem of coordination. In fact, such tactics depend for their success on a fairly high level of at least tacit cooperation between the two branches. If the executive and legislature are sufficiently far apart in their views, it may not be possible for the president to negotiate any understanding with a foreign power that will be acceptable to Congress. If Congress changes its position once an agreement has been reached, or if the president is unable to "deliver" it, heading off a threatened action in return for concessions, then the utility of the good cop–bad cop routine will be sharply diminished in future negotiations. On the other hand, if no harm is ever forthcoming, foreign leaders will begin to doubt that they really have anything to lose by standing firm.

Clever tactics for exploiting the inherent division in the U.S. decisionmaking machinery are a less than perfect substitute for steps aimed at actually reducing that gap.

Increasing Interbranch Coordination

It has been argued that the deterioration in executive–legislative cooperation on foreign policy issues is the result of three factors: the decay of the cold war consensus, the collapse of previous arrangements for promoting coordination between the branches, and the increased frequency of national governments divided along party lines. How likely is it that, in the years ahead, any or all of these tendencies will be reversed?

To take the least fundamental of the three conditions first: there is certainly no reason why the U.S. people could not choose to elect a president and a majority of Congress from the same political party. Neither the Republican grip on the White House nor the Democratic hold on Congress is so tight as to be unbreakable, although the first appears at this point to be more vulnerable than the second. As illustrated by the unfortunate record of the Carter presidency, however, the dominance of a single party does not guarantee effective interbranch collaboration on foreign affairs, still less the formulation and execution of effective policies. These will depend on the size of the majorities a president can assemble in Congress and, even more important, on his capacity for leadership.

There is probably no way of reconstructing the institutional conditions that permitted relatively close interbranch collaboration on foreign policy in the forties, fifties, and sixties. Both the changes within Congress and the shift in the balance of executive–legislative power have deep and fundamental causes; neither one will be easily or quickly reversed. Individual members have learned to profit from and have come to expect a situation in which congressional power is widely diffused rather than concentrated in the hands of a small group of "barons." There is no reason to expect them to accept a reversion to previous practices, even if, in some ways, this would make life easier for the executive. The notion that, having reclaimed its constitutional role as a co-equal partner in foreign affairs, the Congress would now be willing to give it up is also farfetched.

Congressional power is going to remain dispersed, and Congress is going to continue to insist on a substantial role in shaping foreign policy. In the face of these conditions the typical remedy proposed is consultation—some reconditioned mechanism for enhancing interbranch communication and thus, presumably, cooperation. But increased communication does not, in and of itself, necessarily lead to enhanced cooperation. Indeed, when the differences between two parties are great enough, more contact can mean more friction and even less understanding.

In the long run, reestablishing a consensus on the various aspects of foreign policy will be the key to improving the country's strategic performance. Without it schemes for increased consultation will come to nothing. Where it exists the U.S. system may yet prove capable of greater flexibility than the gross anatomy of its institutional structure would seem to permit.

The initial postwar consensus was forged in the aftermath of a terrible international upheaval and sustained, for a time, by a shared sense of external threat. Whether the changes that are now occurring are sufficiently dramatic to provide the preconditions for the formation of a new consensus remains to be seen. For the time being what is most likely is a period of drift and disagreement during which the country's policies will be pulled in several different directions simultaneously. By bringing long-submerged disputes more clearly to the surface recent events could even make things much worse, perhaps triggering a series of divisive debates over such issues as how best to manage economic relations with Japan. But [recent] developments . . . will also speed the dissolution of old divisions, thereby opening the way for realignment and, perhaps, ultimately, renewal. If that happens the United States could emerge better equipped to deal with the challenges of the coming era than it appears to be at present.

NOTES

1. Kenneth N. Waltz, *Theory of International Politics* (Reading, Mass.: Addison-Wesley, 1979), p. 168.

2. [Avinash Dixit, "How Should We Respond to Other Countries' Trade Policies?" in Stern, *U.S. Trade Policies*] p. 279. . . .

3. See [I. M.] Destler, *American Trade Politics* [Washington, D.C.: Institute for International Economics, 1987], pp. 9–36.

9 POST–COLD WAR POLITICS

Norman J. Ornstein and Mark Schmitt

As dramatic political changes continue throughout Eastern Europe and the Soviet Union, the world may indeed be witnessing the virtual disappearance of communism as a political ideology. The decline and fall of communism has proceeded so smoothly that so far this geopolitical shift has presented few hard choices in American foreign policy. But as communism recedes, American politics faces a strange new dilemma: How will the U.S. political system operate without anticommunism as its central organizing principle?

Especially since World War II anticommunism has defined not only U.S. foreign policy but also the competition between the two leading American political parties. Debates over the federal budget have been driven by the perception of an immediate Soviet communist threat to the United States. Even toward regions or on issues untouched by Marxist-Leninist dogma, American foreign policy has been guided by worries about communism. Both John Kennedy and Ronald Reagan owe their success as politicians in part to their unyielding rhetoric against the evils of Soviet communism, particularly as practiced in Eastern Europe. (However, their willingness to shelve that rhetoric when it came to actual negotiations with the Soviets was responsible for their stature as presidents.)

In the immediate postwar era of Harry Truman, the Democrats' combination of anticommunism and assertive internationalism worked to their electoral advantage, enabling them to compete evenly with the Republicans on foreign-policy questions. But for at least the last 20 years, the Republican party (GOP) has consistently used anticommunism to its advantage. The GOP edge stems not from every Republican being more anticommunist than every Democrat—no one could have been more staunchly anticommunist than Kennedy or Democratic Senator Henry "Scoop" Jackson—but from the GOP's internal consensus on the magnitude of the communist threat and on how to deal with it, combined with the Democrats' disarray on these questions.

Long after communism had lost whatever appeal it had for most American leftists, liberal Democrats remained divided between anticommunists and those who called themselves anti-anticommunists—noncommunists who often reacted with more fury to the excesses of McCarthyism than to the excesses of Stalinism. This division of the 1950s evolved in the following decade into an increasingly bitter conflict between Democratic hawks and doves over American involvement in Vietnam, fueled by the suggestion from the right that those who opposed U.S. military action really preferred a victory by Hanoi. Years later in Nicaragua, the Reagan administration again took advantage of the Democrats' divisions and, despite repeated surveys showing wide public opposition to *contra* aid, managed to plant the suspicion that Democrats who opposed aid to the *contras* actually welcomed the Sandinista government and would hand El Salvador over to another pro-Marxist gang.

While Republicans focused unblinkingly on the threat of communism, some Democrats tried to shift the debate to North-South relations, human rights, and international economic structures. Although these concerns may seem more realistic and relevant for the 1990s, during the preceding decades they were no political match for the Republican drumbeat of anticommunist rhetoric and commitment to an ever-stronger national defense. By late 1989 51 per cent of voters polled by NBC News said they trusted the Republicans to better handle national defense, compared to a mere 15 per cent for the Democrats. On the question of which party could better manage relations with the Soviet Union, those polled preferred the Republicans to the Democrats 43 per cent to 13 per cent.

The 1988 presidential campaign, to the extent that it addressed foreign policy at all, was fought entirely on the traditional ground of anticommunism. Except for a brief tirade against foreign ownership of U.S. assets at the end of the campaign (unwittingly addressed to Missouri auto workers employed by an Italian firm), Democrat Michael Dukakis only halfheartedly attempted to shift the terms of debate on foreign policy. Instead, he sought to demonstrate that he could be just as tough on the communists as any Republican. Dukakis decided to convey that image by riding in a battle tank as it rumbled around a field. The event created an unforgettable image, though one useful only to his opponent.

Dukakis' strategists correctly perceived that past Democratic attempts to shift the foreign policy debate away from communism to newer, more complex issues usually failed to stir voters. Still, by 1988 the struggle with communism was not dominating Americans' perceptions of foreign policy as it had for decades. The electorate's sense of U.S. weakness and Soviet militancy, so acute in 1980, lessened as the Reagan administration's two terms neared their end. That administration's massive military expenditures thoroughly sated popular demands for a stronger defense. The completion of the defense buildup, the revolutionary changes in the Soviet bloc, and a sweeping arms agreement on intermediate-range nuclear missiles—together with high trade deficits—started to shift the public's international concerns. As a result, by 1988 some nontraditional issues were beginning to show up on the electoral radar screen, even without the candidates making a sustained effort to talk them up.

In March 1988, one in a series of public opinion polls sponsored by Americans Talk Security (ATS) revealed this shift in American attitudes. Asked whether the greatest threat to America came from "military adversaries like the Soviet Union" or from "economic competitors like Japan," 59 per cent of those polled said the economic threat was greater, while only 31 per cent remained more concerned about the military threat. The most important goal of U.S. national security policy, according to those polled, should be combating international drug traffic, followed by reducing the trade deficit. Cutting the U.S. and Soviet nuclear arsenals finished third. The goals of stopping communism in Central America and containing Soviet aggression were fourth and fifth respectively—still high on the list but a rather striking change from 1980.

While the Republican party continues to hold an overwhelming 3:1 advantage on the basic question of which party would do a better job dealing with national security, the parties have been more evenly matched on these nontraditional issues. Those questioned by ATS were split almost evenly on which party was more likely to stand up to countries that engaged in unfair trade practices and on which party could better assist free-enterprise economies around the world. Democrats were seen as better at promoting democracy globally and at ending poverty and hunger.

Public perceptions of each party's abilities in handling these newer issues, however, are likely to be much more mutable in coming years than were views of Republican and Democratic versions of anticommunism. Since neither party has established a firm record on issues such as dealing with unfair trading partners or stopping the drug plague, voters are likely to respond on the basis of their overall party preference. By themselves, the ATS polls do not indicate that Democrats have an advantage in these issues, rather they have no disadvantage: The parties start with a clean slate.

A CHANCE FOR THE DEMOCRATS

There are some reasons, however, for believing that the Democrats are better positioned to take advantage of the post-communist political climate. Since the ATS polls . . . were taken, world events have caused the importance of the anticommunism issue, which favors Republicans, to diminish even further, thus highlighting the nontraditional issues on which the parties are more evenly matched. The sound domestic economy has shifted concern from unemployment and inflation to America's decreasingly competitive position in the world economy, especially in comparison with Japan, emerging East Asian countries, and the European Community. Meanwhile, popular uprisings in the Warsaw Pact . . . toppled one communist government after another. American political debate has [moved] directly to the issue of encouraging the development of strong democracies in their place.

All but one of the few countries that continue to espouse and practice communism are small or isolated—like Albania, Cuba, Ethiopia, North Korea, and Vietnam—and the only remaining major communist power—China—is an economic partner of the United States. Even Nicaragua, the country that for eight years had been the obsessive focus of Reagan's hemispheric anticommunism, suddenly has emerged as a democracy, with an elected, anti-Sandinista government.

Nicaraguan President Violeta Chamorro's victory . . . touched off a small squabble in the United States over who really won—Reagan and the *contras*, or former Costa Rican President Oscar Arias Sanchez and his peace plan (assisted by Congress). This debate inevitably will end up moot, but more important, there is no indication that American voters have any interest in determining who deserves the credit for the . . . turn of events in Nicaragua, or that their political preferences will be shaped by history's verdict. This applies not only to Nicaragua but to all the mind-numbing arguments about who won the Cold War.

That said, however, the so-far peaceful transition in Nicaragua probably could not have occurred without Bush's decision, early in his presidency, to break off the all-out battle with Congress over *contra* aid. Instead, he concentrated on the goals in Latin America that he and congressional Democrats could agree on, ignoring complaints from the far right. These goals are those that just [a few] years ago were emerging as the nontraditional dimensions of foreign policy: peacefully establishing democracies and regimes respectful of human rights in El Salvador and Nicaragua. Senate Republican leader Bob Dole of Kansas endorsed a similar adjustment in priorities in January 1990 when he proposed shifting U.S. foreign aid from major military powers in positions of geostrategic importance, such as Egypt, Israel, and Pakistan, to emerging democracies in Eastern Europe. Dole, who once used the pejorative term "Democrat wars" to describe American military actions in this century, now favors what have historically been "Democrat policies" of using foreign aid more as an economic instrument for democracy and less as a military weapon against communism. And yet, given the pace of change in the world, Dole's reappraisal is not surprising.

Even as new concerns about trade, democracy, human rights, and the environment continue to rise in importance as foreign-policy issues, they cannot yet fill the vacuum being created as anticommunism disappears from American politics. This is because anticommunism was never simply an *issue*—it was (and is) a basic American *value*. Polls taken for the Times Mirror Company by the Gallup Organization in 1987 found that 70 per cent of Americans identified themselves as strongly anticommunist and a majority affirmed that the best way to ensure peace was through military strength. The answers to such questions would not be very different today; all that has changed is their real world implications. Just as earlier generations considered themselves "abolitionists" long after the demise of slavery, Americans will continue to think of themselves as anticommunist, at least until they coalesce around a new international purpose that is clear, complete, moral, and necessary.

The issues emerging in the wake of anticommunism are a mixed bag of incomplete and sometimes incompatible ideas: protectionism, competitiveness, economic cooperation, democracy, human rights, the drug war, environmental protection, and shifting military and foreign aid expenditures to domestic programs. Alone, each one is too narrow a foundation for building either a complete foreign policy or a political message compelling enough to replace anticommunism. Combining and reinterpreting these elements, however, will eventually produce at least one political message with the earlier appeal of anticommunism. It is unlikely that such a message will arise through an evolutionary process of deliberation and debate, or even through the political parties per se. Absent a dramatic crisis, it is the nature of American politics to await a politician with the clarity of vision of a Truman, Kennedy, or Reagan.

Because the two parties start out with a clean slate on these issues, this new foreign-policy message would seem as likely to come from a Republican as from a Democrat. There are five reasons, however, to expect that it will be a Democrat who frames the new message:

- The next two likely Republican presidential candidates, George Bush and Dan Quayle, both have invested their careers in anticommunist politics. Given anticommunism's continuing importance in some conservative circles, . . . they show no signs of giving that up.

- Many of the new causes, especially trade protectionism or assertive economic nationalism, will not fit comfortably into the GOP philosophy of free markets and free trade.

- Democrats know that their party needs a new foreign-policy message. Republicans so far are still winning elections with their old message.

- Of the few politicians who so far have shown an awareness that a new global mission for America is desirable—Senators Bill Bradley (D-New Jersey) and Al Gore (D-Tennessee), and Representative Richard Gephardt (D-Missouri) among them—most have been Democrats.

- Anticommunism, to the delight and advantage of the GOP, has been a wedge dividing Democratic hawks and doves in the presidential nomination process and during congressional sessions. The diminishing relevance of anticommunism provides an opportunity for new unity in the Democratic party. Richard Perle, one of the most combative hawkish Democrats, who served as an official in the Reagan Pentagon, said recently that "there is a real chance for significant healing within the party." Still, this chance will not necessarily become reality. Each party still has an opening to craft a resonant and lasting message that will incorporate these new issues.

Republicans might find an edge in the electorate's lingering distrust of

Democrats at the national level.   Large numbers of voters, including many Democrats, have grown skeptical of the Democratic party's ability to manage the domestic economy, as well as foreign affairs.   The absence for more than 20 years of a Democratic president who passed muster on these counts does not help either.   A new Democratic party theme will have to overcome greater initial skepticism than a comparable message articulated by the Republican party.

The Republicans may also be able to take advantage of the fact that the revolutionary and positive changes sweeping the communist world have taken place during Republican presidencies.   However, political parties often fail to receive long-term credit for events during their time in power, as Winston Churchill discovered after World War II.   A desire for change can overwhelm a sense of gratitude; "What have you done for me lately?" is a common refrain among voters.   But a sense of goodwill toward the GOP for changes that took place on its watch might buy the party some time to develop a fitting theme for the future. . . .

ECONOMIC NATIONALISM

To many Democrats, it has seemed clear for some time that the only viable foreign-policy message is economic nationalism, broadly defined.   Policies that fall under this rubric range from protectionism (import barriers to cut the trade deficit and protect specific industries, and limits on foreign ownership of U.S. assets) to competitiveness (using education, workplace democracy, innovative management, industrial policy, and other "soft" tools that, while requiring heavy government investment, could strengthen American business without compromising free trade).

In practice, protectionist policies are usually more modest than the rhetoric behind them, since most attempts to limit imports or capital flows are diluted somewhere along the way by someone who once took a course in economics. In addition, most of the competitiveness proposals seem benign.   Indeed, education and research and development should be seen as desirable goods in themselves; Americans probably do not and certainly should not need the specter of a foreign enemy to spend money on them.   Economic nationalism can give Americans a healthy dose of competitive zeal and a commitment to domestic reforms, as well as offering a model for the world of fair trade on an even playing field.   Yet is is difficult to hold back the darker, emotional side of economic nationalism, namely xenophobia.

Japan-centered economic nationalism has an intuitive appeal for some Democrats because it can *look* a lot like anticommunism—yet seems a mirror image of anticommunism in that it helps Democrats instead of Republicans. In this emerging mythology, Japan, like the Soviet Union, becomes a foe whose distinct corporate culture and economic system are seen as mocking the rules of international conduct and stifling individual liberty.   The public clearly responds to this image: In a 1989 Gallup poll conducted for Times Mirror, 58 per cent of Americans said that Japan was the top economic power in the world, compared to 29 per cent who assigned the lead to the United States, which has a gross national product almost twice as large.

Despite its gut-level appeal in the body politic, economic nationalism probably lacks sufficient staying power as a political message. It has some serious problems that probably will prevent it from replacing anticommunism as an American value and as a consensual goal of policy. First, it depends on significant exaggeration to stir voter anger. For example, the Times Mirror poll found that most Americans considered foreign investment in the United States a threat, making it a seemingly potent political issue. But the poll also found that most Americans have an inflated view of the extent of foreign ownership. Most Americans surveyed thought foreigners controlled more than 15 per cent of privately owned U.S. real estate, when in fact they own less than 5 per cent. It is doubtful that Americans will have the same high degree of concern once they understand the true level of foreign investment in the U.S. economy.

Second, large numbers of Americans benefit from foreign trade and investment, whether as consumers buying Japanese VCRs or cars, or as employees working for companies that sell inexpensive foreign textiles or distribute foreign car parts. On the investment side, some Americans have benefited from the sale of property at inflated prices, others through a new job with a Japanese or other foreign company. . . .

Third, scaring people about the dangers of a trade deficit is the kind of "doom and gloom" message for which Republicans take such glee in mocking Democrats. Democrats consistently fail to persuade voters that the prosperity they have enjoyed since 1983 is illusory. . . .

Finally, economic nationalism is doomed as a full substitute for anticommunism because it resembles anticommunism on only one side—it identifies a distant, different-looking, different-sounding foreign adversary. Anticommunism endured as a value precisely because there was more to it than just a diabolical enemy. Anticommunism also envisioned a strong and positive purpose for America, a leadership role not just in containing Soviet communism but in expanding and perfecting democratic capitalism. Economic nationalists conceive of their mission as creating a United States that would be number one in a Hobbesian, zero-sum world of finite economic resources. That is not the same as being a leader in a world of expanding economic opportunities and political freedoms. The guiding principle of economic nationalism is that the United States should be "king of the hill." A comparable metaphor for anticommunism, as expressed by Reagan, was America as the "shining city upon a hill." The difference in the attitudes underlying the "shining city" and the "king of the hill" embodies the differences between anticommunism and economic nationalism as emotive political themes.

Economic nationalism can be seen as a variation of a trend toward isolationism that has emerged in some circles as anticommunism has faded.

The isolationist reaction can be found in almost identical forms on the left and the right.   On the left, echoing George McGovern's 1972 campaign plea "Come home, America," it takes the form of impatient social-spending claims on the "peace dividend," and a demand that the vast bulk of the money saved from reducing U.S. defense commitments abroad and from pushing Japan and Western Europe to assume a larger share of the burden of their defense, be promptly reinvested in domestic programs.   John Jacob, president of the National Urban League, reflected this brand of isolationism in his call for a rapid transfer of $50 billion from the military to a "domestic Marshall Plan."   Representative Barney Frank (D-Massachusetts) laid out the strategy most explicitly in a recent forum on the Democratic party: "We can now say, 'Harry Truman, we succeeded.   Containment has worked, the Marshall Plan has worked, and the occupation of Japan has worked.' It's time to come back home.   We can reorient those resources toward education, improve our international competitive strategy, and be nicer to ourselves."   Of course, the idea of a peace dividend is not outlandish and neither is the figure of $50 billion, at least by the mid-1990s.   It is the singular focus on shifting priorities so sharply inward that earns the label of isolationism.

Republican isolationists, too, figure a hefty peace dividend into their political calculus, but they would use it to fund a new round of tax cuts, which along with anticommunism underwrote much of the GOP's success in the 1980s.   "Put the money back in the hands of the people who won the Cold War: the American taxpayer," Senator Phil Gramm (R-Texas) has argued. . . .

That . . . an isolationist strain should emerge in the aftermath of the Cold War is not surprising.   Every twentieth century war has brought in its wake a powerful isolationist faction, usually in Congress, that clashed sharply with the postwar internationalism of the executive branch.   (Two such clashes resulted in the rejection of the League of Nations in 1920 and the unsuccessful resistance to the Marshall Plan in 1947.)   What is surprising, given the public's instinctive approval, is that the post–Cold War isolationist faction is so poorly represented in government.   This is probably because the Cold War cost few American lives, and because U.S. lawmakers are better traveled and better educated than ever.

The new internationalists who hold sway in Washington are neither naive nor overly idealistic; they do not dream of ending conflict among nations. Instead, they are looking for a way to build cooperative international structures to address three interrelated global problems: economic development, nurturing of democracies, and environmental protection.   The economic angle is exemplified by Bradley's diligent efforts to ease the crippling debt burden of Latin American economies.   Dole's foreign aid proposal is likewise economic, but its primary aim is to encourage new democracies.   Gore has taken the lead in pursuing international agreements to reduce global warming.   As environmentalist factions gain governmental influence throughout Europe, and as it becomes clear that the USSR cannot repair the catastrophic pollution of its rivers, lakes, and forests without Western help, Gore's multilateral approach will become more necessary and more useful.

This brand of politics has the advantage of envisioning a strong and positive leadership role for America in the world. The two things the United States builds best—democracy and prosperity—it can help other nations build. And on environmental issues, which must be addressed globally, Americans can take the lead in bringing countries together for mutual benefit. Although it lacks a foreign enemy to demonize, this kind of internationalism may be the most promising of the foreign-policy messages vying to fill the vacuum left by anticommunism's diminishing relevance. It is also the most embryonic, largely because the opportunities to address environmental problems globally and to assist in the building of democracies in Eastern Europe have been thrust upon the United States so recently.

However, it is already possible to discern some potential pitfalls for these themes. As was the case with some of the global negotiations during the 1970s, multilateral environmental negotiations could take the form of international conferences at which smaller countries engage in endless America-bashing—and perhaps Japan-bashing and Soviet-bashing. If this were to happen, a backlash by the American public against Third World ingratitude and American weakness would almost certainly ensue—a backlash that would probably hurt the Democratic party. . . .

Whether internationalist themes will hold sufficient appeal as a political message for the American public remains to be seen, even though they will surely dominate foreign policy as practiced. So far, the media seem to have concluded that these internationalist themes are too complex and dull to inspire voters. . . . Such skepticism may stem from the same widespread but shortsighted assumption that a strong foreign-policy message requires a clear-cut enemy.

POLITICAL NOVELTY AND DEMOCRACY

Beyond simple isolationism and internationalism, the decline of communism and the emergence of new democracies could enliven American politics a third way. A message could evolve that would exploit the sheer power of newness or novelty in politics. . . .

Political novelty . . . has its appeal in the United States. For several years basically satisfied voters have been showing signs of restlessness amid what soon will be twelve consecutive years of moderate-to-conservative Republican leadership. This vague yearning for change underlay Dukakis' 17-percentage-point lead over Bush in July 1988, when Dukakis was still little known. It showed up again in a January 1990 *Wall Street Journal*-NBC News survey in which 54 per cent of those polled said they want Bush and Congress to "shake things up." The sight of East Europeans opening new frontiers of political freedom, while Americans wring their hands over whether they can risk adding to the federal deficit, will probably accelerate this desire to join in the global celebration of political change.   It is as if Americans as a nation had volunteered diligently for 40 years on a political campaign, then had to watch the victory party on television at home. . . .   A novel message keyed to the emergence of democracy throughout the world could be substantive and lasting but still attractive to voters looking for excitement, inspiration, and change.

This message would start from the premise that as the world becomes more democratic, so should the United States.   As democracy expands globally, American democracy should expand and evolve so that it remains the model for the world.   In the workplace, more democracy would mean giving employees a personal stake in the goods and services they provide and incentives to make them more competitive.   School systems could become more democratic by giving parents and teachers control of school buildings (as Chicago and Miami have done) and by giving parents more choice in selecting schools for their children.   Housing projects, unions, interest groups, and corporations all might function better if they operated more democratically and responsively.   Some of these proposals were foreshadowed in the position papers of such unsuccessful presidential contenders of 1988 as Democrat Bruce Babbit and Republicans Pete du Pont and Jack Kemp.   They come variously from the wish lists of liberals and conservatives, but they remain under the common umbrella of extending American democracy.   Pollster Daniel Yankelovich and former Under Secretary of Commerce Sidney Harman brought together many of these ideas in their 1988 book *Starting with the People*, suggesting that citizens become "stakeholders" in the structures of public life.

Central to such an approach would be the promotion of these values abroad, in keeping with a long tradition that includes Kennedy's Peace Corps. The Peace Corps helped make Kennedy's anticommunism palatable to skeptical Adlai Stevenson liberals in his party.   Reagan similarly used the creation of the National Endowment for Democracy to lure trade unionists and other conservative Democrats onto the bandwagon of his hardline, Goldwater-style anticommunism.   In both cases, encouragement of democracy abroad worked alongside anticommunism, helping to build a bipartisan consensus that might otherwise have been lacking.

Yet the question remains: Is democracy promotion by itself robust and expansive enough to succeed anticommunism as the cornerstone of U.S. foreign policy?   It seems at this point that, with much work left to be done, democracy promotion could become the keystone of Americans' sense of purpose in the world. . . .

In the 1980s the United States expanded the role of the capitalist marketplace in domestic economic life and then, operating mostly by example, extended pro-market values and policies to scores of countries in Latin America, Asia, and Africa.   As the 1980s was the decade of democracy, the 1990s could become the decade of democracy.   As with free markets, the best way to encourage the establishment of American-style institutions abroad will be to perfect them and demonstrate their potential at home.

The domestic political message of extending democracy's reach could be linked to economic nationalism in a way that would give it a more positive gloss. This path was sketched by writer James Fallows in his 1989 book *More Like Us*. Fallows argues that the United States will compete most effectively with Japan not by imitating that country's centrally planned industries, protectionism, and conformity, but by drawing on and facilitating aspects of the American character—risk-taking, mobility, flexibility, and democracy—that are chiefly responsible for the success of the U.S. economy and national experiment.

In conjunction with international cooperation, a call to extend American-style democracy worldwide would resemble the affirmative, purposeful side of anticommunism in much the way that economic nationalism resembles its negative, antipathetic side. Like anticommunism, extending democracy embodies long-held American values, especially the ideas of perfectibility and continuous progress. Like anticommunism, it reaches deep into America's domestic political life to define the nation's purpose in the world. Finally, by involving more Americans in participatory institutions, democracy promotion would forge a sense of community that would make both the internal and international purpose of the United States not just a "government policy" but a source of national identity. All Americans, not just policymakers, could feel as though they had a stake in such a pursuit.

Neither party's basic ideology is antithetical to such an approach; it belongs as much to the tradition of Kennedy's Peace Corps as to Reagan's National Endowment for Democracy. Democrats probably have a head start—if they use it—in putting forward such a post–Cold War approach. . . . But Democrats also suffer from a poor public image and an almost compulsive tendency to offer up presidential nominees who are weaker than Democrats at other levels of government. Given their history, it would be imprudent to predict that Democrats can assume a leading role in international affairs, even if the Bush administration leaves a political vacuum.

Republicans now may have less drive to shape a new political message, but they still hold an edge with voters through the GOP's reputation for competence in managing risky situations. . . . Republicans will also be able to point out that the decisive and favorable changes in Eastern Europe and Latin America have taken place on their watch. It will be difficult for a Democrat to contend that a more activist administration could have accelerated those changes.

Given the weaknesses and flaws of both parties, it is conceivable that no coherent or workable political message will emerge; instead, the domestic politics of American foreign policy may be driven not by a powerful underlying theme but by situational and emotional tactics in Congress and in presidential campaigns. Foreign policy and political themes are not necessarily closely connected, but lack of coherence in political dialogue probably would presage a lack of coherence in U.S. foreign policy.

However, that outcome is unlikely to occur. Voters and politicians alike want and need a set of organizing principles to harmonize American values with the realities of America's power and limitations in the world. In looking ahead to the wide open landscape of American politics after anticommunism, Americans will probably agree with Bradley that they are a people in need of a "big ambition." This ambition is a blank space that Americans should not fill in rashly. But this space eventually will be filled. Whoever does so will succeed in shaping the post–Cold War world and reorienting American political life toward a new global purpose.

10 PUBLIC OPINION: THE PULSE OF THE '90s

John E. Rielly

The mood of the American public and its leaders has shifted. The Cold War and the U.S.-Soviet competition are passing from center stage, and a new age of global economic competition has emerged. Americans enter this new era with increased confidence about their military preeminence, but with a growing sense of economic vulnerability.

These are the most important general conclusions of the latest quadrennial survey of the American public and of elite opinion makers sponsored by the Chicago Council on Foreign Relations, conducted in mid-autumn 1990.

Four years ago [in 1986] the Council's survey confirmed that Americans were giving foreign affairs an increasingly high priority compared to domestic issues. Americans were affirming their desire for a stronger U.S. role in the world, and they remained preoccupied with a military confrontation with the Soviet Union.

Although Americans still remain committed to an active U.S. role in the world, concern about the Soviet Union as the principal threat has receded, especially among leaders. The leaders perceive the United States as vastly superior in military power to the Soviet Union, although the public sees the balance as more equal. They support a wide array of cooperative measures with the Soviet Union. Most astonishing, rather than as the principal adversary, Americans now view the Soviet Union as one of the three leading countries where America has a vital interest. The public ranks the Soviet Union fourth in favorability on its "feeling thermometer" in terms of warmth or coolness toward various countries, and Soviet President Mikhail Gorbachev enjoys a popular regard that places him as one of the three most highly esteemed world leaders, ahead of even President George Bush. Issues linked to the U.S.-Soviet competition, such as increased defense spending, have sharply declined in priority. However, it is unclear how deeply rooted this change in attitudes toward the Soviet Union will prove to be. By late

January 1991, indications were emerging that news of the Soviet military intervention in the Baltic republics may have been cooling American attitudes toward the Gorbachev government.

As they did four years ago, the public and leaders want the United States to continue playing an active role in world affairs, but there is a growing sense of economic vulnerability. Both are divided on whether the United States plays a more important role today than it did 10 years ago. In this respect, the confidence in U.S. global leadership shown in the 1986 survey has eroded. Both the public and leaders now believe that because of its inability to solve economic problems, the United States has declined as a world power. Although presently militarily preeminent, the United States is viewed as losing the economic competition with Europe and Japan.

Europe and Japan continue to receive a high level of attention, though the attitude toward Japan is now increasingly critical. While the majority of the American public continues to support the use of troops in a crisis situation in Europe, less than half of the public favors the use of troops to defend against an attack on Japan. By substantial margins, both the public and leaders believe the economic power of Japan will be a more critical threat to American vital interests in the next few years than will Soviet military power.

Support for key military alliances such as NATO [the North Atlantic Treaty Organization] has diminished substantially, as has support for increased defense spending. Americans favor substantial troop cuts in Europe. And although European unification continues to be viewed positively, concern about economic competition from that source is rising.

After a decade of relative obscurity, and well before the outbreak of war with Iraq, the Middle East had emerged in the public mind as the biggest foreign-policy problem facing the United States. Iraq is viewed as one of the principal threats to America's vital interests. Willingness to use U.S. troops to defend Saudi Arabia, however, is markedly higher than willingness to use force to drive Iraqi forces out of Kuwait. Both public and leadership attitudes toward Israel are more critical than they were four years ago. Yet willingness to use American troops in Israel's defense is greater.

A substantial shift in foreign-policy goals is also evident. Among the public, support for defending weaker nations against aggression and for defense of human rights is up—a shift undoubtedly influenced by Iraq's August 1990 seizure of Kuwait. Support for protecting the jobs of American workers has declined from 1986, but, together with protection of the interests of American businesses abroad, is one of the top two foreign-policy goals listed by the public [see Table 10-1]. Among opinion leaders, concern about Soviet military power and containing communism dropped sharply, while support for the United Nations increased.

Once again large gaps divide the public from leaders on a number of issues. Leaders are more convinced that the Cold War is over, more critical of Israel, and more concerned about Japan's growing power. Leaders favor sharper cuts in American troop strength in Europe and in the defense budget. While

Table 10-1. Foreign-Policy Goals Considered "Very Important"

	Public	Leaders
Protecting the jobs of American workers	65%	39%
Protecting the interests of business abroad	63	27
Securing adequate supplies of energy	61	60
Defending our allies' security	61	56
Preventing the spread of nuclear weapons	59	94
Promoting and defending human rights in other countries	58	45
Improving the global environment	58	72
Protecting weaker nations against foreign aggression	57	28
Reducing our trade deficit with foreign countries	56	62
Matching Soviet military power	56	20
Containing communism	56	10
Worldwide arms control	53	80
Strengthening the United Nations	44	39
Helping to improve the standard of living of less developed nations	41	42
Helping to bring a democratic form of government to other nations	28	26

the Bush administration's overall public rating on foreign policy is lower than the public rating of Reagan's foreign policy four years ago, leaders react more favorably to Bush's foreign policy than they did to Reagan's.

The nationwide survey that generated these findings was conducted by the Gallup Organization between October 23 and November 15, 1990. During this period 1,662 men and women were interviewed in person. In addition, 377 leaders were interviewed either in person or by telephone between October 19 and November 16. The leadership sample included officials from the Bush administration, Congress, international business, labor, the media, academic and religious institutions, private foreign-policy organizations, and special interest groups. In addition, these data were supplemented by selected Gallup opinion polls in January 1991, both before and after the outbreak of war with Iraq, and after the Soviet government's military intervention in Lithuania.

This is the fifth Chicago Council study of American foreign-policy attitudes, and the first not dominated by Cold War issues. The initial study was conducted in December 1974, soon after the resignation of President Richard Nixon. The one previous to this new survey occurred in the fall of 1986, a time of economic prosperity, six years into the Reagan administration and slightly more than one year after Gorbachev's accession to power in Moscow.

In the 1986 Chicago Council study, the American public and leaders were still preoccupied with the competition with the USSR. The mood has changed radically. When the public is asked to identify the two or three biggest U.S. foreign-policy problems, the U.S.-Soviet relationship does not appear in the top 10, though four years ago it was ranked first. Among leaders it still comes in third, but with a big 25 percentage-point drop from four years ago. For leaders, the Cold War is clearly over, and leaders' responses on a variety of questions reflect this belief.

Both the public and the leaders feel that domestic problems are the greatest that face the country today. The public is more concerned in the aggregate with social problems than are the leaders; the leaders are slightly more concerned in the aggregate about the economy and unsatisfactory government performance than is the public. Among the individual items that draw concern, drug abuse and the budget deficit lead the public's list, while the budget deficit, the state of the economy, Iraq, and the Middle East generally top the leaders' list.

The decline of the Cold War has clearly led to decreasing concern about arms control and the threat of nuclear war. Among foreign-policy issues, the leaders' concern about Iraq and the Middle East takes precedence. Uncertainty about industrial competitiveness also ranks high. Concern about domestic economic issues remains high among both public and leaders; concern about such recession-related issues as inflation and unemployment, the biggest issues of the late 1970s and early 1980s, is lower. Not surprisingly, dependence on foreign oil is considered a significant foreign-policy problem.

Despite this preoccupation with domestic issues, almost two-thirds of the public (62%) continue to favor an active U.S. role in the world, a figure down only slightly from four years ago. Awareness of global interdependence has grown as substantially more Americans believe that foreign policy makes a major impact on the overall economy at home, including food and gasoline prices. The public's interest in news about U.S. relations with other countries has also risen substantially. For the first time, interest in international issues is comparable to that in local and national news. American global predominance may be diminishing, but America is not abandoning internationalism.

The last four years have also seen a significant shift in the way the public and leaders perceive America's role in the world. Four years ago the proportion who believed that America played a more powerful role in the world rose noticeably, while the proportion who perceived a less-influential U.S. role declined. Now the numbers are about even. Only 37% believe the United States plays a more important role compared to 41% in 1986, while 35% believe the United States is playing a lesser role compared to 26% four years ago. The shift among American leaders is sharper, with a decline of 7 percentage points among those who think America plays a more important role and an increase of 16 percentage points among those who hold the opposite view. Similarly, 66% of the public and 71% of the leaders believe that America's inability to solve its economic problems has caused the country's decline as a world power. Although the United States has emerged in the 1990s as the only military and economic superpower, there is decidedly less confidence about America's future. Whether the outcome of the war with Iraq will affect such confidence is still unknown.

This change follows the decline in the perceived priority of the U.S.-Soviet military confrontation, and the increase in importance of economic issues. The perceived magnitude of U.S. economic problems, coupled with the growing economic power of Europe and Japan, has lowered expectations about the U.S. global role. In the past, the U.S. role was linked closely to the public's impression of the military balance with the Soviet Union. This is no longer the case. Since 1982 a growing share of Americans have believed the United States is militarily stronger (21% to 32%) and, conversely, a declining share (29% to 15%) feel the Soviet Union is stronger. Among American leaders, 71% think the United States is militarily superior—a prodigious rise of 51 percentage points since 1982—while only 3% believe the Soviet Union is stronger. In addition, only 18% of the public and 8% of the leaders in 1990 considered the Soviet Union to be the principal adversary of the United States. Thirty-three per cent of the public and 20% of leaders regard Soviet military power as a "critical threat" to U.S. vital interests in the next 10 years. In comparison, 60% of the public and 63% of leaders believe the economic power of Japan will be a "critical threat." At the same time, 30% of the public and 41% of the leaders feel that economic competition from Europe will pose a "critical threat."

The reduced Soviet threat and increased confidence in American military superiority have led to a substantial rise in sentiment for cutting the defense budget and reducing American military commitments in Europe. In the fall of 1990 a thin majority of the public (53%) wanted to maintain the current level of defense spending, while 12% wanted to expand it and 32% favored reducing it. On the leadership side, 21% preferred to keep it the same, only 2% wanted to expand, and 77% wanted to cut back, a large shift of 40 percentage points over a four-year period.

A similar trend was evident in support of America's principal regional military alliance, NATO. As with defense spending, a majority (56%) of the American public wanted to preserve the present level of commitment, while 22% wanted to reduce it, an 11-point increase over the last four years. On the leadership side, 35% approved of maintaining the commitment at the present level, while 57% favored reducing it, a sharp increase of 44 percentage points over four years that again reflected the strong impact on leadership opinion of the winding down of the Cold War.

When the public and leaders were presented with a precise set of alternatives for troop strengths in Europe, the public favored a mean level of 181,300 troops, or roughly half the current deployment. Leaders favored sharper reductions for a mean level of 101,200 over the next few years. Thus the decline of the Cold War brought an understandable drop in support for security alliances and stationing troops in Europe, particularly among leaders who are more convinced of the decline of superpower competition. At the

Table 10-2. Attitudes on the Use of U.S. Troops Overseas

When asked about various hypothetical situations, the following percentages of
people responded that they would favor the use of U.S. troops . . .

	Public	Leaders
If Soviet troops invaded Western Europe	58%	87%
If Iraq invaded Saudi Arabia	52	89
If the government of Mexico were threatened by a revolution or civil war	48	19
If the Soviet Union tried to overthrow a democratic government in Eastern Europe	44	29
If North Korea invaded South Korea	44	57
If Arab forces invaded Israel	43	70
If Iraq refused to withdraw from Kuwait	42	55
If Japan were invaded by the Soviet Union	39	73
If the government of El Salvador were about to be defeated by leftist rebels	28	13
If the government of the Philippines were threatened by a revolution or civil war	22	7

same time the majority of the American public, and a smaller percentage of
leaders, still favor at least the current level. A majority of both groups favor
a substantial continued American troop commitment in Europe for the foreseeable future. Only a small percentage of the public (12%) or the leaders
(10%) favor a complete troop withdrawal.

Public support for using American troops in crisis situations continues to
be selective [see Table 10-2]. A contrast persists between willingness to support their use in Western Europe and reluctance elsewhere. There are two
hypothetical exceptions: a North Korean invasion of South Korea and an
Arab attack on Israel. In the case of Korea, for reasons that are not clear,
public support for such a defense rose from 24% to 44%. Although both
the public and leadership have adopted increasingly critical views about Israel
over the past four years, the percentage in both groups who support using
American troops if Israel were attacked by an Arab state rose by more than
10 percentage points. A strong majority of the American public continues
to oppose the engagement of American forces if the government of El Salvador
were on the brink of defeat by leftist rebels, or if the Philippines were threatened by revolution. Leaders' opposition to military intervention in those
two instances is even higher. Leaders also strongly opposed the use of troops
in Eastern Europe, or if the government of Mexico were threatened by revolution. Not surprisingly, in countries involved in the Persian Gulf crisis

(i.e. Saudi Arabia and Israel), support for troop use grew; in most other cases it declined.

On the question of Congress's role in determining foreign policy, a plurality of both the public and leaders believe that it is "about right." Although there are still more members of the public who feel Congress's role is too weak (25%), there has been a steady increase in the number of public respondents who believe the role of Congress in foreign policy is too strong, from 10% in 1974 to 22% in 1990. Among the leaders, however, there has been an increase in the number who feel Congress is too weak, from 25% in 1986 to 33% in 1990, compared with 27% who feel it is too strong. In the period since mid-November when these polling data were collected, Congress has once again become a forum for debate on the administration's Persian Gulf policy. Nevertheless, in the end, a majority of both houses supported the president's policy.

As support for American military commitments in Europe and Asia declines, some have urged that Japan and Germany enlarge their military role. Our survey found little support for this approach. Fifty-nine per cent of the public and 65% of the leaders oppose a larger military role for Japan and Germany, while only 29% of the public and 33% of the leaders favor a larger role.

When it comes to identifying areas of U.S. vital interest, there were some significant changes as well as important continuities. Saudi Arabia and the Soviet Union came out at the very top of the public's ranking, this time followed by Japan, Great Britain, Kuwait, Canada, and Germany. On the leadership side, Germany and Japan once again came first with a 95% rating, followed by Mexico, the Soviet Union, Canada, Saudi Arabia, and Great Britain. When public attitudes were gauged on a "feeling thermometer," Canada and Great Britain once again came out on top, followed by Germany, the Soviet Union, and Italy. Most noteworthy, again, is the dramatic shift in attitude toward the Soviet Union, which consistently ranked near the bottom on these scales throughout the 1970s and 1980s.

Aside from the Soviet Union, which rose 27 "degrees" on the thermometer, the biggest change in attitudes toward a single country was the 9 degree drop for Japan, back to levels recorded before 1986. Although Japan clearly remains seen as a country of great importance to the United States, a number of negative indicators are apparent. As noted, Japan's economic power is considered a critical threat to America's vital interests in the next decade by almost two-thirds of both the U.S. public and leaders. A sharp drop is evident in both public and leadership support for using American troops if Japan were invaded by the Soviet Union. About three-fourths of the public and leaders believe that Japan practices unfair trade with the United States. This negative shift in attitudes toward Japan is stronger among leaders than among the public. For the first time, opinion leaders listed Japan as one of America's most important foreign-policy problems. This is consistent with the higher priority given to global economic competition and to leaders' growing worry about economic competitiveness.

Public attitudes toward foreign economic aid are considerably more negative than they were four years ago, evenly divided between those in favor and those opposed. Leaders continue to be strongly supportive, with 90% again supporting foreign aid. Applied to specific countries, sharp differences between the public and leaders emerge. Three-fourths of leaders favor an increase of aid to Eastern Europe, while only one-fourth of the public does. Just less than half of the public and just more than half of the leaders believe aid to Israel should be either decreased or halted altogether.

Military aid commands even less support from the public, with roughly two-thirds opposing it and less than one-third supporting it. Among leaders, a big shift occurred, with less than half (39%) supporting it and 57% opposed to it. Even for countries like Egypt, which is directly affected by the Persian Gulf crisis, five times as many people favor decreasing military aid as favor increasing it. Similar negative attitudes apply to government sales of military equipment to other countries. Just under two-thirds of the public oppose them and less than one-third favor them, with leaders equally divided.

Support for military and economic aid to Israel and Egypt, the two largest recipients of American assistance, decreased despite the Gulf crisis. Both the public and leaders generally favor cutting economic aid, military aid, and military sales to these two countries more than they favor increasing them. Israel also generated less sympathy among the public and leaders in its dispute with the Palestinians. In 1990 only 34% of the public and 33% of the leaders said they sympathized with Israel over the Palestinians. Four years ago, before the start of the *intifada*, as the Palestinian uprising in the Israeli-occupied West Bank and Gaza Strip is known, and in responding to a slightly different question, 61% of both public and leaders sympathized with Israel over Arab nations. While only 20% of the public favor reducing economic and military assistance to Israel if it does not negotiate a settlement with the Palestinians, 50% of the leaders favor reducing such assistance. Throughout the survey American leaders tended to take a more critical attitude toward Israel than did the public at large. Given the shift in both public and leadership opinion identified here, American pressure on Israel to seek a settlement of its conflict with the Palestinians may well increase—notwithstanding Israel's restrained initial response to Iraqi missile attacks and the close U.S.-Israeli cooperation that developed in the early days of the [Persian Gulf] war.

Despite America's perceived economic weakness, the public shows no significant change in its attitude toward protectionism despite the expectations of numerous commentators. More than half (54%) of the public believe that tariffs are necessary, while 25% favor their elimination. Among leaders two-thirds favor eliminating tariffs and one-third believe tariffs are necessary. Yet a long-term trend toward increased protectionist sentiment among leaders continued. From 1978 to 1990, the proportion of leaders favoring tariffs increased by 10 percentage points. When asked about trade policy with neighboring Mexico, however, an impressive 71% of the public and 86% of the leaders favored a free-trade area with Mexico similar to that in place with Canada.

On the issue of oil dependency, a decisive percentage of leaders and public favor developing alternative energy sources and requiring cars to get better gas mileage. Less than one-third of the public favor building more nuclear power plants, while more than half of leaders do. An overwhelming 85% of the public oppose the addition of a 25-cent-per-gallon gasoline tax in order to reduce oil imports, while two-thirds of the leaders favor such a tax. Once again, as in 1974, at the time of the first oil crisis, the public strongly opposes increased gas taxes designed to reduce dependence on foreign oil.

Overall, the public's assessment of the Bush administration's foreign policy after nearly two years in office (though before the outbreak of war with Iraq) is more critical than the comparable evaluation of Reagan four years earlier. The percentage of those who rated American foreign policy as excellent or good fell from 53% to 45% in that period. The percentage rating it as fair or poor rose from 43% to 50%. Meanwhile, 61% of leaders rate Bush's foreign policy as good or excellent and only 39% rate it fair or poor—a substantially more positive rating than under Reagan four years ago. The leaders' evaluation reveals more positive evaluations of the Bush administration's handling of arms control issues, the Middle East, and relations with the Soviet Union, and more critical evaluations of trade policy and counter-terrorism.

On Bush's response to Iraq's invasion of Kuwait, 58% of the public and 70% of the leaders surveyed in November 1990 rated it either excellent or good. Thirty-eight per cent of the public and 29% of leaders rated the response fair or poor. By early January 1991, however, support for the Bush policy had weakened somewhat. Ten days before the war started on January 16, 1991, 52% of the public supported U.S. military intervention to oust Iraq from Kuwait and 39% were opposed. Thus the close votes in the U.S. Congress supporting Bush's policy were a reflection of sentiments in the country at large.

In conclusion, the American public and its leaders do not seem to be backing away from their commitment to U.S. leadership internationally. With the breakdown of Soviet economic, political, ideological, and military strength, America's preeminent relative power position may even have been strengthened. Yet despite a renewed confidence in the ability of the American military to check aggression, as seen in early war successes against Iraq, a growing awareness of economic and social challenges at home will probably lead most Americans and their leaders to be selective in supporting U.S. overseas intervention in the 1990s. Even a U.S.-led victory in the war with Iraq is not likely to reverse the inclination toward cautious internationalism among the public and opinion leaders.

Part II: RELATIONSHIPS

During the height of the Cold War, American policymakers had little difficulty distinguishing friends from foes. The world was thought to consist of three groups: allies who shared American fears of communism and the Soviet Union; the Soviet Union, sometimes China, and others who aligned themselves with America's enemies in the so-called international communist movement; and neutral and nonaligned states that sought to stay out of the contest between the superpowers but who often became the objects of their competition for clients.

These distinctions, blurred for some time, have now largely vanished. To be sure, the United States still enjoys the support of some more than others, and it remains both wary of its former communist adversaries and concerned about developments in the Third World that affect its interests. But today the relationships between the United States and others hinge on a more varied agenda than they did during the Cold War. The issue is how best to define U.S. national interests vis-à-vis others in an environment where the communist menace and Soviet expansionism no longer order priorities.

The issue is nowhere more striking than with respect to U.S. relations with the Soviet Union itself. Is it in the interest of the United States to drive an already weakened Soviet Union into further decline and perhaps disintegration in hopes it will be relegated to the status of a minor player on the world stage? Or are U.S. interests better served by programs designed to promote democracy and revitalize the economic health of the Soviet Union, much as the United States did with its German and Japanese adversaries after World War II?

Policymakers face analogous cost-benefit calculations as they assess the future of U.S. relations with Germany and other states in both Eastern and Western Europe; with Japan, China, South Korea, Taiwan, and others in the Far East; and with a host of Third World states in South and Southeast Asia, the Middle East, Africa, and the Western Hemisphere. As we might expect— and as the essays that follow demonstrate—opinions differ widely regarding the wisdom or folly of alternative policies and courses of actions.

THE UNITED STATES AND THE SOVIET UNION

Especially perplexing to American policymakers now that the Cold War has concluded victoriously is the kind of relationship the United States should forge with the Soviet Union. They worry that the Soviet economy is in ruins and that the centripetal forces in its constituent republics and among its dissident nationalities may rend America's historic adversary asunder at the same time that the U.S.S.R. remains powerful militarily and the only state capable of mounting a credible military threat against the United States. They also worry that Mikhail Gorbachev's initiatives toward political and economic liberalism may fail and culminate in a reversion of the Soviet Union to dictatorship, domestic repression, and, perhaps, external aggressiveness.

The Bush administration for a time talked hopefully of a full political and economic integration of the Soviet Union into the community of nations in the expectation that it would then play a constructive world role in concert with the United States. Soviet-American collaboration in the United Nations Security Council in organizing a response to Iraq's aggression against Kuwait was consistent with that view. On the other hand, Moscow's seeming intransigence in the face of the aspirations for greater freedom expressed by Lithuania and others in the Baltic area and elsewhere in the Soviet Union compromised the Bush administration's promise that the United States would be the vanguard of democracy in the post–Cold War world. The dilemma the administration faced was a paradoxical variant on that which its predecessors confronted when they found themselves sometimes supporting dictators whose only claim to U.S. allegiance was their anticommunist credentials.

In "Coping with Victory," John Lewis Gaddis explores the choices and dilemmas presented by America's Cold War victory, which has meant that "for the first time in more than a century there is no clear challenger to the tradition of liberal democratic capitalism according to which [the United States] and much of the rest of the West organizes itself." Gaddis warns that "if history is any guide, what [U.S. leaders] will probably do is fritter away the fruits of victory by failing to think through what [they] want victory to accomplish." The legacy of the Cold War is part of the danger, he observes, because it colors and distorts clear thinking about how the United States might productively develop the kind of relationship with the Soviets so obviously in its fundamental interests. "Old answers," he opines, "will not suffice."

Placing the choices policymakers now face in a broader historical context, Gaddis reaches some surprising conclusions. He explains why it is in the interest of the United States to "seek the survival and rehabilitation of the Soviet Union" as a great power, for example. He also determines that "it would be to the advantage of the United States and the Soviet Union . . . to retain their nuclear superiority over the rest of the world, albeit at much reduced levels," and advises that the North Atlantic Treaty Organization (NATO) and the Warsaw Pact be preserved as "stabilizers" designed to bring "order and predictability to Europe" even as their deterrent functions lapse. And he concludes that the Cold War victory—"the triumph of liberty"— while cause for celebration, "will almost certainly be transitory" as "new forces will eventually arise that will swing the balance back to power once again."

Andrew C. Goldberg, in "Challenges to the Post–Cold War Balance of Power," addresses the future of the Soviet-American relationship from the systemic perspective. He examines how the retreat of Soviet military power will affect the global balance of power and its relevance to U.S. security. Perceiving no other "power or constellation of powers" likely to "challenge U.S. security and its primacy as a superpower," Goldberg nonetheless argues that "it is possible to construct . . . scenarios in which the geostrategic threat to the United States, with or without the Soviet Union, could become very pronounced." Berating U.S. "detachment" and "aimlessness in defining its own interests" prevalent in the early 1990s—a drift reinforced by the Persian Gulf conflict—Goldberg considers the "effect the prospective balance of cooperation and competition between the United States and an enfeebled Soviet Union may yet have on containing future threats to U.S. security." Because "the United States and all of its erstwhile cold war allies and adversaries are now in uncharted waters, stripped of the certainties that made the course of the Cold War predictable," Goldberg concludes that "how the United States handles the balance of power problem over the next several years may well determine the patterns of interstate competition for generations to come."

THE UNITED STATES AND EUROPE

American foreign policy has often been described as Eurocentric, for obvious geostrategic and historical reasons. The region was the scene of two world wars in the twentieth century as well as the "battleground" of the Cold War. In all three wars American participation was decisive in determining the outcome.

It was the crisis in Greece and Turkey that led to the enunciation of the Truman Doctrine in March 1947. Three months later Secretary of State George Marshall announced the creation of a multibillion-dollar plan designed to help rebuild war-torn Europe in an effort to strengthen it against communism and to provide a market for American exports. And in 1949 the United States became a party to NATO, its first military alliance with European powers since the American Revolution and its first permanent "entangling alliance" of the sort George Washington had warned against in his Farewell Address a century and a half earlier. The alliance served multiple purposes; it "kept the Russians out, the Americans in, and the Germans down."[1]

Together these three acts more than any other gave definition to an American grand strategy captured in the themes of globalism, anticommunism, and containment. Isolationism was rejected, and the lessons of the 1930s that political leaders learned, particularly those relating to the dangers of appeasing aggressors and to the linkage between economic prosperity and international peace, formed the bases of "liberal internationalism" as a definition of the nation's world role. Enthusiasm for NATO and overt military intervention in Korea, initiated by the Truman administration in June 1950, waned late in 1950, and both NATO and the Korean War came under attack during the "Great Debate" over American national security policy in 1950–1951, in which Senator Robert Taft, the outspoken conservative Republican critic of Truman's policies, was a leading protagonist. But NATO survived, the Korean War continued to be prosecuted, and eventually the conservative critics of a policy built on the premises of globalism, anticommunism, containment, military might, and interventionism fell by the wayside. The tenets of liberal internationalism thus became the core elements of the Cold War consensus operative within the United States from the late 1940s until the 1970s, when it was shattered by domestic discord over the Vietnam War.[2]

Liberal internationalism in the period following World War II "meant first and foremost U.S. leadership."[3] More broadly, liberal internationalism embodied "the intellectual and political tradition that believes in the necessity of leadership by liberal democracies in the construction of a peaceful world order through multilateral cooperation and effective international organizations."[4] The viewpoint came under sharp attack during the 1980s,[5] but it reemerged in the aftermath of the Cold War among those who saw a continuing need for U.S. leadership in world affairs, "although now with a much greater sharing of costs and decision making with new power centers in Europe, Asia, and the developing world."[6]

Strains of the international ethos punctuate concern over the future of U.S. relations with Europe, and in particular the debate over Europe's "new architecture." The problems are frequently cast as the possible resurgence of Soviet power and aggressiveness combined with German revanchism. The alternatives for dealing with the twin fears typically focus on two institutional structures: NATO, in which the United States would presumably remain dominant among its sixteen members; and the Conference on Security and Cooperation in Europe (CSCE), in which the Soviet Union would play a potentially key role among its thirty-four European states, Canada, and the United States. Variants exist,[7] but it is clear that a continuing U.S. role in

Europe would be greatest if NATO continues to play a dominant role in Europe's political and security future.

Critics of the liberal alternative focus on neither NATO nor the CSCE. Instead, they see the end of the Cold War as an opportunity for disengagement. "Withdrawal of the Red Army from Europe would remove . . . the military instrument of Marxist restoration," according to former presidential adviser Patrick J. Buchanan. "The compensating concession we should offer: total withdrawal of U.S. troops from Europe. If Moscow will get out, we will get out. Once the Red Army goes home, the reason for keeping a U.S. army in Europe vanishes. Forty years after the Marshall Plan, it is time Europe conscripted the soldiers for its own defense. . . . The day of the realpoliticians, with their Metternichian 'new architectures,' and balance-of-power strategems, . . . is over."[8]

Complicating the future of U.S. relations with Europe is the emergence of the European Community (EC) as an economic rival of the United States. Promoting European economic integration has long been a goal of American foreign policy, and officially it remains so, but the steps the EC has taken toward a single market have helped to create an economic giant whose combined gross national product rivals that of the United States and whose population exceeds that of the United States. The fear is that the EC will pursue protectionist trade strategies and related fiscal and monetary policies that will lead to a European-based economic bloc from which the United States is effectively excluded.

As the foregoing synopsis indicates, America's Eurocentric foreign policy promises to be buffeted and strained in the years ahead as the end of the Cold War removes much of the glue that has cemented the transatlantic alliance since World War II. Our next two essays address many of these issues and the policy responses they invite. The essays also suggest something of the differing perspectives that analysts bring to the question of the future of U.S.-European relations in the post–Cold War world.

Asserting boldly that "the Europe of the Cold War has dissipated into the background of history," Ronald Steel, in "Europe after the Superpowers," explores the consequences likely to result now that "the American role as Europe's protector and power broker is finished." Seeing those who equate the end of the Cold War with the end of tensions as mistaken, Steel urges that the United States jettison "Atlanticism—the organizing principle of U.S. postwar policy toward Europe"—as the dependence of Europe on America, the foundation of Atlanticism, has given way to new realities that require new thinking. Many trends speak to the importance of this challenge, including the revival of the "German Question," the emergence of the European Community as a serious economic and political competitor, and the "devolution" of responsibilities for security to the Europeans themselves. Predicting that "NATO is as doomed as the already . . . defunct Warsaw Pact" and that Eastern Europe is unlikely to be either pacific or democratic, Steel maintains that "it would be desirable to bring both the United States and the

Soviet Union into the equation" to preserve European peace. Asserting that U.S. interests are in "a Europe that is peaceful, prosperous, open to trade and investment, and a menace neither to itself nor to others," Steel concludes that the U.S. role must be an active one that will require the United States to "readjust [its] ways of thinking, discard obsolete relationships and ideological blinkers, embrace new opportunities, and act upon a wider and more imaginative concept of [its] interests."

A variant on this perspective is offered by David Calleo, a longtime and articulate advocate of the view that the United States should devolve greater responsibility for European security on Europeans themselves. Calleo draws attention to the probability that the Western victory in the Cold War was "so complete" that it "threatens to destabilize many habitual relationships, the transatlantic alliance among them." He explains in "American National Interest and the New Europe: The Millennium Has Not Yet Arrived" why the Cold War served to limit interstate conflict, and why the "Soviet retreat has greatly confused America's geopolitical strategy" at the very time that "the United States itself manifests too many characteristics of national decline for comfort."

Against this backdrop, Calleo examines the new threats and opportunities that both the Europeans and Americans now face. Predictably, the Soviet Union and united Germany figure among the concerns, but Calleo also addresses the role that the EC may play in the creation of a new Europe characterized by broader unity and equilibrium than in the past, and the sources of contention that already plague U.S.-EC trade relations. NATO and America's future in the Cold War alliance also figure prominently in his analysis. "America's fiscal problems will almost certainly lead to drastic cuts in U.S. forces in Europe," he argues. Two paths to understanding the fate of America's hegemonic role in NATO follow: scrap it, or reform it. Calleo prefers the latter but concludes that "both military and geopolitical factors favor a more European NATO." Finally, Calleo concludes that the U.S. response to a possible future in which the United States might be excluded from Europe must begin with attention to its own problems. The message that "today's greatest threat to the liberal Pax Americana is . . . from the financial disorder of the United States" permeates all of Calleo's analysis.

THE UNITED STATES AND THE PACIFIC RIM

As in Europe, security concerns have for some time figured prominently in U.S. relations with nations on the Pacific rim. The United States has been linked in mutual defense arrangements to Japan, South Korea, and Taiwan since the 1950s, for example, and it was in the Asian theater that twice since World War II the United States became embroiled in a major land war. Recently, however, the Pacific rim has figured as prominently in American thinking about its economic health as it has in its thinking about national security. The persistent U.S. trade imbalance with Japan and with four newly industrializing Asian nations popularly known as the East Asian "tigers"— South Korea, Taiwan, Hong Kong, and Singapore—is a primary source of concern. In 1989, for example, U.S. imports from Japan and the four tigers totaled $156 billion, and the trade imbalance between them and the United States accounted for over two-thirds of the overall U.S. trade deficit.

The imbalance with Japan has been an especially contentious issue in the United States, where it is believed that protectionist practices in Japan work against U.S. companies trying to sell their products there, thus denying them the same advantages that Japanese firms enjoy in the United States. Although Japan shifted in the late 1980s away from its earlier export-led growth strategy toward a domestic demand-based strategy,[9] penetrating the Japanese market has remained difficult. Furthermore, Japan spends only about 1 percent of its gross national product on national defense compared with the 6 percent or more that the United States spends,[10] but at the same time it enjoys the protection of the United States under a 1960 U.S.-Japanese mutual defense pact. The frequent charge, therefore, is that Japan does not bear its fair share of the burden of the defense of the Western alliance even while it enjoys the economic benefits of the security assured it by the U.S. military presence in the Far East and by its nuclear and conventional deterrent.

In the case of the other Pacific rim countries, the concern is how to compete with manufacturers whose wage rates are significantly lower than those of the United States and to whom, therefore, the United States effectively "exports" jobs. A preferred response has been an aggressive "protectionist" trade policy designed not only to promote the historic U.S. objective of "free trade" but also to ensure the more recent objective of "fair trade," one that seeks to ensure that U.S. businesspeople compete on a "level playing field." Thus, the United States has sought through specific reciprocity (sometimes called aggressive reciprocity) to open foreign markets through bilateral negotiations and has used the threat of protection against foreign imports to win voluntary export restraints and other concessions from its trade partners. "Strategic trade" policy, in which the United States aggressively seeks to promote advantages for U.S. firms, has also been urged by many.

The growing economic and political importance of Japan, the Newly Industrialized Countries (NICs), and China is part of a global transformation of power relationships underway for some time but now greatly stimulated by the end of the Cold War.[11] As the United States seeks to cope with these fundamental changes, it has confronted the timeless tradeoff between guns and butter. In "Pacific Agenda: Defense or Economics?" Selig S. Harrison and Clyde V. Prestowitz, Jr., begin with the premise that part of the economic difficulties the United States has experienced with its allies in Asia stem from its emphasis on military rather than economic security. They show how the wisdom of "the single-minded American focus on security concerns in the Asia-Pacific region" has become anachronistic now that Soviet military threats to the region have vanished. Today, they argue, "it is the danger of [American] economic insolvency, reflected in budget deficits, an eroding industrial base, and the growing American inability to compete with newly formidable economic rivals" that must capture Washington's attention and be the point of departure for a sensible policy response.   The authors review the incentives for and obstacles to the policy reorientations they recommend insofar as they relate to Japan, China, Taiwan, the two Koreas, and the Philippines.   Bemoaning the Bush administration's disregard of the "opportunity now emerging to restructure the obsolete postwar order in East Asia," Harrison and Prestowitz also make a convincing case for disentangling economic and security issues and putting economic priorities first.

The prudence or impracticality of this prescription will be tested most visibly in America's relationship with Japan—a Pacific rim superstate of critical importance to U.S. security and prosperity.   I. M. Destler and Michael Nacht note in their essay, "Beyond Mutual Recrimination: Building a Solid U.S.-Japan Relationship in the 1990s," that "the United States and Japan entered the 1990s with both the security and the economic sides of their relationship at some risk."   They diagnose the underlying causes of this deterioration and propose a number of policy departures that could mend or reverse it.   And they conclude after examining a number of possible alternative futures that the challenge is to make "competitive interdependence" a reality by rejecting the impulse to embrace economic nationalist measures.   "The main lesson of the last forty years" that should guide American policymakers' interests in building a constructive relationship with Japan is "that welfare gains come not from competition in armaments, but from progress in production and in global economic integration."

THE UNITED STATES AND THE THIRD WORLD

The emergence of the East Asian tigers and other Newly Industrialized Countries as primary exporters of manufactured products attests to the dramatic changes that have taken place among the developing nations of the Third World during recent years.   Once courted primarily as partisans in the superpowers' Cold War contest, the relationships that the United States and others in the industrial world now maintain with Third World nations and the interests they have there are so varied that it is increasingly difficult to think of the developing world as a cohesive unit with common characteristics.[12]   Some members of the so-called Third World remain of strategic concern; others are important primarily as economic partners (or competitors); and still others command attention primarily for humanitarian reasons.

John W. Sewell examines, in "The Metamorphosis of the Third World: U.S. Interests in the 1990s," how the changed and changing nature of the Third World as well as the changing nature of Soviet-American competition will affect U.S. relations with developing nations.   The agenda of North-South relations continues to be crowded, as issues of poverty, the environment, population, urbanization, common social problems, and technological developments as well as a host of short-term issues promise to link the United States and the Third World to a common future. Reflecting the ethos of liberal internationalism, Sewell argues that U.S. leadership will be required to meet the challenge of these emergent issues, but he recognizes that the changed international economic position of the United States will also impose constraints on what can be accomplished "without condemning future generations of Americans to paying off an unprecedented level of foreign debt." Thus, at the same time the United States finds that "developing countries are much more central to important U.S. interests" than previously, it also finds that its "relations with the developing countries . . . will be played out in a much different policy environment than in the past."

In contrast to Sewell, some see the end of the Cold War as an opportunity to disengage from the Third World, much as they urge disengagement from Europe. Buchanan, for example, describes foreign aid, long an important instrument of U.S. policy toward the Third World, as "an idea whose time has passed."[13] He also urges removal of U.S. troops from Korea and elsewhere. "It is time we began uprooting the global network of 'trip wires' planted on foreign soil to ensnare the United States in the wars of other nations, to back commitments made and treaties signed before this generation of American soldiers was born."[14]

Still others see U.S. national interests in the Third World as continuing but less varied than in Sewell's broad agenda. For them, the maintenance of peace remains paramount. Advocates of this school of thought concede that promotion of democratic government, economic development, and related goals are important, but they emphasize the preservation of regional stability above all else, for without peace, neither democracy nor growth nor other values are likely to take root and develop. This places a premium on arms and security, traditional objectives in U.S. relations with the Third World.

In "Regional Security, Arms Control, and the End of the Cold War," Geoffrey Kemp examines developments related to the traditional thrust of U.S. Third World policies. Kemp identifies "three good reasons to be . . . skeptical about the prospects for reducing regional conflict and implementing regional arms-control agreements." First, he argues, superpower retrenchment will create a vacuum that will tempt regional powers to use force to settle disputes (as seen by Iraq's invasion of Kuwait). Second, conditions conducive to war in such troublespots as the Near East and South Asia are growing. Third, most Third World countries are engaged in ambitious armament programs that will inhibit incentives to reduce tensions through collaboration.

Recent developments among Third World countries related to these trends lead Kemp to conclude that "a new age of internationalism cannot be assured" now that the Cold War has ended. Given this, it is unlikely that the United States will be able to "distance itself from the traumas of this new world and retreat to a neo-isolationist posture with international involvement primarily focused on economic matters." Geopolitics destine the United States "to remain a key world power" in a regionalized, competitive world. In consequence, the United States will sometimes face dilemmas. "U.S. policy toward regional conflict and arms control," for example, "will remain torn between the desire to limit weapons proliferation and the need to continue to support friends and allies and to be prepared, as a last resort, to intervene in certain contingencies with U.S. military force." To reduce the dangers inherent in this circumstance, Kemp recommends that the United States work through multilateral channels to encourage regional powers to negotiate arms control agreements.

NOTES

1. Cited in Walter LeFeber, *The American Age: United States Foreign Policy at Home and Abroad Since 1750* (New York: Norton, 1989), pp. 467, 469.

2. See Eugene R. Wittkopf, *Faces of Internationalism: Public Opinion and American Foreign Policy* (Durham, N.C.: Duke University Press, 1990).

3. Richard N. Gardner, "The Comeback of Liberal Internationalism," *Washington Quarterly* 13 (Summer 1990), p. 23.

4. Gardner, p. 23.

5. See Thomas L. Hughes, "The Twilight of Internationalism," *Foreign Policy* 61 (Winter 1985–86), pp. 25–48.

6. Gardner, p. 23. See also Stanley Hoffmann, "A New World and Its Troubles," *Foreign Affairs* 69 (Fall 1990), pp. 115–22; Stanley Hoffmann, "The Case for Leadership," *Foreign Policy* 81 (Winter 1990–91), pp. 20–38.

7. See, for example, Joachim Krause and Peter Schmidt, "The Evolving New European Architecture—Concepts, Problems, and Pitfalls," *Washington Quarterly* 13 (Autumn 1990), pp. 79–92.

8. Patrick J. Buchanan, "America First—and Second, and Third," *National Interest* 19 (Spring 1990), p. 79.

9. Bela Balassa and Marcus Noland, *Japan in the World Economy* (Washington, D.C.: Institute for International Economics, 1988).

10. For comparative data on defense spending performance, see *World Military Expenditures and Arms Transfers 1989* (Washington, D.C.: Arms Control and Disarmament Agency, 1990).

11. See Robert Gilpin, "International Politics in the Pacific Rim Era," *Annals* 505 (Summer 1989), pp. 56–67.

12. See Richard Bissell, "Who Killed the Third World?" *Washington Quarterly* 13 (Autumn 1990), pp. 23–32.

13. Buchanan, "America First—and Second, and Third," p. 81.

14. Buchanan, "America First—and Second, and Third," p. 80.

11 COPING WITH VICTORY

John Lewis Gaddis

One day in September of 1946 an as yet little-known George F. Kennan found himself trying to explain to State Department colleagues what it was going to be like to deal with the Soviet Union as the other great power in the postwar world. Traditional diplomacy would not impress Stalin and his subordinates, Kennan insisted: "I don't think we can influence them by reasoning with them, by arguing with them, by going to them and saying, 'Look here, this is the way things are.'" They weren't the sort to turn around and say, "By George, I never thought of that before. We will go right back and change our policies."

But by [1988] leaders of the Soviet Union and Eastern Europe were saying something very much like that. Once confident of having mastered the "science" of politics and history, the successors to Lenin and Stalin have had to acknowledge that the system those "founding fathers" imposed on Russia after the First World War and on its neighbors after the Second World War simply has not worked. They have now in effect turned to the West and said, "Tell us what to do. We will go right back and change our policies."

We have witnessed one of the most abrupt losses of ideological self-confidence in modern history. The once impressive façade of world communism no longer impresses anyone: those who lived for so long under that system have at last, like Dorothy in *The Wizard of Oz*, looked behind the curtain; they have found there, frantically pulling the levers, pumping the bellows, and pontificating into the speaking tubes, a few diminutive and frightened humbugs. As a result, Eastern Europe has come to resemble the stage set for *Les Misérables*, but with the revolutionaries this time winning. And most remarkably of all, it is the leader of the Soviet Union itself—the current chief wizard, if you will—who seems to be playing simultaneously the roles of Dorothy and Jean Valjean.

The resulting situation leaves the United States and its allies—preoccupied so recently with visions of American decline—in a position of great and unexpected influence. For not only have we prevailed, by peaceful means, over our old Cold War adversaries; it is also the case that for the first time in more than a century there is no clear challenger to the tradition of liberal democratic capitalism according to which this country and much of the rest of the West organizes itself.   We are at one of those rare points of leverage in history when familiar constraints have dropped away; what we do now could establish the framework within which events will play themselves out for decades to come.

Unfortunately we are almost certainly not up to this task.   There exists in the West something we might call the dog-and-car syndrome: the name refers to the fact that dogs spend a great deal of time chasing cars but very little time thinking about what they would actually *do* with a car if they were ever to catch one.   Our leaders are not all that different: they pour their energy vigorously into the pursuit of victory, whether in politics or in war, but when victory actually arrives, they treat it as if it were an astonishing and wholly unforeseen development.   They behave like the senator-elect in Robert Redford's movie *The Candidate* when he takes an aide aside at the victory celebration and asks incredulously, "What do we do now?"

If history is any guide, what we will probably do is fritter away the fruits of victory by failing to think through what it is we want victory to accomplish. The Athenians defeated the Persians in the fifth century B.C. only to defeat themselves through their own subsequent ambition and arrogance.   The Turks spent centuries trying to take Constantinople for Islam only to see world power passing at the moment of their triumph, in 1453, to secular European states for whom the question of which faith ruled the "Eastern Rome" meant very little.   The British drove the French from North America in 1763 but then alienated their own colonists, who in turn drove them out of their most valuable possessions on that continent.   Victory in the First World War brought only dissension and disillusionment among the victors, and a purposeful urge for revenge among the vanquished.   An even more decisive victory in the Second World War produced a long, costly, and nerve-wracking Cold War for those who won, and the mutually reinforcing benefits of peace and unprecedented prosperity for those who lost.

This depressing pattern of victories gone awry is almost enough to make one wish we were commemorating Cold War defeat.   It certainly ought to make us think seriously, and rather quickly, about how not to squander the opportunities that now lie before us.

We should begin by recalling that the Cold War was a new kind of great-power rivalry, one in which the possibility of going to war always existed, but in which the necessity for doing so—at least in a form that would pit the Soviet Union and the United States *directly* against each other—never arose.   As a result, that conflict took on the paradoxical character we associate with the name history has given it: the Cold War contained most of the anxieties, animosities, and apocalyptic exhortations that one tends to find in "hot" wars, but without the rubble or the body count.   In time people became so used to this situation that some, myself included, began using the equally paradoxical term "long peace" to characterize it. Whatever the merits of the label, the importance of what it describes ought not to be minimized: a great-power competition carried on without great-power war is a distinct improvement over the way most such rivalries have been handled in the past.

But we also need to remember that the long peace grew out of a relationship between two superpower adversaries. If they are no longer to be adversaries—or if one of them is no longer to be a superpower—then the conditions that gave us the long peace will change. We need to make sure as we put the Cold War behind us that we do not also jettison those principles and procedures that allowed it to evolve into the longest period of great-power rivalry without war in the modern era. If a long peace was in fact the offspring of the Cold War, then the last thing we should want to do, in tossing the parent onto the ash heap of history, is to toss the child as well.

We will need a strategy that does not waste time and energy trying to turn back irreversible changes, but also one that is imaginative enough to find ways, within the limits of what is possible, to preserve the stability the Cold War has given us. The very concepts we employ in thinking about international affairs grew out of the now antiquated circumstances of superpower rivalry: if all we do is to apply old categories of thought to the new realities we confront—if we limit ourselves to trying to teach new dogs old tricks— we could find our approach to world politics to be as outdated as was the approach that certain now-defunct Marxist regimes took toward their own internal affairs prior to 1989.

The following are some new issues we will face as we seek to extend the long peace beyond a Cold War the West has now won. Old answers will not suffice in dealing with them.

SHOULD WE WELCOME THE DECLINE AND POSSIBLE BREAKUP OF THE SOVIET UNION?

The most astonishing fact facing us as the 1990s begin is that we can no longer take for granted the continued existence of the USSR as the superpower we have known throughout the Cold War. Its economy is in ruins; its government is unsure of its own authority; its leaders confront nationalist pressures far more deeply rooted than the "socialist" values the Soviet state has been trying to implant for more than seven decades. There are those in the West who welcome these developments as the consummation of a wish long and devoutly held. Second thoughts, one hopes, will produce more-mature reflections.

Among them should be the realization that it takes two to tango, and that the United States has no particular reason to want to conclude the bipolar superpower dance that has been going on since 1945. For by comparison with the multipolar international systems that preceded it, Cold War bipolarity has served the cause of peace remarkably well: the First and Second World Wars arose from failures of communication, cooperation, and common sense among several states of roughly equal strength, not from situations in which two clear antagonists confronted each other. The relative simplicity of postwar great-power relations may well have made possible their relative stability, and a situation in which the Soviet Union is no longer such a power would mean an end to that arrangement. War might not result, but instability, volatility, and unpredictability almost certainly would.

It is also worth noting that military hardware does not simply vanish into thin air as a nation's position in the world declines, or as its internal authority crumbles. The means by which a new war could start—and indeed, with nuclear weapons, the means by which we ourselves could be destroyed—will remain in the hands of whoever rules the Soviet Union. If that country should break apart, these lethal instruments might well come under the control of competing factions whose caution with respect to their use might not exceed the intensity of the rivalries that exist among them.

We confront, then, an apparent paradox: now that we have won the Cold War, our chief interest may lie in the survival and successful rehabilitation of the nation that was our principal adversary throughout that conflict. But a historian would see nothing odd in this: Napoleon's conquerors moved quickly to reintegrate France into the international community after 1815; Germany and Japan received similar treatment after their defeat in 1945. It was the failure to arrange for Germany's reintegration after the First World War, some scholars have argued, that led to the Second World War. Power vacuums are dangerous things. Solicitude for a defeated adversary, therefore, is not just a matter of charity or magnanimity; it also reflects the wise victor's calculated self-interest, as confirmed by repeated historical experience.

But to say that the United States should seek the survival and rehabilitation of the Soviet Union is not to say that we should do so in its present form. That country's future is in question today not because anyone has attacked it but because its own internal structure has proved unworkable. If the USSR is to recover, it will have to change that structure; the only question is how. And although the Soviet people themselves will, in the end, decide that question, we in the West are not without influence in the matter: consider the regularity with which Soviet officials now solicit our advice.

Americans have long questioned the wisdom of trying to maintain multinational empires against the will of their inhabitants. The collapse of the Russian, Ottoman, and Austro-Hungarian empires during the First World War vindicated that skepticism, as did the dismantling of the British, French, Dutch, and Portuguese empires after the Second World War. Soviet officials have argued, of course, that the analogy is imperfect, that their non-Russian republics are not colonies at all but rather constituent parts of the USSR, linked to it by their own free will. But the French used to insist, with equal lack of credibility, that Algeria was part of France itself and content to remain so. A mother country's claims of filial devotion do not establish its existence.

The French experience also shows how close a state can come to destroying itself by trying to hang on to an empire for too long. It would hardly strengthen the Soviet Union to have several simultaneous insurgencies going on within its borders; just one, in Algeria, was enough to persuade that most imperious of modern statesmen, Charles de Gaulle, that imperial devolution had its advantages. France's position in the world has hardly declined since then, and many of its former colonies have chosen to maintain economic, linguistic, and cultural ties with their former ruler—as have many of Great Britain's—even as they have broken political ties. Denying autonomy ensures the absence of allegiance; allowing it at least leaves possibilities open.

A Russia that embraced a De Gaulle solution would remain a great power: even if the Russian federal republic alone were all that survived under Moscow's rule, it would still control 76 percent of the land area and 52 percent of the population of the present USSR. Bloated boundaries have never provided very much security in a nuclear age in any event, but with nationalism rampant and with the means of suppressing it no longer effective, they are certain in the future to provide even less.

It would appear to make sense, therefore, for the United States to favor as much of a breakup of the Soviet Union as would be necessary to leave it with a reasonably contented as opposed to a disaffected population, *precisely because we should want to see that state survive as a great power.* And who knows: in a post–Cold War world Kremlin leaders might actually acknowledge the sincerity of our motives in taking such a position (although we should probably not count on that).

WHAT IS GOING TO BE LEFT FOR NUCLEAR WEAPONS TO DETER?

As areas of agreement in Soviet-American relations have expanded, the occasions on which either side has felt the need to deter the other have become rare, and that trend has in turn raised the possibility of getting by with far fewer nuclear weapons and delivery systems than each side has now. Reductions have already begun, and there is every reason to think that they will continue.

We and the Russians would do well, though, to resist the temptation to abolish nuclear weapons altogether, or even to reduce our stockpiles to a level approximating that of the next largest nuclear power. The reason for this is simple: nuclear weapons have played a major role in bringing about the evolution from Cold War to long peace. They have made each side think twice before taking action that might risk war; they have served as a kind of crystal ball into which statesmen can look to see what the consequences of a future conflict will be, and that vision has induced caution.

Nuclear weapons also sustained Soviet-American bipolarity beyond the time that it might otherwise have been expected to last. Given the Soviet

Union's chronic economic difficulties, its claim to superpower status would have lost credibility long ago had that country not possessed a tremendous nuclear arsenal. But because of the stability that bipolarity brings, it is not at all clear that the world would have been a more peaceful place had the USSR become an "ordinary" power.

The relationship between nuclear weapons and superpower status is, to be sure, poorly understood. No one has ever been quite certain how to define just what a superpower is, apart from this characteristic of having a large number of nuclear weapons. But no one has ever been quite certain either just how nuclear weapons made the United States and the Soviet Union superpowers in the first place. What we do know is that the caution nuclear capabilities encourage and the bipolarity they sustain have created the framework for a reasonably stable international order. It might be best not to inquire too deeply into how.

Witch doctors, after all, produce their cures largely by psychological effect: their powers evaporate if examined too closely. The psychological effects that nuclear weapons have provided may well have cured the great powers of a very dangerous illness indeed, which was their propensity to rush blindly into wars without considering the consequences. We would do well to accept this result gratefully, and without challenging too directly the means by which it has been brought about.

It would be to the advantage of the United States and the Soviet Union, therefore, to retain their nuclear superiority over the rest of the world, albeit at much reduced levels, and with maximum cooperation to avoid surprises and accidents. But we might well rethink targeting doctrines, for as the physicist Freeman Dyson has wisely observed, just because a nation has nuclear weapons does not mean that it has to point them at anyone in particular. Their purpose, rather, should be to maintain a healthy fear of incautious action on the part of everyone, and a healthy respect for a major method by which we have achieved a long peace. If that fear and that respect come from the contemporary technological equivalent of rattling bones and chanting incantations around a campfire, then so be it.

[WHAT ROLE MIGHT NATO AND THE WARSAW PACT PERFORM?]

If the Soviet Union and the United States are no longer to confront each other as adversaries, then the original purpose of NATO and the Warsaw Pact—deterring military attack—will have passed away. It is worth recalling, though, that these alliances had secondary purposes as well: both were intended to overcome old nationalist rivalries in Europe; both were instruments by which the superpowers sought to integrate those portions of Germany that they controlled into those parts of Europe that fell within their influence. The two alliances served as stabilizers in that they brought a certain order and predictability to Europe; and although that stability was not always based on justice—witness Soviet behavior in Eastern Europe—it did secure peace for almost half a century on a previously war-prone continent.

But with self-determination triumphant among former Soviet satellites and with German reunification [complete], we . . . confront a task quite unfamiliar to our generation (although not to those of our parents and grandparents), which is cartographic revision: the map of post–Cold War Europe is not . . . the one to which we have become accustomed since the end of the Second World War. Soviet-American rivalry, it is now apparent, simply suppressed nationalism in Europe; it did not end it, and it will not take long for the effects of resurgent nationalism, both in reality and on maps, to manifest themselves. Europeans are entering uncharted territory, and in such circumstances it may be wise to hold on to what is familiar, even if it is a bit out of date.

We should therefore seek to preserve the secondary stabilizing functions of NATO and the Warsaw Pact, even as their original deterrent purposes disappear. It is always easier to modify existing institutions than to create new ones; preserving the Cold War alliances but shifting their roles could ensure that resurgent European nationalism does not, in these new and volatile circumstances, once again get out of control.

One way to accomplish this might be for [the] reunified Germany to link itself to both alliances at the same time. Such a solution would have seemed ludicrous when NATO and the Warsaw Pact confronted each other as Cold War adversaries, but is it so implausible in a post–Cold War era? People have learned to live with stranger things: consider what happened to Germany itself, and to its former capital, in the years that followed the Second World War. If one keeps in mind that we are talking about a world in which once-competitive alliances have taken on the common task of preserving the stability Europe achieved during the Cold War—and if we remember that stability will be the prerequisite for any Europe-wide economic integration—then it might well be [advantageous] to . . . [keep] NATO and the Warsaw Pact around for a while—even if their role resembles that of nursemaids more than that of warriors. . . .

SHOULD WE HELP TO REPAIR THE DAMAGE MARXISM HAS CAUSED?

Economic distress obviously encourages political instability: as Paul Kennedy, the Yale historian, has pointed out, uneven rates of economic and technological development are what cause great powers to rise and fall. If one accepts the argument that the United States and its allies should want Russia to remain a great power, then it would hardly make sense to welcome an economic collapse there or in Eastern Europe, however misguided the policies were that produced that prospect.

But the West has an ideological as well as a material interest in wanting to see *perestroika* succeed: the cause of democracy throughout the world can only prosper if that ideology—and not Marxist authoritarianism—provides the means by which the USSR and its neighbors at last achieve economies capable of satisfying the needs of their peoples. And if the emergence of even partly democratic institutions inside the Soviet Union makes the prospect of war less likely—there is strong historical evidence that democracies tend not to fight each other—then that would be an important reinforcement for the role nuclear deterrence has already played in discouraging the incautious use of military force.

Few people today remember that a similar combination of geopolitical and ideological motives impelled Secretary of State George C. Marshall in 1947— at Kennan's suggestion—to offer to include the Soviet Union and Eastern Europe in the plan for economic assistance that came to bear Marshall's name. Stalin, with characteristic shortsightedness, rejected the idea, and the Marshall Plan went on to become a program for the rehabilitation of Western Europe—one that was so successful that editorial pages ever since have resounded with calls for its revival, however dissimilar the circumstances might be to those that existed at the time of its creation.

Now, though, the way is open to implement Marshall's original vision. For although it lies beyond the power of anyone in the West to ensure the success of economic reforms in either the Soviet Union or Eastern Europe, those countries are already asking the United States to provide much of the training and technology without which failure will be certain. We will need to think carefully about just what we can do, and how we should do it.

One thing is apparent at the outset: any new aid program for the Soviet Union and Eastern Europe will have to be multinational in character. The United States is well beyond the point at which it can take on a burden of this magnitude by itself, as it did in 1947. Fortunately, though, it can now enlist the very considerable resources and skills of former recipients of Marshall Plan aid in Europe, notably [former] West Germany, and also those of Japan, another past beneficiary of American assistance. All these states have cause to welcome an integration of Soviet and Eastern European economies with those of the rest of the world; none of them has any good reason to want to see *perestroika* fail.

A multinational aid program would have several advantages over older, unilateral forms of aid. It would maximize the resources available while minimizing the burden on an already overstretched American economy. It would be less susceptible than past foreign-aid programs to the charge that it serves the political interests of a particular state; it would also be less vulnerable to the volatility of domestic politics in any one state. It would soak up surplus products and capital from two large-scale exporters of these commodities—Germany and Japan—whose success in exporting has periodically strained their relationship with the United States. And such a program might also help to heal political differences that still exist between

Japan and the Soviet Union and that might well exist between [the] reunified Germany and the Soviet Union.

We might also consider encouraging corporate rather than government sponsorship for at least a major portion of this assistance, where profitability and propriety make it feasible.   Corporate management could provide faster action and greater efficiency than would otherwise occur; it might also be more sensitive than official initiatives to those market forces in the Soviet Union and Eastern Europe whose emergence we want to encourage.   Some such activity is already under way, most conspicuously with a project that surely marks a turning point of some kind in the history of our times: I refer to the . . . opening of McDonald's in Moscow, a project that [is] particularly interesting to watch because of the corporation's decision to develop its own network of farms, processing plants, and training centers inside the USSR. The resulting contest is sure to be a titanic one, and whether Russia will overwhelm McDonald's or McDonald's will overwhelm Russia is far from clear.   But the fact that it is taking place at all can only warm the heart of anyone who has ever been to the Soviet Union and felt the urge to shout, out of sheer exasperation: "What this country needs is a good service economy!"

WHAT HAPPENS AFTER GORBACHEV?

No one, not even [Gorbachev], is indispensable (although he comes about as close as any person in recent memory).   The frailties that flesh—or a political career—is heir to can only increase with the passage of time; we in the West must be prepared for the moment when the most imaginative Soviet leader since Lenin is no longer on the scene.   To fail to do this—to assume that everything that is happening hinges on Gorbachev alone—would in itself be to fall into an outmoded way of thinking.

There is at least one reason to think that the post–Cold War era will continue into the post-Gorbachev era: it is the fact that the roots of the long peace were in place well before Gorbachev came to power.   Whatever their dissimilarities, neither Stalin nor Khrushchev nor Brezhnev wanted a war with the United States; the likelihood of such a conflict has declined steadily over the years, regardless of whether tyrants, reformers, or stagnationists ruled in the Kremlin.   It is true that Soviet domestic and foreign policies are harder to separate today than they once were: an abandonment of *perestroika* or a crackdown on dissent would obviously undermine Moscow's improved relations with the West, just as the Tiananmen Square massacre undermined Beijing's. . . .

The West's strategy, therefore, ought to be to do nothing to undermine Gorbachev's authority, but not to be wholly dependent upon it either.   Because the forces that have ended the Cold War are deeply rooted—and because the problems that beset the Soviet Union will remain after Gorbachev leaves the scene—we have some basis for confidence that the initiatives he has taken to deal with both domestic and foreign-policy issues are not going to disappear after he does.

The names that we attach to things—which in turn determine the categories we use in thinking about them—are only representations of reality; they are not reality itself. Reality can shift, sometimes more rapidly than the names we have devised to characterize it. Concepts like "communism," "capitalism," "deterrence," "credibility," and "security" only approximate the conditions we confront; but words like these tend to take on a life of their own, thereby constraining imagination. . . . We need to avoid letting the categories that exist in our minds blind us to what our eyes are seeing.

At the same time, though, there is at least one thing to be said in favor of retaining old names, even as one accommodates to new realities. Cloaking change in the appearance of continuity is a time-honored technique of political leadership, for it allows those at the top to alter their thinking and shift their policies without seeming to be inconsistent. Cloaking change in the garb of continuity eases transitions; it can be a way of making revolution look like evolution, which is sometimes a useful thing to do. We should not, therefore, do away entirely with the terminology of the Cold War, or even with all the institutions that reflect that terminology; but we should welcome the opportunity slowly but steadily to shift the meanings we attach to them.

Who is it that we have defeated in the Cold War? It is not the Russian people, whom we never saw as enemies, and toward whom we bear no ill will. It is not the Soviet Union, for we should want to see that state survive as a great power. It is not communism, because that doctrine has proved so malleable over the years that it has long since lost any precise meaning. It is certainly not Gorbachev and [his] Soviet government, who have had the wisdom to recognize reality and the courage to adjust to it. It is not even the Cold War, because that experience brought us the long peace. Indeed, it is odd that there should be so much talk of victory and so little specificity as to at whose expense it actually came.

It might help clarify things if we recall what appears to be a recurring competition in human affairs between coercive authority and individual autonomy, between what the sociologist John A. Hall has referred to as the forces of power and those of liberty. The tension is as old as recorded history, and it will no doubt be with us as long as history continues. But power and liberty are rarely precisely balanced: one or the other predominates most of the time, with only occasional shifts back and forth.

The century has not, on the whole, been kind to liberty. The forces of authoritarianism overcame those of autonomy in most parts of the world most of the time during this period: witness the respective triumphs of fascism, communism, and all the varieties of dictatorship that lay between. It appeared until quite recently to be the fate of most people to have most of their lives managed for them, to lack the means of controlling their own affairs.

What happened in the revolutionary year 1989 was that liberty suddenly found itself pushing against an open door. The balance swung away from power with breathtaking speed; the authoritarian alternatives that have dominated so much of twentieth-century history were revealed to be, for the most part, hollow shells. We have good reason to hope that liberty will flourish in the next few years as it has not in our lifetime; and it is in that context that the real nature of the West's "victory" in the Cold War becomes clear. For it was authoritarianism that suffered the real defeat, and in that sense all of us—including our old Cold War adversaries—have won.

But history will not stop with us, any more than it did with all the others—Marx and Lenin among them—who thought they had mastered its secrets. The triumph of liberty will almost certainly be transitory; new forces will eventually arise that will swing the balance back to power once again. It is not clear at the moment, though, where they will come from, or when they will arrive. It would be prudent to be on the lookout for them; it would be wise to be prepared for their effects. But the fact that the forces of resurgent power are not yet in sight—that we have the luxury of at least some time to savor the liberties that all of us, Russians included, have won—ought to be an occasion for ecumenical, if wary, celebration.

12   CHALLENGES TO THE POST-COLD WAR BALANCE OF POWER

Andrew C. Goldberg

Does the recent retreat of the Soviet military threat signal the declining relevance of the balance of power to U.S. security? For much of modern history statesmen have spent considerable time attempting to calculate the relative balance of political, economic, and military power among the major states out of concern that one might use its capabilities to attain hegemony over the others.   The United States reluctantly fought in two world wars to forestall such a development and preserve a global equilibrium conducive to its interests.   It spent much of the Cold War performing the same role against the likelihood that the Soviet Union would accomplish what Germany and its allies failed to.

In the space of barely five years, however, the Soviet Union, the bête noire of U.S. statesmen since the end of World War II, has become virtually irrelevant to U.S. military planning.   Its empire in Eastern Europe is in ruins, its domestic society is wracked by economic collapse and national separatism. The Soviet Union does not look like a good candidate for survival, let alone great power status in the future.

With the decline—and maybe fall—of the Soviet empire, what will Americans really have to worry about when it comes to the security of their homeland and their own status as a superpower? . . .

Defining post—cold war security threats . . . involves some initial, and at this early stage somewhat intuitive, judgment as to whether or not a balance of power among the major powers matters any longer as a criterion for judging where U.S. interests and concerns lie.   Throughout much of this century U.S. policymakers and policy analysts have debated whether the United States government should work under the assumption that relations among the great powers would always involve the potential for military conflict, or whether the process of economic integration and a growing sense of community would pacify relations to the point where the military component of politics would disappear.

With the attenuation of the Soviet military threat, it is harder to imagine a situation in which any power or constellation of powers would present the appropriate combination of military and economic muscle that would challenge U.S. security and its primacy as a superpower. Saddam Hussein's adventure in the Persian Gulf demonstrates that U.S. leaders can have plenty of military involvements that do not engage the opposition of the Soviet Union or any other great power. Yet at the same time, we are still years away from the time in which almost any state apart from the major industrial powers will have the capability to defeat—as opposed simply to disturb—U.S. power. What, then, defines the major security challenges to the United States in the post–cold war era?

This [essay] takes the skeptical view that we are still far from a time in which one can say safely that the balance of power—in both its economic and military facets—is no longer relevant to U.S. global concerns. It is possible to construct a variety of scenarios in which the geostrategic threat to the United States, with or without the Soviet Union, could become very pronounced.

The analysis here begins with the state of U.S. security, whose defining characteristics as it enters the 1990s are a new sense of detachment from global military dangers—despite the Gulf conflict—and of aimlessness in defining its own interests. The [essay] then considers a range of scenarios in which the changing character of the superpower relationship either exacerbates emerging threats or gives birth to qualitatively new ones. These scenarios are not meant to exhaust the varieties of possible security concerns but only to be illustrative. Finally, the question is raised as to what effect the prospective balance of cooperation and competition between the United States and an enfeebled Soviet Union may yet have on containing future threats to U.S. security.

SETTING THE CONTEXT: THE NEW U.S. INSULARITY

Much as in the periods before the two great wars of this century, the United States is experiencing the feeling of security that comes from its relative strategic insularity on a continent devoid of adjacent military challengers. During the decades of intense military competition between the United States and the Soviet Union along the forward lines of containment in Europe and in Asia, this feeling of insulation from attack was diminished, at least in the minds of U.S. leaders and to some degree also in the public mind. The perception that the United States might be drawn into a conflict that might lead, perhaps not to invasion but to a nuclear attack on the U.S. homeland, was a pronounced if not imminent concern.

Yet, with the contraction of Soviet military and political power in Eastern Europe and its substantially diminished role in regional turbulence beyond Europe, Soviet invasion of Europe—and therefore the most likely cause of nuclear escalation—is now of almost insignificant concern. Although it is true that Soviet nuclear capabilities remain awesome, it is hard to link their use to any immediate political trigger. U.S. leaders and political commentators are therefore experiencing a distance from world conflict that is both satisfying and troubling at the same time. The satisfaction comes from more than a sense of security and advantage. Although world politics may be increasingly pluralistic in an economic and political sense, militarily the United States is the only power with true global reach. Now, with the Soviet retreat from global military competition, the United States also has the freedom of action to use its capabilities with the kind of impunity only dreamed of a decade ago.

The sense of unease comes from an inability to define what this insularity means from the standpoint of defining U.S. security interests. Even the casual observer of international affairs recognizes that there are problems with the potential for violence in almost every region in the world, including Europe. In the absence of a clear danger to the United States, however, it becomes harder to decide what any of this turbulence has to do with that country as opposed to the wider world of less fortunate powers. Much as in the debates before World Wars I and II over defining the national interest, once again no clear consensus remains on what defines the nature of the external threat or the role of military power in shaping a world conducive to American political and economic well-being.

In defining future threats one might usefully offer three illustrative scenarios, each of which could hold the potential for disrupting U.S. strategic insularity over the next several decades. . . .

The first illustrative scenario may be described as "Soviet Weimar." In this scenario, the Soviet Union is able to master its domestic political and economic troubles sufficiently to again wield considerable coercive political and military influence in Eurasia and perhaps beyond. Like Weimar Germany in the 1920s and 1930s, this new Soviet Union (or whatever it may yet be called) would feature domestic political forces that felt disadvantaged, deprived of prestige during a period of weakness, and anxious to challenge the post–cold war status quo. The Soviet Union may eventually come to be dominated by policies that reflect these influences.

The second category of threat assumes that protracted Soviet weakness would create a political and military vacuum that Germany would fill. This Germany would resemble less the Third Reich than the Second. It would remain parliamentarian in its politics—as did its nineteenth-century predecessor. This new Germany would, nevertheless, be subject to increasingly nationalist and interventionist passions occasioned by its involvements in Eastern Europe and its absorption of 17 million East Germans with different cultural and political inclinations. It would also be economically far stronger than its historical predecessors and would have the additional advantage of being the core of a more economically integrated—and therefore dependent—Europe.

The third category we might describe euphemistically as the "Byzantine" scenario, although it draws on many comparable examples of the past. Here the collapse of the Soviet Union would occasion the emergence of large successor states or alliances whose values were alien to the West but whose military capabilities were such that they would eventually come to pose a serious military threat even to the United States.

THE SOVIET UNION AS WEIMAR

The revival of the Soviet Union as a danger to the international order along the lines of Germany after World War I is a popular candidate among threat scenarios. Like Germany after the Great War, the Soviet Union is beset by economic dislocation, is burdened with the costs of dismantling its huge military establishment, and faces widespread social unrest. Also, as in Weimar Germany, underneath a basically liberal leadership lies a wellspring of nationalist resentment with authoritarian inclinations. Such forces may grow stronger as economic failure breeds social reaction against reformers at the top.

Finally, like Weimar, there is powerful evidence that many in the Soviet populace perceive themselves as having "lost" the Cold War not through any failure of Soviet military prowess, but because intellectual reformers in Moscow capitulated out of cowardice and political weakness. Weimar had its myth of the "stab in the back": here the scapegoats are the Westernizing intelligentsia, Jews, even the Communist Party.

The simultaneous disintegration of domestic well-being and international influence provides circumstances ripe for the creation of a backlash within the Soviet state. Such a backlash, it might be surmised, may come in the form of a right-wing dictatorship—perhaps a very capitalistic one, such as Korea in the sixties and seventies, or Pinochet's Chile—bent on recouping its lost clout in global affairs. As Weimar gave birth to Hitler, so might the Soviet Union create its own autocratic champion.

What limits, but does not eliminate, the potential recurrence of the Weimar model in Soviet clothing is not so much any inherent virtue in President Mikhail S. Gorbachev's leadership or that of any of his rivals but rather the polyglot nature of the Soviet state, which confounds the emergence of such a threat. Post–World War I Germany, whatever its economic constraints, was nationally homogeneous, and, with the minor exceptions of Alsace-Lorraine and a bit of East Prussia, territorially integrated. By contrast, the cohesion of Soviet society and its integrity as a state is diminishing rapidly. As each individual Soviet republic, including the Slavic core of Russia, the Ukraine, and Byelorussia, declares its sovereignty, the difficulty of preserving even a semblance of integration becomes more acute.

The Soviet economy in the postindustrial era, moreover, represents an unmitigated disaster. Weimar Germany, whatever its economic burdens, remained the most important economy in the Europe of its day and maintained a modern base upon which to reconstruct its war machine. Gorbachev's Soviet Union cannot boast an equivalent technological or economic base.

For the Weimar scenario to unfold, two factors are essential. The first is the preservation of some form of national integrity. This does not mean that the Soviet state as it exists today must remain unchanged: the Russian empire and its Soviet successor have held many different borders in the last three centuries and yet remained important in international affairs. It does mean, however, that the resource-rich Russian Republic and the Ukraine must somehow remain an integrated territorial base.

Second, the Soviet Union requires radical economic reconstruction that will marry technologies and assistance imported from abroad with the sort of ruthless economic transformation that has yet to occur in the five years of Gorbachev's rule. Absent these elements, it is hard to imagine the Soviet Union will survive.

Yet the possibility remains that the country will pursue policies that will galvanize its technological and economic base, despite past failures. . . . If so, then the marriage of capitalist reform, social convulsion, and a feeling of deprivation in terms of international prestige and influence may yet give birth to the Weimar scenario.

AN "IMPERIAL" GERMANY AND A DECAYING SOVIET UNION

Another scenario presents an alternative protagonist. Instead of a Weimar Soviet Union, one can imagine an "imperial" Germany that would replace the Soviet Union as the dominant power in Europe. . . .

In an irony not lost on those with a historical bent the United States has fought two hot wars, and one cold one, to prevent the resources of Europe from falling under the control of a single manager. With the deterioration of Soviet power and the increasing economic dependence of Europe on a united Germany, however, the prospect of Germany emerging as a political hegemon looms very large indeed. Unfortunately, then, the example of . . . benign [former] West Germany is no guarantee against economic and foreign policies that may prove to be disadvantageous to others, not least among them the United States. If one believes that greater German political and economic power will create opportunities for competition as well as cooperation, then the balance of military power in Eurasia is an important element in shaping Germany's relationship with the United States. . . .

The role of Soviet–German relations becomes extremely problematic in this strategic era. Germany is the leading candidate, by virtue of geographical proximity and political inclination, to be the central banker for both East European and Soviet reconstruction. It also has the potential for acting as an interventionary political and military force in the unsettled politics of Eastern Europe. For a weak and battered Soviet state, Germany is not only an object to be coopted but also an ascendant political rival to be feared.

The political terrain across which these two nations stare at each other is hardly promising. Throughout Eastern Europe, the forces of national discord remain in tense competition with a tenuous liberalism. The apparent remoteness of near-term economic rejuvenation of the region will only intensify the propensity for political turbulence from the Baltic to the Balkans. A giant transmission belt of political dissatisfaction runs from East Germany to the Ukraine. The potential for a misstep by Germany, the Soviet Union, or both in the crisis-prone affairs of this region may increase over time. . . .

Within this context, the future relationship between German leaders who are just beginning to build a new state with newly defined interests and a Soviet government that is trying to preserve a collapsing system becomes a major worry for the United States. Economic nationalism and political instability remain forces to be reckoned with that, if not managed prudently, can still lead to a German–Soviet military confrontation. That such a confrontation would involve the United States is not unlikely, because it would raise the specter of a major land war in Europe and a convulsive alteration of the balance of military power.

BEYOND EUROPE: THE SOVIET UNION AS A DECLINING BYZANTIUM

Just as Japan's 1931 invasion of China provided a foretaste of things to come, Iraq's invasion of Kuwait creates an unpleasant reminder of the ugly uncertainties that afflict U.S. diplomacy in the wider world. To a great extent, the idea that stability would increase in regional trouble spots once the Soviet Union was in retreat has been cast into doubt. This development comes as no surprise to those who have been warning for many years that the mixture of unrequited nationalism, high-technology weaponry, and socioeconomic turmoil in the Middle East, South Asia, North Africa, and elsewhere would provide more than enough trouble for the United States for years to come.

In an ironic turnabout, it has become the hope of many inside and outside the Bush administration that Soviet power might actually play an interventionary role in some of these areas—on the U.S. side. Countering the Iraqi adventure has indeed been portrayed in the press as a test for such cooperation. Soviet support in the United Nations (UN) was useful in creating the economic embargo against Saddam Hussein, while its declaratory policies and token deployments of military force created the appearance of adding symbolic muscle to the U.S. military involvement.

It is, therefore, sometimes popular to view the Soviet Union today as a kind of Ottoman empire in decline. Embracing the Soviet Union, much as Great Britain once embraced the decaying Ottoman empire as a partner in preserving stability in the semisavage regions of the non-Western world, has a charming quality. At the risk of adding another potentially invidious analogy, however, one might suggest that the Soviet state may also resemble Byzantium in its decline.

Like the old Eastern Roman Empire, the Soviet Union is an uneasy amalgam of East and West. It is also one of the main territorial buffers between the populous, quarrelsome, and increasingly militarily sophisticated states of the Middle East and Southern Asia and the wealthy Western democracies. As Byzantium crumbled in the Middle Ages, leaving Europe open to the depredations of the militant East, the Soviet Union might be succeeded by states that would accentuate the existing competition between these two alien worlds.

Whether one chooses the Byzantine analogy, that of the Ottoman empire, or some other, it is becoming clear that the United States may have a vested interest not only in containing a resurgence of Soviet power but also, ironically, in averting the collapse of the Soviet Union in the face of rising nationalism.

In this regard what stands out about the "new thinking" emanating from Moscow regarding the promotion of East–West cooperation on maintaining regional stability is not its good intentions. Instead it is the Soviet's new dependence on the West—particularly the United States—for the regional peacekeeping increasingly essential to Soviet security: many of the world's most explosive actors sit hard by Moscow's troubled Central Asian regions.

Due to Soviet weakness, the United States and the Soviet Union now share a common concern for taming regional confrontations and thwarting the rise of new regional adversaries. While differences will emerge over specific policy responses, the community of interest is evident and was most recently reflected in Soviet cooperation in the embargo of Iraq.

Unfortunately, this weakness sharply limits Soviet ability to render much more than token support to U.S. peacekeeping endeavors. Not only is the Soviet government absorbed in its own troubles; it cannot afford interventions in the Persian Gulf or South Asia that might spill over to fuel the restiveness of its own non-Slavic nationals.

The obverse side of Moscow's declining imperial condition is also problematic for the United States. If a stable Soviet Union is a precondition for joint action in global peacekeeping, then an unstable Soviet empire is itself part of the peacekeeping problem.

U.S. policy still avoids the tough questions of the linkages between future global stability and breakaway successor states of the Soviet empire. How would U.S. decision makers respond to alliances or fusions between Soviet Central Asia and Islamic states such as Iran and Pakistan? Would an independent Ukrainian Republic be a welcome addition to the family of nations if it cast into doubt the legitimacy of frontiers in the Balkans or the Caucasus? Would the United States care more or less if such new territorial formations were armed with long-range weapons of mass destruction, such as SS–18 missiles from the presumably defunct Soviet Strategic Rocket Forces?

Were the United States to attempt to prop up the Soviet Union in somewhat the manner of British assistance to the Ottoman empire during the eighteenth and nineteenth centuries, the complications would be enormous. The problem with an Ottoman-style marriage of convenience is that it tends to be an unhappy one. Like Great Britain before it, the United States may find itself confronted with the choice of intervening, perhaps militarily, to support the Soviet Union against the national aspirations of its subject peoples. If it does not bolster Soviet control, U.S. leaders may find themselves acquiescing in the formation of unpredictable, potentially hostile territorial and military formations with no track record of moderation.

CONCERTS, CONDOMINIUMS, AND CONTAINMENT

Each of the preceding scenarios presents a picture of a world most U.S. officials would probably see as threatening to the security of the United States and to its position as a great power. A resurgent and aggressive Soviet Union, with perhaps a more efficient economy and a thirst for territorial, political, or economic compensation for perceived cold war losses would be a serious cause for alarm. So, too, would be a hegemonic Germany were it to undermine U.S. political and economic influence or unilaterally involve itself in regional crises. Finally, the absorption of large chunks of Soviet territory, and along with them substantial amounts of their military capability, into the family of radical, anti-U.S. regimes would create an ugly new dimension in the already worsening problem of North–South strategic relations.

Admittedly, each scenario represents the sort of worst case that today's conventional wisdom seems to reject as overly pessimistic. Yet assuming that a variant of one or more of these cases were to unfold, what are the options for maintaining an equilibrium that minimizes the potential for conflict or war involving the United States?

One ready candidate is true isolationism in the realm of security. Abandoning its twentieth-century role as the guarantor of the Eurasian balance would minimize U.S. exposure to risk. It would, however, constrain U.S. ability to shape an international political and economic order congenial to its prosperity and long-term security.

Another option, popular among a number of today's observers, is the formation among the great powers—including the Soviet Union—of a system similar to the Concert of Europe that emerged after 1815. Here the assumption is that there are no longer any important differences among the major states and that all have an interest in preserving the status quo.

While a greater measure of great power cooperation may be the case at the moment, the foregoing analysis suggests that the contradictions among major powers may intensify rather than diminish as they are subjected to new post—cold war challenges. Just as in the earlier concert system, which fell apart with the rise of the Second Reich, a concert is viable only if everyone can stay in tune.

Equally problematic is reliance on a Soviet—U.S. condominium in maintaining global order. So long as the Soviet Union remains a crippled power, no truly equitable partnership is possible. On the other hand, were the Soviet state somehow resuscitated from its current condition, we might find ourselves less a partner than a renewed adversary.

It is impossible, however, to arrive at a truly satisfactory formula for deciding on the scope of U.S. involvement in an international system that will be in flux for some unknown period. Yet the essential objectives of U.S. policy seem apparent. It must attempt to nurture a political balance among the major powers in Eurasia that mitigates, to the greatest extent possible, tendencies toward both hegemonism and disintegration.

Ironically, this means that the United States will find itself occupying an odd middle ground in its relationship with its long-time adversaries and allies. It must stay in the containment business, maintaining a healthy, forward-deployed military posture, and in associated alliance commitments, embodied primarily in the North Atlantic Treaty Organization (NATO), that allow it to constrain the development of a revanchist Soviet Union. At the same time, however, the United States is almost compelled to cultivate opportunities for cooperation with the Soviet Union that would prevent or at least slow a Soviet slide into an anarchy that would throw Eurasian stability into doubt. To a large extent, then, the ability of the United States to preserve equilibrium in the international system rests on the future health of the Soviet Union. Far from being marginalized by the end of the Cold War, the Soviet Union stands at the heart of the emerging balance. . . .

Tying the United States to the preservation of the Soviet Union or, failing that, to assisting in its graceful decline requires as much a leap of faith as it does political calculation. This is so not only because the odds on the accelerated crackup of the Soviet empire grow day by day, but also because the policies the United States might employ to bolster Soviet stability are so painful within the context of the current U.S. political system.

The easiest aid to render the Soviet Union is declaratory. The United States could align its public policy on the side of Soviet unity against the aspirations of dissatisfied ethnic and national groupings. Such a policy tends to run counter not only to liberal U.S. political culture, but also to a recent history in which "captive nations" were portrayed as heroes. As demonstrated in the Bush administration's schizophrenic handling of the Baltic separatist crisis of 1990, U.S. policymakers are often left in an uncertain suspension between a reflexive desire to support national determination and an equally strong desire to control the instabilities inherent in a Soviet collapse.

The second type of aid—and the one that is talked of most—is economic. Here the problems are obvious. U.S. leaders, burdened by incipient recession, the national budgetary deficit, and the seemingly intractable savings and loan crisis, may perceive themselves at the point of financial overload. The Soviet Union, with its inability to move assertively toward a market economy, seems an undesirable locus for U.S. aid and investment. This confluence of factors was felt in the lukewarm U.S. response to the extension of economic aid to the Soviet government during the July 1990 economic summit. Nevertheless, it seems hard to imagine that the Soviet economy can be salvaged without determined U.S. leadership.

In addition, there is the possibility of military intervention on behalf of the central government in Moscow. Fantastic as this may sound, it is not without precedent. In 1919 U.S. forces were on the ground in Siberia partly to prevent Japanese territorial aggrandizement. Not all the territorial amalgamations in Central Asia and the Far East one might imagine rising from the ruins of the Soviet state would be beneficial to long-range U.S. security interests, and some could compel a military action. This would especially be the case if alliances of Islamic states arose that had access to many of the long-range nuclear weapons that might be seized during the dismemberment of the Soviet Union.

The attempt to preserve some global equilibrium in conjunction with the Soviet Union ought not to prevent U.S. statesmen from preparing for the eventuality of Soviet collapse. If the analysis presented here has any validity, future U.S. leaders should not assume that the balance of power will end with the demise of the Soviet Union, nor that the community of interests among the remaining or emerging powers in a new system will be strong or enduring. For the moment, the weight of history is still on the side of the skeptics.

It is possible, then, that the 1990s represent a period of transition much like the 1920s. How the United States handles the balance of power problem over the next several years may well determine the patterns of interstate competition for generations to come. The United States and all of its erstwhile cold war allies and adversaries are now in uncharted waters, stripped of the certainties that made the course of the Cold War predictable. Certainly one should fervently hope that the evolving state system will be a great improvement over past eras. No prudent statesman, however, should bank on it.

13 EUROPE AFTER THE SUPERPOWERS

Ronald Steel

The Europe of the Cold War has dissipated into the background of history. None of the ineluctable "realities" we took for granted during the past four decades carries much meaning any longer. The division of Europe, the partition of Germany, the hegemony of the superpowers, the deadly competition of rival alliances—all this is now outdated. The old American role as Europe's protector and power broker is finished. . . . Much of American policy toward Europe has, like the assumptions that guide it, become irrelevant.

While the Cold War divided Europe into two hostile blocs, one dominated by the United States and the other by the Soviet Union, it also imposed order and stability on a Continent that for much of this century has known neither. Throughout most of the Cold War, Europe was remarkably quiescent, one of the few areas of stability in a world rocked by regional, tribal, and postcolonial warfare. The rival pacts into which Europe was divided, the evident determination of the giants to shield the heartland from their joustings for influence, indeed their contentment with a status quo that ensured their preeminence over a divided Europe—all these factors reinforced a structure of stability.

But the ending of the Cold War removes the very structure of European stability. Imposed from the outside, that stability was maintained by a European psychology of acquiescence to the superpowers and reinforced by the arms race. The collapse of the Soviet Empire in Eastern Europe and the emergence of a unified German state have eroded the political balance on the Continent. Europe, for so many decades an instrument of the policies of others—willingly so in the West, unwillingly in the East—has forced Washington and Moscow to the sidelines. Rather than setting the agenda for Europe and deciding the parameters bounding the new Europe, they have become little more than spectators in the great unfolding drama of Europe's future.

For the first time since 1945, the question for these two great powers is not the place that Europe plays in their rivalry. Rather, it is how they can protect their interests in, and ultimately even against, a Europe that is defining itself independently of them. For American policymakers, lulled by more than four decades of Atlanticism into assuming an identity of purpose between the United States and Western Europe, an adjustment to the new realities of power will be wrenching. But such an adjustment is urgent if the power to influence events, and thus to protect the future, is not to be dissipated. . . .

The end of the Cold War means not only the abatement of tensions, but the demise of the entire political order that stemmed from it. The political order, insofar as Europeans were concerned, was dominated by the United States and the USSR. It is finished. For some time it has been both politically and economically obsolete. Its continuation over the past decade has been a result of cultural lag and of unimaginative, uninformed leadership by both superpowers. But it took the action of the Soviets and the Eastern Europeans finally to bring it down.

The Cold War world has collapsed, first of all, because of Mikhail Gorbachev. His determination to respond to the economic needs of Soviet society, to reform rigid ideological and political structures, and to reinterpret the requirements of Soviet security has transformed the relationship of the Soviet Union to Eastern Europe and to the nations of the Atlantic Alliance. He set in motion forces far more powerful than he or anyone else could have imagined. . . . He surely did not intend that communists would be discredited and forced from power in Eastern Europe; that East Germany, the star of the Soviet diadem, would be swallowed up whole by the Federal Republic; that republics of the Soviet Union itself would demand independence from the Kremlin; or that the scepter of power in Europe would pass from Moscow to Berlin. Yet this [happened], and the Soviets, like ourselves, [were] powerless to prevent it.

The second force that undermined the Cold War is the declining importance of military power. Nuclear weapons have proved to be not only a great equalizer—making the Soviet Union, a nation with a third-rate economy, the "equal" of the United States—but a great neutralizer as well. The superpowers find their nuclear might unusable not only against each other, but even against recalcitrant lesser states they seek to control, such as Afghanistan and Vietnam. Unlike previous technological innovations, such as tanks or dreadnoughts, nuclear weapons are not even useful to intimidate the weak. The kind of military force marshaled by the so-called superpowers (even the term has begun to sound ironic) is no longer an effective measure of global influence. Power today is measured increasingly by productivity, trade surpluses, and technological innovation rather than by nuclear throw weight. Effective, usable power has been shifted from the nuclear musclemen to the more agile trading states.

A third factor is the economic fatigue of the superpowers. The weapons race has left them, like exhausted gladiators in an arena abandoned by a bored crowd, less—rather than more—able to influence events and defend their broader interests. This is dramatically so for the Soviet Union, but also true for the United States. The profligate rearmament programs of the 1980s, combined with unfavorable trade balances and an unwillingness to tax for public expenses, weakened American competitiveness and with it the economic base of American power. Even without a Soviet initiative, the United States must inaugurate its own version of perestroika. The challenge to American economic interests, both from the actions of the United States itself and from its allies and clients, dictates an about-face from an obsession with the Cold War.

The dissipation of the psychology of the Cold War has, like an earth tremor rumbling beneath a seemingly impregnable building, shaken the mighty structures we have taken for granted. Foremost among these structures is a Europe divided between the United States and the Soviet Union. It has become as anachronistic to speak of the "communist bloc" today as it would be to refer to the "Axis" or the "Central Powers." It is even getting difficult to speak with clarity of Eastern as distinct from Western Europe. Day by day we witness the transformation of the "other Europe" into what must be called simply Europe. Not long ago it was considered arrogant or insensitive to speak of "America's Europe" or "Russia's Europe." Today such terms are simply meaningless. History has passed them by.

As the Cold War power blocs have crumbled, the structures that delineate them—NATO [the North Atlantic Treaty Organization] and the Warsaw Pact—have become functionally irrelevant. A Soviet leadership that allows communist parties to be swept from power in Eastern Europe cannot expect Warsaw Pact membership to be a high priority for the hard-currency nationalists who have replaced them. . . .

While the Pact is . . . defunct, NATO could remain formally intact for some time longer. It asks little of its members, except for military expenses many today consider redundant, and the Europeans are now finding a new use for it as an insurance policy against one of its members: Germany. For some time, it has been inertia rather than fear that has held the Alliance together. Once the door to political change in the East was opened, the issue of Europe's defenses took a back seat to the question of Europe's political future. NATO is by nature a reactive alliance. By reacting to the decline of the Soviet threat, it unavoidably undercuts the reason for its own existence.

The result of this has been to magnify a development that has been gathering force for more than a decade, but has been masked by Cold War rhetoric and the inflation of Cold War rhetoric during the last years of Carter and the first term of Reagan: the reduction of America's dominant place in Europe's affairs. Our control over Europe was directly related to the degree that Europeans believed they needed our protection. What was once so eagerly solicited by them now seems a bit of a nuisance—even though the desire for some form of American connection remains. With the Soviet threat retreating into the history books, with Germany rising to become one of the world's great powers, and with Europe itself—like some restless adolescent—proclaiming its independence and demanding gratification of its needs, the notion of Europe as a junior partner and dependency of America seems as quaint as it is self-deluding.

Atlanticism—the organizing principle of U.S. postwar policy toward Europe—was built on such dependency. It was the form in which the United States saw itself in relation to Western Europe, and it inspired a host of institutions and bureaucracies that encouraged and managed that relationship. NATO, the linchpin of Atlanticism, was always conceived as the instrument by which the United States, with Europe's consent and assistance, would provide for the protection of its allies. In so doing, it also retained ultimate direction of Europe's defense and diplomacy. This is the system that such European nationalists as General de Gaulle inveighed against and labeled "hegemony." But it also served Europe's interests. Atlanticism worked so long as Europe's division seemed insurmountable and Europe's dependency inescapable. As these conditions have eroded, so has Atlanticism. With the Soviet Union transformed from a present menace to an impoverished and confused supplicant, the United States has become less important to Europe and exerts less influence over it. The end of the Cold War has meant the extraction of the United States from the European equation. As we assume the role of bystander at the political and economic reorganization of Europe, we find ourselves having moved, however regretfully, into a post-Atlantic world.

The passing of the old order signals the resolution of certain problems—such as a Soviet Union that threatened to impose its will on Western Europe. But it also unleashes others: some new, some until now repressed or concealed. These are likely to replace the Cold War as a focal point of our anxieties toward the external world.

First among these is the emergence of a European entity, constructed on the base of the European Community (EC), that will be a serious economic and political competitor. Already the EC is a larger market than the United States, its industries often more productive, and its standard of living at least comparable. In an earlier time the United States could, and often did, use Western Europe's military dependency as a lever to gain economic or political concessions. But beginning in the early 1980s, with the Soviet gas pipeline imbroglio, the Europeans made it clear that they would pursue their interests even where this risked straining relations with Washington. This focus on self-interest at the expense of Atlanticist pieties will inevitably increase after the creation of a single European market in 1992. Europe may speak in one voice, or perhaps in several, but its cues will not come from Washington.

Second, it is abundantly clear that European nationalism, at least in the East, is growing. Together, we and the Soviets imposed an unnatural calm upon Europe. People who had been at one another's throats for centuries lived together in peace, if not in harmony. Europe has been a tranquil place for the past 45 years, whether under democratic governments in the West or imposed communist dictatorships in the East. But the relaxation of central control in Eastern Europe and the removal of the fear of Soviet intervention have allowed long-suppressed resentments and ambitions to burst open. Deep-seated ethnic fevers have not abated in the East, and even national frontiers are once again being called into question. These fevers will be hard to confine to Eastern Europe. Indeed, as German unity proceeds, they could shake even the hitherto stable and pacific Federal Republic as it tries to absorb 16 million people who have lived for three generations under totalitarian systems. The "peaceful revolution" that shook Eastern Europe in the fall of 1989 could yet come to bear some resemblance to its forebear of two centuries earlier. We may come to look back with some nostalgia on these past decades as a time when Europe was stable.

Third among the problems posed by the waning of the Cold War is the reemergence of the German Question. Long confined to the realm of the hypothetical by the U.S.–Soviet competition and Europe's partition, it has once again become an active issue. The German Question was never re-solved, but merely repressed. It was always at the center of Europe's stage, like the rhinoceros in Ionesco's play that everyone walked around and pre-tended did not exist.

NATO was brought into being not only to deter a marauding Soviet bear, but to reassure the other Europeans that the Germans would be kept in place. The division of Germany was, in the eyes of most Europeans, the one happy result of World War II. Germany's postwar partners refrained from saying this openly, and gave lip service to the dream of unification so long as it seemed infinitely distant and unlikely. They learned to live quite comfortably with a democratic West Germany of roughly the same size and economic strength as Britain and France.

Just as Germany was crucial to NATO, so did the trans-Atlantic Alliance play an important part in dealing with the German issue. For the Americans, it offered a way of harnessing German industry and manpower in the struggle against the Soviet Union. For the Europeans, the presence of a large Amer-ican army on German soil gave reassurance against all potential aggressors. Thus, just as partition reduced German power and ultimately served to "con-tain" it, so did an American-dominated NATO keep Germany within an Atlantic framework tied to U.S. leadership.

The Germans, too, benefited from such an arrangement. They gained protection from the Soviets, U.S. economic assistance, reconciliation with their Western neighbors, sanction for rearmament, and leverage—on that distant day, from which their gaze never fully strayed, when the Soviet hold on East Germany loosened—for the ultimate unification of Germans under a common flag. Thus, in an apparent paradox, it was only by unflinching allegiance to the West and the incorporation of the Federal Republic into Western military and economic institutions that the ending of Germany's partition and her reconciliation with the East might one day be brought about.

That seemingly unattainable time has now come, and the long-dormant German Question is upon us. . . . We are witnessing the emergence of what was once called Mitteleuropa: an Eastern Europe dominated economically, culturally, and politically by the powerhouse of Germany.   Germany's interests, like its sense of identity, require it to look east as well as west, and in the East it has no serious economic or even political competition.   In a German-dominated Eastern Europe there would even be a special place for the Soviet Union, most likely as a workshop and source of raw materials. In its role as economic junior partner, or even apprentice, the USSR would, like any semi-developed country, benefit from German know-how and investment.   The Cold War relationship between these two countries would, in other words, be turned upside down; or, looking at it another way, they would return to their pre-1941 relationship.

This raises the question of whether it is possible to construct a Europe large enough to channel and dilute German power.   The EC, impressive though it is, lacks the weight.   A unified Germany will dominate the Community, encouraging separatists in Britain and elsewhere who are already wary of European integration.   In one sense the problem is not that Germany is too large, but that Europe is too small.   The reason for this is that it is divided and that the Soviets were, during the entire Cold War, written out of the equation as though the USSR were a non-European power.   But historically, culturally, and geographically it is a part of Europe.   More important, it is central to the creation of a viable European balance.

Cold War politics dictated that the only way the USSR could be brought back would involve opening the entire Continent to Soviet military dominance.   Such a fear has always been exaggerated, given the Soviet Union's economic backwardness and military caution.   But today the very notion seems fanciful.   The Soviet Union is a troubled, ethnically divided, semi-industrial country.   It needs association with Europe in order to emerge from its backwardness and pursue the democratic evolution of its political system.

A quarter-century ago de Gaulle envisaged a Europe extending "from the Atlantic to the Urals."   At that time, in the heyday of Atlanticism and of American expansionism, such a concept was deemed unrealistic and even anti-American.   But today . . . the notion of a Europe responsible for its own security and stability is more than appealing.   It is necessary.   It provides the best hope for avoiding the breakdown of the European idea into a congeries of contentious and jealous power groupings of the kind that have been so disastrous in Europe's past.   It also offers a framework for enveloping Germany in a structure it cannot dominate and that is not threatening to it.

For the United States, the challenges posed by an evolving and potentially volatile situation in the heart of Europe are clear.   The first is to keep Europe stable at a time when the Cold War blocs have become unraveled.   Second, the United States needs to maintain its influence on the Continent in a situation where the Western Europeans, less dependent on U.S. protection, are also less responsive to U.S. economic and political interests.   Third, the United

States must assist the liberalization of the Soviet Union in order to prevent its regression to Cold War militancy. The fourth challenge is to ensure that the evolving European balance will not become hostile to U.S. interests. Although the United States is not a European power, it is very much of Europe, and it has a crucial stake in the manner by which Europe emerges from the Cold War.

How these goals can be accomplished will involve considerable argument, shoving, and reordering of priorities, for an adjustment to new realities cuts to the heart of long-cherished assumptions and entrenched bureaucracies. In every area the most ruthless "new thinking" will be essential.

NATO

Here it will be impossible to carry on as before, even with sharply reduced U.S. forces on the Continent and the "devolution" of more responsibilities to the Europeans. The Alliance is simply worth far less than it used to be: both to Americans and to Europeans. An American troop presence is desirable in the short run to reassure both Europeans and Soviets that the old balance will not suddenly be overturned. It also serves as an instrument of American influence in Europe. But the purpose of the Alliance has to be redefined from primarily one of deterrence to that of mutual security.

In the long run, however (where long means two or three years), NATO is as doomed as the already . . . defunct Warsaw Pact. It is simply not possible to sustain an alliance such as NATO without an enemy such as the Soviet Union has been. We will have to stop thinking about how to reform NATO and start thinking about how to move beyond it. This means moving from a relationship of power and authority to one of equality and mutual dependency. This will not be an easy adjustment, especially for U.S. national security bureaucracies grown rich and fat on nearly a half-century of imperial management.

Eastern Europe

For all the justifiable euphoria that has greeted the downfall of Stalinist dictatorships in most of the region, the fact remains that the states of this region are, for the most part, without a democratic tradition or modern economy. Some are quite likely to revert to previous forms of militarism and authoritarianism. All will probably be plagued by unemployment, inequality, and the consequent social unrest. The states of this traditionally unstable region have been frozen in an authoritarian mold for at least four decades, and some for many more. They have been cut off from the forces of democratization and modernization that have transformed Western Europe. They have a long history of anarchy, ethnic violence, endemic hatreds, regional warfare, and authoritarianism. The fact that they have been liberated from communist dictators does not mean that they will be pacific or democratic. For the time being Eastern Europe is a no-man's-land, detached from Soviet control but not yet capable of being absorbed into the democratic West without dangers for all concerned. It needs to be put into a political quarantine while its fevers subside. The Soviets kept the peace in Eastern Europe, albeit at terrible human cost, for more than four decades. The region will not be stabilized easily now that Soviet, and even communist, control has been removed. Stabilization requires not only Western patience and firmness, but also the cooperation of Moscow. This means a return to some of the principles of great power peacekeeping that were enunciated in the World War II conferences at Yalta and Potsdam but ignored and then repudiated by the passions of the Cold War. Eastern Europe may well need some external force to keep the peace and prevent nationalism from destroying the emerging European union. Historically, this role has been played by Germany, but this has also posed problems of hegemony. For that reason it would be desirable to bring both the United States and the Soviet Union into the equation.

Western Europe

Although U.S. influence has been sharply reduced by the decline of the Soviet threat, it is not negligible. The Europeans continue to need the United States for balance: not only against the Soviets, but against each other, and particularly to counterbalance the ascending weight of the Germans. It is not in the interest of the Europeans to lock the United States out of the emerging new power balance, and they should be made aware of this. The U.S. role in Europe is not only to nurture and protect, but also to participate in the Continent's evolution. American policy should be directed toward keeping the EC open, not only to U.S. trade and investment, but also to Eastern Europe and the Soviet Union. Within the framework of a wider European community open to the East lies the possibility for bringing an evolved Soviet Union into a continental balance.

Germany

The Cold War began with Germany, and it is ending with Germany. Because the World War II allies could not agree on the political orientation of Germany, along with that of Eastern Europe, they partitioned the former reich and built fortresslike spheres of influence on either side of it. The unification of Germany marks not only the end of the Cold War, but the expulsion of both America and the Soviet Union from the positions of power they have occupied for more than four decades. Confronted with a resurgent Germany that seems likely to dominate the Continent, they seek to maintain their privileges and, more important, some measure of control of a renascent great power capable of challenging them both. . . . [Germany] will not consent to be occupied by foreign armies, and in short order both the Americans and the Soviets will be sent home.   To try to contain a unified Germany through NATO is like trying to contain Bismarck through the Congress of Vienna. The framework is outdated and functionally meaningless.   If Germany is to be "contained," that must be accomplished through a political, economic, and even military structure of which it is a determinant part.   This means a wider European security order that would supersede the outdated Cold War alliances and would include the two declining superpowers, America and the USSR.

Soviet Union

If the Cold War was the confrontation between the United States and the USSR, the post–Cold War period will be marked by their guarded cooperation in pursuit of common interests.   It will mean, in effect, a return to the logic of the World War II alliance, into which Washington and Moscow were forced because they faced a greater threat to their interests.   During the 40 years of the Cold War they defined the world as being divided between them. That definition was never accurate, and now it has no meaning at all.   Other challengers are rising—Japan, Germany, a unifying (or perhaps splintering) Europe—and more will follow.   The Soviets need the United States to keep Europe calm, to restrain a revived Germany, and to prevent the creation of an anti-Soviet alliance that would threaten their existence.   But the United States also needs a cohesive Soviet Union that does not itself become a "power vacuum" sucking in foreign intervention.   It is not in our interest that the Soviet state collapse into a congeries of bitterly feuding ministates organized around ancient ethnic hatreds.   American security requires not anarchy and violence, but stability and calm in Eastern Europe.   This means the maintenance of a power in the East to flank and to balance the turbulent forces of nationalism now roiling what was once the Soviet Empire.

The balance of power is not an outdated concept. . . . Just as the Soviets have begun to realize that we are not so much the "enemy" as we are a potential partner in a quest for security that has assumed very different forms than it took during the Cold War, so we must readjust our thinking.   Instead of devoting our energies to devising ways of weakening and disrupting the Soviet Union, we will, because of the radical changes in the world power structure that have become unavoidable, grow increasingly preoccupied with efforts to strengthen and stabilize our former nemesis.   We will, that is, have to start thinking about the Soviet Union the way we did about Germany and Japan once World War II was over and a new challenge to our interests began to emerge.

The focal point of the U.S.–Soviet competition has been Europe, and it is concern over the future of Europe that must force the United States and the USSR into at least a tacit cooperation.   The United States does not need, and cannot expect, a compliant Europe.   But it does require a stable one, as do the Soviets.   We should use our waning authority over our European allies to attain this objective. We cannot lackadaisically assume that the Europeans will work things out among themselves. They have not done so well at this in the past. Nor can we assume that whatever the Europeans— or the strongest powers in Europe—decide will be in our interests as well as theirs. We shall have to play as active a role in the coming European set- tlement as we played in building a Western European Cold War bloc. We have interests in Europe, for Europe, and in some cases against Europe. To say merely that we want a strong, unified Europe is simplistic and even possibly self-defeating. We need a Europe that is peaceful, prosperous, open to trade and investment, and a menace neither to itself nor to others. We need, as do the Soviets, a Europe that will not return to its patterns of ethnic violence, revanchism, and civil war.

We are witnessing today in Europe a return to history: a return to ethnicity, to nationalism, to self-determination, to the struggle for influence and power. Such goals in the past have not always led to tranquility. They may not do so now unless the Europeans show restraint, unless a workable power balance is established, and unless the United States recognizes and acts upon its interests in the coming European settlement. This is an astonishing moment in European history, one comparable to that of the eruption of the great forces in 1848. Whether it leads, as earlier revolutions have, to disillusion and reaction or to a freer and more peaceful Continent depends to a significant degree on our own ability to readjust our ways of thinking, discard obsolete relationships and ideological blinkers, embrace new opportunities, and act upon a wider and more imaginative concept of our interests. To say that the Cold War is over is simply to express a cliché; to act upon it unsenti- mentally and in response to the new forces of change will require that rarest of qualities: statesmanship.

14 AMERICAN NATIONAL INTEREST AND THE NEW EUROPE: THE MILLENNIUM HAS NOT YET ARRIVED

David Calleo

Future relations between America and Europe will depend heavily on how the overall global situation evolves and what general geopolitical roles and strategies the United States and the Europeans choose to pursue. The global situation has remained essentially static for so long, and national strategies have remained so constant, that this truism about the interdependence of regional and global policy is perhaps harder to grasp than it ought to be. Throughout the long postwar period, with its bipolar global dispensation, America's commitment to European defense was never seriously in question, nor was Europe's desire for it. And both were firmly committed to the liberal world political economy of the Pax Americana. It was this harmony of transatlantic interest that made the postwar global system possible. Thanks to the transatlantic alliance, a Eurasian balance contained the Soviets on their own home ground and left the United States the predominant power throughout the rest of the globe. Today, in the last decade of the twentieth century, the Soviets have rapidly abandoned the Cold War, retreated from Central Europe, and embarked on profound if uncertain reforms to democratize their politics, liberalize their economy, and federalize the remainder of their empire. In effect, the bipolar global dispensation has collapsed.

A NEW WORLD ORDER

So complete a Western victory threatens to destabilize many habitual relationships, the transatlantic alliance among them. The destabilization has been, first of all, intellectual. The Cold War provided a simplistic but highly serviceable way to view the problem of order in the world. It focused American efforts on building the military forces to deter Soviet aggression, and the military, political, and economic coalitions needed to contain Soviet ambitions.

For our West European allies, America's anti-Soviet preoccupation was preferable in many respects to the diffuse and relatively unlimited American aims of the wartime period. President Franklin D. Roosevelt and Secretary of State Cordell Hull had dreamed of a global system of free trade, where Europe's old colonies would become liberal democracies, Germany and Japan would be severely punished, and the United States, together with its Western allies and the Soviets and Chinese, would use the United Nations Security Council to enforce collective security against "aggression." This early vision of the American century elicited grave reservations in Western Europe. The British and French, as well as the Soviet government, felt threatened by the overwhelming military and economic power of a United States beginning to enjoy its hegemonic destiny.

Stalin asserted dreams of his own and brutally imposed Soviet predominance in Eastern Europe. By allying with a newly communist China, he appeared to have cemented a vast Eurasian bloc, an "evil empire" that was, potentially at least, a global challenger to the Pax Americana. It was certainly a real enough threat to Western Europe. But the resulting Cold War had advantages from a West European perspective. It restrained America's universalistic pretensions within the more manageable goal of containing the Soviet challenge. Building a grand anti-Soviet alliance inclined the United States into a series of compromises with European and Japanese aspirations. Out of this came the Marshall Plan and Germany's rearmament, as well as America's support for Japan's resurrection, and the European Economic Community. As the United States contested Soviet influence in the Third World, anticommunism modified anticolonialism and aid supplemented free trade.

In some respects, the Cold War probably limited interstate conflict. A Europe clearly divided into two blocs, both heavily armed with nuclear and conventional forces, made a new European war extremely improbable. Dividing the Third World into U.S. and Soviet clients gave a much-needed definition to relations among the bewildering crowd of uncertain states emerging from the old European empires. The two superpowers, mesmerized by their nuclear balance of terror, drew back from direct confrontations with each other and tried to restrain their respective clients from challenging what were perceived as the vital interests of the other. After Korea at least, wars in the Third World were mostly instigated by local clients for their own purposes, as in Arab-Israeli clashes, or resulted from a superpower's miscalculation of the strength and determination of indigenous, nationalist forces, as in Vietnam or Afghanistan. While it seems perverse to wax enthusiastic over the benefits of an order that brought so much oppression, and wasted such huge resources on armaments, the Cold War's restraints were certainly preferable to the violent military conflicts and economic convulsions of the twentieth century's first half.

The sudden end of the Soviet "threat" now requires a redefinition of the fears, ambitions, and policies of both the Americans and the Europeans. The nature of the future world order will very much depend on the degree to which those redefinitions are harmonious with each other. For the United States, one immediate tendency is to turn back the intellectual clock to the more universalistic aspirations of the wartime era. Without the Soviet threat to provide focus and discipline, America's global mission can once more be defined as stopping "aggression" in general. The ever-serviceable Munich analogy can become a sort of intellectual hair trigger, ready to invoke retribution at any use of force to settle grievances against the status quo.

This tendency is encouraged by America's present exceptionally high degree of military readiness. The Soviet retreat, following the great Reagan military buildup, leaves the United States with a relatively high capacity to impose its will through superior military force. Gorbachev's retreat, leaving the United States the lone superpower, entices us into the role of world police, perhaps even more than did Stalin's relentless probing.

In a world full of thwarted national aspirations, unsettled grievances, artificial boundaries, and reckless dictators, the risks of such a police role are considerable. Becoming a sort of global Metternich seems a formula destined to alienate a good part of the world, Europe included, and exhaust ourselves in the process. Avoiding such risks will presumably require a world vision more receptive of change, more discriminating about defining and protecting American interests, and more alert to the possibilities for using the initiatives of others.

If the sudden Soviet retreat has greatly confused America's geopolitical strategy, it has revolutionized the perspectives of the Europeans. For a start, America's geopolitical weight in Europe is now considerably depreciated. So long as the formidable Soviet army was deployed in the middle of Germany, a Western Europe that wished to preserve its independence and prosperity urgently needed the Atlantic alliance. Today's Soviet Union may possibly remain a military colossus, but it has a very different posture in relation to its West European neighbors. These neighbors now begin to look on the Soviet Union, with its vast undeveloped resources and hunger for consumer goods, more as a target of economic and political opportunity than as a military threat. America's military and political role in Europe is thus devalued from being the almost indispensable protector against an urgent danger to being a prudent insurance policy against a remote contingency.

Toward Global Pluralism

While the Soviet Union's sudden retreat has brought the need for new American and European roles and strategies to a head, the need has, in fact, been long anticipated. The trend away from a bipolar world has been a longstanding one.   Signs of a more plural distribution of economic prowess and political vitality have been abundant in recent years.   Japan's spectacular industrial and financial development has been followed by the rise of highly competitive manufacturing in other Asian countries, not too long ago classified as underdeveloped.   This has had profound implications for American and European economies.   Revolutions in every postwar decade—from Algeria in the 1950s to Iran in the 1970s—have also made manifest the dynamic energy and the unstable structures of postwar Moslem civilization.   Iraq's assault on Kuwait challenged not only the regimes and economic relationships but the state system itself left over from the era of Western domination.

Over the past decade, Europe has produced perhaps the most beneficent signs of pluralist vitality.   Progress toward a more integrated West European Community has taken several significant steps, among them the European Monetary System and the Single European Act.   The Soviet Union's retreat has brought Germany's peaceful unification and Central Europe's return to its traditional Western orientation.   Even the less developed Balkan states are being drawn into Europe.   At the same time, the halting Soviet progress toward a liberal economy and democratic federation presents Europe with huge long-term economic prospects.   The political dangers are obvious, but so is the enormous promise.

Any trend toward a more plural world implies a concomitant relative "decline" of the superpowers.   For the United States at least, this relative decline is not in itself undesirable.   That Europe is richer and stronger in relation to the United States than in 1950 or 1960 is hardly surprising and can be attributed in good part to the success of deliberate American policies. The same might be said of the rise of Japan or other rapidly developing Asian states.   But relative decline can also become absolute and pathological—a weakening of the springs of national strength.   For the superpowers, the principal cause for this absolute kind of decline is not the rise of others but their own inappropriate policies.   In a world growing more plural, superpowers trying to continue their traditional roles without adapting to the new circumstances risk overstretching their resources to the point where they do real harm to their own long-term national prospects.

It seems self-evident that the Soviet Union has been its own worst enemy. Many analysts suspect that the United States is on a similar course.   The most obvious evidence of America's overstretching lies in its twin deficits— fiscal and external—that must be largely financed by capital borrowed from abroad or inflation.   These chronic deficits have now endured well over a decade, going back to the unbalanced fiscal policies and unsound financial practices of the 1970s and before.   Behind these accumulated problems lies an erratic contest for priority between military and civilian aims, resolved too frequently by a resort to easy money that the dollar's international position has made too possible.

These practices have increasingly damaged the American economy's long-term prospects.   The litany of weaknesses has grown familiar.   The federal government now struggles with an exceptionally high level of debt service that progressively constrains its resources. Neglect of the country's physical infrastructure, education, and health needs over several years continues to weaken the economy's productive base. So does crime, drug addiction, and a swelling underclass. Excessive credit creation, often to offset fiscal short-falls, has discouraged saving and encouraged a dangerous level of debt among firms and too much speculative investment in general. Thanks to the consequences of macroeconomic malpractice, the American economy now has a high propensity for inflation that needs to be repressed by periodic bouts of savagely tight monetary policy. This stop-go policy, coupled with the sharply oscillating exchange rates that are one of its consequences, discourages long-term investment. Low and misdirected investment saps the growth of productivity needed to keep American industry competitive at home or abroad. High debt, low savings, and the regular urgent need to borrow from abroad all greatly constrain the flexibility of macroeconomic policy in the face of future recessions; at the same time, the high level of public and private debt makes any deep recession dangerous for financial stability. Conditions of this kind make the United States increasingly unattractive for foreign investors; at the same time, it has grown highly dependent on a regular inflow of foreign capital to finance its swelling debt. Under these circumstances, the United States is not only unable to participate actively in recapitalizing Central and Eastern Europe but must fear the diversion of European capital away from financing American debt.

In short, the retreat and apparent collapse of Soviet power is not the unequivocal American victory that might have been expected. The United States itself manifests too many characteristics of national decline for comfort. Soviet decline has to be counted, then, as less a sign of American triumph than of a more plural world in general. The problem for the United States is how to foster a new order out of those plural elements, while avoiding a fate for itself similar to that of the Soviets.

Keeping the Peace

America's economic improvement and geopolitical redesign are, of course, closely interdependent. The Soviet retreat seemed to offer the United States some fiscal relief through cuts in military spending, but the Persian Gulf crisis that erupted in the summer of 1990 made clear that any such relief will prove ephemeral without basic changes in American geopolitical strategy.

The Persian Gulf crisis demonstrated rather clearly what seems to be the basic characteristics of the new post–Cold War order. At the outset, the United States was unable to deploy a vast force without fear of Soviet reaction. On the contrary, the Soviet Union voted in the United Nations Security Council to legitimize the presence of the American forces and to impose severe economic sanctions on Iraq. The Soviets even hinted that they might supply forces to a collective peacekeeping effort under United Nations command.   The old dream of cooperation between the superpowers to impose world order suddenly revived.   But while the Soviets undoubtedly have large military forces, their political and economic disarray made it unlikely that they would or could deploy them, let alone risk a lengthy campaign.   Their large and restless Moslem population and the recent disaster in Afghanistan make them leery of any superpower combination smacking of traditional great-power imperialism against the Moslem world.   All these constraints suggest that even with Soviet goodwill, superpower condominium is an improbable organizing principle in the more plural system that is emerging.

As it happens, the bulk of non-American forces to counter Iraq had to come from Britain and France or from certain states of the region—principally Egypt, Saudi Arabia, and Syria.   The entire, slow unfolding of the crisis demonstrated the difficulties of combining pluralistic peacekeeping with traditional American hegemony.

Caught unprepared for this particular crisis, the American military proceeded to deploy its huge forces according to an operational plan originally drawn up to counter a massive Soviet or Iranian invasion of the entire Persian Gulf area.   Military decisions also seemed to reflect putative lessons from the Vietnam War.   Since gradual escalation did not work there, it is said, overwhelming force had to be applied in the Persian Gulf from the very outset.

At the same time, the limits to American means were made vivid by the spectacle of the American secretary of state and the secretary of the treasury traveling around the world raising funds to defray the military costs.   Through the broad support marshaled around the world for the Persian Gulf intervention could also be seen a continuing diffidence toward a unilateral American military role.

Political conditions seem unusually propitious for developing a concert of powers to maintain order against the more flagrant and brutal forms of aggression, at least in places critical to the collective national interests of Americans, Europeans, Japanese, and Soviets.   The United States, however, is inhibited from genuinely pursuing a coalition strategy because it believes that timely and decisive military action requires preemptive American leadership and initiative.   At the same time, whatever the practical difficulties of collective peacekeeping, the costs and dangers make it unlikely that the United States will sustain a unilateral policy for very long.   Moreover, the United States acting unilaterally risks putting itself in the position of the world's principal reactionary power, the great enemy of all the forces around the globe urgently pressing for change.   It remains to be seen whether the lesson can be grasped in advance or has to be learned through painful and costly experience.

However the lesson is learned, and whatever the final consequences of the intervention in the Persian Gulf, America is in no position to return to its hegemonic dreams of 1945.   Financially, the United States has grown dependent on the inflow of foreign capital and can reduce its dependency only by reducing its fiscal deficit—a difficult course quite incompatible with sustaining its present military establishment, let alone transforming it into a world police force. In fact, the United States is unlikely to follow such an ambitious geopolitical course, if for no other reason than that the American public is unlikely to support it through any prolonged test of strength, and properly so. America's global problem, then, is how to build an effective concert. While the United States undoubtedly still has the leading role in building the new machinery, Europe, as during the Cold War, remains the partner needed for success. Western Europe is still the principal region in the world, and in some respects the only one, that combines economic, financial, and military power on anything like the American scale. Whether the transatlantic partnership endures obviously depends on how Europeans, as well as Americans, assess its value in the more plural world now emerging. That assessment depends at least partly on how well the partnership adapts its inner arrangements to fit the new world.

NEW EUROPEAN PERSPECTIVES

Throughout the Cold War, the Atlantic alliance ensured Europe's independence as well as America's global predominance. On balance, Europeans had good reason to find the terms favorable. With the Soviet Union's retreat, Europe is unlikely to feel the same urgent need for the American alliance; the transatlantic relationship is thus fated to change its character. But both the West European states and the United States will continue to have vital interests in each other. They share profound cultural ties, and they remain the only parts of the world where liberal political and economic traditions are deeply implanted and reliably practiced. But the new European scene, transformed by the Soviet retreat, now has different threats and different opportunities for both European and American policy.

The principal common threat is that the recent changes in Europe will prove too great for either the European or the international system to contain. The worst danger might come from the disintegration of the Soviet Union itself. While a genuinely federated Soviet Union, with its elements open and liberal, ought to prove a great boon for Europe, a Soviet Union that breaks up in domestic chaos and internecine conflict could easily bring Europe closer to war than it ever was during the Cold War. No one can say how Gorbachev's grand experiment will evolve. But the extremely pessimistic expectations for his economic reforms, widespread among the experts, do not permit any facile optimism about the stability of the Soviet Union, the longevity of its nascent democracy, or even its current friendly posture toward its Western neighbors. In any event, whatever regime evolves will remain a military giant. Europe's political safety will require that Soviet military power be balanced in some effective fashion.

The Soviet Union is obviously not the only potential source of instability.

Those Central and East European states now free of Soviet tutelage will have enormous difficulty transforming their economies rapidly enough to relieve the long frustrated expectations of their populations.

While Eastern and Central Europe have been struggling with their new freedom, the nascent West European confederacy has been riding a wave of optimism about its own prospects. But troubles in Central and Eastern Europe can easily cause dissension among the West European states and blight those prospects. The most critical issue for West European solidarity will be what happens within united Germany. West Germany was the great anchor of Western Europe's liberal prosperity and democratic stability. Together with France, the Federal Republic led the European Community throughout its history. But absorbing the old German Democratic Republic now presents the Federal Republic with a challenge that can be expected to absorb a good part of its energy and wealth for a generation. Under the circumstances, Germany's traditional role in the European Community can hardly be taken for granted. Germany is more important for Europe than ever, but its policies will be less stable and predictable, and it will have far fewer resources for resolving other people's problems.

German unification also poses a challenge to the rest of the European Community, France in particular. The threat of German hegemony dominated French policy in the time of the Third and Fourth Republics. Under the Fifth Republic, a more robust and confident France shifted from a policy of hostile containment to one of intimate partnership with Germany. This change was possible partly because the French felt themselves stronger. Even if former West Germany was somewhat richer and more populous, France's economic performance was impressive. Whatever economic disparity existed seldom seemed great enough to make the partnership seriously unbalanced and uncomfortable. France's superior status as an independent nuclear power with considerable global outreach, bolstered by the exceptionally creative elan of French diplomacy, seemed to more than compensate for any economic gap. In recent years, moreover, the French economy has grown even stronger. The French have restructured many of their leading industries and brought their inflation rate slightly below Germany's.

The united Germany undoubtedly affects this Franco-German balance, but calculating the effect is not easy. For the near future, absorbing the east will more likely weaken Germany's economic weight than strengthen it. For the German government's finances, East Germany will be a heavy liability well into the future. For private firms, the economic possibilities in the east are nearly all long term at best. French firms, of course, have not been inactive in looking over the more lucrative possibilities. Insofar as German firms are under greater constraint to invest in eastern enterprises generally, it may not prove an advantage to them. In the long run, the real value of acquiring several million well-educated and presumably hard-working and ambitious citizens should not be underestimated. But the short-term economic costs may be very high.

Politically, the new Germany is even more elusive. Historically, the Germans—east, west, south, and north—have not got on particularly well with each other. Prussian domination was much resented in the old Reich, and the return of even a radically truncated eastern region is not welcomed as an unmixed blessing, even now. But the former West German political system has deep resources of tolerance and balance, and underneath its partisan waves flows a stable current of common sense. Still, Germans and their neighbors can hardly be blamed for some apprehension.

So far, the principal common reaction among the West Europeans has been to press forward more frantically with plans for tightening integration within the European Community (EC). This merely reinforces a trend well under way before the Soviet retreat united Germany and opened up Eastern Europe. The Single European Act of 1986 had already committed EC states to major new steps toward monetary union and general economic and political integration. Logically, however, Europe's new situation just as easily favors delaying as speeding up any "deepening" of the community. A disparate crowd of eastern states is now desperately eager to adhere to the West. Complicating matters further, Austria, Sweden, Switzerland, and Turkey would also like to join the community. Faced with this situation, the EC is trying to deepen and widen simultaneously. But the declared priority has so far seemed to go to deepening. The prevailing theory has been that only by intensifying its Western core can the EC have enough inner strength to reach out and eventually incorporate the east. This has been preeminently the French view; and the Germans, eager to reassure their Western neighbors, and perhaps themselves, have been at pains to cater to it.

It is not clear how long this priority will prevail. From the start, the British, never enthusiastic about a Europe bound tightly together, have openly argued that the community should forbear its internal tightening in order to incorporate the Central and East European states. The British position has a certain obvious logic, and its appeal has been growing. On balance, it seems probable that the community will strengthen its integrating structures somewhat, but not as much as many had hoped.

Institutional progress within the EC in recent years, combined with fear of the destabilizing effects of the Soviet retreat, has promoted a revival of the old dream of a federal community whose structures will somehow replace the nation-states. That dream is likely to remain as great an illusion in the near future as it has been in the past. The community is not a centralized state, nor does it seem about to become one. But by a more practical standard, the EC is an extraordinary success. Its success derives from the working balance it has achieved between national self-determination and collective needs. Its real progress has depended on Europe's national governments, elites, and publics developing an extended sense of self-interest in building a regional system. Building this system has not made Europe's nation-states disappear into a new superstate. The old states remain the ultimate centers of political legitimacy and administrative authority, but they have developed among themselves remarkable openness and cooperation, kept functioning by a structure that provides for constant negotiating among the governments and bureaucracies. The success of the EC thus stems from its practical machinery for negotiating and harmonizing national interests. In the process, a considerable degree of common European feeling has most certainly grown up among both elites and the public at large. But this European feeling is not so much a diminishing of national loyalty as an extension of it.

In effect, Western Europe has not been creating a new superpower on the American model but a new political form whose constitution embodies a balance between national and collective interests and identities. It has grown into a working constitution for much of the European continent. As a continental constitution, it is highly flexible, and for that reason more robust than it seems. It may prove ideal for absorbing the intense pressure in Europe to accommodate so many new forces. In the long run, it may prove better able to regulate the affairs of a whole continent than the more rigidly centralized national structures of the earlier continental systems, the United States and the Soviet Union. Certainly the troubles of the Soviet Union make evident its structural limitations. Unfortunately, the growing problems of governing the United States also suggest the limitations of a federal as opposed to a multinational continental system.

Whatever its advantages, a confederal system will not hold together unless its states have reached a certain acceptable equilibrium of power among themselves. Germany's unification will inevitably encourage tentative new alignments within the community. The anti-German France of the Fourth Republic can be expected to revive sufficiently to look with new interest on relations with its old allies—Britain, "Latin Europe," or Eastern Europe, including the Soviet Union itself. Heavy North African emigration will continue to remind the French not to ignore their Mediterranean neighbors. The Italians, too, have a Mediterranean preoccupation, but also historical ties to German Mitteleuropa; they have begun to promote a revived "Habsburg Europe"—to forge the states of the old empire into a cooperative bloc within the new enlarged Europe.

These sorts of constructions are no substitute for the European Community. But insofar as they develop, they will inevitably make for a different EC, with different alignments and centers of initiative. But whatever the new stresses and strains within the EC, it presents what is, by far, the most hopeful and attractive vision of how the new Europe should develop. West Europeans are not at all likely to throw away the immense political and economic capital they have invested and developed within it.

For many obvious reasons, Europe will have a tendency to grow more inward-looking over the next few difficult years. But Europe's interdependence and vulnerability will not permit it to ignore the rapid changes and increasing troubles around it. The troubles of a more plural world should reinforce the impulse for European states to formulate compatible and concerted foreign and defense policies. This will require new institutional structures—logically in the EC framework but perhaps more probably in a format with more restricted formal membership and less cumbersome procedures. Depending on American policy, a troubled world should also prove a strong incentive for Europeans to maintain the transatlantic alliance.

AMERICA AND THE NEW EUROPE

As the European states struggle toward a broader unity and a new equilibrium among themselves, what should be the European role of the United States? Within the political-economic structures of the European Community, the United States remains a privileged outsider. Over the years, U.S. efforts to make a place for itself inside the structures of the European Community have been contentious but unsuccessful. So long as the EC is primarily an economic coalition, these efforts are not likely to succeed in any serious way. Inevitably, the United States is seen not only as a political ally but as a major economic rival. Given the great diversity and conflicting interests within the EC already, admitting the Americans inside the community is bound to seem a formula to paralyze the already too cumbersome bargaining process. If the larger U.S. interest lies with a stable order for the new Europe, acquiring a stronger bargaining position over trade issues at the expense of weakening the community's structures and solidarity makes for a bad exchange.

American trade interests, however, have an important political significance. The United States is inclined to blame its huge and chronic trade deficit on the mercantilistic protectionism of its allies. Disputes with the EC have been long and bitter. But American trade with Europe has, in fact, improved sharply in recent years. The heavy growth in demand likely to follow from German unification and Central and Eastern Europe's liberalization should improve the American position still further. At the same time, traditional American goals, like an end to European agricultural or aircraft subsidies, are less likely than ever to be met. With all their other concerns, Europeans will not cut back their agricultural sector any more rapidly than they have been doing. Nor are they going to abandon subsidies to high technology. Moreover, a real trade war might well harm the overall American trade position much more than Europe's.

In any event, the real problem with U.S. trade lies in the accumulating imbalances and malformations of the domestic economy. The tendency to substitute advocacy of international trade reform for internal structural and macroeconomic reform is a dangerous evasion, likely to embitter our diplomatic relations without improving our trade. It seems particularly unjustified in U.S.-EC trade relations.

The Future of NATO

Even though the Cold War seems near its end, the United States has a natural tendency to try to preserve its North Atlantic Treaty Organization (NATO) hegemony—both because the new Europe still needs some kind of security structure and because NATO remains the principal way that the United States has institutionalized its role as a European power.

Hanging onto the traditional NATO role is not, however, a good long-term strategy. NATO was formed to counter an urgent Soviet military threat. Negotiations have now institutionalized the Soviet military retreat. While there are still relatively few in Europe who would deny the legitimacy or usefulness of some American role in European defense, the traditional overweening hegemony of the United States in NATO begins to seem inappropriate and even oppressive. And to Americans, moreover, the huge cost of the NATO deployment—roughly half the defense budget in recent decades—also seems increasingly anomalous and insupportable. Even without arms control negotiations, America's fiscal problems will almost certainly lead to drastic cuts in U.S. forces in Europe. What then happens to America's hegemonic role in NATO?

Basically, there are two ways to resolve the issue: one is to scrap NATO and find some new way for the United States to participate in European security arrangements. The other is to reform NATO in some fashion that preserves its usefulness, along with an acceptable American role. Those who advocate ending NATO generally propose folding it into a pan-European security structure in which the United States participates. Thus, some analysts want the apparatus of the Conference on Security and Cooperation in Europe (CSCE) to evolve into a "security community" that would include the United States, but dissolve the old alliance blocs completely. Those who propose keeping NATO tend to want to either transform it into a more European organization with a lesser American role or expand its scope to global concerns that would freshly legitimize the old American role. Each solution has problems.

Scrapping NATO seems unwise so long as the Soviet Union remains a military superpower. While the major European NATO states bound together in alliance could make a reasonable military and political counterweight to Soviet power, a structure that dissolves NATO without creating at least a West European substitute would not be a very strong guardian for Europe's long-term security. This is not to deny the usefulness of some general pan-European security organization. A more structured form of CSCE could monitor Europe's security balance and negotiate the periodic adjustments needed. It might also conceivably give legitimacy and direction to some collective force to preserve order within Europe itself.

A collective structure without a Western bloc could not, however, give stable resolution to Europe's major security problem—the military imbalance between the Soviets and the individual states of Western Europe. Disturbing political-economic events in Eastern Europe would probably provoke the major Western states to rearm. Serious German rearmament on a national rather than bloc basis would logically include nuclear forces. Preserving the Western military bloc as an integral part of the structure of European security from the very start seems a more prudent long-term strategy.

Continuing Soviet military potential makes it unwise to scrap NATO entirely, but with the Soviet threat now much more remote, should the Atlantic alliance be restructured to preserve both an American military presence and a European consensus on security? Two solutions jostle for attention. The Persian Gulf crisis and ensuing war revived the old idea of changing NATO's focus from European to global security—a move that would presumably restore a range of threats great enough to justify America's traditional hegemonic role, even if the United States no longer maintains a huge European army.

The idea has been discussed since the beginning of the alliance but never got anywhere. European and American interests in other parts of the world, while often parallel, have not seemed sufficiently convergent to justify an alliance so closely structured and hegemonically organized as NATO. Some serious differences have surfaced over the years, principally in the Middle East, where many European governments have found the United States too tied to Israel, but also in Southeast Asia and even Central America.

Americans, too, have been diffident. A global NATO would tend to limit U.S. global policies to suit the European allies. Such a commitment risks paralyzing American global policy, and the United States seems far from ready for it, as the Persian Gulf crisis made quite clear.

Such complications suggest the danger of trying to refocus NATO on any global agenda. The United States and Europe share a deep common interest in maintaining a military balance within Europe itself. Straying beyond this common purpose seems less likely to strengthen the alliance than break it up. Countries like Germany, if pressured by NATO to join global policies that have little public support, will soon generate powerful opposition to the alliance itself. European powers disposed to join the United States in global peacekeeping, like Britain or France, can do so outside NATO and can tailor their collaboration to the degree of consensus between their aims and American ones.

If enlarging NATO's scope seems a dubious way to preserve it, what about a Europeanized NATO? In its more extreme version, the Americans would withdraw and some kind of European institution would replace NATO entirely—a military dimension to the European Community or a drastically rejuvenated West European Union. At present, such a course seems too radical for European governments—partly because they are not used to the idea, but more fundamentally because a continuing American presence seems good insurance against a Soviet or nationalist German military revival.

The basic outline of arrangements to shift primary responsibility to the Europeans is not so difficult to imagine. Over time, the United States should withdraw all but one or two divisions. But more difficult questions follow. With the U.S. contribution limited, and Europe's standing armies and reserves providing the bulk of NATO's forces, the United States cannot expect the same leading role in the command structure. But can the American forces remaining in Europe be expected to serve under foreign commanders?

In recent years, the American military has been notably opposed to serving under any direction but its own. This is an increasingly dysfunctional view. To say that U.S. military forces can never serve under foreign commanders effectively limits U.S. military deployments to situations in which they will be the principal force. It deliberately renounces a good part of our potential diplomatic influence and military strength in the plural world that is fast coming upon us. It discourages genuine multinational military forces and handicaps any sharing of military labor among a concert of powers. It will prove particularly discouraging for efforts at global peacekeeping. For the American military to hold fast to such a position under all circumstances suggests a deficient understanding of the relationship of military force to political power. It seems a serious intellectual and doctrinal deficiency at odds with the national interest.

Within NATO, however, the nuclear question greatly complicates the problem of a non-American commander. Traditionally, the United States has been unwilling to station ground forces in Europe unless accompanied by short- and intermediate-range nuclear weapons—first, because the conventional balance in the region always seemed to favor the Soviets; second, because the Soviets themselves deployed such weapons. For obvious reasons, the United States has insisted on controlling the use of American nuclear weapons, even when they were deployed among allied forces. With a European SACEUR [Supreme Allied Commander Europe], what happens to the chain of command between the [U.S.] president and [U.S.] nuclear weapons?

To raise these questions is not to assume that they can never be answered. Before the Soviet retreat, nuclear weapons were needed to compensate for an overweening Soviet conventional superiority that posed, in itself, an urgent threat. Europe's new arms control regime will severely limit Soviet capacity for any westward attack before a long and obvious buildup of forces. Under these circumstances, the need for deploying short- and intermediate-range nuclear weapons has to be reconsidered. The Germans, on whose soil the bulk of these weapons are deployed, will certainly do so.

Some longer-range American "theater" systems, capable of striking the Soviet Union, will no doubt continue to be a welcome contribution to Europe's "strategic" nuclear deterrence. But these systems could remain under American command. It is no longer clear, in any case, why NATO's collective deterrent needs to be provided so exclusively by the Americans. Now that both the British and French are rapidly acquiring major strategic deterrents of their own, they can assume a more prominent role in Europe's general strategic defense.

Problems of nuclear control are obviously complex and cannot be resolved without prolonged reflection and negotiation. But with an entirely different European military balance in prospect, they do not form the same intractable impediment to a more European NATO as during the Cold War. In short, both military and geopolitical factors favor a more European NATO. If the old alliance is to be saved, this is probably the only way to do it.

Europe without America?

America has a primordial interest in keeping Europe from again becoming a major breeding ground for war. Confederal cooperation seems the best bulwark against European destabilization, but the United States also fears being excluded from the new Europe. Intensifying European cooperation sometimes enhances that fear. Europe is not only America's closest military and political ally, but also America's principal commercial rival. A "European space" that encompasses Scandinavia, the old Soviet sphere in Eastern Europe, and the southern Mediterranean countries poses economic threats as well as opportunities for the United States. Over the longer term, a newly opened Soviet Union is itself a prime candidate for incorporation into a Eurocentric bloc. With vast natural resources and great appetite for capital and consumer goods, a transforming Soviet Union offers tremendous opportunities to its rich Western neighbors. The danger that a Soviet Union whose economy does not develop rapidly risks being destabilized politically, and returning to its old ways or worse, constitutes a further incentive for Europe to reach out to the Soviets, politically as well as commercially.

Disquiet over this potential new alignment is already visible in fears that the Germans, ransoming their eastern half with economic blandishments, will be drawn too deeply into Eastern Europe, at the expense of their old links to the West. Other Western countries, such as France, Britain, or Italy, might also feel compelled to compete with the Germans for Soviet favors. The Japanese could hardly remain indifferent to such developments. In due course, a Russo-Japanese rapprochement would imply a further isolation of the United States. In the end, a vast Eurasian bloc might emerge. The end of the Cold War, in effect, might usher in the end of the American century.

Given the current economic disarray of Eastern Europe and the Soviet Union particularly, such fears seem highly exaggerated. Over the longer term, however, they should not be ignored. The real issue is the appropriate strategy for addressing them. Trying to hang onto America's traditional military predominance over Western Europe is one familiar strategy: thus the impulse to make NATO into a globally oriented alliance. Another is to oppose vociferously the European Community's "inward looking tendencies" or its reaching out to incorporate its neighbors. Another is to cultivate our own special relationship with the Soviets, perhaps around the old Cold War dream of a global condominium. Yet another is to reinforce the Cold War special relationship with Germany.

The United States can be expected to explore all of these impulses over the coming years. Each will have its appeal, but also its limits. Turning NATO into a global alliance run by the United States will not deflect Europeans from recognizing their own distinctive interests in the Third World. If the United States pushes too hard, it may well accelerate the process of transatlantic estrangement.

As for Soviet-American condominium, while the Soviets will certainly want to maintain good relations with the Americans, they are not likely to be drawn into a policy that estranges them from the Europeans. It is the Europeans who can offer most of what the Soviets need. The brutal truth is that the United States no longer has the financial resources to play a dominant role in transforming the Soviet economy. And since the Russians are themselves in the process of renouncing an empire, their enthusiasm for a partnership designed to keep order around the globe will be more polite than fervent. They can be expected to remain firmly preoccupied with themselves for the foreseeable future.

For the United States to adopt a spoiler's role in Europe at this late date seems a strategy with limited appeal and dangerous risks. Trying to play off one European state against another would more likely embitter transatlantic relations than succeed in preserving American predominance. Europeans have innumerable rivalries and frictions but also a deep common stake in their collective prosperity and stability. They have been developing that stake for over three decades and are unlikely to be lured away from it by anything the United States has to offer.

Trying to take advantage of the uneasiness in Europe over German unification seems a particularly unwise course. While continued close relations with Germany are obviously in America's interest, treating Germany as our particular ally in the European Community and neglecting other links — particularly with the French — is not. Notions of Germany as the master of the new Europe are greatly exaggerated, and it is hardly in our interest to encourage delusions of this kind among the Germans. Nor should we try to manipulate the jealousies of Germany's neighbors to limit European cohesion.

We should not forget that Europe remains probably the one place in the world whose destabilization could still easily trigger a general nuclear war. Europe's postwar progress toward inner stability has been an incomparable advance toward world stability. Trying seriously to reverse that progress would be a crime against history and a frivolous disregard of our own vital interests.

For these and other reasons, the United States will need to temper its assaults against the [European Community's] "mercantilism." For the United States to attack the European Community too severely risks a disintegration of European cooperation that would not be in anyone's interest. In any event, the United States does not have a compelling economic case. If the United States could get its own fiscal, financial, and industrial house in order, the trade problem would take care of itself. Indeed, the opening of the Soviet economy, and the huge rise in world demand that it implies, could provide a heaven-sent opportunity for the United States to reverse its chronic current-account deficit. But to eliminate the chronic imbalance between domestic production and absorption, we also need to resolve our fiscal crisis. Again, the problem abroad starts at home.

The same point may be made about the most effective strategy to prevent a Eurasian bloc from forming at the expense of transatlantic ties. So long as the world economy remains open and liberal, it is not in any nation's interest to be bound too exclusively into a relationship with another power or bloc of powers. The Europeans treasure their own union, but they are happier with each other if the Americans are nearby. Certainly Europeans would prefer to keep their relationship with the United States and limit their dependence on the Soviets. Nor will the Soviets, or others in Eastern Europe, wish to make themselves too exclusively dependent on anyone—the Germans, Europeans generally, or the Japanese. They will naturally welcome anyone with something to offer. A pluralistic approach to economic relations is not only the best way to guard political independence, it is manifestly the most efficient way to maximize economic benefits. So long as the world economy remains tolerably open, everyone's obvious enlightened interest is to keep it that way.

Should the liberal world economy collapse, however, it will be difficult to avoid the growth of blocs. If the world's market mechanisms break down generally, thanks to a depression or financial crisis, states can be expected to create limited zones of protected order within which they can hope to restart their stricken economies. Trade will become exclusive within these zones, and thus trade and investment will grow more and more intimately tied to competing political systems. This was the pattern for the imperial world of 1910 and, to a much greater extent, for the bloc world of the 1930s. Those were the kinds of world that the Pax Americana was meant to banish.

Ironically, today's greatest threat to the liberal Pax Americana is not from the Soviet Union but from the financial disorder of the United States. Belatedly, the Soviets have started adjusting to the inexorable realities of a more plural world. The Soviet Union's defeat as the rival superpower may thus mark its rejuvenation as a nation. It is not clear, however, that the United States has seriously begun its own adaptation. On the contrary, the Soviet defeat seems to have revived the old postwar dreams of world hegemony. If those dreams prevail in American policy, America's triumph in the Cold War may prove a very expensive victory. And one of the principal and earliest costs is likely to be the transatlantic relationship.

15 PACIFIC AGENDA: DEFENSE OR ECONOMICS?

Selig S. Harrison and

Clyde V. Prestowitz, Jr.

As fears of Soviet military power have declined . . . , the United States has initiated sweeping changes in its approach to Europe and to global arms control. But the Bush administration is completely ignoring the equally important opportunity now emerging to restructure the obsolete postwar order in East Asia and the Pacific.

Even before the Berlin Wall fell, it was increasingly apparent that the fundamental challenge facing the United States is not Soviet military might. Rather, it is the danger of economic insolvency, reflected in budget deficits, an eroding industrial base, and the growing American inability to compete with newly formidable economic rivals, especially Japan, South Korea, and Taiwan.

The continuing shift of economic power to East Asian competitors has been due in significant measure to the single-minded American focus on security concerns in the Asia-Pacific region. Since the Truman administration, successive presidents have subordinated U.S. economic interests to perceived geopolitical requirements. As the price for their military and diplomatic cooperation, the United States has actively promoted the economic power of its East Asian allies. Critical American technology and industrial know-how have repeatedly been transferred at little or no cost. At the same time, Washington has accepted trade and investment relationships based on an implicit understanding that U.S. markets would be relatively open while those of its partners would be much more restrictive. Whenever this asymmetry has caused economic disputes to reach a crisis the United States has generally avoided pressing the issue to a conclusion.

Was this unavoidable in the context of the Cold War? Whatever the ultimate verdict of history, Soviet President Mikhail Gorbachev has now made it possible for Washington to put economic priorities first and to strengthen its leverage with the East Asian capitals hitherto regarded as indispensable pillars of U.S. security.   Since 1987, Gorbachev has offered time and again to negotiate a far-reaching mutual reduction of American and Soviet forces in the Far East—and the Indian Ocean as well—as part of global arms control trade-offs.   Regrettably, American officials have consistently brushed off these Soviet overtures.   Defense Secretary Richard Cheney, announcing in February 1990 a unilateral 10 per cent reduction of U.S. military personnel in the Pacific, rejected regional arms control.

The United States now spends an estimated $42 billion a year on the direct and indirect costs of its Far East military forces.   Thus, the budgetary impact of major force reductions would be significant.   However, the most important benefit of a Pacific détente with Moscow would be the opportunity to refocus on economic priorities.

In a more relaxed security environment, the United States could formulate an integrated national economic strategy designed to meet the competitive challenge without worrying about whether it would jeopardize military links. Even with a strengthened posture, however, major reductions in the trade imbalance with Japan would take many years in the absence of a substantial effort to make American industries more competitive.   Charges of economic inequity are justified only in selected areas of the relationship.   The major thrust of a shift in priorities would therefore be to revitalize the economic base of American power.   This would presuppose a wide range of new domestic economic policies.   But it would also require, above all, an end to self-defeating technological transfers made in the name of security, as well as appropriate U.S. countermeasures to mercantilist East Asian policies that threaten the survival of strategic industries such as aerospace, electronics, semiconductors, supercomputers, and telecommunications.

The . . . controversial decisions [in 1990] to join in co-development and co-production of the Japanese FSX and South Korean FA-18 fighter aircraft are only the latest examples of a 40-year behavior pattern in which the United States has sacrificed its economic interests for what it regarded as military imperatives.   Throughout much of the postwar period the United States accepted a substantial overvaluation of the dollar in relation to East Asian currencies in order to strengthen its allies economically and induce them to stay in the American camp.   U.S. laws regulating unfair trade practices were rarely applied to the East Asian allies.   Thus, in the late 1960s the Nixon administration ignored the dumping and collusion that led to the virtual disappearance of the U.S. consumer electronics industry.   In the 1970s the Carter administration promoted co-production by approving the joint de-velopment of the F-15, then the most advanced U.S. fighter plane.   Later, the General Accounting Office concluded that a massive transfer of tech-nology had greatly strengthened Japan's aircraft manufacturers, both military and commercial, as well as its electronics industry.   In 1985 the vast illegal dumping of semiconductor chips by Japanese manufacturers threatened the survival of the U.S. industry.   Yet a high-level White House task force agreed only to a limited U.S. response after warnings from then National Security Adviser John Poindexter that any firm U.S. action might endanger potential Japanese support of the Strategic Defense Initiative (SDI) program.

PATRONIZING ASIA

The United States fell easily into this pattern in the immediate postwar period when it struck a tacit bargain to exchange economic largesse for defense cooperation.   American leaders took a patronizing view of the war-devastated East Asian countries.   Insensitive to their social strength and nationalist dynamism, Washington did not view them as potential competitors even in the remote future.   The opening of the American market on a nonreciprocal basis seemed of little consequence because at that time few thought the East Asians could make goods Americans would want.

Tokyo, Seoul, and Taipei were quick to recognize the opportunity to milk the security relationship for economic advantage.   Until recently, however, Washington, mesmerized by the communist specter, was blind to the shift in economic power that was occurring.   Japan's military "free ride" is a favorite target of American critics.   But South Korea's meteoric economic rise has also been accelerated by American economic and military aid, U.S. tutelage in export promotion, and the subsidy provided by U.S. military protection.

Preoccupied with China as a military threat, the United States pumped massive aid into Taiwan to build it up as a counterweight and sought to discourage its natural economic tilt toward the mainland.   Washington helped orient Taipei's exports to the United States by actively fostering U.S. investment in Taiwanese industries geared to the American market.   Taiwan, like South Korea, continued to receive trade concessions under the Generalized System of Preferences until January 1989.   Now the island has piled up $71 billion in foreign exchange reserves.   Out of a $109 billion U.S. trade deficit in 1989, Tokyo ($49 billion), Taipei ($13 billion), and Seoul ($6.3 billion) accounted for $68.3 billion, nearly two-thirds of the total.

Perhaps the most damaging legacy of American policies is that the United States embraced the fiction of an essential similarity between the principles and purposes of the U.S. economy and those of its East Asian protégés.   While these countries pursued mercantilistic policies at odds with American free-market and free-trade doctrines, for purposes of grand strategy the United States averted its eyes and clung to the fiction of similarity, even as its industries succumbed one by one to East Asian competitors who were not behaving at all as Western economic principles said they should.

This fiction was necessary to sustain American public support for the Pacific alliances in the face of the severe economic dislocations resulting from East Asian competition.   Indeed, uneasiness over these alliances has grown in recent years with the realization that America's military allies are economic adversaries with greatly differing systems. But refusal to acknowledge that an adversarial trade relationship exists only adds to the built-in tensions now multiplying in both the defense and economic aspects of America's East Asian relationships. More important, it prevents the United States from responding effectively to the competitive challenge.

Most Americans believe that the East Asians are not observing the rules of the trading game. In reality, however, the East Asians never accepted the American version of the rules. Their own cultural, social, and political priorities have led them to organize and run their economies on the basis of principles different from those of the United States. To achieve American-style openness in these economies, the United States has often demanded what would amount to a social or industrial revolution in East Asian societies; not surprisingly, East Asians have responded with irritation and counterattacks.

The American response to the challenge of the East Asian economies should come in the economic arena. Instead, Washington has been making ever more strident demands for greater defense "burden sharing" to offset high U.S. trade imbalances. By emphasizing burden sharing, the Bush administration is inadvertently and dangerously exacerbating trade frictions, given basic differences in how Washington and East Asian capitals perceive their relationships. For example, Americans generally believe that South Korea should feel indebted to the United States for its economic and military help. Rejecting the idea of such a debt, however, most South Koreans think of themselves as the victims of a partition imposed by the superpowers. While grateful for American help, especially in the Korean War, they feel that the United States owes them military protection and special economic treatment in return for the use of their territory for nuclear-equipped military bases directed at the Soviet Union as well as North Korea.

Similarly, as many Americans see it, the United States showed a rare benevolence in helping a defeated Japan to its feet, and the affluent Tokyo of the 1990s should feel indebted for past economic assistance as well as for its military "free ride." In this view, without American capital and technical help, not to mention Japanese profits linked to the Korean and Vietnamese wars, Japan never could have achieved its "economic miracle." This concept of a "debt" is flatly rejected by Japan, however, because most Japanese believe that the United States rebuilt Japan for its own strategic reasons as an industrial bulwark against the Soviet Union and China.

TOKYO TRADE-OFF

Far from feeling indebted for the U.S. military presence, many Japanese resent American bases, not only because they serve as a reminder of Japan's defeat in the war, but also because they have been used for military purposes in Vietnam and elsewhere in Asia that were repugnant to most Japanese. Despite significant continuing popular opposition to the Japanese-U.S. security treaty, successive conservative Japanese governments have been able to sustain their "special relationship" with the United States by portraying it as a trade-off in which Tokyo has provided military privileges and foreign policy support in exchange for U.S. solicitude in economic matters.   For many of the ruling conservatives themselves, the treaty has had a specifically military rationale. But for the broader Japanese public, with its diversity of foreign policy views, the alliance has been politically digestible primarily in economic terms.   Most Japanese have viewed the treaty as a tacit precondition for assuring access to the American market as well as for securing stable supplies of foodgrains and a variety of American—or American-controlled—natural resources, notably oil, enriched uranium, and coking coal.

Increasingly in recent years, Japan has sought to redefine the meaning of security in economic and political rather than in military terms.   "Comprehensive security" is the new watchword.   Even the conservatives accept "burden sharing" only as a rationale for increasing the size of Japan's own defense forces.   The security treaty, in this view, should relate solely to the defense of the Japanese home islands.   The United States, however, has continued to press for even larger Japanese payments to offset the cost of the 63,000 American military personnel, including sailors of the Seventh Fleet, still stationed in Japan.   It is also pushing the Japanese to expand their commitments to join U.S. forces in defending the Pacific against a diminishing Soviet threat.

Nationalism is growing in Japan and is likely to take an anti-American direction if the United States fails to keep pace with growing sentiment in favor of a reduced superpower military presence.   The U.S. Marine commander in Japan, Major General Henry Stackpole III, stirred up a storm in March 1990 when he said that the American force presence is "a cap in the bottle" to prevent a resurgence of Japanese military power.   "Some Japanese," responded a *Yomiuri* newspaper columnist, "cannot feel good about paying for a watchdog that watches them."

Both rightists who seek a more independent military posture and Socialist-led forces on the left who advocate looser ties with the United States are gaining strength.   Socialist leader Takako Doi, who opposes burden-sharing payments to Washington, advocates the removal of American and Soviet nuclear weapons from all of Northeast Asia and urges acceptance of the Soviet proposal for three-way discussions on regional arms control with the United States and Japan.

Moscow is openly linking its arms control overtures with exploration of a deal in which some or all of the disputed Kurile islands would be returned to Japan if Washington and Tokyo agree not to use them for military purposes. . . . Moscow appears to be moving toward a resolution of the Kuriles issue in order to obtain badly needed Japanese help in developing Siberia. But any agreement on how many islands would be returned and on the terms for assistance would presuppose demilitarization of the islands with American concurrence.

Instead of seeking to block a Soviet-Japanese rapprochement, the United

States should recognize that improved relations between them would serve American interests as part of a larger process of reducing regional tension. The first step in such a process should be the inclusion of naval arms control measures, embracing the Pacific, in global Soviet-American arms control agreements. The United States should also encourage a Japanese-Soviet territorial settlement and a variety of East Asian arms control negotiations encompassing China, Japan, and the two Koreas.

Japanese arms control specialist Tsuyoshi Hasegawa has warned that . . . projected Soviet-American cuts in land-based intercontinental ballistic missiles . . . could aggravate military tensions in Northeast Asia unless they are reinforced by wide-ranging naval arms control measures. Cuts in land-based missiles, he observes, would enhance the importance of submarine-launched ballistic missiles (SLBMs) on both sides. This would have a special relevance for Northeast Asia because Moscow deploys nearly half of its missile-firing submarines (SSBNs) in and around the Sea of Okhotsk north of Japan.

To avoid destabilizing effects, the Strategic Arms Reduction Talks (START) agreement would have to include deeper cuts than the United States is now ready to make in the number of SLBMs both sides deploy globally. But such missile reductions and resulting SSBN cutbacks would expose the remaining SSBN forces to an increased threat unless cuts in the SLBMs were accompanied by cuts in the number of attack submarines and other anti-SSBN forces. The threat would be greater to Soviet SSBNs than to American SSBNs, given the superiority of American submarines in evading detection.

At present, the START negotiations do not contemplate any reductions in anti-SSBN forces. Yet both Moscow and Washington would benefit from reducing worldwide deployment of attack submarines to a common ceiling of 50 or 60 each. . . .

Significant reductions in Soviet nuclear capabilities in the Sea of Okhotsk would enable the United States to reduce a broad range of offensive forces in the Far East designed to attack SSBNs, including carrier-based forces. . . .

Continued American foot dragging on naval arms control could foreshadow a cycle of escalation that would greatly complicate American relations with Japan and the USSR. More important, a change in the U.S. posture on naval arms control may prove necessary to avoid a breakdown of negotiations on conventional force reductions in Europe. Marshal Sergei Akhromeyev, Gorbachev's principal defense adviser, warned in July 1989 that the United States cannot expect to get force reductions in Europe "and then build up its naval forces without any constraints, especially its carrier battle groups, thus gaining military superiority in order to dictate its will to the USSR from the position of strength." . . .

The U.S. Navy attaches special importance to its Japanese bases as part of its "maritime strategy." In the event of a war, the United States could attack the Soviet homeland with nuclear weapons from close-in forward positions. Soviet missile-firing submarines based in and near the Sea of Okhotsk and its environs would also be major American targets.

One of the many anachronistic assumptions underpinning the maritime strategy is horizontal escalation. The United States would retaliate against Soviet moves in Europe or the Persian Gulf by using Japanese bases for strikes at nearby Soviet forces and bases. But would Tokyo cooperate? While the United States is committed to the defense of Japan under the security treaty, Japan does not have a similar obligation to help the United States in military operations against a third party. Applied to Japan, horizontal escalation was never much more than a slogan. It is increasingly meaningless against the background of a changing Japanese-Soviet relationship. Moreover, as the Soviet threat in Central Europe declines, the basic rationale for horizontal escalation vanishes.

In pursuing arms control initiatives, the United States would be in greater harmony with a public opinion trend in Japan favoring foreign and defense policies that are more independent. This trend cuts across right and left alike. By showing its readiness for looser security links with Japan attuned to progress toward a relaxation of Soviet-American tensions, the United States can strengthen centrist Japanese political elements favoring a continuation of nonnuclear, defense-oriented military forces with a limited reach. Conversely, by pushing for closer defense ties, accompanied by greater burden sharing, Washington will feed the fires of nuclear nationalism, since some hawks argue that Japan may as well go it alone if it has to pay for its own defense.

In South Korea, too, public opinion would warmly welcome U.S.-Soviet arms control initiatives. . . . A reduction in the regional superpower profile is widely seen as the key to defusing North-South tensions. A more relaxed regional climate, in this perspective, would encourage the Soviet Union to step up its pressure on North Korea to be conciliatory, while the United States would no longer need to keep forces in the South directed at the Soviet Union, notably nuclear-equipped F-16 aircraft. A North-South arms control agreement would then become easier, since the United States would be more disposed to trade U.S. force withdrawals for such arms control measures as the North-South force reductions offered by Pyongyang, a North Korean pullback from the demilitarized zone, and a more defense-oriented North Korean force posture.

The American nuclear presence has become increasingly controversial in the South in the wake of indications that the North may be seeking to acquire nuclear weapons. Pyongyang has long urged the establishment of a nuclear-free zone on the peninsula and has signed the nuclear nonproliferation treaty. But it has conditioned international inspection of its nuclear facilities on the removal of U.S. nuclear weapons. While some hawks in the South want Seoul to go nuclear, public opinion strongly favors a nuclear-free zone.

. . . Just as some vested military interests in Washington and Moscow resist arms control measures, entrenched power groups in Seoul and Pyongyang would like to see the status quo continue. In the South, the same military elite that directly ruled the country for 26 years, until 1987, still enjoys special economic perquisites and exercises powerful behind-the-scenes political influence. The force reduction measures envisaged in a North-South arms control agreement would threaten this bloated officer corps and would lead to reduced defense budgets. In the North, some of the more realistic leaders in the ruling communist Workers party, apparently with the blessing of President Kim Il Sung, have initiated cautious, Chinese-style economic reforms in the face of bitter opposition from hardliners centered in the military. These Pyongyang reformers are also pushing for mutual North-South force reductions in order to liberate funds and labor for increased consumer goods production. Regional Soviet-American arms control measures, in short, would promote democratization in the South and moderation in the North, especially if Washington joined with Pyongyang, Seoul, and possibly others in concurrent negotiations on the Korean peninsula.

China's reaction to Soviet-American force reductions in the Pacific would in all likelihood be positive. It is the superpower arms competition, Beijing contends, that has forced China to build up its military forces at the expense of economic development. Moscow and Washington should thus "take the lead" in reducing their own arms before expecting China to negotiate with them from an inferior position.

Beijing has taken a benign view toward the presence of the U.S. Seventh Fleet as an offset to Soviet power. However, reductions in the American naval presence would no doubt be welcome if they are accompanied by parallel Soviet cutbacks. More uncertain is whether China would enter into talks that could impose multilateral constraints on its own forces. Beijing is pointedly vague about what level of superpower reductions would make its participation possible. Given this ambiguity, the superpowers should proceed with their own regional dialogue while keeping the door open for possible Chinese and Japanese participation. At the same time, the superpowers should encourage separate Sino-Japanese exchanges. As China specialist Michel Oksenberg has observed, growing Chinese uneasiness over Japan's expanding military potential may make Beijing more amenable to regional arms control measures if they would constrain Tokyo.

Defense Secretary Cheney has attempted to justify an indefinite continuation of the "major portion" of the U.S. presence in the Pacific by warning that "a vacuum would quickly develop" in its absence. "There almost surely," he said in Tokyo on February 23, 1990, "would be a series of destabilizing regional arms races [and] an increase in regional tension." Pointing to potential internal instability in Burma, Cambodia, China, North Korea, and Vietnam, he declared that "it's an open question as to how those changes will affect regional stability." China and India, he added, "continue to emerge as regional powers.   We don't know what the regional effects will be. . . . Given these potential dangers to regional security, it should be clear that the United States could not ever think of a withdrawal from Asia."

The principal argument made privately by administration officials is that Japan will eventually dominate Asia militarily as well as economically unless the United States maintains countervailing power.   China and Japan, it is argued, are likely to be rivals, and the United States should play a balancing role.   As Cheney stated, "We would want to be engaged in the Asia-Pacific region even if the Soviet Union were not."

The concept of a vacuum that has to be filled smacks of the colonial era and the "white man's burden" mentality.   It reflects a lingering self-image of the United States as a world policeman.   Instead of inviting continuing collisions with nationalism by injecting itself into Asian regional rivalries, the United States should concentrate on building positive bilateral relationships that cut across these rivalries.   This will be difficult enough at a time of high trade deficits without adding the political and military stresses that would result from actual or perceived attempts to manipulate the regional military balance of power.

Cheney's assumption that "regional arms races" would follow Soviet and American force reductions is open to question.   In the case of China and Japan, many indications suggest that an economic partnership with aspects of a defense alliance is more likely than a military rivalry.   In any event, it cannot be taken for granted that Japan would step up defense spending in direct proportion to Japan-related U.S. force reductions.

In some areas of Japanese defense, American withdrawals might lead to increased Japanese expenditures.   In others, where Japan has often had access to sophisticated U.S. technology at preferential prices, Tokyo might well move cautiously in the absence of the special relationship.   The net effect of American withdrawals would be to sharpen Japanese budget battles in which growing welfare demands would tend to restrain the pace of military expansion.   Hard choices between welfare and defense priorities would compel Japan to reevaluate its regional relationships.   In this reassessment, the specifically Japanese interests that would then govern bilateral relationships with the Soviet Union, China, and North Korea would have to be distinguished from the derivative Japanese interest in Cold War American policies toward these countries—policies that were economically rewarding for Japan but were nonetheless American in conception.

Negotiating force reductions with the USSR and promoting a parallel process of détente in Korea with Soviet support need not mean the termination of the U.S. security treaties with Japan and South Korea during the transition period ahead.   On the contrary, the United States should keep a small residual military force in the Pacific designed to mesh with a continuing but greatly reduced presence in the South China Sea and the Indian Ocean, where Moscow is also eager for arms control.

The value of keeping U.S. bases in the Philippines is related to the Indian Ocean as much as it is to the Pacific. In the context of force reductions in both theaters, the Subic Bay naval base could be converted into a commercial shipyard, and massive outlays for alternative installations could be avoided.

As part of a more detached American posture in East Asia, the United States should also begin to extricate itself from the unresolved conflict between China and Taiwan. American policy should not be based on the implicit assumption that it is desirable to keep the island separated from the mainland whatever the economic and other consequences.

The . . . U.S. trade deficit with Taipei can be reduced only marginally by harder bargaining because the island's population of 20 million is too small to be a significant market. What would make a major difference over time would be a reorientation of Taiwan's export thrust from the United States to China and Japan, encouraged by Washington.

Taipei, with its superiority in many areas of technology and in management skills, and Beijing, with its vast resources and market, are natural partners. Economic links have been growing despite the Tiananmen Square massacre. Rapid development of this partnership would be desirable for the United States for security as well as economic reasons. Increased economic interaction reduces the danger that hardliners in Beijing will use an invasion of Taiwan to divert attention from domestic grievances. . . .

Although the United States characterizes its policy toward the future of Taiwan as one of noninvolvement, Washington is deeply embroiled in the military rivalry between Taipei and Beijing. In recent years, in the name of the Soviet threat, Washington has agreed to sell China $602 million in weaponry and aircraft technology that could be used against Taiwan. The United States ended its security treaty with Taiwan when it recognized China. However, combined sales of weaponry and military technology to Taiwan now range from $700 to $800 million yearly, notwithstanding bitter Chinese complaints that the quantity and technological level of these sales violate the American commitment in the 1982 second Shanghai communiqué to phase them out. This arms sales policy helps offset the trade deficit with Taipei and is perceived by many Americans as a moral obligation in the absence of the security treaty. But one of its important unintended consequences has been to aggravate tensions between Taiwan and the mainland. In Taipei it emboldens advocates of independence, and in Beijing it strengthens militant nationalists who call for annexation of the island militarily before the independence movement gets too strong.

The United States is now reducing its arms sales to Taiwan by $20 million a year. Thus, it would take nearly 40 years to phase them out at the current rate. Until recently, Pentagon officials privately justified even higher sales to Taiwan by saying that a naval base on Taiwan might be needed to counter the Soviet Pacific buildup in the event that the United States lost Subic Bay. A faster reduction process and a termination of major arms sales to China would both be facilitated by a relaxation of regional Soviet-American tensions.

TEMPERING TECHNOLOGY TRANSFER

By testing Soviet arms control initiatives and going as far as Moscow is ready to go in phasing out the Soviet-American confrontation, the United States can acquire the freedom of action needed to shape new policies that safeguard U.S. economic interests while at the same time avoiding needless conflict with East Asian countries. The most urgently needed policy departure is a much more cautious approach to military co-development and technology cooperation arrangements. The United States would not propose co-production or co-development of aircraft or any other weapon or technology unless the United States clearly got back as much in technology and value added as it gave. It would not trade advanced U.S. technology to achieve the goal of military interoperability with allied forces. For example, the proposed co-production of the South Korean FA-18 would have to be justified on its economic merits rather than as a gesture to an ally. It could then be determined whether its economic advantages outweigh diplomatic factors during a period when arms control efforts are underway between the two Koreas.

Similarly, Washington would not solicit foreign participation in SDI, as it does now, by offering the sweetener of technology transfer. Instead it would redirect the resources now being allocated to SDI to the revitalization of American industry. A wide range of research and development spending, now focused on military priorities, could be diverted to critical civilian needs in the context of force cutbacks embracing the Pacific as well as Europe.

In some areas new policies should be tougher, while in others they should be more flexible, as the administration's ill-advised Structural Impediments Initiative (SII) illustrates. Launched in response to the requirements of the new U.S. trade law of 1988, SII represents a change from the traditional U.S. effort to open the Japanese market industry by industry. Under the SII banner, the U.S. government is making a wholesale assault upon the fundamental structure of the Japanese economic and social system. The United States has urged Japan to adopt American-style antitrust policies that would break up or curb the power of industrial and commercial conglomerates such as the Mitsubishi, Mitsui, and Sumitomo groups. Washington has also called upon Tokyo to revolutionize its distribution system by sharply reducing the number of "mom-and-pop" stores and allowing the unrestrained opening of large mass-merchandising outlets to replace the smaller stores. In a direct attack upon the power of Japanese officials, American negotiators have demanded curtailment of the practice of "administrative guidance" through which the long-entrenched bureaucracy exercises its vast informal power. The United States has pressed for dramatic increases in spending on public works as well as taxes and other measures that would increase Japanese consumer spending while reducing savings and investment. In other words, the United States has come out baldly and boldly to urge that Japan become much more like the United States. Despite recent assurances by Japan, such changes are unlikely to occur.

This kind of approach will serve only to provoke the resentment of many Japanese who interpret it as American bullying stemming from jealousy of Japan's success. Ironically, by trying to tie Japan ever more tightly to itself, the United States is likely to alienate Japan more than ever. Under a more realistic policy, SII and other efforts aimed at changing the nature of the Japanese system would be abandoned. Indeed, the whole moralistic framework of the current relationship would be dropped. Because it would no longer need to prove that Japan is a good ally that shares American values, the United States would be able to accept the Japanese system for what it is: a non-American form of capitalism that is neither good nor bad.

Without the compulsion to change the Japanese system, the United States could focus on harder bargaining in certain areas of the traditional trade relationship where inequities exist. For example, many Asian agricultural quotas (such as Japanese and Korean restrictions on rice imports) violate the spirit of the General Agreement on Tariffs and Trade (GATT). The United States, eyeing its security links, has generally hesitated to push disputes over these issues to a resolution.

Under a new approach, if a given issue is not important on its own merits, the United States should drop it. If it is, American negotiators would have greater freedom of action in pressing for full resolution through formal procedures. At the same time, it should be recognized that the United States is not lily-white. Agricultural quotas and legislation requiring many state and federal government agencies to buy American also violate the spirit of GATT and should be rescinded.

While adopting a less combative stance on issues that result from differing economic philosophies and structures, the United States should begin to deal forthrightly, for the first time, with the impact of Japanese and other East Asian industrial policies on American industries. Suppose, for example, the United States concluded that its industry in a certain field might never achieve substantial penetration of the Japanese market. Suppose that Japanese competitors might have a good chance to make deep inroads into the market in question in the United States. All other things being equal, this asymmetry in real market access would put the U.S. industry at a long-term competitive disadvantage. The U.S. government would then have to make a case-by-case assessment to determine whether or not effective American participation in a given industry is a vital interest or not.

In cases where the decision is no, these sectors would not become the subject of trade disputes. Where the decision is yes, American negotiators still would not proceed in a combative manner. They would not accuse the Japanese of being unfair, and they would not demand unconditional opening of the Japanese market or wholesale changes in the Japanese industrial structure. But they would assert a new U.S. policy, based on reciprocity, designed to assure the survival of strategic industries.

Aerospace, electronics, semiconductors, supercomputers, and telecommunications all have been mentioned as possible examples of such industries. Others are biotechnology, advanced ceramics, and engineered plastics. When the industrial policies and closed markets of other countries threaten the existence of such industries, the United States would make clear that it will do what is necessary to sustain them both through positive domestic programs and appropriate countermeasures. At this point, a range of responses on both sides would be possible. Other countries might respond by opening their markets and dropping industrial promotion policies. In some cases, the United States might decide to make entrance into its market conditional on entrance to the other market on similar terms.

Some may call this protectionism, but a look at an actual example of this approach suggests a different perspective. Most countries, big and small, have airlines, often reflecting considerations of prestige and national security rather than of economics. Many countries have national airlines and others have flag carriers, in many cases subsidized. Even the United States prohibits the foreign acquisition of U.S. airlines. Significantly, the United States never offers unilaterally to open its skies in international airline negotiations. It does not accuse trading partners and allies of being unfair because they subsidize their airlines and restrict access to their markets: It knows that such protests would only engender recriminations.

The United States also believes that a viable airline industry is an important component of national security. It will not agree, for example, that all American passengers be carried on foreign airlines; yet it knows that this could happen if the American market were open while foreign markets were closed and foreign airlines were subsidized. The United States does not pursue a laissez-faire, open-market policy, but neither is it protectionist. Rather it negotiates the structure and conditions of the market. Deals are made specifying numbers of destinations and flights and the amounts of landing fees. The result is not a market-share arrangement. Competition remains and no one knows at the conclusion of a deal what share of passengers the U.S. airlines will carry. In practice, the market shares fluctuate and passengers have meaningful choices. At the same time there is little chance that a nation's airlines will go wholly without business or that the nation will lose its airlines. In short, a market-oriented compromise is struck that reflects both the desire for competition and the imperatives of national policy.

While some may say that this arrangement is peculiarly suited to the airline business, a similar approach is in fact already being taken, without official acknowledgement, in the case of supercomputers. In response to below-cost Japanese export pricing and restricted market access in Japan, the U.S. government has pressed the Massachusetts Institute of Technology and other institutions not to buy Japanese supercomputers. Similar informal pressures have been applied to block the procurement of Japanese fiber optics systems.

Such surreptitious, arbitrary tactics undermine the whole concept of rules-based international trade. In a new environment, the United States would openly negotiate bidding conditions, numbers of institutions open to foreign bidders, terms of distribution, and other market parameters in strategic industries.

Putting economic priorities first does not mean that the United States could or should adopt a unilateralist approach. American dependence on East Asia for debt financing and some types of industrial technology rules out a table-pounding, take-it-or-leave-it approach. By the same token, however, it would be incorrect to assume that the United States is now at the mercy of Japan because Tokyo helps subsidize the U.S. budget deficit by buying Treasury bills. Japan makes these purchases primarily because they are a good investment. If the price is right, these purchases will probably continue, regardless of the American posture in disputes over technology and trade. In any case, Japanese threats to withdraw financing or technology would have limited credibility because such actions would involve many private actors, such as insurance companies, banks, and individual investors, who are not easy to control and are subject to U.S. as well as foreign administrative authority.

The American bargaining position in dealings with East Asian countries is still powerful, but it is rapidly eroding. Precisely for this reason, the United States should strengthen its leverage and expand its room for maneuver by negotiating a large-scale mutual reduction of Soviet and American forces in the Pacific. Ironically, in a more relaxed security environment, greater U.S. leverage can lead to a moderation rather than an increase in trade frictions. Freed from the necessity to pretend that the U.S. and East Asian economic systems are the same as a rationale for the alliances, the United States could acknowledge the reality of systemic differences and deal with them in a more pragmatic and flexible manner. It could drop the misleading practice of insisting either that they do not exist or that "good allies" must accept the American version of the rules.

By disentangling economic and security issues, the United States could clear the air in relations with East Asian countries, avoiding collisions over burden sharing. More important, by drawing down the Soviet-American military confrontation, the United States could escape from its fixation with the communist specter and begin to focus on the economic dimensions of its security. Just as the peculiar psychology of the Cold War helped undermine American competitive power, so the end of the Cold War could become the catalyst for a new American global role keyed to emerging economic and political realities rather than a declining military threat.

16 BEYOND MUTUAL RECRIMINATION: BUILDING A SOLID U.S.-JAPAN RELATIONSHIP IN THE 1990s

I. M. Destler and Michael Nacht

. . . As we enter the nineties, Americans face a number of alternative futures—and Japan figures importantly in them all. Conceivable scenarios for the U.S.-Japan relationship range from maintaining—perhaps even deepening—current security and economic interdependence, on the one hand, to growing economic—and perhaps, ultimately, political-military—rivalry and conflict on the other. The preferred outcome is clearly the former. Given the severe costs to U.S. interests of the alternatives, achieving a balanced and durable interdependence is, we believe, a first-order priority for U.S. foreign-policy-makers over the coming decade, equal in importance to the redefinition of the NATO/European alliance structure, and to keeping the Soviet Union headed toward political and economic reform. It could also prove very difficult.

To bring about this relatively happy outcome, the United States needs a strategy that includes:

1. A basis for retaining security cooperation under a condition of reduced threat and increased concern about technological competition;
2. Shoring up areas of weakness in the U.S. domestic economy, to strengthen the U.S. foundation for cooperation and competition with Japan;
3. Continued U.S. efforts to open up the Japanese economy through proc-

Note: Footnotes have been deleted.

esses and substantive agreements that become progressively more two-sided in substance, as well as form;

4. An explicit strategy of reinforcing and deepening economic interdependence; and

5. Articulation of "competitive interdependence" as an explicit alternative to U.S.—and Japanese—economic nationalism.

We develop our case for such a strategy in the pages that follow.

POLICY BACKGROUND

The Strengthening of Security Cooperation

Twice since World War II, in 1951 and 1960, the United States has affirmed through formal treaties its commitment to maintain the security of Japan. This commitment made very good sense thirty years ago; Japan had emerged from World War II struggling to establish democratic institutions under close American supervision and was encouraged by Washington to focus on rebuilding its economy and society, while the United States took care of Japanese security.

The American security commitment was intimately connected to the policy of global containment, and the stationing of U.S. forces on Japanese territory was seen as the principal manifestation of this policy in the Western Pacific. Their presence not only protected Japan but facilitated the projection of American military power on the Asian mainland. U.S. naval power in the region aimed at denying the Soviet navy access to open ocean areas and countering the Soviet attack submarine fleet. American bases in Japan served as staging bases for actions taken during the Korean and Vietnam Wars.

There was persistent anti-American sentiment among leftist and extreme rightist Japanese groups in the 1950s and 1960s. These brought sporadic outbursts against the alliance and the Liberal Democratic Party (LDP) that supported it, peaking in the mass demonstrations which forced President Dwight Eisenhower to cancel his planned visit in 1960. The Vietnam War also became a rallying point for opposition to the United States, particularly in the late 1960s, just as in many other countries around the world.

But by the early 1970s, the security relationship had won broader support in Tokyo as well as in Washington, with the U.S. agreement to return Okinawa to Japan, the American (and Japanese) openings to China, and the promise of a Soviet-American détente symbolized by the signing of the Strategic Arms Limitation Treaty (SALT) in May 1972. Based on an asymmetric economic and strategic relationship between the two nations, a still-threatening international environment, and a sense of mutual respect, the U.S.-Japanese security relationship came to be seen as healthy and mutually beneficial.

This relationship survived a few rough moments in the latter 1970s. The Carter administration's nuclear nonproliferation policy threatened initially to place severe restrictions on Japanese reprocessing of spent nuclear fuel. Carter also mistakenly sought to withdraw American forces from South Korea without consulting the Japanese—fueling post-Vietnam anxieties that the United States was "leaving Asia." Finally, the Carter administration made the mistake of pressuring Japan to spend more than one percent of its gross national product on defense without concrete recommendations for how these funds should be spent.

Nonetheless, by the 1980s it was clear that the U.S.-Japan security relationship had grown much stronger. Bilateral defense cooperation had evolved to include real operational cooperation between U.S. and Japanese forces. It evolved also from U.S. military and commercial sales in the 1960s (e.g., of the F-104 fighter, Airborne Warning and Control System aircraft [AWACS], and CH-47 attack helicopters), to licensed production of American systems in Japan in the 1970s and early 1980s (e.g., F-15 aircraft and Sidewinder missiles), to co-production in the late 1980s (e.g., Aegis destroyers and the Boeing 767). Major U.S. aerospace firms such as McDonnell Douglas and Raytheon became deeply entrenched in cooperative efforts with the Japanese Defense Agency. The Reagan administration eased frictions over Japan's relative contribution by shifting the debate from the level of Japan's defense budget to the "roles and missions" the Japanese Self Defense Forces should perform. Some of the concepts, such as the determination that Japanese naval forces should defend the sea lines of communication (SLOCs) out to 1000 miles from Japan's territorial waters, were of limited operational utility, but the overall health of the security relationship could not have been better. The strong personal ties between President Ronald Reagan and Prime Minister Yasuhiro Nakasone—the "Ron-Yasu" relationship—added an important stabilizing element that sustained bilateral security cooperation through the decade.

The Broadening of Economic Competition

As defense ties grew, so did economic interaction, but here the net impact on bilateral relations has been less salutary. The breadth of the change has been enormous. As recently as [1970], the United States and Japan were enmeshed in a quarrel over textile trade, a matter central to the economy of neither. Today, the economic issues between them involve high-technology industries critical to the economic futures of both, and huge financial flows on which each is highly dependent. Yet while old-style issues involving the impact of Japanese exports no longer hold center stage, they have not disappeared. Instead, they share billing with four other broad and overlapping categories of economic issues (listed here in rough order of their historical emergence):

1. *Import issues* (1955–), resulting from the impact of Japanese products on U.S. producers and markets. These have moved steadily from labor-intensive to capital- and knowledge-intensive goods: from textiles, to steel and consumer electronics, to automobiles and semiconductors;

2. *Export issues* (1969–), typically initiated by U.S. officials seeking to expand trade by breaking down Japanese barriers to American products. Beginning with pressure for tariff reduction, these officials moved in the late seventies to emphasis on non-tariff barriers to U.S. sales of such products as beef and citrus, telecommunications equipment, satellites, semiconductors, supercomputers, and wood products. Increasingly, these have been punctuated with Congressional and industry demands for specific reciprocity and a "level playing field";

3. *Macroeconomic and structural issues* (1971–), raised in response to persistent Japanese trade surpluses and growing U.S. deficits, and involving efforts to influence policies that affect overall balances: monetary and fiscal policies, "structural" measures with impact on savings rates and business practices, and intervention in foreign exchange markets;

4. *Technology-related trade and investment issues* (1982–), arising particularly from Japanese success in high-tech, triggering anxieties in the defense establishment about U.S. technological leadership and security leakage, and broader concerns about overall U.S. "economic security" and leadership; and

5. *Financial, investment and related issues* (1987–), a product of now-massive capital flows from Japan to the United States, reflecting the overall shift in relative economic power.

The emergence of issue types 2–5 has coincided, of course, with Japan's rise over two decades to across-the-board manufacturing pre-eminence and financial power. And over these two decades, the two governments became much more skilled in the management of economic conflict. Many specific crises have been defused through timely agreements; substantial policy changes were in fact negotiated, particularly in Japan's trade and regulatory regimes.

But as the number and diversity of conflicts grew, so did their political difficulty. It was much harder to crack Japanese import markets than to negotiate export restraints; it was a new challenge to engage in meaningful bargaining over "domestic" fiscal and monetary policies or "structural" matters such as savings incentives and land use policies. And the massive cross-border capital inflows of the eighties were without parallel in America's twentieth-century experience. They financed record U.S. trade and budget deficits, with the Japanese Ministry of Finance literally saving the dollar from collapse in 1987. But this represented a financial dependence that both constrained American freedom and multiplied American discomfort. Signaling these developments at the popular level were visible Japanese investments like the purchases of Columbia Pictures and Rockefeller Center.

THE CURRENT SITUATION

The Security Relationship

As we enter the 1990s, the tangible elements of the U.S.-Japan Treaty of Mutual Cooperation and Security remain intact. U.S. Forces–Japan is maintained as one of two subordinate unified commands (the other being U.S.

Forces–Korea) under the U.S. Pacific Command (USPACOM) headquartered in Hawaii. This command includes 2000 army personnel; almost 24,000 Marines; 16,500 airmen and 120 combat aircraft including 72 F-15 C/Ds and 48 F-16s; and 8300 naval personnel who operate several facilities including the naval base at Yokosuka, headquarters for the U.S. Seventh Fleet. American forces extend from Okinawa in the south of Japan to the Misawa Air Force Base in the northern part of Honshu.

Despite the heavy criticism that has often been leveled against Japan for not investing sufficiently in defense, the facts tell a different story. By 1989 Japan's defense budget (approximately $30 billion) was on the verge of surpassing those of the Federal Republic of Germany, France, or Great Britain. The Japanese Ground Self Defense Forces (GSDF) included more than 160 tanks, 180 artillery pieces, 170 armored personnel carriers, and a variety of surface-to-ship guided missiles, anti-tank helicopters, transport helicopters, and surface-to-air guided missiles. The Maritime Self Defense Forces (MSDF) boasted more than 60 destroyers (twice as many as are in the Pacific-based U.S. Seventh Fleet), including two equipped with the Aegis defense system. Consequently, Japan's forces in the northern Pacific are not trivial when compared to the American commitment. The MSDF have also deployed 100 P-3C anti-submarine aircraft (just 23 are in the U.S. Pacific Fleet). The Air Self Defense Forces have 200 F-15s and 100 F-4s. Moreover, Japan provides roughly 40 percent of the costs of stationing U.S. forces in-country and is likely to increase this contribution, in part to assuage American pressures.

The future trends in the security relationship turn on narrower issues of defense technology competition and on broader issues concerning the rapidly changing geo-strategic environment. With respect to issues of technology competition, two recent examples serve to illustrate the long-run problem: semiconductors and the FSX. It is obvious even to casual students of contemporary military affairs that sophisticated weapons systems are increasingly dependent on advanced micro-electronics. Information processing and target acquisition are especially dependent upon the capabilities of advanced semiconductors. A major Pentagon review of the semiconductor industry pointed out that Japanese firms have become dominant across a range of crucial products and technologies. Some analysts have been relatively relaxed about this development, but the authors of the report sounded the alarm that the United States was in danger of becoming excessively dependent on Japanese suppliers for critical elements of its national security capability and that this trend needed to be reversed. This concern was underscored when Japanese Diet member Shintaro Ishihara asserted in 1989 that the provision of Japanese semiconductors to the Soviet Union could change the global balance of power.

The semiconductor controversy highlights one longer-term trend in defense relations with Japan. It is likely that future military power will rely increasingly on three capabilities: sophisticated information processing techniques; the use of directed energy, such as lasers and particle beams, as weapons of precision (in target acquisition) and high-confidence command and control; and the ability to utilize space for military platforms. Besides the superpowers, only Japan is well-positioned to play a leading role in this emerging security environment. Therefore, Japan has, by definition, military potential, and this potential is increasingly seen in Washington as a threat to American predominance in this field.

The FSX controversy that greeted President Bush upon his assumption of office in early 1989 illustrates a related problem. The FSX program involves the development of a new, advanced fighter aircraft that would be deployed by the Japanese Air Self Defense Forces in the mid-to-late 1990s. Tensions in U.S.-Japan relations materialized over whether the aircraft would be a modified version of the F-16 or a new aircraft developed primarily by the Japanese. In Washington, the issue triggered a struggle between the Departments of State and of Defense, on the one hand, and on the other, the Commerce Department, the Office of the U.S. Trade Representative (USTR), and the Office of Management and Budget (OMB). Representatives from State and Defense felt that the deal—in which General Dynamics would be a major subcontractor to Mitsubishi Heavy Industries—was the best the United States could get. Moreover, they had negotiated it with their Japanese counterparts over several years and were committed to defending the results. Commerce, USTR, and OMB, however, saw the FSX as a major stimulus to the establishment of a Japanese aerospace industry that would pose a long-term challenge to American domination of this industrial sector. Urged on by members of Congress, they succeeded in persuading Bush to reopen the matter and win further Japanese concessions.

If in Tokyo, therefore, the controversy grew to symbolize American inconstancy and unpredictability, from the Washington perspective what the FSX came to symbolize more than anything else was the fear that defense collaboration with Japan would jeopardize the pre-eminent U.S. position in the development of military technology and the manufacturing of advanced weapon systems. Technology transfer to Japan could also, it was argued, nourish future commercial competition in the one major high-tech trade area where the United States remained dominant.

In sum, the emerging Japanese economic prowess has now clearly spilled over into the defense sector. As in other areas of economic activity, the bilateral defense technology relationship will likely be marked by complex patterns of cooperation and competition.

In broader terms, the U.S.-Japan security relationship has rested on the shared sense of the threat posed by Soviet military forces to Japanese territory and to the East Asian region generally. For years both felt genuine concern about potential Soviet strikes against Japanese military targets, a "grab" of the northern island of Hokkaido, and the use of the Soviet theater nuclear forces deployed in the Soviet Far East to coerce Japan into making economic and political concessions. In the mid-to-late 1960s there were also expectations that the People's Republic of China (PRC) might mount a serious challenge to Japanese sovereignty.

By 1990 these prospects had lost virtually all credibility. The PRC has not been seen as a military threat to Japan for many years, and its economic and domestic political difficulties are likely to occupy the full attention of its leadership well into the next century. The panoply of major Soviet concessions in arms control negotiations and Gorbachev's permissive and even encouraging attitude toward the collapse of communism throughout Eastern Europe have largely stripped away the sense of Soviet threat felt in the West, including Japan.

Soviet-Japanese relations have improved relatively little under Gorbachev, in part because of continued Soviet control of the four small islands north of Hokkaido and, more deeply, because of the century-old Russo-Japanese animosity symbolized by Russia's humiliating defeat by Japan in 1905. Even Gorbachev's meeting with South Korean President Roh Tae Woo in June 1990 was not wildly applauded in Tokyo, because it raised the prospect of a possible step toward Korean reunification which many Japanese find threatening. The Soviet president's . . . visit to Tokyo in 1991, however, could greatly improve Soviet-Japan relations if Gorbachev's desire to rescue the Soviet economy from near-collapse were to push him to relinquish the northern islands in return for Japanese financial aid, technical assistance, management training, and investment in Siberian development. Indeed, the [1990] Soviet offer to return two of the islands is perhaps a harbinger of a more flexible policy toward Japan. On the other hand, the Soviet move toward Seoul has stimulated Tokyo to enhance its dialogue with *North* Korea, reflecting inherent tensions among the major powers in Northeast Asia. On balance, although the bilateral relationship between Tokyo and Moscow is not warm, the decline of the Soviet threat has unquestionably undercut the primary strategic rationale for the U.S.-Japan security relationship.

The Current Economic Relationship

Meanwhile, the lightning rod for economic relations remains the bilateral trade imbalance. This totaled $49 billion in 1989, with U.S. imports from Japan at $93.6 billion, roughly double U.S. exports to Japan of $44.6 billion. Contrary to conventional political wisdom, this is an improvement in recent years. . . . As recently as 1987, U.S. imports of $84.6 billion from Japan were *triple* U.S. exports of $28.2 billion, and the rise of Japanese imports was much slower from 1986 to 1989 than it was from 1983 to 1986. But . . . the proportionate imbalance with Japan remains substantially greater than that with the world as a whole, as has been true since the sixties.

The bilateral imbalance rises and falls with the overall U.S. deficit, but would persist even if overall global accounts were squared. There is nothing wrong with this *per se*: there is no particular reason why U.S.-Japan trade should balance bilaterally. In fact, experts generally agree that a significant imbalance in Japan's favor is normal.   Given the nation's strong comparative advantage in high-quality industrial products and its dearth of natural resources, Japan naturally runs surpluses with major importers of manufactured goods (e.g., the United States and the European Community) and deficits with sources of food and raw materials (e.g., Australia, Canada, and Indonesia).   As for the overall American trade imbalance, the proper remedies remain home remedies—as the Japanese keep reminding us.   Americans should cut demand by reducing the federal deficit and increasing private savings.   Together with the decline of the dollar that such policies—and multilateral macroeconomic cooperation—might facilitate, this is the route to bringing overall U.S. trade into balance. . . .

. . . Exerting heat have been the provisions of the Omnibus Trade and Competitiveness Act of 1988.   Designed not to assert direct Congressional control, but to force the executive branch to try harder, it institutes a series of deadlines; the most visible and controversial is a new provision of Section 301 of the Trade Act of 1974, as amended.   "Super-301," as it is labelled, calls upon the administration not just to pinpoint barriers to specific American exports that are "unreasonable" or "unjustifiable," but to single out and name "priority foreign countries" for the "number and pervasiveness" of their "acts, policies, or practices" that impede U.S. exports.

Since the provision was written with Japan in mind, the Bush administration had little practical choice in its first year but to declare Japan a trade "sinner." This it did in May 1989, though it limited its bill of particulars to three product cases: supercomputers, satellites, and wood products.   Reaction was strong in Japan, but a way was found to negotiate on these three specific issues, and settlements were reached on all of them in the spring of 1990, before the deadline built into the Super-301 law.   The two nations also joined in a new negotiation, the so-called Structural Impediments Initiative (SII). Undertaken as an alternative to overall indictment of Japan's economy under Super-301, these talks targeted deep-seated behavior patterns in Japan (and the United States) which lay behind Japanese import resistance (and U.S. noncompetitiveness).   Consultations continued on the yen-dollar exchange rate, bilaterally and within the "Group of Seven" (G-7) advanced industrial nations. . . .

While reciprocal in form, the SII talks were one-sided in fact.   They followed the venerable pattern of employing *gaiatsu*, or foreign pressure, as trigger and pretext for Japanese policy change.   This pattern featured U.S. initiative and Japanese deference.   Exploited and refined by officials in both nations through the postwar period, it had gotten the two nations through many economic crises.   And it produced results again in 1990—a preliminary agreement on SII in April, and a final agreement in June.   The latter, facilitated by Bush's domestic concession on taxes, included a Japanese commitment to increase public works expenditures over a ten-year period.

Yet the *gaiatsu* pattern was based on two now-obsolete presumptions: the predominance of American power and the soundness, in Japanese eyes, of

U.S. policies.   It worked one more time in 1990.   But neither Washington nor Tokyo can long defer the challenge of explicitly addressing Japan's emergence as an economic, technological, and financial superpower and the challenge this poses to both.

In the phrase of Ezra Vogel, Japan has become "Number One" in a wide range of manufacturing industries—from automobiles to consumer electronics to semiconductors—and is clearly the world's leader in the technology and management of the production process. . . .

Under these circumstances, there was a certain droll absurdity to the notion, prevalent in the Japanese press, that current United States demands in the SII talks represented the third American reshaping of Japanese society.[1] There is a similar unreality in the standard Capitol Hill rhetoric, threatening dire U.S. actions if Japan doesn't finally act on trade.   Americans must stop talking as if they can reshape Japan, though pressure at the margins can reinforce trends we find promising.   And Japanese advocates of domestic change must stop waiting for Americans to do their political dirty-work for them.

ALTERNATIVE FUTURES: AN AMERICAN PERSPECTIVE

For the U.S.-Japan alliance, both the geostrategic and the economic contexts have been transformed.   The United States no longer dominates the economic relationship.   Nor do the two nations still share a perception of a strong threat in the international security environment.   And with persistent economic conflict, the core sense of trust between elites of the two societies has been somewhat shaken.   A pessimist might conclude from these changes that the very basis for constructive U.S.-Japan relations has been undermined. But this interpretation is one-sided because it emphasizes only the centrifugal forces that are pulling us apart and does not highlight the centripetal forces that tend to keep the relationship intact and functioning. . . .

Despite efforts to diversify its markets, Japan remains highly dependent on access to the American market to maintain its economic health.   Indeed, the rise in Japanese investments and financial interests in the United States has acted to increase Japanese dependence in important respects.   Moreover, many influential Japanese remain uneasy about the potential resurgence of militarism in their society and see the continued American military presence as a stabilizing force.   Indeed, the long-time support of "unarmed neutrality" by the Japan Socialist Party was predicated, in part, on the desire to constrain such militarism.   In the United States, an enormous appetite has grown up for Japanese goods, not just among connoisseurs of video-cassette recorders but among sophisticated American producers who rely on Japanese inputs or Japanese capital.   There are also important cultural and organizational linkages between the two societies, ranging from Japanese affection for baseball, Kentucky Fried Chicken, and American rock stars, to the work of such organizations as the Japan Society, the Asia Society, the Japan Center for International Exchange, and others that promote positive interactions including student and university exchanges, between the two cultures. We must also not forget that we are dealing here with complex relations between two democracies. The Japanese have weathered a number of difficult political and economic storms in the post–World War II period and their democratic system has continued to flourish.

In the short run, a strong inertia and an interaction of mutual interests tend to keep the overall relationship reasonably steady and healthy, notwithstanding the storms of visible political conflict that grab the headlines. For the present, this more than offsets the forces driving the countries apart. But given this balance of centripetal and centrifugal forces, what might the future portend? Three scenarios seem plausible: across-the-board confrontation; competitive techno-nationalism; and competitive interdependence.

Across-the-Board Confrontation

Under this scenario, the image of "Japan As Economic Rival" comes to dominate the relationship. Its underlying premise is that the strength of national economies will be, sooner or later, the determinant of future political power. Japan and the European Community are increasingly recognized as the main U.S. economic, and hence, political competitors. In this future it is also assumed that Japan's alleged uniqueness—its cultural exclusivity in particular—will limit the prospects for cooperation and will reinforce the tendency toward greater inter-state conflict. As conflict grows, so will support in the United States for the argument that Americans must recognize the "zero-sum" nature of the relationship and mobilize for the competition, rather than wait for further gains by Japan (and perhaps by the European Community as well).

This future would pose serious economic and security problems. On the economic side, the United States would incur, at least in the short term, substantial losses as Americans consciously sought to "contain" economic interaction with Japan and to subsidize U.S.-based competition. This would cause particular difficulties for an open economy without the institutions or mechanisms geared to promote either economic insulation or an industrial policy. Sooner or later, it would appear that across-the-board confrontation would lead to the collapse of the post–World War II international economic order, including the General Agreement on Tariffs and Trade (GATT) and the liberal trade regime, the G-7, and other institutions for cooperative economic leadership.

In security terms this scenario would severely erode the U.S. geostrategic position in East Asia. In an across-the-board economic confrontation, anti-Japanese sentiment in the United States could easily translate into severe protectionist legislation against Japanese imports that would greatly damage Japan's economy, at least in the short run. This legislation would in turn trigger enormous anti-American sentiment in Japan. It is hard to visualize support in either Washington or Tokyo for the maintenance of U.S. forces in Japan under such circumstances. The U.S. withdrawal from Japan and from the security alliance would then stimulate a new defense debate in Japan. Without American military protection or the explicit U.S. guarantees of Japanese oil deliveries from the Persian Gulf, there is a serious risk that Japan would become a major new military rival capable of equalling or even surpassing the United States in the development and deployment of high-technology weaponry. The renewed sense of threat from Japan would, in turn, stimulate an arms buildup in Korea, the People's Republic of China, Indonesia and elsewhere in East Asia.

A variant of this scenario envisages the United States and Japan sliding into confrontation without an explicit intention on the part of either to intensify the rivalry. As economic conflicts continue, over time they could undermine commitment to the broader relationship. Government leaders in Tokyo and Washington would become increasingly frustrated with trying to patch over differences and bearing the burden of the relationship in domestic politics. After a while, these differences might extend beyond economic and technological competition to fundamental disagreements over policies toward third countries in the Middle East, Europe, or elsewhere. At some point leaders in one of the countries would decide that it was in their nation's strategic interest or in their own personal political interest to visibly resist or confront the other, or perhaps even to renounce the alliance.

Movement in this direction could be fueled by arguments that the U.S. geostrategic position in Asia no longer served any useful purpose. With the removal of the Soviet threat, some claim that American forces in the region are configured to counter an enemy that no longer exists and are incapable of influencing other troubles in East Asia—turmoil in China or the conflict in Cambodia, for example. But this logic is faulty. The United States retains enormous interest in the stability and prosperity of the region, with which its trade now substantially exceeds trade with Europe. And this stability depends on a continuing U.S. political-military presence.

In contrast to Europe, with its web of long-standing and substantial multilateral institutions and relationships (particularly the North Atlantic Treaty Organization and the European Community), multilateralism in Asia is very weak. The Association of Southeast Asian Nations (ASEAN), which includes Indonesia, the Philippines, Singapore, Malaysia, Thailand, and Brunei, has not moved beyond limited economic cooperation. The newly formed Asia-Pacific Economic Cooperation Council (APEC), which includes all the ASEAN members plus the United States, Canada, Japan, South Korea, Australia, and New Zealand, has yet to define its purposes. The Southeast Asia Treaty Organization (SEATO) collapsed after the American defeat in Vietnam, and it never included East Asian nations.

Instead, what has endured in U.S.–East Asian security policy has been bilateral security relationships, carefully developed and nurtured, with Japan,

South Korea, and the Philippines, as well as strong bilateral ties with Australia, Thailand, and Taiwan. In Europe, it may be possible for the United States to curtail sharply its military presence and redefine its security role within a redefined set of multilateral institutions, but this option is not now available in Asia. Some trimming of U.S. forces may well prove feasible, but an American withdrawal and a U.S.-Japan confrontation would put the entire East Asian security balance "up for grabs." Notwithstanding the receding of the Soviet threat, the U.S. political-military presence is the one broadly-accepted stabilizing force.

This stabilizing role is especially noteworthy on the Korean peninsula, where U.S. forces not only serve as a tripwire to deter a North Korean attack on the South, but discourage the development of adventurism in Seoul toward the north. While much has changed since the outbreak of the Korean War in 1950, the situation remains tense and volatile; the border is one of the most heavily militarized areas in the world. It would be foolhardy and dangerous to remove U.S. forces now.

Finally, there are no guarantees that Chinese or Soviet militarism in the region will not reemerge. The brutal force used by the Chinese leadership to put down the pro-democracy student movement in 1989 demonstrates that not all communist regimes are willing to fade quietly from the scene. The coming succession crisis in Beijing could bring about enormous instability and civil strife; the political situation in the Soviet Union is in extraordinary flux. While U.S. forces would not be directly engaged in shaping developments in either of these great nations, it is difficult to see how reduction or removal of the American presence could lend stability to East Asia.

Competitive Techno-Nationalism

Under a second scenario, the two nations might eschew the risks of confrontation and seek to maintain a general geopolitical alliance and relatively open trade, but simultaneously intensify their competition for global technological leadership. Seeing this as the key to power in the twenty-first century, they might strengthen governmental efforts both to protect and to develop technology on a national basis, with official programs supporting private firms and research and development consortia that exclude or limit participation by foreign firms.

Like mercantilism, "techno-nationalism" views development of new products and processes as a competition among nations, whereas traditional liberals see it as a competition among firms. Advocates of this approach for Americans often see it as doing unto the Japanese what they have been doing to us—or, more benignly, doing *for* ourselves what the Japanese have been doing for themselves.

In addition to its plausibility as a strategy, techno-nationalism has two sorts of domestic political appeals. It offers a rationale to mobilize Americans to change their public and private behavior: to attack the federal deficit, to save more and spend less, to invest for the future. And for Democrats, it offers an appealing marriage of nationalism and government activism.

Critics of such an approach, in turn, see it as a blend of protectionism and counterproductive government meddling in matters better left to markets. Advocates counter that some losses in short-term economic efficiency would be well worth taking if, over the longer term, the American economy can be "restored" or "rebuilt" into the unquestioned global leader it once was. Even if this is beyond reach, America (and the world) might still be a gainer if the relative U.S. position could be stabilized, and interdependence limited and managed. The managed trade likely to be part of such an approach might even serve to damp the fires of U.S.-Japan conflict. After all, "good fences make good neighbors."

The techno-nationalist option responds to undeniable Japanese industrial and financial power. But is it feasible, given the internationalization of the global economy and the openness of American society? Is it desirable, given the rising share of economic and technical innovation that takes place outside our borders?

Feasibility problems begin with deciding what is "national" or "American." What economic institutions should a techno-nationalist policy support? Or to put the question in Harvard economist Robert B. Reich's words, "Who is Us?" Certainly a General Motors plant in Michigan would be included, or a U.S.-owned semiconductor enterprise operating in Silicon Valley. But what about IBM/Japan, or the North American Honda Company? American multinational business would opt for including the former and excluding the latter. Labor has understandably taken the opposite view: encouraging some Japanese investment here and criticizing offshore operations by American firms. But from the techno-nationalist perspective, both vessels—foreign firms operating here, and American firms operating abroad—are leaky.

Even if this problem can somehow be surmounted, consider the fact that industrial process technology has a strong engineering component. How would American techno-nationalism cope with the fact that 50 percent of new U.S.-trained engineering PhDs each year are foreign-born? Given the need for capital, how would the United States "protect" its enterprises from the pull of Japanese technology or the lure of Japanese money? The U.S. Semiconductor Manufacturing Technology consortium (Sematech) may exclude Japanese firms from membership, but it cannot exclude its American members from far-reaching joint ventures with those very same Japanese firms—business interest, and financial need, are just too strong. And we have not even reached the classic problems of deciding *which* technologies government should underwrite, and at what stage in the movement from development of product and process technology to construction of specific plants the public subsidies should stop.

If feasible, is techno-nationalism desirable for the United States? Would it maintain or restore U.S. pre-eminence? By fencing U.S. technologies in, do Americans not simultaneously fence others out, cutting themselves off from the growing volume of innovation that takes place elsewhere, particularly in Japan? Doesn't this risk protecting the second-rate?

Even if pursued with great intensity, a U.S.-Japan technological competition might prove hard to contain. It could well spill over into the security and political sphere, leading in time to confrontation.

Competitive Interdependence

A third approach would be to work consciously at building "competitive interdependence." The U.S. and Japanese governments would work to mute "us-versus-them" stereotypes, by stressing the benefits that citizens of each nation are bringing to the economic welfare of both. To counter the prevalent mercantilist, zero-sum, U.S.-versus-Japan perspective, national leaders would find it in their interest to build a future on the benefits of interdependence. Because both nations are so rich in economic assets and institutions, they gain much if these institutions become intertwined.

This is obviously the preferable future. It is also the choice, we believe, of most of those who weigh the alternatives carefully. In such a scenario, the maintenance of strong ties between the United States and Japan is seen as part of a broader pattern of promoting economic interdependence and of protecting the national security interests of major states. The lesson that endures is that economic growth and great-power peace have been achieved over the past forty years through security cooperation and a growing global economy, not through narrow nationalism. It is these conditions that need to be sustained for the maintenance of American welfare and power.

National governments still have a stake in increasing the returns, absolute and relative, from factors of production based within their territory; because this increases their citizens' welfare, and because it contributes to overall national power and influence. But this interest—the "competitive" concern—would be pursued in ways aimed at muting economic conflict between nations and maximizing the gains from cooperation.

MAKING "COMPETITIVE INTERDEPENDENCE" A REALITY

The front page of the April 6, 1990, *Washington Post* may be a harbinger for the future: the announcement of the dates of Gorbachev's forthcoming Washington visit was upstaged by a report of the interim results of the SII talks between Japan and the United States. In the 1990s, America's place in the world may depend more on working out continuing, constructive relationships with economic allies-cum-competitors, than on our dealings with a declining strategic adversary. Some brief guidelines follow.

Maintain the U.S.-Japan Security Treaty

It is hard to see any reason not to continue the mutually beneficial arrange-ment of the U.S.-Japan security treaty. It is easy to see large costs in breaking it off. The geostrategic changes that swept across Europe in 1989 are also being felt in Asia—Gorbachev met with South Korean President Roh Tae Woo in San Francisco in June 1990, Sino-Soviet relations have improved, and polarization in the Philippines is growing over the American military presence at Subic Bay and Clark Field—but the withdrawal of American military forces from Japan would not serve U.S. interests. Not only does the American military presence reassure our allies in that region against a possible resurgence of the Soviet military threat, it also serves to dissuade the Japanese from acquiring power-projection forces of their own. U.S. forces in Japan have a political and psychological "pin-down" effect, constraining the relatively small but potentially influential circles in Tokyo—some senior officials in the Ground Self Defense Forces, militant nationalists within the Liberal Democratic Party such as Shintaro Ishihara, some key members of the business community, a few journalists and intellectuals—who resent the American-authored Japanese constitution, believe that the days of the United States as a superpower are numbered, and argue that Japan needs to begin to acquire military and political power commensurate with its economic might.

The residual animosity toward Japan throughout Asia remains substantial, and the termination of the U.S.-Japan security treaty would multiply security anxiety throughout the region. It would almost certainly trigger a funda-mental reappraisal of Seoul's security position and would strengthen the arguments of those in Korea who would defend the need to acquire ballistic missiles or nuclear weapons. Thus, even if Japan initially had no plans to enhance its armed forces, the removal of the American military presence from the Japanese home islands would risk provoking a regional arms race that would be in no one's interest.

It is desirable to broaden the Japanese defense contribution through op-erational and technology cooperation, and through increases in Japanese financial support of U.S. defense activities based in Japan. But the United States should not pressure Japan to increase its defense spending further as a share of GNP.

There remains the genuine dilemma of U.S. defense dependence on Japanese technology. Dependence on foreign sources for critical components is ob-viously a problem—it would be better for American interests, certainly, if everything our military needed were "made in USA." But the globalization of defense-related industries is a fact of life, as is the position of Japanese firms in the forefront of technological and product development. The way to cope with this is not by narrow "buy-American" policies, but by encour-aging multiple sources of supply, by strengthening U.S.-based technology development, and by pursuing the strategy of competitive interdependence.

Shore Up the American Economy

Since the distribution of nationally-based productive power does matter, for the welfare of citizens as well as the place of the nation in the world, the United States needs to strengthen its capacity to hold its own in future economic growth, and to eliminate areas of obvious and unnecessary weakness. Above all, the United States should end its $100 billion per year financial dependence on Japan (and the rest of the world), by steps which increase domestic savings and reduce consumption by $150–200 billion per year (3–4 percent of current U.S. gross national product).   The best way to do this is to end public "dis-saving" by moving the total federal budget (Social Security included) from deficit to surplus.   This requires, however, a painful exercise in domestic political burden-sharing, with Republicans sharing responsibility for new taxes and Democrats consenting to restraints on Social Security and other programs that serve their constituencies.   Any budget agreement . . . will be, at most, a first step along a rocky road.

Such a restoration of macroeconomic sanity should be reinforced by selected microeconomic steps.   Since private firms pursuing their own interests tend to underinvest in research and development, the United States should strengthen governmental support of technology development, particularly on production processes, in broad areas of present (and likely future) economic importance to U.S. and other advanced industrial economies.

Also necessary are stronger public programs in such critical areas as education and infrastructure development.   Concerning investment, Americans might shelve the current sterile debate about the capital gains tax and try to find out what really does move business and individuals to save and invest. This could lead to realistic incentive packages encouraging long-term business investment in productive assets, and longer-term planning and profit horizons.

Continue Pressure for Opening Up Japan

Americans should continue their efforts to open up and internationalize Japan's enormously productive but still relatively closed economy.   This goal should be pursued, however, through processes and substantive agreements that become progressively more two-sided, involving reciprocal pressure, as appropriate to a relationship of equals (or near-equals).   In this sense, the SII talks are correct in form, though insufficiently balanced in practice.

Work Explicitly to Deepen Interdependence

Rather than mobilizing as if for economic warfare, and rather than crying with alarm at each new Japanese international economic venture, Americans should seek ways to reinforce and reward Japanese internationalists.   Continuing pressure for investment access in Japan, for example, should be joined by encouragement of Japanese and other foreign direct investment here, particularly that which underwrites high-value-added economic activity within our borders.   Joint ventures should be, in most instances, welcomed.   They are particularly welcome in manufacturing, since the operations of Japanese firms in the United States can be a particularly effective means for the transfer of technology from Japan to the United States.

Government support of research and development programs should extend to all firms, U.S.- and foreign-owned, that are carrying out important research and development and technology-intensive production on U.S. soil, although it might be appropriate to insist that the government-supported activity be carried on within our borders.   Learning from the technological progress of Japan-based firms requires a strengthened U.S. capacity for ongoing dialogue with them and the people who make them work.

Speak Out for Competitive Interdependence

Finally, leaders in both nations should offer a rhetorical alternative to economic nationalism, by giving voice to the goal of competitive interdependence and developing programs in its name.   To hold their own, Americans need to correct their economic policies and shore up their institutions.   But to get the maximum gains from the dynamic global economy, with minimum risks of future interstate conflict, Americans should want the Japanese involved in the U.S. economy, just as Americans should be involved in Japan, and both in Europe.   There should be top quality economic activity going on in all of them.

Such an approach serves to vindicate the main lesson of the last forty years: that welfare gains come not from competition in armaments, but from progress in production and in global economic integration.   Leaders in Washington—and Tokyo—should keep reminding us of these lessons and adopt policies that put them into practice.

NOTE

1. The first two, of course, were Commodore Perry's opening of Japan in the mid-nineteenth century, and the U.S. occupation under General Douglas MacArthur after World War II.

17 THE METAMORPHOSIS OF THE THIRD WORLD: U.S. INTERESTS IN THE 1990s

John W. Sewell

As the United States enters the last decade of the twentieth century, it faces a policy environment unprecedented in postwar history. The U.S. economy is still the world's largest and wealthiest, but the heightened interdependence of the international system has eroded the ability of the United States unilaterally to dictate its own interests.

Unlike earlier periods, the developing countries are much more central to important U.S. interests. The developing world, however, also has changed, and U.S. relations with the developing countries in the 1990s will be played out in a much different policy environment than in the past.

The United States has interests in the developing world in the 1990s that are multiple, complex, overlapping, and often conflicting. Economic and political interests in many developing countries will sharpen, and security interests—as traditionally defined—may diminish.

The diminution of security interests is in and of itself a major change, as U.S. policies toward the developing countries have been dominated by concerns about military security since the 1950s. Hopefully, the evolving U.S.–Soviet relationship will reduce threats to American interests in the Third World and open diplomatic possibilities to reduce tensions. . . .

This [selection] is based on the assumption that traditional U.S. international economic interests that have been sustained in the postwar period are valid; and that U.S. interests lie in fostering an expanding and relatively open global trading and financial system that meets the needs of all countries that participate in it. In addition, the United States now has an urgent interest in ameliorating a set of common global problems—poverty, environment, population, acquired immune deficiency syndrome (AIDS), and drugs—that in different ways threaten our own well-being.

In the decade ahead, however, the United States no longer has the power to dominate and "manage" the international system by itself; and currently it is constrained by its own economic mismanagement. In addition, the developing countries must be more centrally involved if the United States is to further its own interests. In the last two decades many developing countries have:

- emerged as important trading partners—particularly as export markets at a time when trade has become more important to the United States—and as competitors in manufactured goods, such as steel, autos, and light aircraft.

- become important participants in the international financial system, most notably as borrowers from the commercial banking systems of the industrialized world.

- emerged as politically important in their own right. Few countries are as important to the United States as is its neighbor, Mexico.

- developed much greater capacities to manage their own affairs, and are less likely to be dictated to from abroad.

- become important potential partners in addressing the international "global agenda" problems of poverty and environment, and common social concerns, such as narcotics and AIDS.

THE "THIRD WORLD" HAS CHANGED AND THE PACE OF CHANGE WILL CONTINUE

From 1950 to 1980 the developing countries compiled a spectacular record of economic growth. As a group, they grew at a faster rate in the postwar period than the developed countries did during their own industrial revolutions. As a result, the developing country share in real gross world product grew from 15 percent in 1960 to 22 percent in 1985. In the same period, many of these countries became important participants in the expanding global trading system. In 1965 they accounted for only 7 percent of exports of manufacturers; by 1985 their share of global manufactured exports had risen to over 16 percent.

The composition of Third World industrial exports also changed, with traditional labor-intensive products, such as shoes and textiles, diminishing in importance compared to exports of electric machinery, chemicals, and transport equipment. In 1986, for the first time, developing countries as a whole earned more foreign exchange selling manufactured exports than fuels or nonfuel primary products. Manufactures now account for more than one-half the foreign exchange earnings of large middle-income countries, such as the Philippines and Thailand.

But economic progress has been shared unevenly among developing countries, and there is now a growing differentiation among and between countries.

In the 1960s and 1970s Latin America experienced quite respectable growth, particularly in countries such as Brazil and Mexico. And a number of other middle-income countries succeeded in enhancing their status in the international economy. But Asia is the real success story. Between 1970 and 1986 the newly industrialized Asian countries outpaced average world trade and output growth. Real output of these economies increased at an annual average of 6 to 8 percent between 1980 and 1987. The volume of merchandise exports of the newly industrialized Asian countries expanded at an average of about 12.7 percent a year between 1980 and 1987, or more than three times as fast as world merchandise trade volume. In 1986 . . . the dollar value of Asian countries' merchandise exports increased by 13 percent to reach $465 billion, or about 22 percent of world merchandise exports. Asian countries' trade surpluses rose as the volume of their imports lagged far behind exports in the 1980s.

In contrast the low-income countries—concentrated in sub-Saharan Africa, but also in South Asia and Latin America—have remained producers of primary commodities and are heavily dependent on flows of concessionary resources. But even sub-Saharan Africa posted respectable records of economic growth in the 1960s and early 1970s.

In the 1970s the pattern of financial flows to the developing countries also changed; total transfers grew rapidly and diversified. Private bank lending (fueled by surpluses from the Organization of Petroleum Exporting Countries—OPEC) and foreign investment swamped Official Development Assistance (ODA). Resource flows from OECD (Organization for Economic Cooperation and Development) nations to developing countries nearly tripled between 1970 and 1983. In the five years prior to 1982, developing countries received positive net resource transfers of $147 billion in medium- and long-term lending—with most of the increase coming from private commercial sources. As a result, by 1983 Official Development Assistance accounted for less than one-third of total financial flows from rich to poor countries.

This progress came to a halt in most parts of the developing world in the early 1980s, and in terms of economic growth, the 1980s have been a lost decade. Only Asia has escaped.

High interest rates, falling commodity prices, heavy debt burdens, negative net transfers, volatile exchange rates, and restricted markets in the developed economies plagued a faltering international economy. World recession, and then crippling debt-service payments, caused growth among Latin American countries to slow to annual average rates of 1.9 percent between 1980 and 1987. Per capita income is roughly 8 percent lower today than in 1981, and wages have dropped by 30 to 40 percent in some countries. Sub-Saharan Africa grew more slowly than other developing regions in the 1970s, and the situation worsened drastically over the period from 1980 to 1987 as Africa's real gross domestic product grew by less than two-tenths of one percent annually. As national income dropped and populations climbed, per capita incomes in some African countries have fallen by as much as 25 percent since 1981. Like Latin America, Africa's export performance continues to be plagued by restrictive debt burdens and a lack of net capital inflows. Moreover, the sharp decline in prices of primary products, which comprise 90 percent of the region's exports, slashed export earnings.

According to most forecasts for the period to 1995, developing country growth will remain restrained. The World Bank projects real gross domestic product growth for developing countries as a group at about 4.2 percent— higher than earlier [in the 1980s], but significantly below the rate achieved during the 1970s. Low-income countries' growth rates—particularly for sub-Saharan Africa—are expected to be barely sufficient to keep pace with population increases. . . .

As a result of these changes, both favorable and unfavorable, the construct of the "developing world" is itself no longer adequate as a basis for defining U.S. interests and determining U.S. policies. Indeed, these countries now exhibit such diversity as to raise questions about the validity of the very concept. The developing world now can be disaggregated for purposes of policy analysis into at least three rough groupings; but even these contain a wide diversity of countries:

- the *industrializing countries*, including the six newly industrializing countries of East Asia and Latin America, but also a much larger number of countries that have increased their industrial production as a share of gross domestic product;

- the *low-income countries* of sub-Saharan Africa, South Asia, and Latin America;

- the *"Giants"*—India and China—that are rapidly modernizing industrial economies held back by large rural and still very poor populations.

Each of these categories, however, encompasses a variety of countries. The "industrializing" category includes the Asian countries, which have piled up substantial financial reserves, and the debt-burdened economies of Brazil and Mexico in Latin America. Similarly, Kenya, Zimbabwe, and the Ivory Coast in Africa have compiled very respectable records of increasing manufactured output based on their agricultural resources. Finally, countries in all these categories face problems of poverty and environmental deterioration.

In the 1990s policy makers should look at the developing countries not by income categories, but by the issue areas in which individual countries are important to U.S. interests. For instance, discussions on commercial debt should mainly involve Latin America, as only a few African countries borrowed from commercial banks; trade negotiations should touch on various groups of developing countries, depending on the particular trade issue; and U.S. foreign aid should be concentrated in the countries that do not have access to global markets or nonconcessional capital.

THE CHANGED POSITION OF THE UNITED STATES

The health of the U.S. economy will have immense implications for the policy environment of the 1990s, and therefore for U.S. relations with the developing countries. As the United States still accounts for 28 percent of the world's gross national product (GNP), an expanding U.S. economy can create an international environment conducive to progress and growth; but a faltering U.S. economy cannot provide the markets necessary to absorb growing developing country exports, and will not have the resources needed to deal with the issue and assist renewed growth and progress in the developing countries.

The United States, however, now is in an international economic position unprecedented since 1945. Like many debt-burdened developing countries, the United States must balance its trade accounts, service its foreign debt, and rebuild its industrial base. Although its position is undeniably more favorable than that of any developing country, the United States, too, needs to develop.

Most analysts believe that the external deficit of the United States can be brought under control and the U.S. economic position restored only with a substantial reduction in the federal budget deficit. Equally important, coordinated policy action by the main industrial economies, particularly Japan and Germany, will be needed to reduce trade imbalances to sustainable levels . . . and to set the stage for steady growth worldwide during the [1990s].

Conventional wisdom currently holds that the U.S. trade imbalance will be closed if these measures are taken. The role that could be played by the developing countries—or, more specifically, by the countries that are important participants in the international economy—is virtually absent from current policy discussions. According to Overseas Development Council (ODC) estimates, however, renewed growth in those countries could raise U.S. exports to developing countries by as much as $30 billion by 1992. . . . The industrialized countries of Western Europe present only modest opportunities for increased U.S. exports. Even under optimistic assumptions about increased openness in Japan, that country is not large enough to be the only expanding market for U.S. exports.

ODC's analysis shows that resumed growth in the industrialized countries will be necessary but not by itself sufficient to increase U.S. exports and reduce the U.S. trade deficit to manageable proportions. In addition, the current debt-induced outflow of resources from the developing countries will have to be reversed to expand developing country import capacity—and our own export potential. Contrary to the thrust of the current debate raging in this country, U.S. trade problems with most developing countries are far more due to their current debt predicament and weakened import capability than to either unfair trade practices or any fundamental decline in U.S. competitiveness.

The hard fact is that neither the U.S. merchandise trade account nor the current account is likely to be balanced in the next several years. But sustained and rapid growth in the industrializing developing countries is a key element in making significant progress toward reducing the trade deficit without inducing a global recession.

THE EMERGENCE OF A GLOBAL AGENDA OF INTERRELATED PROBLEMS

Along with growth, debt, and adjustment, poverty, environmental sustainability, rapid population growth, urbanization, AIDS, and drugs are now central issues in U.S. relations with the developing countries.

Poverty

Just as developing countries made important advances in economic growth during the 1960s, important achievements also were made in human well-being. Life expectancy rose and infant mortality rates fell in most developing countries. People in developing countries in 1985 could expect to live an average of about sixty years, compared to about fifty-one years in 1965. Literacy has spread dramatically: primary school education is now a reality for most children in the developing world, and secondary school enrollment rates have also improved.

Nevertheless, the problem of poverty looms larger than ever. Despite measurable progress, the stark reality is that the poor are still very poor, and, because of population growth, there are now more of them. Roughly one in five of this planet's 5 billion people lives in absolute poverty, struggling with malnutrition, illiteracy, disease, infant mortality, and short life expectancy. In addition, a disproportionate number of people living in poverty are women posing a new challenge for those concerned with alleviating poverty. In a September 1988 address to the World Bank Board of Governors, Barber Conable, president of the World Bank, pointed out:

> Poverty on today's scale prevents a billion people from having even a minimally acceptable standard of living. To allow every fifth human being on our planet to suffer such an existence is a moral outrage. It is more: It is bad economics, a terrible waste of precious development resources. Poverty destroys lives, human dignity and economic potential.

The incidence of poverty varies markedly from region to region. In East and Southeast Asia, slower population growth rates and steady advances in per capita income have contributed to a significant reduction in poverty. In South Asia, where roughly half of the world's poor live, modest rates of growth have barely kept pace with the expanding population. And in sub-Saharan Africa, where two-thirds of the people live in poverty, rapid population growth rates combined with sustained economic deterioration, falling or stagnant agricultural production, and natural disasters all have contributed to widespread malnutrition and decreased social welfare.

In addition, the economic stagnation of most developing countries in the 1980s has reversed many hard-won gains of earlier decades. For sixteen African and Latin American countries, per capita income was lower in 1985 than in 1965. In another dozen countries in these two regions, per capita income grew by less than 1 percent during the same period. In twenty African countries, the average calorie supply, already inadequate, was lower in 1985 than in 1965. With slow growth predicted for most of these economies in the 1990s, the prospects for recovery of living standards in the future is questionable.

Environment

Massive and potentially irreversible environmental destruction is consuming the earth's resource base. Between 1950 and 1983, 38 percent of Central America's and 24 percent of Africa's forests disappeared. Logging, agricultural expansion, and urban growth contributed to the destruction of forests. Deforestation undermines development by destroying watersheds, reducing fuel and material availability, destroying species, and affecting global climate.

The temperature of the earth's atmosphere appears to be rising, posing a serious threat to virtually all natural processes on which human life depends. The so-called greenhouse effect expected to result from rising atmospheric concentrations of carbon dioxide and other gases is already under way. Between 1950 and 1983 the level of carbon dioxide emissions tripled. The largest portion is due to industrialized countries, but the fastest growth of emissions has been in developing countries.

The report of the World Commission on Environment and Development, chaired by Norwegian Prime Minister Gro Brundtland, concluded that

> Major unintended changes are occurring in the atmosphere, in soils, in waters, among plants and animals, and in the relationships among all of these. The rate of change is outstripping the ability of scientific disciplines and our current capabilities to assess and advise: The security, well-being, and very survival of the planet depends on making the necessary institutional changes, now.

Population

Environmental problems are exacerbated by population growth. Each of the 86 million people added to the population each year will consume additional land, water, and energy, thus further straining the environment. The world's population doubled in less than thirty years, passing the 5 billion mark in 1987. An additional 3 billion people will inhabit the globe by 2025.

Almost all of the growth in global populations has been concentrated in the developing world, where human demands often overtax local systems. Although population growth per se is not always harmful, when annual population increases are coupled with heightened stress on local ecosystems, shortages of food, fodder, and fuel can emerge almost overnight. If the demands of local populations surpass the sustainable yields of forests, grasslands, and croplands, the systems will continue to deteriorate even if population growth stops. Shortages of fuelwood—which affect 1.5 billion people in sixty-five countries—and the search for crop and pasture land contribute to the rampant devastation. In India, well over half the lands suffer from degradation and face steadily declining productivity without major new investments.

Urbanization

Since 1950 Third World cities have been growing approximately three times faster than those in the industrialized world. By the turn of the century, half of the world's population will be urban, and eighteen of the world's twenty-one largest cities will be located in the developing world. Third World cities are growing very fast, but squatter settlements, shantytowns, and low-income neighborhoods within cities are growing about twice as fast. In the poorest countries, such as Haiti and Burundi, as many as one-half of all city dwellers live in absolute poverty; in India, about 40 percent; and in less poor countries, such as Morocco or the Philippines, about 30 percent.

Common Social Problems: AIDS and Drugs

An increasing share of the global total of AIDS cases has been identified in developing countries where limited resources inhibit the ability to respond to the AIDS challenge with effective prevention campaigns. In per capita terms, a number of developing countries already have statistically more severe AIDS epidemics than does the United States. Globally, AIDS epidemics appear to be most serious in Africa, the Caribbean, Europe, and North America—with seventeen of the nineteen most afflicted countries found in Africa and the Caribbean. In Uganda, for example, the number of people with AIDS may be doubling every four to six months, and if present rates continue, more than half of all sexually active Ugandans may be infected by 2000.

The impact of AIDS on social and economic development in the developing world, though difficult to forecast, may be critical. A preliminary study by Harvard University showed that economic losses due to AIDS in five seriously affected central African countries could . . . exceed total foreign aid to those countries by 1991. Poor health resulting from poverty may intensify the impact of AIDS in many developing countries, since malnutrition increases a person's susceptibility to infectious disease.

The rising tide of illicit drugs entering developed country markets represents a significant and increasingly divisive factor in relations with the developing world. The main consumer countries are rich and industrialized; the main producer countries are poor and predominantly agricultural. Producer and consumer countries blame each other for the accelerating drug traffic and advocate, respectively, demand-side and supply-side solutions.   Efforts to control drug cultivation and production overseas often impinge on nationalist sensitivities.   Political elites in some developing countries view antidrug crusades as imposing significant economic and social costs and as creating new and formidable political challenges.   Inevitably, narcotics control drains political and financial capital that could be used to pursue other policy goals.

A "THIRD INDUSTRIAL REVOLUTION" MAY TRANSFORM RELATIONS BETWEEN DEVELOPED AND DEVELOPING COUNTRIES

If the United States deals with its immediate economic problems and adjusts to a changed international economic position, it can end up in a relatively more powerful position by the mid-1990s.

This does not mean, however—as some seem to assume—that if the adjustment task is accomplished, the world will revert to the *status quo ante*. Nor is it clear that, even if the United States makes the transition, prospects for many developing countries will be particularly favorable.   Not only do they have to work their way out of the debt situation; but at the same time, developments in economics, environment, science, technology, and industrial organization are rapidly changing the structure of the international economy, with profound implications for both the United States and the developing countries.

Technological developments, such as qualitative advances in information processing, industrial robots, and new high-speed global communications networks, are contributing to fundamental shifts in relations between the United States and the developing countries.   This "Third Industrial Revolution" has the potential to enable the United States to reestablish economic supremacy, but it also threatens to increase the gap between industrialized and developing countries.   The prospect of a developing world lagging further and further behind technologically—and unable to compete globally on any significant scale—is not in the political and economic interests of the United States or the developing countries.

By the mid-1990s, the impact of the new industrial technologies will be felt.   The components include virtually simultaneous developments:

- Micro electronics is drastically reshaping patterns of industrial production and already has led to the introduction of totally new products. Welding and painting in the auto industry, for instance, are almost exclusively done by robots.

- Leaps in global communications link together the world virtually instantaneously, allowing industry to be geographically dispersed.

- New management techniques pioneered by the Japanese are transforming industrial production in the United States. These include "just-in-time" inventory practices, an emphasis on quality production, and the development of new, closer links between suppliers and producers.

• Finally, new advanced synthetic materials developed for specific purposes and the new products resulting from our vastly expanded understanding of genetics already are appearing in the marketplace.

These technologies can work to the advantage of the United States. American workers are skilled and flexible; and the U.S. labor force will grow slowly between now and the year 2000. U.S. research and development capacity is strong, and the United States has Third World neighbors that can provide close, lower-cost manufacturing sites. One major stumbling block is the fact that these developments require capital and technological skill, which developing countries lack. Likewise, many of these new technologies require fewer workers. Yet a country like Mexico faces the difficult choice between investing in these technologies to remain globally competitive, and the need to create a million new jobs a year to accommodate its growing population.

Developing countries that do not have a significant industrial base and that do not already export to industrialized countries will find their economic problems compounded. This poses tremendous challenges for the United States. If these countries are not equipped to assimilate new technologies, their deepening economic malaise will exert the same kind of drag on American exports in the 1990s as it has since the early 1980s.

POLICIES FOR THE 1990s

Choices taken in the period immediately ahead will determine the broad shape of the policy environment in the developing countries by the mid-1990s. There are various possible outcomes. At one extreme, a series of difficult policy decisions can be taken to deal with the debt issue and with continued liberalization of the global trading system that will restore economic growth rates in the developing countries (and the industrialized world) to levels approaching those of the 1960s and 1970s. At the other, global growth rates could well continue at the low levels of the 1980s, leading to widely divergent country experiences. Continuing population growth combined with stagnant economies could lead to a developing world containing many countries marked by increasing tension and growing human misery.

The current U.S. economic predicament has focused political attention on the need to take policy action swiftly. To revitalize its economy and restore its ability to exercise international leadership, the United States would be wise to devise measures to support renewed global growth, including rapid growth in the developing countries. In the immediate future, financial measures will be of utmost importance to this effort.

Meanwhile, however, the longer-term economic trends driven by the technological revolution continue unabated.   The kinds of policies needed to address these problems generally have longer lead times than the short-term financial measures that can stimulate growth, making it imperative to proceed on both fronts at the same time.   The following policy recommendations focus on measures to deal with the present economic crisis. . . .

Managing the Short-term Financial Crisis

The United States has a very strong interest in pursuing a short-term global economic strategy that emphasizes renewed global growth, particularly in the developing countries.   Furthermore, if this growth is to have the necessary, positive impact on global trade imbalances, it is vital to design policy actions to help channel it into expanded trade.   From the perspective of the United States as well as developing countries, these actions must pay particular attention to growth in developing countries.   These policies will have to be developed and implemented in cooperation with other industrialized countries and with the developing countries most concerned.   In this setting, U.S. leadership remains pivotal.   The policies described below can be implemented only if the United States, despite its current economic problems, takes an active role in designing and supporting them.

The central short-term issue for U.S. policy makers is to identify politically feasible new initiatives to help the developing countries resume and sustain economic growth.   The imperatives of narrowing the U.S. budget deficit currently make any major expansion of resources for international programs politically difficult.   And the commercial banks and private equity investors are highly unlikely to expand current lending levels or strengthen their investment positions until growth resumes in those countries.   But new programs are possible if the need is important enough.

Renewed and sustained growth in the developing countries requires that these countries themselves adopt appropriate economic policies, and that the net transfer of resources to those countries be at a level that supports growth.

A globally coordinated, U.S.–led debt policy designed to reverse the net drain of resources from the debtor countries is essential to this end.   Such a policy should allocate the costs of adjustment among banks, debtor countries, international institutions, and lending countries without destabilizing the international banking system.   A central element of such a strategy would be the establishment of target figures, perhaps under the aegis of the World Bank and International Monetary Fund, for individual debtor countries to reduce resource drains in ways supportive of more equitable economic growth. The strategy would include measures both to promote economic efficiency and to protect particularly vulnerable groups of poor people within developing countries.   Creditors—whether governments, international financial institutions, or commercial banks—would have discretion to decide either to extend new loans or to cut debt-service requirements. . . . A strategy containing these elements not only would spread the costs of adjustment more equitably but would also considerably improve the U.S. trade balance, enhance American leadership in international economic relations, and improve U.S. diplomatic relations with the developing countries.

Management of the debt crisis will be a central issue well into the 1990s. The key to resumed growth is a combination of tough policy choices by developing countries, an amelioration of the debt situation as discussed earlier, and a heretofore elusive degree of global macroeconomic coordination. Sustained economic growth in the developing countries will be necessary to expand world trade and long-term investment. Leaders of the developed countries will need to take coordinated action to avoid volatility in exchange rates and in interest rates, and to ensure that their macroeconomic policy choices provide an environment for global growth.

If this growth strategy is to happen, policy makers will need to design creative ways to stimulate the flow of additional public and private resources to the developing countries. Among the steps that need to be taken are the following.

INCREASE TRANSFERS FROM COUNTRIES IN SURPLUS. Countries with large financial surpluses, most notably Japan, must begin to play a more important role in global finance. The Japanese government has expanded its aid program dramatically in recent years. Measured as a percentage of GNP, Japan's level of aid is already higher than that of the United States, and Japan has now passed the United States as the world's largest donor in absolute terms. But Japan has been reluctant to assume international economic leadership and generally has deferred to the United States. One of the creative challenges facing policy makers is to devise measures to encourage the Japanese and surplus countries in Western Europe to use more of their surpluses for restarting growth in the developing world. For both Japan and the United States, this task is not, however, without political problems. The Japanese surplus is largely in private hands, and measures will have to be devised to channel it to international purposes. The United States faces a different problem. The international financial institutions should have a major role to play in recycling these surpluses, but the United States would inevitably have to yield more of its influence in these institutions to the Japanese and other new contributors.

GENERATE NEW RESOURCES WITH MINIMAL BUDGETARY IMPACT. The exigencies of the current crisis should stimulate policy makers to look for nontraditional ways of providing capital to restore growth in the major debtor countries. The current crisis also calls for more imaginative use of guarantees to foster greater capital flows and debt service reduction—as suggested by U.S. Treasury Secretary Nicholas Brady—into the developing countries. A special issuance of the [International Monetary] Fund's Special Drawing Rights (SDRs) for allocation to developing countries under the aegis of the World Bank and the International Monetary Fund is another potential source.

REDIRECT RESOURCES AVAILABLE THROUGH THE U.S. INTERNATIONAL AFFAIRS
BUDGET. The United States can restructure its existing international affairs
budget to respond to these challenges. During the first half of this decade
[the 1980s], this budget (generally known as the "foreign aid" program) more
than doubled, but all of the increase has gone to military and security aid—
to the neglect of programs designed to foster American interests in the developing countries through economic growth and long-term development.
Economic and development assistance has in fact declined. The imbalance
between the military and the economic in current programs represents a
misallocation of scarce resources that the United States can no longer afford
in this period of budgetary stringency. U.S. interests in the developing world
today by and large do not stem from concerns about military security; they
are largely economic, political, and humanitarian. Even a modest reallo-
cation of funds within the current budget—in the range of 10 to 20 percent—
could free a substantial amount of resources to support global growth in the
developing countries.

EXPAND TRADE. Policy makers will need to give priority to expanding exports
to the developing countries, particularly to those that are rapidly industrializing. . . . Two quite different sets of policies will be important to that end.
Some developing countries will continue to run surpluses and will need per-
suasion to open their markets to imports from both industrialized and developing countries; others, however, will still be working their way out from
under the debt overhang through receiving trade surpluses. Their ability to
import will depend on the availability of capital inflows.

EXPAND EXPORTS. Ensuring the continued growth of export markets in the
developing countries will have to remain a central priority of U.S. foreign
policy throughout the 1990s. In industries such as microelectronics-based
manufacturing and in agriculture, American producers need to look to markets in the developing countries for future growth. . . .
    Other trade issues will loom large as a result of the changes in industrial
technology and organization. These include the need to develop new rules
to govern the disputes that will inevitably arise as more developing countries
seek to take advantage of an open trade system, especially in the areas of
intellectual property and investment promotion measures, and also as a much
more creative effort to increase trade among developing countries themselves.

Policies toward Those Left Out: Poor People and Poor Countries

Despite the shifts that have gone on in relations between the United States
and the developing countries, development assistance still will have a major
role to play in the period ahead in promoting the development of the poorer
nations and in addressing the global agenda issues described earlier. This
will require considerable redesign and restructuring of current U.S. development cooperation policies.

Currently, only 40 percent of all aid from the OECD countries goes to the poor, low-income countries; the U.S. share going to lower-income countries is 24 percent.   In most industrialized countries, budgetary resources for development assistance will be scarce, and the acute needs of the low-income countries make it imperative that concessional assistance be directed to them. The need for this shift is analogous to the importance of preserving a domestic "safety net" for disadvantaged groups in our own society, even in the face of economic adversity.

In addition, a new U.S. development cooperation program is needed that focuses on the address of a limited number of specific global problems, seeking to provide U.S. leadership in a concerted international effort by developed and developing countries to attack poverty and sustain the environment.   It would be helpful to focus U.S. programs on internationally correlated and agreed upon goals for achievement by the end of the century to give focus to the programs and to attract public support.   Possibilities include: food security and the significant reduction of chronic hunger; primary health care for a majority of the world's people on a sustainable basis; literacy for the new generations of children without discrimination on the basis of sex; halving existing high population growth rates; helping to build capacity in the developing countries to adapt and to utilize for their own revolutionary scientific and technological developments; and institutional development, education, and training to improve the capacity of developing countries to better manage their own environment and natural resources.

A concrete problem-solving mode of operation is important because U.S. resources are limited and represent a declining proportion of larger aid flows from other donors, and because developing countries themselves have acquired the competency to implement their own development choices.

U.S. leadership and leveraging on selected global problems would be a key element in a new development cooperation strategy, both in bilateral and multilateral aid programs, as well as on broader international economic policies.   A much stronger leadership on donor coordination will provide the United States with greater influence on the amount and direction of resources provided, as well as on the content of programs of other donors and the multilateral development institutions.

In the 1990s, aid policies also will need to be radically redesigned to take account of the technological revolution and to ensure that its benefits do not bypass low-income countries and poor people.   Countries that do not already have an industrial base and do not already export to the industrialized countries will find it increasingly difficult to compete in world markets unless they have some particular resource—material, human, or geographic—that will give them an edge.   Low-income countries by and large will not be able to reap the benefits of the new industrial technology.   In addition, past experience with dramatic technological innovations—most notably, some of the lessons learned in the introduction of the successful "Green Revolution" crops—illustrates that such innovations must be very carefully launched so as to avoid increasing social inequity.

The precise impact of the new technologies is still very difficult to predict; they are not yet in widespread use in developing countries, and their potential for improving human well-being through applications to health, education, and agriculture is far from fully understood. There is, moreover, a strong possibility that at least some of their side-effects will be adverse, especially in the near term. The reason lies in the nature of the technology. Fewer new jobs will be created, and those that are will be at a higher skill level— for which the majority of people in the developing world will not be qualified. As a result, in countries that achieve competitiveness, middle-class workers benefiting from the new technologies are likely to form "islands of prosperity," with a resulting aggravation of income disparities within the country.

On the other hand, the potential of the new technologies for vastly improving human well-being is also great. The microelectronics technology can be applied to development problems in even the poorest countries. For instance, remote sensing by satellites can be used for identifying resources, demographic planning, and early warning of drought. Personal computers can have a great impact on government planning and data collection, as is already the case in Nigeria and Kenya. The new telecommunications technologies make remote areas more accessible, permitting village-level education to spread widely and inexpensively. The new developments in biotechnology have vast potential for improving human welfare. As mentioned earlier, these include a range of new agricultural products, vaccines and medicines, and new sources of energy. Many potential biotechnology applications are of great significance for developing countries because they are relatively less capital-intensive, less energy-demanding, and less sophisticated than most of the current physical-chemical industrial methods.

LESSONS FOR POLICY MAKERS

The United States is entering a new era. Policy makers cannot ignore the constraints that the changed international economic position of the United States imposes on a broad range of its foreign policy choices without causing further long-term erosion of this country's international position—or without condemning future generations of Americans to paying off an unprecedented level of foreign debt.

The changes in the policy environment have implications for policy makers as they begin the redesign of U.S. development cooperation programs and lay out broader international economic policies.

Most importantly, the United States will have to implement expansionary, noninflationary monetary policy in conjunction with budget cutting to avoid the recessionary impact of lowering the federal budget deficit. This requires coordination with the central banks of the major industrialized countries.

In addition, leaders of the developed world will need to take coordinated action to avoid volatility of exchange rates and in interest rates, and to ensure that their macroeconomic policies provide an environment conducive to global growth. If the world drops into another major recession, the impact on the developing countries will be disastrous, with heavy costs to U.S. interests.

Addressing the debt crisis should have priority in U.S. relations with the developing world. Third World debt has altered international trade flows and added to the U.S. trade deficit by forcing developing nations to trim their imports. Debt has also become a central issue in America's relations with its hemispheric neighbors and with sub-Saharan Africa. The overall aim of U.S. policies toward the developing countries should be to stimulate the flow of resources needed to resume growth in those countries.

Sustained and rapid economic growth in the Third World, particularly in the middle-income developing countries, is now of direct importance to the United States because it could be a key element in making significant progress toward reducing the U.S. trade deficit without inducing a global recession. As a result of debt and slow growth in the developing world, U.S. exports to all developing countries dropped from $88 billion in 1980 to $78 billion in 1987. The impact on employment also was dramatic. The actual and potential employment loss (if exports had grown in the 1980s as they did in the 1970s) amounted to nearly 1.8 million U.S. jobs—or nearly 26 percent of total official unemployment in 1989.

Trade openness remains crucial both for the United States and the developing countries. The industrialized countries must fight protectionist impulses and bolster world export earnings and buying power. It will not be possible for the developing countries to grow and service their debts if they are denied access to markets for their goods. In turn, the U.S. trade deficit will not decrease substantially without increasing the purchasing power of the developing world.

The trend in the developing world toward democracy and market oriented policies needs to be supported. Democratic regimes typically attempt to reconcile the developmental goals of economic growth, decreasing income inequality, and management of external dependencies. But democracy has proven an elusive goal over the long run in most of the Third World. For that reason, it is important that democratization and "openness" in the developing world be assisted.

The new developments in science and technology present opportunities for U.S. development programs. The pace of change and the specific outcomes to arrive in the wake of technological developments are still unclear. Aid policies will need to be redesigned to take account of the technological revolution and to ensure that its benefits do not bypass poor people and poor countries. Aid programs need to focus on assisting developing countries, particularly the poorer ones, to strengthen their national capacity to develop and utilize new technologies for their own benefit.

The growth in the number of aid donors and the relative decline in U.S.

development assistance actually opens opportunities for the United States but also implies that development policy must be much more strategic.   Countries with large financial surpluses, most notably Japan, must play a more important role in global finance.   The Japanese and surplus countries in Western Europe should be encouraged to recycle their surpluses for restarting growth in the developing world.   This task is not without political problems.   The international financial institutions (IFIs) should play a major role in recycling these surpluses; the United States would, however, inevitably have to yield more of its influence in these institutions to the Japanese and other new contributors.

In an era of scarce U.S. resources, greater U.S. participation in the IFIs also has the advantage of leveraging large amounts of lending with small amounts of cash.

In the next decade [the 1990s], U.S. bilateral aid programs will not be essential to middle-income countries' growth, but they will continue to play a major role in the development of the low-income countries.   U.S. aid should be targeted predominantly on those countries.

The emerging "global agenda" of interrelated problems and their world-wide repercussions should set the agenda for the U.S. aid program in the 1990s.   The importance of these global problems demands a vigorous national and international response.   The United States is the logical candidate to spearhead the effort to deal effectively with this nascent global agenda through renewed leadership in the international organizations.   This is one area in which U.S. actions and leadership will be more important than U.S. funds.

18 REGIONAL SECURITY, ARMS CONTROL, AND THE END OF THE COLD WAR

Geoffrey Kemp

The end of the Cold War has raised expectations in the United States, Europe, and the Soviet Union that military budgets will be cut, arms-control agreements will be signed, and a peace dividend will allow for retrenchment and greater investment in domestic programs. There also is great hope that the appeal of arms control and force reductions, as well as democracy and the free market, will spread to other regions of the world.

A case can be made for optimism. The pressures on national defense budgets are intense, and the only question remaining is which components of the force structures of the North Atlantic Treaty Organization and Warsaw Pact will take the greatest cuts. No politicians are going to argue against such cuts unless there is an international crisis directly impinging on Western security. The unconstitutional removal of Soviet president Mikhail Gorbachev would be the event most likely to prompt a more conservative attitude to defense retrenchment. Likewise, in Eastern Europe and the Soviet Union, it will take a disaster of great magnitude to increase defense investment.

Furthermore, in recent years there has been an encouraging easing of many problems of international security in the developing world. The Soviet Union has pulled its forces out of Afghanistan and has agreed to major cutbacks of forces in East Asia, especially along the Sino–Soviet border. Vietnam [has withdrawn] from Cambodia. The superpowers have helped broker an end to the Angolan war and Namibian independence is now a reality. In Latin America the appeal of Marxist guerrilla movements armed and supported by the Soviet Union is on the wane. On the more functional issues of arms control, the Soviet Union has agreed to abide by the terms of the Western-sponsored Missile Technology Control Regime (MTCR) to limit missile trans-

Note: Footnotes have been deleted.

fers to conflict regions and, with the United States, has agreed to significant cuts in its arsenal of chemical weapons.

There are, however, three good reasons to be more skeptical about the prospects for reducing regional conflict and implementing regional arms-control agreements. First, superpower retrenchment itself will create a vacuum, and regional powers will move quickly to fill the void. Second, sources of conflict in key regions of the world have not gone away and in some areas, such as the Near East and South Asia, the prospects for war are growing. Third, and perhaps, most telling, there is no sign that countries in regions of conflict have the political incentives at this time to work together to reduce tensions; in fact, the evidence points in the other direction—many of them are rearming with top-of-the-line military equipment.

SUPERPOWER RETRENCHMENT AND THE REGIONALIZATION OF CONFLICT

The end of the Cold War will accelerate a process that has been underway for some time, namely the regionalization of regional conflicts. Each region is likely to adapt to retrenchment in its own way. In some cases, for example Latin America, the United States will retain considerable influence. In other areas, such as Africa, neither the United States nor the Soviet Union is likely to have much impact on events in the [1990s]. In important regions such as the Middle East and East Asia, however, the United States and the Soviet Union will retain vital interests even as their capacity to influence events diminishes, compelling increased cooperation with major regional powers. This is likely to lead to new strategic alignments and a continuation of classical geopolitics and balance of power policies.

With the diminution of superpower power has come a gradual removal of the collective security shields that both the Atlantic alliance and the Eastern bloc have provided to regions around the Eurasian landmass and, on occasion, have extended to areas in Africa and Latin America. Collective security not only has carried with it the assurance of superpower support in times of crisis—including the occasional use of superpower military forces—but it also provided subsidized access to arms, supplies, and economic aid. As the collective shield, the arms, and the aid all begin to wither, those regions formally protected by these cold war accoutrements will seek alternative means to assure their security.

U.S. allies in Europe and Asia are worried about a cutback in U.S. forces that is too precipitate. They fear that the drawdown of U.S. forces in Europe, the Mediterranean, the Indian Ocean, and Southeast Asia will compel states in those areas suffering local rivalries and conflicts to increase their own military capabilities or to look for another hegemon for protection. Fears of U.S. withdrawal are most apparent in Europe, where the concern is tied to the issue of a united Germany and its potential for domination of the continent. In the Pacific and East Asia there is concern that if the United

States reduces its presence and abandons its military bases in the Philippines and Japan, it will be only a matter of time before Japan or China emerges as the hegemonic regional power.

There also are parallel concerns that the breakup of the Soviet empire will create instability around its huge border. Long-muted regional conflicts in Eastern Europe already have reemerged all around the region, as well as inside the Soviet Union. Poland, in particular, feels vulnerable as it views the prospects of a united Germany, a breakup of the Warsaw Pact, and uncertainty over the future of the Baltic states.

Along the southern periphery of the Soviet border, ethnic violence is prevalent. Fighting between Azerbaijanis and Armenians at one point called into question the Soviet army's ability to protect nuclear weapons installations in the region. There is speculation about the Balkans once more becoming a potential catalyst for conflict. The Soviet Union's decision to cut back on support for radical regimes in the Arab world has caused a geopolitical earthquake in that region.

Who will be the new hegemons, aside from Germany, Japan, and China? If the Koreas ever reunite, a third regional superpower could emerge in East Asia with potentially traumatic implications for regional security. The leading candidates in Southeast Asia must be Indonesia and Vietnam, with India playing an increasingly assertive role in the more westerly precincts. All three of these countries, however, are so burdened with economic problems that their capacity to expand defense capabilities may be limited.

On the subcontinent itself, India already dominates its neighbors. In fact, it is seen by some as a regional bully. Sometimes Pakistan's importance is brushed over too quickly, although by any standards, Pakistan is a potentially important regional military power, especially in the context of Gulf geopolitics. It is, after all, a nuclear weapons state.

In the Gulf, the current focus is on Iraq's emergence as a hegemon, a prospect that [has sent] both thrills and chills throughout the Muslim world. On the one hand, Iraqi leader Saddam Husayn is seen as a strong man capable of standing up to Iran, Israel, and the West; on the other hand, he is viewed as a rapacious bully determined to use his military might to force the smaller Arab oil-rich states to pay his bills and the rest of the Arab world to accept his leadership pretensions. [The author's observations about Iraq, which proved remarkably on target, were made prior to its invasion of Kuwait and the subsequent Persian Gulf War of 1991.—*Eds.*]

Eventually, Iran once more will reemerge as a power to be reckoned with in the Gulf, irrespective of the nature of its regime. In their more somber moments the Iraqis are aware that the best ally they had toward the end of the fighting with Iran was the late Ayatollah Ruhollah Khomeini, whose impact on the conduct of the war led to disastrous military decisions. A more "moderate" Iranian leader would pose serious problems for Iraq and the smaller states of the Gulf Cooperation Council (GCC). How the GCC countries try to juggle their security needs in the face of two such antagonistic and strong powers will be a test of their diplomatic ingenuity in the future.

In the Arab–Israeli context, Arab countries are struggling to adapt to the impact on their security of Soviet retrenchment.   In the short run this has been beneficial for Israel.   Not only has the Soviet Union cut back on arms supplies to radical states such as Syria, but it also has opened its doors to Jewish emigration to Israel. . . .

Latin America presents a different case.   It never has been plagued with the ethnic and religious rivalry common to the Near East, Asia, and Africa. Furthermore, most of the guerrilla and radical movements in Latin America have been influenced primarily by Marxist ideology rather than nationalism and ethnicity.   As a consequence, the collapse of Soviet power and authority has led to a shift on the part of the mainstream Latin radical movements toward politics rather than violence as a way to achieve social change.

In Africa it is possible that Nigeria and a politically stable South Africa could emerge as the dominant powers south of the Sahara, but this is far from clear.   Africa is so overwhelmed by economic and social problems that its importance on the geopolitical stage is likely to decline in the coming decade [the 1990s].

TRADITIONAL CONFLICTS WITH NEW INGREDIENTS

Despite the surge to democratic rule in Europe and parts of Latin America and the hope that the freedom virus of 1989 will spread, the basic sources of conflict in most regions of the world remain unresolved.   Moreover, new sources of antagonism have emerged as well.   At the top of the list is the gap in the rate of economic development.

In the Gulf states and East and Southeast Asia, several countries have prospered due to either the export of oil or the development of high technology industries.   The small countries of the Arab Gulf are modern, affluent societies.   To be sure, they face serious problems in the years ahead, but these are more political than economic in origin.   Singapore, Hong Kong, Taiwan, and Korea are now referred to as newly industrialized countries (NICs); Thailand and Malaysia have shown strong economic potential in the past few years.   In Latin America, Chile has reemerged with a strong economy.   Elsewhere in the Western Hemisphere, however, the absence of economic growth and a parallel rise in the conditions of social chaos, including rapid population growth and an educated but unemployed youth, suggest increasing political instability.   The same is true for the Arab countries not exporting oil, whose youthful populations are becoming more and more discontent with the status quo.   This has led to a rise in Islamic fundamentalism.

Without sustained economic growth and the resolution of the debt crisis, political discontent is bound to grow.   Yet, there is unlikely to be enough capital to finance the huge debt burden of the poor countries while at the same time finding the funds to bail out the bankrupt Communist regimes in

Eastern Europe and the Soviet Union. The financial needs for the reconstruction of the Eastern bloc are huge. While the prospects for an economic bonanza are attracting Western capital, there remain enormous environmental costs to be met. One estimate is that it will take $200 billion to deal with industrial pollution alone.

In addition to problems of debt and population dynamics, most regions, including parts of Europe, are still bedeviled by historic disputes over borders, economic zones, water sources, and immigration. These issues, together with new environmental problems such as deforestation, flooding, and industrial pollution, have emerged as important factors on the national security agendas of many countries. For instance, what initially may appear to be an environmental issue often can manifest itself as a national security issue at the regional level. For example, if as a result of flooding in Bangladesh, caused by the cutting of forests in Nepal and the gradual rise in sea levels in the Bay of Bengal, less and less land is available to cultivate, illegal immigration from Bangladesh to India is likely to increase. This poses burdens for local authorities and further antagonizes relations between immigrants and the indigenous population. It is easy to see how in such circumstances violence can erupt and relations between poverty-stricken states can be stretched to the breaking point.

At a more general level, the efforts by environmental movements in the West to stop such activities as cutting down the rainforests of Latin America and Asia often alienate the countries in those regions, who argue that they cannot afford to pay the price for pristine environmental activity unless they receive economic help from the industrial powers, who, they contend, are responsible for most of the global pollution.

REGIONAL CONFLICT AND REGIONAL ARMS RACES

The evidence in the key regions around the Asian landmass is that regional conflict is alive and well. The best hard data to confirm this point relate to fears about new wars and the statistics of arms proliferation, which reflect in a very clear and ominous way the investment many countries are making in their military forces at a time when the talk in Washington is of disarmament. . . .

. . . There are at least three elements of the regional arms races that are new and disturbing. First, the quantity and quality of arms found in regional conflict areas have reached unprecedented levels and the ability of local military forces to project power far beyond their borders has increased. Second, the Iran–Iraq war demonstrated the effectiveness, under certain conditions, of chemical weapons and surface-to-surface missiles (SSM) and has raised fears about the further spread of weapons of mass destruction, including nuclear weapons. Third, new suppliers—the so-called second tier— have entered the arms market and can provide some of the weapons that previously were the monopoly of the superpowers and the Europeans.

Force Levels and Proper Projection

The regional powers spend most of their defense budgets on modern conventional weapons, not on the more publicized surface-to-surface missiles and weapons of mass destruction that have captured attention in the recent past. The numbers are impressive. Egypt, India, Iraq, Israel, and Syria all have more main battle tanks in their inventories than either Britain or France, the former colonial powers. Israel and Iraq have more armored personnel carriers and India has more combat aircraft than all NATO countries with the exception of the United States. India has the world's third largest army and the seventh largest navy. Syria and Egypt have forces far larger than Spain.

While raw numbers are not as large in other regions of the world, there has been a significant trend toward force modernization and the expansion of defense budgets. Military developments in East Asia are particularly significant. Japan already possesses the fifth largest navy in the world and has plans to acquire a number of guided missile destroyers and two aircraft carriers, which would make it the preeminent naval power in the region.

With 394 combat aircraft, 1,600 main battle tanks, and armed forces 1,249,000 strong, Vietnam remains a formidable military power, although whether it can afford to modernize its forces remains to be seen. Indonesia, Malaysia, and Singapore have begun to cooperate on matters of defense. In February 1989, a memorandum of understanding was signed to give Singapore's armed forces extensive training in Indonesia. Singapore has commissioned its first West German–designed corvette, and has received 8 U.S. F–16 aircraft. Thailand, which already has 18 F–16 fighters, has acquired 400 new armored personnel carriers of Chinese design. . . .

Numbers alone provide merely a broadbrush view of the arms race. In terms of the quality of the weapons, the picture is equally striking. The array of conventional equipment includes top-of-the-line American-made items such as the Abrams main battle tank, F–15 and F–16 fighters, and the improved Hawk SAM. The best Soviet equipment also has been transferred, including MiG–29s, which have gone to India, Syria, and Iraq, and SU–24s, which have gone to Libya, as well as a Soviet Charlie–I class nuclear submarine that was received "on loan" by India, bringing up to 17 the number of submarines in the Indian navy.

Britain, France, and China have sold their best fighter aircraft to a number of countries. In addition to the deal with Malaysia, Britain concluded two agreements with Saudi Arabia in 1986 and 1988 covering the sale of 118 Tornados, 48 Hawk light fighters, 90 Black Hawk helicopters, and a number of trainer aircraft. These two agreements, worth $10 billion and $20 billion respectively, represent the largest aircraft sale ever between the United Kingdom and a Middle Eastern country. China also has supplied a large number of fighter aircraft to North Korea, Pakistan, and Egypt.

Several regional countries now have conventional military forces that can operate at increasing distance from their borders, posing potential threats to a wider number of neighbors, as well as to other forces operating in these regions.   Of particular interest is Iraq's . . . military buildup. . . . India's growing power projection capabilities, demonstrated with interventions in Sri Lanka and the Maldives, are indicative of India's determination to become a major regional power.

Chemical, Biological, Nuclear Weapons and Missiles

The spread of weapons of mass destruction and their delivery systems, especially missiles, is at the focus of new concerns about proliferation.   Although nuclear weapons remain in a class by themselves, the use of chemical weapons in the Iran–Iraq war and the low-keyed response of the international community have made them an attractive alternative to nuclear weapons for technically deprived countries wishing to develop military capabilities for both deterrence and war-fighting. . . .

Chemical weapons do not equate with nuclear weapons in terms of destructive power.   Against a well-protected, forewarned population or military force, the effects of even the most lethal nerve agents can be limited.   Thus, for chemical weapons to be most effective, they have to be used without warning against defenseless, unprotected populations.   It is this characteristic that makes them so abhorrent.

Even more frightening than the prospect of chemical weapons use is the prospect that there will be greater efforts to develop and use biological weapons.   Biological weapons are comprised of living organisms that can cause often infectious, incurable diseases such as anthrax, the plague, or tularemia. Only tiny amounts of these bacterial agents are necessary to create widespread infection; in an aerosol attack, 0.077 ounces of tularemia would produce a cloud 325 feet high, taller than a 20-story building, and 0.62 miles square, with infectious doses multiplying every minute.   More than 400,000 people could die within five days of such an attack, with many more deaths following in the surrounding areas.   Biological weapons have the potential to be much deadlier than chemical weapons and, according to [then] CIA Director William Webster, yield the widest area coverage per pound per payload of any weapon system in existence.

The CIA has stated that at least 10 countries in the world currently are working to produce biological weapons, and any nation with a pharmaceutical industry conceivably can assemble biological warfare agents.   Although biological weapons have not been attributed specifically to any countries in the Near East and South Asia, it has been reported that Iraq possesses a biological warfare facility near the village of Salman Pak, 35 miles southeast of Baghdad.   An Israeli official has stated that the Iraqis have developed a military capacity without having manufactured actual weapons, that less-advanced Syrian biological research exists, and that Libya has attempted to buy information on biological warfare.   The charges have been denied by Iraq, one of the 111 signers of the 1972 Biological Weapons Convention (BWC) that bans such weapons.

Advances in biotechnology also are making possible the eventual mass production of toxins for weapons use. These are chemical substances found in living organisms that can be reproduced with genetic engineering techniques. A good example is rattlesnake venom, an organic toxin, which when mass produced could act as a chemical weapon for which there is no antidote. Toxin weapons represent a dangerous blurring of the distinction between chemical and biological agents, as they are derived from living organisms, but the toxin itself, whether collected from the living organism or genetically reproduced in a laboratory, is not alive and acts as a poison rather than as a disease.

Biological weapons, although more deadly and potentially much more destabilizing than chemical weapons, possibly rivaling nuclear weapons, have not been given the same attention that chemicals have received. This is perhaps because they do not pose as immediate a threat as do chemicals and, indeed, their potential—and limits—are not yet fully understood. Biological weapons also are perceived as "unusable," in the same sense that nuclear weapons are unusable, meaning that the cost of their use so far exceeds any gains that it seems unthinkable. However, as with nuclear weapons, the cost of failed deterrence with biological weapons could be devastating.

Surface-to-surface ballistic missiles with widely varying ranges, payloads, and accuracies are present in the arsenals of Algeria, Egypt, Iraq, Iran, Israel, Kuwait, Libya, Yemen, Saudi Arabia, Syria, both Koreas, Taiwan, Argentina, and Brazil. Most of these missiles are obsolescent, Soviet-designed unguided rockets and first-generation guided missiles with limited range and poor accuracy that are not deployed in large numbers. Although most of these systems are far from state-of-the-art missile technology, some countries have been successful at modifying and enhancing their capabilities. Faced with the lack of a retaliatory capability when Iran began to launch missile attacks on Baghdad, Iraq embarked upon an ambitious project to extend the range of its Soviet-supplied Scud-B guided missiles. By reducing the size of the warhead compartment and leaving more room for the missile propellant, Iraq developed the 600–700 km range Al-Hussayn missile and the 900 km Al-Abbas. . . . [The author next provides a country-by-country survey of the missile arsenals of many developing countries, which demonstrates that these states are rapidly acquiring the capability to carry out highly destructive wars with the advanced weapons available—Eds.]

Intelligence reports concerning nuclear weapons present overwhelming evidence that Israel is a fully fledged nuclear weapons power and that India and Pakistan have nuclear weapons production capabilities. Iraq's interest in the acquisition of nuclear weapons has been a continuing source of concern. . . .

Iran and Libya also have sought nuclear weapons in the past. Iran launched an extensive nuclear weapons program under the shah, but the revolutionary government showed little interest in pursuing the program further when it came to power in 1979. . . . Rumors again have begun circulating that Iran is gearing up its nuclear program, with one report stating that Iran is seeking to have nuclear fuel production capability.

North and South Korea, as well as Taiwan, are possible candidates to join the nuclear club. Although Taiwan and South Korea have been dissuaded from acquiring these weapons through U.S. military assurances, North Korea's nuclear energy program remains a major concern. . . . Despite being a signatory to the 1972 Non-Proliferation Treaty (NPT), North Korea has not allowed the International Atomic Energy Agency (IAEA) to inspect its nuclear facility at Yongbyon. Taiwan has signed the NPT and is currently believed not to be pursuing a nuclear weapons program, although it has an extensive civilian nuclear power program and the capability to produce a nuclear explosive device.

New Suppliers

A third reason for concern about the military buildup in regions of conflict relates to the changing relationships among the supplier countries and the impact this will have on efforts to implement arms-control regimes. In the past, the U.S.–Soviet rivalry has provided a bonus for many Third World countries that were able to obtain large quantities of military grant assistance or low-interest loans by playing off one side against the other. In exchange, both countries had the power—used but rarely—to exert great influence over their clients.

Although the drawdown of competitive aid programs will mean less assistance and leverage in the future, it will not mean that the superpowers will opt out of the arms market. Each superpower retains strategic interests in these regions and each will have a large arms industry seeking profitable ventures with regional countries that can pay the price. Furthermore, the Third World arms market not only keeps Britain and France actively involved as weapons suppliers, but it also has attracted a large number of new suppliers, including China, Argentina, North Korea, South Korea, and Brazil. China has emerged as an important arms supplier, providing a wide selection of basic weapons, including combat aircraft, tanks, missiles, artillery, submarines, and small arms. During the mid-1980s, when the Iran–Iraq war was at its peak, China was the largest arms exporter in the developing world. Although its export capacity is in no way comparable to those of the United States and the Soviet Union, China has carved out a corner of the arms market as a supplier of less sophisticated conventional technology sold at cut-rate prices. It also should be remembered that in Eastern Europe and the Soviet Union there are thousands of skilled weapons specialists who now may take advantage of the freedom to travel to work for profit in those countries able to pay hard currency. Trying to put a cap on the transfer of people will be much more difficult than controlling technology.

Argentina, Brazil, and Singapore also are emerging as weapons suppliers to the Third World. From 1977 to 1987, Latin America and East Asia increased their world arms export market shares from 0.4 to 1.7 and 1.3 to 3.2 respectively. Although Brazil and Argentina appear to be concentrating on the high end of the weapons supply spectrum—including missiles, aviation and avionics, and armored combat vehicles—Singapore's strength is in smaller weapons and ammunition. There are growing indigenous arms capabilities in all of these regions, with Israel and India in possession of the most sophisticated industries. Israel has been active in the arms market for many years, and in 1988 it exported a record $1.47 billion in arms to 61 nations. The first half of 1989 saw a 40 percent increase in sales of Israel Aircraft Industries, 75 percent of which was accounted for by increases in exports. [In 1989] India announced that it, too, would begin to promote foreign arms sales. Egypt, Iraq, Iran, and Pakistan also have strong production capabilities in certain categories of weapons, especially ammunition and small arms.

In sum, the diversification of the arms market and the increasing sophistication of some of the weapons produced by new suppliers suggest that although the United States and the Soviet Union probably will remain the most important suppliers, in part due to their great capacity to provide weapons in large quantities in times of war, their dominance is slowly eroding. If the East Asian economic powers, especially Japan and Korea, decide to enter the market in a big way, they quickly could achieve a very strong competitive position. The idea of Honda or Toyota making jet fighters may be premature, but it is not impossible given the anticipated changes in Japan's strategic status.

IMPLICATIONS FOR U.S. POLICY

What do these trends mean for U.S. diplomacy and national security policy in the 1990s? One thing is clear; a new age of internationalism cannot be assured. In the absence of sustained global economic growth it appears less and less likely. If internationalism is not possible, can the United States distance itself from the traumas of this new world and retreat to a neo-isolationist posture with international involvement primarily focused on economic matters?

Although neo-isolationism may be appealing to some, it is unrealistic. The ideological zero-sum games of the Cold War may be over, but geopolitics as an important component of international relations is not dead. Geopolitics may now have to share the spotlight with other items on the agenda, but it will remain a driving factor in the way the world works. In a regionalized, competitive world, with numerous sources of unresolved conflict, the United States is destined to remain a key world power with global interests as well as the need to retain the military capacity to intervene directly or indirectly in those regional conflicts where its interests are most clearly at stake. This means that it will have to adapt to the new regional political and military environment by seeking and maintaining security ties with close friends and allies with whom it shares similar values, as well as others.

For example, although U.S. strategic interests in the Persian Gulf are not preordained or absolute, so long as the United States pursues an energy policy that depends more and more on this region for oil, it cannot "opt out" from the security problems of the region just because it is becoming weaker relative to the regional powers. For the foreseeable future, the United States will remain committed to the security of Israel and some of the moderate Arab countries. Similarly, there is no way any administration can ignore the impact that a dramatic change in the balance of power in East Asia would have on U.S. interests throughout the region, including the all-important economic component. To be able to influence events in this key region the United States must retain a viable, albeit reduced, forward military presence. It also must continue to use arms sales and arms assistance to support key regional players.

How does such a policy coexist with the need to work to limit weapons proliferation and seek regional arms-control arrangements as a way to control the spread and danger of local conflict?

U.S. policy toward regional conflict and arms control will remain torn between the desire to limit weapons proliferation and the need to continue to support friends and allies and to be prepared, as a last resort, to intervene in certain contingencies with U.S. military force. In both the Near East and East Asia, the United States has such enormous interests at stake that arming its friends is necessary, in part at least to assist its own military capabilities should it ever have to intervene to protect Korea, Israel, or Saudi Arabia or to secure Gulf oil supplies. Yet, in doing so, its own assertive policies on arms sales and a forward, if reduced, military presence become part of the problem of implementing regional arms-control arrangements. There is no neat and easy solution to this dilemma. Until there is peace in the Middle East, or an alternative energy source is found, or the Koreas unite, no U.S. administration will or can abandon these two regions.

In the meantime, what can be done about the dangers of regional conflict and arms races? There is a growing consensus among the industrial powers that something should be done to put limits on the transfer to regions of conflict of weapons of mass destruction and of some of the most sophisticated conventional technologies. There is, however, a significant ideological gap between the industrial powers and many of the regional states that see arms-control initiatives as an attempt to interfere with their national security needs at a time when the old collective security umbrellas are being removed.

Most regional states believe that arms-control arrangements must either parallel or follow progress on the resolution of regional conflicts, not precede it. The exception would be informal arrangements to avoid conflict (for example, the so-called "red lines" that have existed between Israel and its neighbors) and the Indo–Pakistani agreement not to attack each other's nuclear facilities.

There also remain analytical problems of relating arms-control measures to regional security needs. It is difficult to separate out the impact of nuclear, chemical, missile, and conventional proliferation and treat each item separately if one takes into account the realities of national security in the region. From a practical perspective, however, disaggregating the components of the arms race so far has proved to be the only manageable—and partially successful—way to focus attention on them.

The United States must continue to work within the framework of several multilateral channels to control nuclear and chemical weapons and surface-to-surface missiles. Efforts to promote a worldwide ban on chemical weapons seem to be making the most progress. . . .

During the May 1990 summit an agreement was signed between the United States and the Soviet Union regarding chemical weapons. Both countries agreed to reduce their current stockpiles to 5,000 agent tons by 2002 and immediately to discontinue production of chemical weapons without waiting for a global ban to come into effect.

Concerning ballistic missile proliferation, a group of seven states—the United States, Canada, France, Italy, Japan, the United Kingdom, and West Germany—formed the MTCR in April 1987, to deal with the growing threat posed by the spread of ballistic missile technology. The MTCR focuses narrowly on those missiles that are considered to be nuclear-capable. . . . The agreement consists of a set of parallel export controls in each member country, dependent for enforcement on the laws of each state. The agreement prohibits the transfer of conventional SSMs, space launch vehicles, key subsystems for SSMs, and facilities to produce them. Other items to be limited are on-board computers, inertial navigation systems, liquid and solid rocket fuel, testing equipment, flight control equipment, materials for rocket body and engine parts, and technology and know-how for the above items. Any of these items sold must be accompanied by the assurance that they will not be diverted to rockets.

Since its inception, the MTCR has become a focal point, specifically in the United States, in the fight to stop the spread of *all* ballistic missile technology in the Third World. Its current status as an export control agreement between states, rather than as a formal treaty, leaves it open to different interpretations by each of the member states. The MTCR is further stymied by the fact that two principal surface-to-surface missile suppliers to the Third World, the Soviet Union and China, are not members, although the Soviet Union has said that it will abide by the "export guidelines of the existing regime." . . . The MTCR also is a highly discriminatory mechanism because it makes no demands on its signatories for cutting their own arsenals and offers no incentives for compliance to those it is directed against.

In the realm of nuclear weapons, the NPT divided the world into the nuclear "haves" and "have-nots" with the purpose of halting the spread of nuclear weapons technology in exchange for promoting the spread of peaceful nuclear energy technology. Embodied in the treaty is a commitment by those nuclear weapon states party to the treaty to work toward global nuclear disarmament. With 139 member states, including three nuclear weapon states—the United States, the Soviet Union, and the United Kingdom (France and China are not members)—the NPT is the most sweeping, comprehensive, and probably most successful technology control regime in existence.

At the same time, however, the NPT has not been signed by Israel, India, Pakistan, Brazil, Argentina, or South Africa. Security concerns and the desire for great power status have proved to be more important considerations for these countries than the amorphous goal of halting nuclear proliferation. India has led the fight against the discriminatory nature of the NPT. After the August 1990 NPT review conference, the treaty will run for five more years, until it expires in March 1995, unless it is renewed or a new agreement is signed.

There presently are no international institutions that deal with conventional arms control—in fact, most of the industrial countries that are working together to control nuclear, chemical, and certain missile technologies are competing with each other for sales of high technology conventional arms. This paradox is exemplified by the fact that the U.S. undersecretary of state for security assistance has *both* the arms control *and* arms sales portfolios in his office.

If there is a lesson to be learned from the European experience on conventional arms-control negotiations, it is that until there is movement toward the resolution of basic political and geographic aspects of the problem, detailed blueprints for arms control will not succeed. Europe at last is making progress on arms control because the political environment has changed.

Indeed, the most promising avenues for serious arms-control arrangements are those that involve the regional players themselves, with or without the cooperation of the external powers. These can take many forms, including both informal and formal agreements. Although the external powers may be able to slow and, on occasion, intervene on an ad hoc basis to prevent certain inherently dangerous activities (for example, chemical weapons programs in Libya), there is little hope for comprehensive agreements without regional cooperation, especially at a time of superpower retrenchment.

The dilemma is most apparent in the case of chemical and nuclear weapons in the Middle East. It might be possible to focus on chemical weapons or nuclear weapons if some proximate symmetry existed between the adversaries, but unlike the situation in Europe, this is not the case. Israel will not give up its nuclear monopoly in the absence of an iron-clad peace treaty, a treaty that would have to extend to relations with Iraq and possibly Iran. On the other hand, the Arabs cannot be expected to support a comprehensive chemical and missile ban as long as Israel has nuclear weapons. . . .

Thus, we have a Catch-22 situation. High-level arms-control initiatives on major weapons systems prior to an ongoing peace process are unlikely to work unless the countries of the region agree to them. However, the political problems of reaching a peace settlement and deciding where one state's security ends and another's insecurity begins are so complex that a decision to postpone major arms-control initiatives encourages a continued arms race that has built-in dangers and can lead to war.

How can these two positions be reconciled?   The practical answer must be to pursue *limited* arms-control objectives *prior* to peace negotiations and to accept that substantive progress on resolving the tough issues of nuclear and chemical weapons and SSMs will have to wait until the political environment improves.   The best time to negotiate a ban or strict limitations on weapons of mass destruction would be the period following a peace settlement between the primary adversaries.   In contrast, the most inappropriate time to raise the issue of, for example, Israel's nuclear weapons, would be during the period when Israel is being asked to make territorial concessions and perhaps to agree to the creation of a Palestinian state.   At that moment, Israel will be preoccupied with security issues and its population will be divided on the correct action to take.   The case for territorial compromise will rest on the types of security guarantees that can be negotiated.   Until the format of a peace settlement finally is settled, no Israeli government will give up nuclear weapons.

In conclusion, it is easy to develop schemes for greater U.S.–Soviet cooperation to end regional conflict, including greater restrictions on the transfer of certain technologies and weapon systems.   This has some encouraging possibilities, but if such actions are undertaken in such a way as to convey a superpower condominium, they will backfire.   Superpower cooperation that ignores the realities of regional politics could end up leading to more conflict and greater efforts to circumvent restrictions on weapons technology. In contrast, superpower cooperation that directly involves the regional powers holds the most promise for success.   In the meantime, the United States will have to plan for continued, although more limited, intervention capabilities in regions crucial to its national interest.

Part III: CAPABILITIES

Containment has been the dominant foreign policy strategy of the United States since World War II. Its intellectual roots can be traced to George F. Kennan's "X" article, "The Sources of Soviet Conduct,"[1] which he published in 1947 while director of the State Department's Policy Planning Staff. In this article, Kennan assessed the way that Soviet history, ideology, and the patience and flexibility of its leaders as they pursued communist purposes combined to pose a challenge to democratic nations. He determined from his assessment of the motives and ambitions of Soviet foreign policy that "the main element of any United States policy toward the Soviet Union must be that of a long-term, patient but firm and vigilant containment of Russian expansive tendencies."[2] He urged that the purpose of containment was "to confront the Russians with unalterable counterforce at every point where they show signs of encroaching upon the interests of a peaceful and stable world." "It would be an exaggeration to say that American behavior unassisted and alone could ... bring about the early fall of Soviet power in Russia," he concluded. "But the United States has it in its power to increase enormously the strains under which Soviet policy must operate, to force upon the Kremlin a far greater degree of moderation and circumspection ... , and in this way to promote tendencies which must eventually find their outlet in either the breakup or the gradual mellowing of Soviet power."[3]

The prescriptions Kennan advanced in his now famous article found expression in the Truman Doctrine and, later, in the series of mutual defense pacts the United States sponsored with nations along the borders of the Eurasian landmass occupied by the Soviet Union and Communist China. Kennan has protested that these military arrangements were a misapplication of his assessments and prescriptions, which called for the political containment of a political threat, not the military containment of a military threat.[4]   Nonetheless, by the early 1950s the view widespread among American policymakers was that the Soviet Union was primarily a military threat bent on a military conquest of the West.   Once more the assessment and prescriptions that followed from it were articulated by the State Department's Policy Planning Staff.   This time the form was a classified document known as NSC-68 (National Security Council paper number 68), written by Paul Nitze, Kennan's successor on the Policy Planning Staff.   NSC-68 concluded that it was not only within the power of the United States to contain the Soviet Union but also to destroy it.   It thus proposed a massive buildup of American military power and called for a nonmilitary counteroffensive against the Soviet Union, which included covert economic, political, and psychological warfare designed to foment unrest and revolt in Soviet-bloc countries.   In many respects the prescriptions of NSC-68 contained the outlines of containment as it has been practiced ever since.   The early 1970s phase in Soviet-American relations, known as détente, saw the United States move in the direction of a political containment of a political threat, but it was a short-lived period that was followed in the 1980s by a resurgence of the militant thrust of postwar American foreign policy.

With the end of the Cold War it is apparent that many of the assumptions on which containment rested and the prescriptions inherent in NSC-68 cry out for reevaluation.   Even before the unfolding of the dramatic changes in Eastern and Central Europe in 1989 and 1990, the growth of defense spending during the Reagan administration fueled controversy over the cost of military preparedness compared with competing priorities.   The budget of the Department of Defense grew from $155 billion in 1980 to twice that amount in 1988, and the nation's debt and trade deficit with other nations mushroomed simultaneously.   Defense spending alone cannot be regarded as responsible for these developments, as the connection between military spending and economic performance is complex.   But neither can it be ignored.   Understandably, therefore, as the Soviet empire disintegrated, intense debate ensued over how to spend the "peace dividend" and how best to downsize and reorient the nation's military and related foreign policy capabilities. What role should military might and interventionism play in America's post–Cold War foreign policy posture? it was asked.   If communism and Soviet expansionism no longer threaten the vital interests of the United States, does this call for retrenchment?   Or is the threat from abroad and the necessity for U.S. leadership as compelling as ever?   If indeed promoting democracy and combating tyranny worldwide become the goals of American foreign policy as the United States approaches the millennium, are even greater effort and sacrifice required, not less?   But at what cost?   And can the United States afford it?

As with other questions central to the debate on America's global role in a post–Cold War world, these were not conclusively answered before events in 1990 and 1991 put the debate on hold, but the combination of challenges from abroad and constraints at home ensures that they must be addressed. Indeed, the questions become compelling as the United States seeks to match capabilities to objectives.

THE MILITARY DIMENSION

A preference for military might and a penchant for overt and covert intervention in the affairs of others have been hallmarks of American foreign policy since World War II.   The ability of the United States to pursue its objectives through such means has depended on policymakers' capacity to draw on a vast array of economic, intelligence, and strategic and tactical military assets.   Public diplomacy abroad (and sometimes at home) and foreign economic and military aid and sales are exemplary.   Militarily, nuclear weapons have figured prominently among U.S. assets, as the United States has depended heavily on the deterrent threat of nuclear weapons to preserve its own physical security and that of its allies against a potential Soviet military attack.   Conventional military weapons have also contributed to the U.S. deterrent posture, most notably in Europe, where they served to enhance the credibility of the U.S. commitment to defend its North Atlantic Treaty Organization (NATO) allies from a Warsaw Pact attack at whatever level it might occur.

Conventional military forces outside of Europe likewise served to enhance the credibility of U.S. promises to protect its allies by practicing "extended deterrence."   These forces also provided the means with which to seek influence over political events in other countries.   By dispatching an aircraft carrier from one theater to another, conducting military exercises near the border of an adversary, sending military aircraft over its capital city at supersonic speeds, or engaging in other shows of force, the United States has repeatedly used its vast military might to shape political outcomes abroad without resorting to the actual use of force.   But on seven conspicuous occasions overt military force has been used: Korea (1950–1953), Lebanon (1958), Vietnam (1962–1973), the Dominican Republic (1965), Grenada (1983), Panama (1989), and most recently, Iraq and Kuwait (1991).   A common characteristic of these interventionist episodes is that all occurred in the Third World.   With the notable recent exceptions of Panama and the Iraq-Kuwait conflict, a second characteristic is that all were motivated by fear of communism and Soviet expansionism.

With the disintegration of the Soviet external empire in Eastern Europe, the demise of the Warsaw Pact as a military threat, and the withdrawal of the Soviet Union from Afghanistan and its disengagement from other Third World hot spots, defense planners in Washington found themselves in the uncomfortable position of having to defend a mammoth budget without the same enemy—communism and Soviet expansionism—that had been used to justify high levels of defense expenditures for more than forty years.   Defense spending critics, in turn, saw new opportunities to reorient national priorities away from military spending toward neglected aspects of "the economic, social, and environmental foundations upon which [America's] security and strength as a nation ultimately rest."   As urged by a group of eminent scientists and intellectuals in early 1989:

> In determining our nation's priorities we cannot ignore that the postwar period is over, that the United States is now a debtor nation in a more competitive global economy, and that a whole new array of economic and environmental threats confronts us.   We cannot ignore the economic challenge posed by the rise of Europe and Japan, nor the environmental challenges posed by the warming of the planet.   And we cannot ignore the opportunity . . . to staunch the hemorrhage of resources to a wasteful arms race.[5]

The onset of the Iraq-Kuwait crisis and the subsequent war in the Persian Gulf dissipated any meaningful discussion of a "peace dividend," and the Bush administration moved only slowly and tentatively toward downsizing the military establishment.   The administration's early budget proposals for fiscal 1992 called for cancellation of some weapons programs and deactivation of some army divisions, but the overall level of defense spending remained (other than for the war against Iraq) largely unchanged, while the budget called for major increases in some programs, such as the Strategic Defense Initiative (SDI).   Progress was made toward a strategic arms reduction agreement with the Soviets that would make deep cuts in the erstwhile superpowers' nuclear arsenals, but there is also evidence that the administration's strategic doctrine continued to carry the United States quietly but surely down the path toward a nuclear war-fighting capability and the planned use of strategic weapons in the event of a conflict with the Soviet Union.[6]

A measured response to the declining Soviet military threat is doubtless in order.   As Charles William Maynes, editor of *Foreign Policy*, observed, "Even though the Cold War is over, history and prudence dictate that at least in its early stages the coming retrenchment not be too sweeping.   Just as individuals prudently purchase insurance, so should nations."[7]   Still, critics of the Bush administration wondered whether the opportunity to set new foreign and domestic priorities might not be slipping away.   Some also worried that the Iraq-Kuwait crisis signaled renewal of the U.S. global policeman role, in widespread disrepute since the Vietnam War.   As one critic put it:

> America's economic and social decline has given birth to the Bush Doctrine, a strategy premised on the vigorous exploitation of the leverage available to the world's unique superpower now that the Soviets have retreated from the center of the global stage.   America is currently enjoying a brief window of opportunity. Saddam Hussein has chosen the precise moment—after the Soviet retreat but before the Pentagon budget cuts—when the U.S. military machine was at the peak of its ability to impose its strategic will upon an uncertain future.[8]

What the U.S. posture toward Saddam Hussein portends for the future remains uncertain, although the evidence points toward a dramatic reorientation of the U.S. military posture toward thwarting Third World threats to its perceived interests.[9]   In this sense the war against Iraq may be only the first in a series of regional conflicts in which U.S. military power will be called on to play a crucial—if bloody and expensive—role.

The first three readings in this part focus on the military dimension of U.S. foreign and national security policy capabilities.   They direct attention to the changing context of American national security policy and raise pointed questions about the thinking that will shape the military posture of the United States in world affairs in the years ahead as it seeks to cope with the Lippmann gap.

In the first selection, "Principles of U.S. Grand Strategy: Past and Future," W. Y. Smith identifies five principles that have governed U.S. national security strategy since World War II and inquires into their continued relevance for the future.   The principles cover a broad spectrum of ideas, including the centrality of the Soviet Union in strategic thinking, the emphasis in military thinking on technology over human assets, the role of civilian leadership in strategic thinking, the growing recognition of the destructiveness of nuclear weapons, and the emergence of arms control as an element of national security policy.   Smith ends by speculating on the possible emergence of new national security principles out of the changing global environment. New patterns, he suggests, will focus on the inability of the United States to pursue unilateral action in the future, on a more assertive role by Congress in policy making, and on the impact of multipolarity on American national security policy.

The ability of policymakers and the bureaucratic organizations on which they depend for ideas and support to devise new modes of thinking, even in the face of radically different circumstances, is by no means assured.   On the contrary, old ways of thinking have the force of habit behind them and are typically reinforced by bureaucratic inertia and sustained by prior political commitments and resources.   In "The Ghost in the Pentagon: Rethinking America's Defense," Fred Charles Iklé examines the thinking in the Pentagon that is likely to shape U.S. strategic doctrine and grand strategy in the 1990s and beyond.   In response to his questions "What, now, are the threats against which the Pentagon should prepare?" and "How should America's strategy and military forces . . . be changed to take account of the transformed environment?" Iklé concludes that a "1947 mindset" continues to dominate thinking in the Washington national security establishment.   Much of Iklé's argument turns on the potential threat to the West from the now defunct Warsaw Pact.   Still, there is a familiar ring in Iklé's argument that speaks broadly of the incapacity of large-scale bureaucratic organizations to adapt their worldviews to new circumstances.   Thus, Iklé's indictment still warrants consideration: "The forty-year-old image of The Threat and our forty-year-old strategy constrict our capacity to grasp the immensity of the global change now unfolding before us."   "Stalin has been buried twice in Moscow," he concludes, "but his ghost lives on in the Pentagon."

Bureaucratic organizations may be slow to change their thinking, but they are also adaptive entities with enormous survival instincts. Thus, at the same time that the ghost of Stalin haunts thinking about the Soviet threat, particularly with respect to nuclear strategy, Iklé observes that Pentagon military planners have also begun to redesign U.S. conventional military forces to deal with Third World contingencies. Although a focus on the Third World has become "fashionable," Iklé reminds us that "the problem of Third World hostilities is not new at all. Every war in which the United States has been involved since World War II—either directly with its forces or indirectly by providing military aid—occurred in the so-called Third World."

Should the United States be involved in the Third World? What are its interests there? The questions have long bedeviled policymakers and critics alike. During the Cold War the answers were often dictated by Moscow. If the Kremlin had an interest in a particular Third World country or region, so did the United States. The bipolar distribution of power ensured that outcome. Because bipolarity dictated that each superpower would be sensitive to the slightest shift in power from one side to the other, neither could be indifferent to efforts to woo the uncommitted to its own camp.

In the eyes of many, the end of the Cold War also implies the end of the Third World as a geopolitical entity subject to superpower entreaties and competition.[10] Does the United States therefore have continuing interests in the Third World? Stephen Van Evera addresses the question of U.S. Third World interests and priorities in his essay, "American Intervention in the Third World: Less Would Be Better." The title conveys the message, as Van Evera sees the range of situations and circumstances that might justify U.S. intervention in the Third World as severely circumscribed. Included in his indictment of past interventions is a critical appraisal of the Reagan and Bush administrations' decisions to involve the United States in conflict situations in Asia, Africa, and Central America, which he finds unwarranted. On the other hand, Van Evera determines that the deployment of U.S. forces to stem Iraqi aggrandizement in the Persian Gulf was warranted, but largely because of the U.S. commitment to Israel: "The U.S. deployment thwarted a serious threat to Israel's security and deflected a threat to the United States that derived from America's commitment to Israel." Although this reason was discussed less than others that were bandied about by various policymakers, Van Evera concludes it probably was the "most important."

In addition to the site of military interventions and shows of force, the Third World has also repeatedly been the scene of U.S. covert intelligence operations carried out by the Central Intelligence Agency (CIA). The penchant for covert activities abroad—secret activities undertaken for the expressed purpose of influencing the outcome of political events—became part of the interventionist thrust characteristic of American foreign policy during the Cold War and derived from the same anti-Soviet containment strategy that rationalized military activities. Again, then, the question becomes, as

Loch K. Johnson asks in the title of the next selection, "Now That the Cold War Is Over, Do We Need the CIA?"

Johnson is quick to point out that "the Cold War may be over, but this nation's need for accurate information about the world remains acute." Thus, the intelligence mission of the CIA—its responsibility for collecting the information necessary for sound policy making—needs to be retained as it "has proven itself, despite the inevitable errors, indispensable to those who make decisions in Washington." But he urges that information gathering be given precedence over "dirty tricks." The reason, according to Johnson, is that "with few exceptions, the CIA's covert actions have done more to harm than to help America's interests abroad."

THE ECONOMIC DIMENSION

Walter Lippmann's concern in 1943, noted in the introduction to Part I, centered on the ability of the United States to match its power and commitments in the post–World War II world. As it turned out, the United States emerged from World War II unrivaled as the world's hegemonic power, with the result that little seemed beyond its reach. The German and Japanese challenges to the existing global order had been turned back as both were decisively beaten in war, and even America's victorious allies in Western Europe and on the Eurasian landmass lay exhausted and in ruins. The Soviet Union would eventually emerge as the principle challenger to the United States, but it was in no position to play that role in 1945. Its industrial, agricultural, and transportation systems had either been destroyed or severely damaged. The death of an estimated 26 million Soviet soldiers and citizens in what the Soviets came to call the "Great Patriotic War" conveys something of its cost. Although the United States had suffered some 300,000 casualties, the ratio of Soviet to American war deaths was more than eighty to one.

Not only did the United States alone emerge unscathed from World War II, it actually prospered as a result. The nation's gross national product grew by 70 percent between 1941 and 1945, and civilian consumption of goods and services rose by half. And in the years immediately following the war, the United States achieved a level of economic and military power unparalleled in history. In 1947 the country accounted for 50 percent of the combined gross world product. The United States was also the world's preeminent manufacturing center and leading exporter, and its monopoly of the atomic bomb gave it military superiority. Thus, the United States did indeed seemed poised on the threshold of the American century.

Concern with how to match commitments and power as the American century wanes takes on special urgency in a global environment that has witnessed a measurable decline of American power relative to other nations since the 1940s, for the United States can no longer control political outcomes at the international level as it once did. The proportion of the combined gross world product accounted for by the United States had slipped to 28 percent by 1960, to 25 percent by 1970, and to 23 percent by 1980.[11]   During the 1980s the proportion hovered around the 24–26 percent mark,[12] but the U.S. share of both "old manufactures," such as steel and automobiles, and "new manufactures," such as microelectronics and computers, continued to decline.[13]   Moreover, labor productivity was often greater in other industrialized nations, which also exhibited personal saving rates that far surpassed those in the United States.[14]

The Lippmann gap implies that policymakers, faced as they are with limited resources, must often make tradeoffs between different policy arenas.   The classic tradeoff is between "guns and butter," that is, between expenditures on national defense and social welfare.   Those concerned about imperial overstretch worry that the tradeoffs faced today will ultimately yield self-defeating choices.   A decision to maintain or increase defense spending at the expense of greater investments in education, for instance, will undermine the ability of the United States to compete effectively with others.   Some, like Japan, will—already have, in the view of many—acquire a competitive edge over the United States, with the result that imperial overstretch will inevitably lead to relative decline.   At issue is whether the "trading state"—the nation that expands its resources through economic development and foreign trade—will ultimately surpass those wedded to the pursuit of power through territorial control and the exercise of force.[15]

Just as the United States today faces a changing political order, it also faces a changing economic order that affects in important ways the complex nexus between national security and economic security.   In "International Economics and U.S. National Security," Theodore H. Moran examines six broadly defined international economic issues in U.S. relations with developed and developing countries that will gain increasing prominence on the national security agenda of the future: the question of financial support of the Soviet Union; relations with Japan; the globalization of the defense industrial base; energy vulnerability; the economic and political fate of the Third World; and international trade in narcotics.   While each of these issues merits attention in its own right—and Moran offers cogent policy prescriptions on all of them—in the final analysis the ability of the United States to exercise a leadership role in the global political economy may depend on its ability to forge a domestic policy consensus to face "the security environment of the future" where the "dangers are likely to be more diffuse, the connections between them and the policies needed to respond to them more murky, and the need for sacrifice in order to advance national interests more opaque than in the period of bipolar antagonism."

Forging that domestic consensus will not be easy, as the economic problems already faced by the United States remain serious.   The afterglow of victory in the Persian Gulf War momentarily pushed these problems to the background, but they remain.   Indeed, Robert Kuttner argues in "Postwar Economics" that "in resurrecting a Pax Americana the Bush Administration has complicated a host of nagging economic issues," including those related to the budget deficit, economic growth, energy dependence, the cost of maintaining peace and security in the Middle East, and a host of domestic problems ranging from banking reform to the cost of health care. Kuttner reaches the disquieting conclusion that "all of these problems will continue to sputter along on automatic pilot as long as a new Pax Americana dominates Presidential attention."

Among the nagging economic problems facing the United States is its seeming inability to compete in the global marketplace, where the competitive advantage in some industries is perceived to have shifted to other nations. Protectionist sentiments run high in the United States and ultimately threaten to unravel the Liberal International Economic Order of which the United States historically has been a primary champion. Paul Krugman examines the political and economic rationale for protectionism in "Free Trade and Protectionism." Included in his analysis is a consideration of the utility of a strategic trade, an often popular proposal for coping with perceived disadvantages the United States experiences in its trade relations with others. The purpose of such a policy, which effectively is a "limited government industrial policy consisting of carefully targeted subsidies," is to create comparative advantages in particular industries. Krugman concludes that the case for free trade remains, although it is "often overstated." In part this is because "the actual prospects for a successful strategic trade policy are not very good." Still, other states have demonstrated a capacity to pursue strategic trade policy. Thus, "it is extremely difficult to maintain a hands-off position in the United States when other countries do not do the same, especially when America is evidently in relative decline."

DECLINE OR RENEWAL?

Can the United States cope with the Lippmann gap? Will it balance its commitments and capabilities into line? The last three essays briefly address these questions, and they arrive at somewhat different answers. Walter Russell Mead recognizes in his essay, "On the Road to Ruin," that the United States has won the Cold War, but he argues that in the process it has lost economic ground to its own allies. Mead foresees the emergence of three economic blocs—Europe, East Asia, and the Americas—with the United States as the leader of "the weakest and most troubled" of the three. Unless the United States undertakes radically new thinking, Mead argues, the three-bloc world portends that the United States will plummet from its position as the world's hegemonic power to a position akin to that of Argentina—"a rich country . . . in many ways similar to ours . . . [whose] economy alternates between hyperinflation and depression; its politics, between anarchy and dictatorship."

Joseph S. Nye, Jr., is among those who have countered the pessimism of the "declinists" with a decidedly more optimistic picture of the future world role of the United States.   In "Against 'Declinism'" Nye warns that "the United States cannot stand alone as the world's policeman," but he also observes that if the United States, the largest power in the world, "does not lead in organizing collective action [against aggressors such as Iraq], no one will."   Maintaining that the ascribed symptoms of America's demise are greatly exaggerated, Nye continues that, in the final analysis, "there is no reason Americans cannot afford both Social Security and international security."

We conclude *The Future of American Foreign Policy* with a brief essay by Paul Kennedy, whose ideas on the rise and decline of great powers have permeated many of the essays in this book.   Even those whose ideas were not directly influenced by Kennedy's—such as Walter Lippmann—would doubtless pay homage to them.   Kennedy's essay here, entitled "A Declining Empire Goes to War," is brief but pointed.   To those who urge that the ability of the United States to wage successful high-tech warfare in the Middle East demonstrates it is a rising power, not a declining power, Kennedy responds as follows:

> So much of the "decline" debate seems to be obsessed with where America is now . . . [including] the way in which current military successes supposedly prove that the U.S. is not "a declining power."   My own concern is much more with the future, a decade or more down the road, if the trends in national indebtedness, low productivity increases, mediocre educational performance and decaying social fabric are allowed to continue at the same time that massive American commitments of men, money and materials are made in different parts of the globe.   Like the late Victorians, we seem to be discovering ever-newer "frontiers of insecurity" in the world that we, the number one power, feel impelled to guard.
>
> . . . it is no use claiming that America is completely different from . . . earlier great powers when we are imitating so many of their habits. . . .
>
> The dilemma that the U.S. faces during the next decade in achieving a proper balance between ends and means—thus avoiding "imperial overstretch"—is awkward enough.   But the last thing that is needed is for its people to be encouraged to seek its self-esteem on the battlefield.

NOTES

1. George F. Kennan ["X"], "The Sources of Soviet Conduct," *Foreign Affairs* 25 (July 1947), pp. 566–82.

2. Kennan, p. 575.

3. Kennan, pp. 581–82.

4. See, for example, George F. Kennan, *Memoirs* (Boston: Little, Brown, 1967).

5. Richard Barnet et al., "American Priorities in a New World Era," *World Policy Journal* 6 (Spring 1989), pp. 203, 204.

6. Desmond Ball and Robert Toth, "Revising the SIOP: Taking War-Fighting to Dangerous Extremes," *International Security* 14 (Spring 1990), pp. 65–92; Strobe Talbott, "Rethinking the Red Menace," *Time* January 1, 1990, pp. 66–72.

7. Charles William Maynes, "America without the Cold War," *Foreign Policy* 78 (Spring), pp. 13–14.

8. Martin Walker, *World Policy Journal* 7 (Fall 1990), p. 796.

9. Richard J. Barnet, "U.S. Intervention: Low-Intensity Thinking," *Bulletin of the Atomic Scientists* 46 (May 1990), pp. 35–37; Michael T. Klare, "The U.S. Military Faces South," *Nation*, June 18, 1990, pp. 841, 858–61; Michael T. Klare, "Policing the Gulf—and the World," *Nation*, October 15, 1990, pp. 401, 416, 418, 420. See also Charles William Maynes, "Dateline Washington: A Necessary War?" *Foreign Policy* 82 (Spring 1991), pp. 1–19.

10. See, for example, Richard Bissell, "Who Killed the Third World?" *Washington Quarterly* 13 (Autumn 1990), pp. 23–32; Mark Falcoff, "First World, Third World, Which World?" *American Enterprise* 1 (July/August 1990), pp. 13–14.

11. Herbert Block, *The Planetary Product in 1980: A Creative Pause?* (Washington, D.C.: U.S. Department of State, 1981), pp. 74–75.

12. Central Intelligence Agency, *Handbook of Economic Statistics, 1988* (Washington, D.C.: Government Printing Office, 1988), p. 30. Hereafter cited as CIA.

13. CIA, pp. 16, 18.

14. CIA, p. 58.

15. See Richard Rosecrance, *The Rise of the Trading State: Commerce and Conquest in the Modern World* (New York: Basic Books, 1986).

19 PRINCIPLES OF U.S. GRAND STRATEGY: PAST AND FUTURE

W. Y. Smith

Since the invasion of Kuwait by Iraq on August 2, 1990, the crisis in the Persian Gulf has dominated U.S. thinking on security matters—and rightly so. Whatever present crisis seriously challenges U.S. interests always seems to have priority in U.S. thinking over longer-run dangers. It is, after all, the danger most immediately threatening to U.S. national interests. One major consequence of recent developments, however, is that they ... diverted attention from a major debate that was taking shape, a debate the United States must come to grips with: the future defense policy and force structure the United States will choose to finance. ...

Sooner rather than later the United States should return to the task of sorting out better what kind of military force it wants in the future, and for what purposes. Budget reductions will dictate smaller U.S. forces, that is certain. In view of this reality, the United States must ensure that these smaller forces are structured to meet well-defined strategic objectives— objectives that are consistent both with the U.S. vision of the future and its pocketbook.

It is helpful in thinking about future U.S. strategy to reflect on the past and evaluate key patterns of earlier thinking in order to ascertain which should be discarded and which remain useful. What follows is an exploration of key principles that have influenced U.S. strategic thinking and the resultant strategy since the end of World War II and a consideration of their future application.

STRATEGY SINCE WORLD WAR II

The Oxford dictionary defines strategy as "the art and science of employing the political, economic, psychological, and military forces of a nation or group of nations to afford the maximum support to adopted policies in peace and

Note: Some footnotes have been deleted, and others have been renumbered to appear in consecutive order.

war."   Liddell Hart devised that definition at the end of World War II, and it is a generally satisfactory one if it is remembered that the word "employ" means "to devote or direct toward a particular activity or person."   That is a tall order.

The concept of strategy used here builds on Liddell Hart's and embodies the answer to three questions:

- What does the United States want to do, that is, what are its *objectives*?
- How does the United States want to do it?   In other words, what *concepts* will guide its actions?
- With what does the United States want to do it, that is, what *means* will it use?

Liddell Hart's definition fits more the concept of what is today most often called grand strategy.   Although that concept remains a matter of great import for the United States, the vast uncertainties relative to the military component of U.S. strategy warrant special attention to that particular component.

In devising and implementing the military component of U.S. national security strategy over the last 45 or so years, five principles or patterns of thinking have stood out.   Some of these principles are obvious; others probably are less so; but all have been influential.   Parenthetically, choosing to concentrate on patterns shaping strategic thinking rather than on the various strategies the United States has attempted to follow over the years precludes a recitation of the history of "massive retaliation," "flexible response," or the overall strategy the United States tried in Vietnam—"winning the hearts and minds of the people."   Nevertheless, these strategies do present themselves for consideration, either directly or indirectly, along the way.

The first principle that has shaped U.S. strategic thinking about the establishment and use of military force is both obvious and accepted: *the primary focus of our strategic thinking until very recently has been the potential for armed conflict between the United States (and its allies) and the Soviet Union (and its client states).*   The overall U.S. strategy was "containment," and the United States followed it successfully for some 45 years.   U.S. military forces were designed, developed, and deployed accordingly.   Moreover, it was believed that if the United States could meet the most challenging military threat, it could with the same forces meet less challenging ones.   That principle is so obvious and accepted that there is no need to spend much time on it. Still, it has been fundamental and, in the view of many, basically sound.

A second principle of central and obvious import to U.S. military strategy runs as follows: *the development of U.S. military forces should emphasize the substitution of technology for manpower.*

In fact, this principle has been influential throughout U.S. history.   It is, nonetheless, fundamental to present U.S. strategic thinking—the emphasis on expending equipment rather than personnel, the emphasis on quality over quantity.   No U.S. political or military leader has yet been willing to send young Americans into battle with inferior equipment—and it is unlikely that that will ever change. . . .

The U.S. military has responded to this verity by aligning doctrinal thinking with the above precept. The U.S. Army's Airland Battle doctrine reflects the belief that U.S. forces must be prepared to fight outnumbered and win. Quality clearly comes into play here—quality of equipment, training, and doctrine.

A third principle, which has been apparent since World War II—and before that, if truth be known—is this: *civilians exercise leadership in strategic thinking in the United States.*

Bernard Brodie, in his seminal 1959 book *Strategy in the Missile Age*, noted that almost all military professionals were more interested in *tactics* than *strategy*. Most military professionals, he said, from Napoleon to Dwight D. Eisenhower, although they seldom expressed it in so many words, believed that handling forces on the battlefield (tactics) was far more challenging and difficult than bringing the forces to the battlefield in a favorable position (strategy).

Brodie noted that military professionals usually believed that strategy could be handled by the application of certain rules or principles that were relatively simple compared to the complexities of tactical problems and the skill needed to deal with them; in other words, military professionals tended to equate strategy with the principles of war, which were simple and easy to grasp; they therefore directed their attention to tactics. Brodie wrote that the prevailing military definition of strategy was much too narrow and excluded consideration of the ultimate objectives of a campaign and, beyond that, those of the war in which the nation was engaged. He was correct, of course, on both counts. The definition of strategy used by the military professionals at the time was much too narrow. More recently, uniformed military have broadened their thinking, but they have rightly concentrated on developing operational plans for the employment of military forces, and military professionals have made only meager contributions at best to U.S. strategic thinking. Broad concepts to guide actions have come from civilians, not from the military. It has been civilians who have coalesced the thinking from both military and civilian sources into cohesive strategic theories that impel new courses of policy.

In this connection, it is instructive to review a partial list of civilians who have shaped U.S. strategic thinking—and the types of military forces the United States has fielded and the purposes for which they are to be used—since World War II. The list is only illustrative and is far from complete.

- Bernard Brodie, in the book already mentioned, made U.S. planners begin to think through much more carefully the implications of waging wars in the era of nuclear weapons.

- Herman Kahn made U.S. strategists begin to "think the unthinkable" and contemplate what might actually happen in a thermonuclear war and how to deal with it.[1]

- Robert Osgood was among the very first to mandate thinking through the possibilities and potential for limited wars in the nuclear age, wars that would be fought for less than total victory with less than total use of available force.[2]

- Albert Wohlstetter caused the U.S. Air Force to rethink its policy and doctrine on surprise attack and on relying on medium bombers based overseas—he demonstrated their unacceptable vulnerability to enemy attack.[3]

- Thomas Schelling took the lead in introducing game theory into U.S. strategic thinking in the late 1950s and especially during the Kennedy administration.[4]

- Robert McNamara, through his control over U.S. strategic nuclear weapon systems programs, led the nation to a strategy of achieving deterrence through "mutual assured destruction" rather than striving for military superiority. A review of his annual strategy and defense budget presentations to Congress makes evident the movement of his thinking away from a counterforce strategy to one of mutual assured destruction as the basic strategic goal.

- James Schlesinger, as secretary of defense in the mid-1970s, in speeches and testimony before Congress formalized the concept of "essential equivalence" with respect to U.S. and Soviet strategic nuclear forces and promoted serious thought about limited nuclear options in such a world.

The one military professional who had a significant role in shaping U.S. thinking was General Maxwell Taylor with his [1959] book *The Uncertain Trumpet*. In that work General Taylor made the case, inter alia, for "flexible response"—a strategy that relied both on conventional and nuclear military forces in theater warfare.

Some important thinkers are not included in the above list, and the contributions of those mentioned are not all of the same value. The basic point that most strategic thinking that shapes public views in the United States comes from the civilian sector cannot, however, be seriously challenged.

A fourth principle is this: *with respect to nuclear weapons, U.S. thinking since World War II has gone from fascination with things nuclear to appreciation of the limitations of such weapons.*

It is tempting to phrase this principle as "from fascination to disenchantment"—at least at the level of theater nuclear war—but such a formulation is too unequivocal. At the political level, some U.S. leaders early on began to have doubts about the utility of nuclear weapons in warfare. They thus centered their activities on deterring war. In military circles, however, planning for the possible employment of such weapons had the highest priority. It was posited that the best way to deter war was to demonstrate the ability to use nuclear weapons if forced to. It is true, though, that the U.S. Navy for some years now has for the most part been less than enamored of the employment of these weapons at sea by surface fleets.   Moreover, as a result of the developments in Europe in 1989 and 1990 and the changing attitudes of many U.S. allies in the North Atlantic Treaty Organization (NATO) regarding battlefield nuclear weapons, the U.S. Army is reportedly reevaluating the need for all nuclear weapons now in the hands of ground forces.

To be sure, nuclear weapons remain central for deterrence.   Strategic nuclear forces and, at least for the time being, longer-range theater nuclear weapons, still have deterrent roles.   But the pattern now unfolding seems likely to feature nuclear weapons primarily as weapons for strategic deterrence.   Moreover, the changing nature of the Soviet Union, the demand for deeper cuts in strategic nuclear forces through arms-control agreements, and budget pressures in the United States all point to drastically reduced strategic nuclear forces for both the United States and the Soviet Union.

It is ironic, however, that as the major world powers seem to be relying less on nuclear weapons for security, the probability of regional powers—Iraq, for instance—achieving a nuclear capability is increasing.   We will, therefore, continue to live in a nuclear world, like it or not, and any war between major powers—and perhaps some wars between regional powers—will be fought in a nuclear environment.   It is a reality from which there is no escape.

A fifth principle that has shaped U.S. strategic thinking over the last four decades is this: *arms-control considerations have become an increasingly central ingredient to U.S. grand and military strategy.*

Disarmament is hardly a new subject.   Nicholas II of Russia initiated proposals for dramatic arms reductions in the final years of the nineteenth century.   His proposals did not achieve actual reductions, but early in this century they did lead to a series of conventions, treaties, and agreements on the conduct of war.   Negotiations and agreements flourished again after World War I, with the Washington Naval Treaty of 1921 establishing a framework for naval reductions that continued to dominate thinking until late in the 1930s.   And the well-known Kellogg–Briand Pact of 1928 "outlawed" war as a means of achieving national objectives.

World War II pushed those initiatives to rear stage, but almost immediately after the war discussions began on the possibilities of controlling atomic energy, and the famous Baruch Plan was presented to the United Nations. The seriousness of the United States in offering the plan and of the Soviet Union in discussing it have long been debated.   However genuine or not the initial proposals and discussions may have been, after India rallied support to forbid atmospheric nuclear testing following the large 1954 U.S. nuclear tests, the United States had to take control of atomic energy more seriously. President Eisenhower appointed Harold Stassen as his White House special assistant for disarmament in 1956, and that action set in motion trends that over time moved arms control—the term and purposes substituted for disarmament during the Kennedy years—to the very center of U.S. strategic thinking.

Schelling had a lot to do with acceptance of the term "arms control," pointing out that in the nuclear age it was as important—if not more important—to have *stability* in the arms balance between the United States and the Soviet Union as it was to have simple reductions in arms. In fact, he offered the proposition that the search for stability might cause the United States to prefer somewhat higher to lower levels of armaments.

All that is well accepted now, but at the time it shifted the focus away from "general and complete disarmament" to more limited objectives. Moreover, during the Eisenhower years, disarmament matters were handled separately from other security matters. They were not handled within the elaborate national security planning and implementation structure the president had established. During the Kennedy years, however, arms-control matters became closely intertwined with strategy. The 1963 Limited Test Ban Treaty epitomized that shift by focusing on the strategic implications for the United States of agreeing to the treaty.

From then on arms control moved fairly directly into the strategy-making process. By the mid-1970s, each new arms program going to Congress had to be accompanied by an arms-control impact statement that outlined for the Congress what effect that program would have on U.S. efforts to reduce armaments. In the late 1970s and early 1980s, the United States took another step linking arms control to strategy—the "dual track" decision—by which it was agreed that the number of Pershing IIs and ground-launched cruise missiles NATO would field would be determined by U.S. success or failure in getting an agreement with the Soviet Union to limit those types of weapon systems. Agreement on the "double zero" number of mid- and long-range weapons in 1987 raised profound questions concerning NATO's strategy of flexible response.

The extent to which arms-control considerations have affected U.S. military planning and operations is dramatically underscored by reference to the State Department document *Treaties in Force*. That document lists as in force some 36 treaties, conventions, and agreements that impinge on military operations. A few of them, admittedly, go back to the mid-nineteenth century, and a number of them came into effect around the turn of the century. Two-thirds of them, however, have been signed since World War II.

These agreements can be divided into five categories: agreements to prevent wars (of which there are 6); to limit peacetime operations (2); to provide rules for the conduct of war (15); to prevent warfare in new environments (6); and to limit armaments (7). Not included in the preceding listing, of course, are the far-reaching agreements on conventional forces in Europe (CFE), signed in late 1990, and on strategic arms in the Strategic Arms Reduction Talks (START). To list these various treaties, conventions, and agreements is to underscore the point that arms-control considerations are central ingredients of U.S. grand and military strategy.

PRINCIPLES OF FUTURE STRATEGY

If these five principles have played important roles in shaping U.S. strategic thinking since World War II, will each principle influence U.S. strategic thinking in the uncertain future?

Principle 1: Primacy of the Soviet Threat

Conflict between NATO and the Warsaw Pact is no longer the primary focus of U.S. strategic thinking. The Soviet Union at present is not able to challenge the West militarily in Europe. The Warsaw Pact has virtually disintegrated. Soviet military leaders are beset by myriad problems—among them force levels, modernization, ethnic composition, source of manpower (conscription or voluntarism), role in government decision making, and public support. Yet the Soviet Union still has massive and modern strategic nuclear forces— it is the only country with the ability to destroy the United States. To date, it is continuing modernization of those forces with no letup. As long as it continues on this path, the Soviet Union will remain *the* primary focus of U.S. strategic nuclear force planning and hence *the* major concern relative to the survival of the United States.

Principle 1, therefore, will continue to influence U.S. strategic thinking because the Soviet Union remains the principal power the United States must deter. Soviet nuclear capabilities remain a unique threat to the United States and require a response. The focus of U.S. planning relative to the Soviet Union may well narrow to center on this threat. Thus, although the Soviet Union probably will not be the all-important central focus of all U.S. strategic and military planning that it was as recently as [1989], it will still be a significant ingredient. Principle 1 will remain a guiding principle of U.S. strategic thinking.

Principle 2: Substitution of Technology for Manpower

This principle will remain dominant in U.S. strategic thinking. Arms-control considerations, however, may increasingly influence the kinds of technology the United States pursues. Early in the CFE talks, primarily at the behest of the Soviets, there was talk of emphasizing "defensive" technologies, that is, technologies that favor the defense of territory. They have argued that armies should rely not on offensive weapons, such as tanks, but on light forces, composed mainly of infantry, because they are more defensive in nature. A number of informed observers have trouble distinguishing offensive from defensive weapons; they point out that it is the purpose for which the weapons are used that determines whether they are offensive or defensive; the weapons themselves are neutral. This argument may never be conclusively settled, but one point can be made. Some quarters will continue to press for more defensive weapons, and they will find at least some sympathetic ears.

Questions about which technologies should be emphasized will linger for other reasons as well. The U.S. military services are today accused of seeking technologies too advanced, too costly, too difficult to use and maintain. More and more often the charge is leveled that U.S. military procurements must be based on technologies more proven and less costly. In an environment that raises questions about which technologies should be pursued for considerations of both arms control and cost and feasibility, technological issues will undoubtedly be around for a long time. Furthermore, experience to date has affirmed the wisdom of U.S. policy in substituting technology for manpower. Thus, this inclination is not likely to change even as there is growing focus on the question of *which* technologies to develop. Arms-control considerations seem likely to increase the political pressures for technologies that are perceived as more defensive in character.

Principle 3: Civilians as the Primary Source of Strategic Thinking

This pattern, also, almost certainly will hold in the future. . . . Most military personnel choose the military profession because they are fundamentally doers, not thinkers. They are generally competent in operational planning and in operating military forces, but they are not great conceptualizers. . . .

Two further reasons why U.S. strategic thinking will continue to reside primarily with civilian analysts merit mention. First, professional military influence is likely to diminish as military budgets shrink. Second, and of more weight, as the strategic problems facing the United States spring more from economic and political than from direct military factors, the military input to strategic thinking will be less needed.

It is noteworthy that no contemporary strategists—civilian or military—have been recognized for their contributions to future requirements of U.S. strategy as were the strategists of the last generation, listed above, for their contributions to U.S. cold war strategy. Certainly, one major reason is that the Cold War is barely over, and it is too early to know what to hope for or expect. Only after some 10 years into the Cold War did plausible, thought-provoking syntheses begin to appear. The period of serious groping for better understanding that preceded them was very similar to the situation in which the United States presently finds itself. The recognized strategists of the future are out there now, developing and articulating their thoughts. It is too early, however, to discern which of them are setting the strategic patterns of the future. That will come with time.

Principle 4: Nuclear Weapons Will Have a More Limited Utility

The trend toward less emphasis on nuclear weapons in planning for possible wars between the major military powers will continue. It is, nevertheless, worth emphasizing that any war between major powers will be fought in a nuclear environment. That does not mean such weapons will necessarily be used, or that forces will necessarily be deployed expecting a nuclear attack at any time, but, at a minimum, it does mean that if one side is on the verge of military collapse on the battlefield, both sides will have to take into consideration the nuclear reality.

Before the disintegration of the Warsaw Pact, it was often posited that NATO's improving conventional military strength reduced the need for NATO to initiate employment of theater nuclear weapons. As a result, any war in Europe probably could be fought conventionally, contrary to NATO's accepted strategy. A counterargument heard at the time, however, could not be dismissed out of hand. Would the Soviets choose to lose a war of conventional forces rather than initiate the use of nuclear weapons themselves? Few would argue that the Soviets would never think such thoughts; clearly nuclear weapons will continue to be a factor in any war between major powers.

It seems likely, however, that the main public interest in things nuclear will not be in the context of superpower confrontation. Rather the focus will shift dramatically to the proliferation of nuclear weapons to regional powers around the world and its political and military consequences. Major world powers will have to consider the possible use by others of nuclear weapons in regional conflicts, a consideration heretofore unnecessary. This reality will keep the nuclear question very much alive. It could change U.S. willingness to deploy forces around the world for fear they might be subject to nuclear attack by a hostile and unpredictable regional power. If it did not affect U.S. willingness to make such deployments, it would certainly affect their nature.

To repeat, nuclear questions are here forever because the weapons cannot be disinvented.

Principle 5: Arms Control Will Influence Grand and Military Strategy

Arms-control matters undoubtedly are also here for the foreseeable future and will continue to be a major element of defense policy-making. In Europe, further reductions beyond CFE seem certain, barring unforeseen developments in the Soviet Union. In the strategic forces negotiations, the momentum in START, combined with budget pressures on the United States and the Soviet Union, seem likely to lead within the next decade to a strategic nuclear force level of no more than several thousand warheads. That will force consideration of the long-term viability of the triad as its component weapons need to be modernized. Hard choices will have to be made, and most likely they will be dominated by the need to ensure the survivability of weapons.

Just as proliferation of nuclear (and other) weapons of mass destruction will dominate thinking concerning the possible employment of such weapons, so in matters relating to arms control more attention will be paid to reducing the possibility that more governments will acquire nuclear weapons and to the dangers of their possible employment in combat.   Indeed, it is highly likely that the major powers will cooperate more and more to damp down dangers they see in regions of the world where their interests may be threatened.   Because the world is in for a period of increased turbulence and turmoil, it is reasonable to expect that the major powers will find frequent need to pool their resources and influence to stem the spread of nuclear weapons.   In brief, arms-control negotiations and agreements will become increasingly important to the major powers as instruments of policy to protect their international political and economic interests.

As the preceding review shows, five principles have had a major influence on strategic thinking in the United States since the end of World War II.   To delineate them is useful not just as a record of the past but also as a guide to thinking about factors influencing U.S. national security policies and strategies in the future.   To be sure, in the future these patterns will not be cast in exactly the same form as in the past; they will necessarily be modified by changing circumstances.   All, however, will be relevant to the strategic issues with which the United States must deal, and all can provide useful insights for meeting the challenges and opportunities of the future.

EMERGING PATTERNS

Patterns from the past may be useful and necessary guides in shaping U.S. strategic thinking in the future, but they will not be sufficient.   As the United States enters the post–cold war era, past thinking must be augmented by additional new concepts that reflect the changed international environment. Events are indeed forcing U.S. thinking forward, more rapidly than many would prefer.   Plainly put, although the post–cold war era is not yet far advanced, its first major crisis, . . . in the Persian Gulf, provides productive insights into patterns of influence likely to take on more importance in the coming years.

The first of these new patterns is very clear: *the United States will be less willing and less able to take unilateral military action than it has been in the past.*   The Persian Gulf crisis is establishing precedents for the legitimate employment of military force in multilateral responses to regional threats. As the [Persian Gulf] episode demonstrates, the United States will increasingly be unwilling to commit resources and accept the overall responsibility in dangerous situations where more than the nation's own interests are at stake. Others affected will be asked to join in a collective effort.   Thus, the United States will more frequently seek a consensus among national governments and international organizations for any use of economic pressure or military force. . . .

Building and maintaining a consistent and effective policy among sovereign nations carries with it a price, however.   Individual government initiatives, no matter how wise or how important the member state that proposes them, must bear the close scrutiny and ultimately gain the support of a broad range of opinion that may be congruent on basic objectives but less united on the means to achieve those ends. This new pattern may well make definitive, dramatic actions to resolve a crisis less likely because the requirements for consensus will almost certainly entail compromises among differing perceptions of the appropriate next steps.

The effect on existing regional and international institutions of the search for consensus among a number of governments remains to be seen. The fact, however, that such entities are in place and provide ready forums for the discussion of issues and the development of courses of action acceptable to a range of opinions certainly places them in a favorable position. We have seen already how the United Nations has gained influence as it served as the focal point for building a globally agreed course of action for meeting the Persian Gulf crisis. It has a good number of new precedents on which to build. On the other hand, NATO . . . declined the opportunity to strengthen its mandate and influence. To be sure, NATO forums [were] used profitably to exchange ideas and information, but as an organization NATO . . . pointedly maintained its regional focus.

A second emerging pattern is this: *the U.S. Congress will insist on a more influential role in decisions concerning war and peace.* . . .

Since the mid- and late-1970s, the War Powers Act and the role of Congress in the overseas deployment and employment of U.S. military forces have been before the American people on many occasions, frequently because of a belief in Congress that the legislative branch has not been adequately consulted in decisions involving the dispatch of U.S. military force into zones of danger or possible hostile action. In an environment in which the United States is seeking consensus from a wide range of foreign governments, it is readily understandable that the U.S. Congress will demand similar attention. And Congress will want a say in the setting of any precedents that would have relevance in the future. Simply put, Congress will more and more want to participate in the making of decisions, not merely to be notified of them after they are made.

A third pattern has been alluded to above but it is one that relates less specifically to the Persian Gulf crisis than it does to the nature of the new, multipolar world. In the absence of the stability and conformity forced on many governments by the Cold War and the dominance of the world's two major powers, individual governments in the future will have greater freedom to pursue their own individual desires. This new situation will not in all cases result in a more cooperative or more peaceful world. Indeed, quite the contrary. It can be argued that Saddam Hussein [was] the first regional leader to take advantage of the new lack of constraints, but he surely will not be the last. The following pattern may consequently emerge: *divergent perceptions of national interests in a world with fewer constraints on actions by national governments will encourage individualism and opportunism that will threaten historic friendships and alliances. . . .*

The third pattern . . . most shows itself . . . in day-to-day competitive economic relations between governments. As the December 1990 collapse of the General Agreement on Tariffs and Trade (GATT) negotiations . . . demonstrated, national economic protectionism is noticeably eroding friendships that have stood stalwart since shortly after the end of World War II. It is thus weakening security arrangements that have helped preserve peace during a dangerous period in world history. Ironically, at a time when the interdependence of the world economy is well recognized, and when the health of each national economy is seen as dependent on the health of the global economy, many governments are seeking unilateral, national solutions to disequilibriums in their own economies at the expense of their trading partners. The debilitating effects of this trend are visible today in U.S. relationships with Western Europe and Japan, the two partners the United States has assisted and encouraged during the years of the Cold War, and with which the nation has had such mutually rewarding friendships and associations. The survival of these long-term friendships in the post—cold war era cannot be taken for granted.

Past, present, and emerging patterns of thought will influence the framework in which the United States does its strategic thinking in the years ahead. Some patterns from the past will work to U.S. advantage, others not. Some of those emerging will not stand the test of time. In any event, the United States must begin now to sort out which of them will guide U.S. thinking and posture in a new world order.

NOTES

1. Kahn's two influential works on this subject were *On Thermonuclear War* (Princeton: Princeton University Press, 1960) and *Thinking about the Unthinkable* (New York: The Horizon Press, 1962).

2. See Robert E. Osgood, *Limited War: The Challenge to American Strategy* (Chicago: University of Chicago Press, 1957).

3. See Albert Wohlstetter, "The Delicate Balance of Terror," *Foreign Affairs* 37 (January 1959), pp. 211–234.

4. See Thomas C. Schelling, *The Strategy of Conflict* (Cambridge, Mass.: Harvard University Press, 1960).

20 THE GHOST IN THE PENTAGON: RETHINKING AMERICA'S DEFENSE

Fred Charles Iklé

From Berlin to Baku, popular revolutions are dissolving the world's last empire—the erstwhile evil one. Upheavals continue. The *annus mirabilis* of 1989 liberated political energy that is now beginning to affect every corner of the globe: hastening the demise of Beijing's outdated dynasty, eroding Fidel Castro's and Kim Il Sung's dictatorships, creating a new German nation, transforming the European Community, and perhaps draining the marrow out of NATO [North Atlantic Treaty Organization].

Routinely, Pentagon planners stake out their work each year with a description of The Threat. Now we see in astonishment that in every arena of confrontation The Threat is being turned upside down. Indeed, our arch-adversary's arch-alliance, the Warsaw Pact, [is now defunct], having lost its ideological glue and Stalinist discipline.

What, now, are the threats against which the Pentagon should prepare? How should America's strategy and military forces, indeed its overall foreign policy, be changed to take account of the transformed environment?

[In 1990], Congress [voted] on the first defense budget since democratic revolution swept through Eastern Europe. The Bush administration [described] this budget as beginning "the transition," in the President's words, "to a restructured military—a new strategy that is more flexible, more geared to contingencies outside of Europe. . . ." But as [this and subsequent] defense [budgets wind their] way through Congress, one must fear [they] will be treated like a big sugar loaf from which to shave off sweet slices: cut more army divisions here, lop off another aircraft carrier there, cancel the new strategic bomber, cut strategic defense by half, and so on—chop, chip, chop.

Note: Some footnotes have been deleted.

One can no more construct a new strategy from canceled defense programs than one can build a house from woodshavings. Alas, any sense of urgency in Washington that has now welled up about defense is aimed at budget cuts, not grand strategy. Stubborn fiscal pressures provide today's motive for changing our military programs and forces. As for America's overall strategy, influential voices in the administration and in Congress maintain that because of vast uncertainty in the world we should change warily. The United States would be rash, it is argued, if it sought to shape the ongoing transformation of the global strategic structure, a transformation that is not only unpredictable but, in any event, largely beyond our influence. A renovation of our security strategy, according to the conventional wisdom in Washington, will have to wait till the dust settles.

This complacency is mistaken. For we should care immensely just how "the dust settles."

To say that the United States can wait to address the fundamentals of our Western security strategy is both too complacent and too unambitious. It is too complacent about the potential losses, the utter disaster that the fragility of today's global transformation could bring. And it is too unambitious and too passive, given the potential gains, the promise for enduring and profound improvement in our security that these pregnant times hold. Both the complacency and the listless passivity stem from a poverty of imagination about the potential for change—indeed, about the impact of the changes that have already occurred. What constricts our imagination are old habits of the mind, an almost unwitting reliance on the strategic concepts that have shaped the ends and means of our defense policy for decades.

THE ENDURING MINDSET

The most influential of these concepts have to do with Europe, precisely the area that has now experienced the greatest change. For more than four decades, year after year, the threat of a massive Soviet invasion of Western Europe has determined the design and purpose of over half of America's resources for defense.

As pervasive as it is obsolete, this mindset took hold [over forty] years ago. In 1947, just two years after the Second World War, planners of the Joint Chiefs of Staff set down some views of a possible war with the Soviet Union. "The Soviet land armies and air forces are capable of overrunning most, if not all, of Western Europe in a short time," warned their memorandum. "The ability of the Allies to meet and retard the Soviet efforts would depend to a very large degree upon the length of the period of warning they receive and the use they made of it." Gloomily, the assessment listed what must be done "if the war is not to be lost." The principal requirement, it argued, is to prepare for "an offensive strategic air effort against vital Russian industrial complexes and against Russian population centers."[1]

All these concepts have survived to this day. The whole mindset is there: the Soviet military threat to the center of Europe, U.S. dependence on warning time, and—to compensate for Western weakness—U.S. strategic bombing of Russia. Like a sturdy genetic code, the mindset propagated itself through generations of technological revolutions in armaments; through the Korean and Vietnam Wars; through the Sino-Soviet split and the build-up of British, French, and Chinese nuclear arsenals; through the economic empowerment of Japan and the growing unity and economic expansion of Western Europe. . . .

. . . Washington's national security establishment continues to see the world in terms of the 1947 mindset. By regarding the basic strategy as an unchanging core, it recognizes improvement only at the edges. It admits—grudgingly—that the Warsaw Pact's massive attack on Western Europe would be somewhat weaker now and preceded by additional warning time. Having figured out that the attack would be weaker, the Pentagon bureaucracy concluded it could still adhere to the same old strategy, even if it sacrificed two army divisions and a few tactical fighter wings on the budget-cutting altar. Second, having discovered increased warning time, the Pentagon bureaucracy now accepts converting some of our forces intended for Europe from active status to the less costly reserve status. While the shift to reserves has merit, how the bureaucracy rationalizes it is preposterous. It totally misses the import of the revolution that has swept through Eastern Europe to conclude merely that we can trim our active forces a bit because our intelligence experts now promise, say, thirty-seven days of warning (instead of fourteen) in the event of the Second Coming of World War II. Since 1989, NATO's warning time is to be measured neither in fourteen days nor in thirty-seven days, but in years—the years it would take to re-Stalinize Eastern Europe. . . .

By postulating that the hoary scenario of the Warsaw Pact onslaught comes packaged with an extra twenty-three days of "warning," the Washington establishment justifies cuts in the defense budget. By trimming the edges of our force posture—cut some divisions here, eliminate some bases there—it can accommodate some further budget cuts. Most of these cuts will be welcomed by most members of Congress—unless and until they hurt vociferous constituents. But the totality of this approach is too passive toward the recent, and still continuing, transformation of the Soviet empire. It fails to cultivate and to secure the hitherto unimagined gains for peace and democracy.

STABILITY WORSHIP

Not to worry, say some U.S. officials, these gains will be secured through arms control agreements, particularly through . . . conventional force reductions in Europe . . . aimed at a treaty that will enshrine the concept of parity between NATO and the [members of the erstwhile] Warsaw Pact and impose the same limits on American forces in Western Europe as on Soviet forces in Eastern Europe. . . .

Why should the United States and its NATO allies labor . . . [to] maintain the Warsaw Pact as a coequal to NATO? Why should the Pentagon bureaucracy still allocate over half its resources to a conventional war in the center of Europe against a Warsaw Pact invasion with only thirty-four days (or whatever) of warning? The answer to both these questions is the same: our arms control policy and our arms policy are dominated by the same obsolete mindset.

The forty-year-old image of The Threat and our forty-year-old strategy constrict our capacity to grasp the immensity of the global change now unfolding before us. We have promoted a "stable balance" between NATO and Warsaw Pact forces for so long that quite a few Westerners have come to think Soviet forces in the center of Europe are needed for the sake of stability. One even hears whisperings in some mossy NATO circles that the Warsaw Pact ought to be preserved to maintain this treasured stability. . . .

Again, those who want to "stabilize" the military confrontation between NATO and the [former] Warsaw Pact [countries] are, in one sense, too unambitious. Beholden to the old strategic mindset, they eschew improvements in our security that an up-to-date strategy could achieve. In another sense, more dangerously, they are too complacent in believing that NATO could protect itself against a "second Stalin" simply by manning its old fortresses again.

Prudently, our defense planners are worried by intelligence information showing that the Soviet Union, despite its acute economic and nationality crises, continues the mass production of a wide array of powerful armaments, including the most modern nuclear missiles. Our planners would be remiss if they failed to project these formidable military capabilities into a less benign political context than we enjoy today. We might wake up some morning to find a new aggressive dictatorship in Moscow, a ruthless tyrant who could order Russian forces to reconquer Eastern Europe and menace NATO more dangerously than Stalin ever did.

But what a fatal error to believe that, in the event of such a catastrophe, NATO could simply pick up where it left off in 1988! It is grossly unrealistic to assume that our Atlantic Alliance would proudly reassemble at the old ramparts, regenerate its military exercises in . . . Germany, deploy new short-range nuclear arms in Europe (as had been planned in 1988), and induce its member nations to increase their defense budgets again.

If the will of all the peoples in Eastern Europe had been crushed under Soviet tanks, if the democratic forces from Sofia to Warsaw had been drowned in rivers of blood, if the profound German aspirations for a unified nation were cruelly affronted by new mine fields and walls, if the expectations for a peaceful, open continent now animating all the nations of Europe were totally shattered—how could NATO then return to "business as usual"? Instead, the Atlantic Alliance would be rent by harsh recriminations. Its governments and its people would have lost confidence in the old strategy; they would recoil from the prospect of another forty years of military confrontation in the center of Europe. With so dark a future, the now ebullient spirit of the European community would falter. The fear of nuclear war would again weigh heavily on the public psyche, a fear the enemy could easily exploit to stir up disunity within the alliance. . . .

CHANGING PRIORITIES

Again it becomes apparent here that our old strategic mindset imposes mistaken priorities on the renovation of America's (and NATO's) defense effort and on the West's arms control policy. Among the top priorities of our defense policy today ought to be the protection and consolidation of the recent political gains in Eastern Europe, and the removal of temptations among Russian "hard-liners" and would-be Stalins to use military force for a new expansion of the empire—all the way into the center of Germany, to the Adriatic, into Afghanistan, and beyond.

This means we must help to hasten the . . . withdrawal of Soviet forces from countries where they are not welcome, even at the price of more drastically and more rapidly reducing U.S. troops deployed in . . . Germany. . . . Of course, we can hope and reasonably expect that a certain presence of American forces east of the Rhine will, for the foreseeable future, be welcomed by the German government and by a majority of the German people. . . . A residual, continuing U.S. troop presence in Germany would symbolize and give reality to a security link between the United States and Europe, thus complementing the enduring spiritual and cultural bonds of the Atlantic Alliance. To preserve a transatlantic security link is an imperative for the long-term benefit of the world.

We can best preserve the global benefits of the Atlantic Alliance by taking the initiative now, in concert with our allies, to shape a new security system for Europe. . . . We should shift more resources and effort to help stabilize democracy in Eastern Europe. . . .

. . . It is conceivable that some new crisis might suddenly tempt Moscow to consider military intervention in Poland, East Germany, or Czechoslovakia, much as Brezhnev stumbled into the decision to invade Afghanistan. *To deter such a decision, under any and all circumstances, is a mission of our national security policy that deserves much higher priority today than the forty-year-old Pentagon mission of deterring the now exceedingly improbable Russian invasion of Western Europe.*

To this end, we must make clear to the leaders in Moscow, whoever they may be, that the West would never accept a new subjugation of Eastern European nations. This means breaking with some shameful past precedents of American indifference. For example, only a few weeks after Soviet tanks crushed the democratic uprising in Hungary in 1956, President Eisenhower stealthily signaled to Moscow that the United States wanted to return to business as usual, despite our vehement public denunciations of the Soviet actions in Budapest. Similarly, after Brezhnev's invasion of Czechoslovakia in 1968, President Johnson's first priority in East-West relations was to resume the strategic arms talks. Prevented from doing so by the incoming Nixon administration, he felt great disappointment; by contrast, he had been much less troubled by Brezhnev's destruction of Czechoslovakia's democratic forces. We now know that this intervention set back democratization in Eastern Europe by twenty years.

Brezhnev's invasion of Afghanistan in 1979 provoked a more coherent and, above all, a more persistent American response. The Carter administration started and the Reagan administration greatly expanded military support for the Afghan resistance. Nine years later, the tenacity of this resistance—and, thanks largely to our help, its effectiveness—compelled the withdrawal of the Soviet forces. Moscow learned a lesson that must have weighed heavily on its decision to abandon its imperial expansionism. If Moscow is not to forget this lesson, the West must continue to remember it as well.

A lesson within this lesson is particularly relevant for the Pentagon's current adjustment to the transformation of the Soviet empire. The Pentagon bureaucracy opposed the Reagan administration's efforts to provide more effective weapons to the Afghan resistance. It held no grudges against the Afghan freedom fighters, of course; it merely wanted to save its weaponry (even some of the oldest models) to meet The Threat it knew since 1947, with its anticipated huge tank and air battles in Germany.

Specifically, the U.S. army bureaucracy fiercely opposed giving the Afghan resistance Stinger missiles, the hand-held surface-to-air missiles with which the Afghans could shoot down Soviet aircraft. Only a minimal fraction of the U.S. army stocks of the oldest version of this missile was needed, and once made available, turned the fortunes of the war in Afghanistan decisively against the Soviet invader. While opposing this small contribution, the Pentagon was unstinting in shoring up the ramparts against a Soviet invasion of the Persian Gulf. That there might be a connection between Soviet success or failure in subjugating Afghanistan and Moscow's appetite for invading Iran, Kuwait, and Saudi Arabia was not apparent to those who jealously guarded the hoard of thousands of old Stinger missiles.

Would it be unfair to see in this story a parable for today's need to set the right priorities between saving assets for World War III and helping to strengthen the forces for freedom now? Many members of Congress and private foreign policy experts are advocating larger and swifter funding for a whole panoply of reconstruction assistance to Eastern Europe—support for new private agriculture, management training for business and government. Clearly, if democracy can be firmly anchored in these countries the security of our European allies will be immensely improved. Efforts by the U.S. government to this end, hence, could reasonably be regarded as complementing or substituting for other U.S. efforts on behalf of NATO. . . .

THIRD WORLD CONTINGENCIES

Over time, of course, the Pentagon will try to redesign its conventional forces for contingencies other than a war against a massive Warsaw Pact attack. The newly fashionable arena for our army, navy, and air force planners is the Third World. All types of armaments have suddenly become "vital" for dealing with Third World conflicts. Undoubtedly, each type has considerable military merit—whether it is the new C–17 transport plane that the air force wants, the new V–22 tilt-rotor plane desired by the marines, or the aircraft carriers treasured by the navy.

Four points need to be kept in mind concerning this now fashionable focus on military contingencies in the Third World. First, for the Pentagon, the problem of Third World hostilities is not new at all. Every war in which the United States has been involved since World War II—either directly with its forces or indirectly by providing military aid—occurred in the so-called Third World. (Korea in 1950 was still a Third World country.) Since the war in Vietnam, American defense experts have conducted innumerable studies of the weaponry and tactics for use in Third World conflicts.

A second point of importance is that the concept of "Third World military conflicts" covers many different contingencies with vastly different circumstances in terms of strategic geography, types of forces, and weaponry used. To be prepared for such disparate contingencies, the United States needs to be able to rely on a wide array of different armaments. The Pentagon's planning, hence, needs to address many different possible threats in Third World situations. Some types of equipment that our military services are wont to neglect may well be essential for some of them; for example, devices to clear land mines in insurgency warfare, ships equipped to clear sea mines, drones for intelligence collection, and other types of unmanned air vehicles.

A third significant factor is the dominant role of military assistance. Should the United States have a major stake in a future Third World conflict, chances are it would seek to rely on assisting its friends, rather than engage its own combat forces. This prospect renders all the more urgent the long overdue overhaul of the awkward patchwork of laws governing military assistance, a task that Congress is reluctant to take up.

A fourth point needs to be stressed, although it may not be welcome in the Pentagon. Only a fraction of the Pentagon budget—less than a third—can be justified in the foreseeable future by the need to prepare for possible U.S. involvements in Third World hostilities. Even though some of the Third World countries are heavily armed, their arsenals are still small compared to the Soviet threat to Western Europe against which we have been preparing all these years.

Yet, much as the "Second World"—the Soviet empire—has changed to a degree and with a rapidity that almost no one had foreseen, we must expect to see surprising changes and major geostrategic transformations in the rest of the world. This potential for revolutionary change confronts Pentagon planners with a tough challenge.   The ratio of the speed of political and diplomatic transformations—revolutions, alliance shifts, imperial expansion, and disintegration—to the speed of weapons development and procurement is about ten to one or even thirty to one.   To complete the research and development of a modern weapons system takes ten years or more, to build and deploy it another ten years, and once deployed the system may remain in our forces for another thirty years.   Who can foresee our strategic requirements for half a century?

NUCLEAR STRATEGY

This epochal time span has particularly frightening implications for nuclear weaponry.   Our nuclear strategy is still under the curse of Joseph Stalin. Few realize the extent to which the design and purpose of our nuclear armaments, doctrine, and war plans date from the same old mindset that since 1947 shaped and governed the bulk of our conventional forces.

In that Stalinist era we sought to deter the Red Army from marching to the English Channel by threatening to drop atomic bombs on Moscow and on Stalin's war industries.   Once we had acquired a great many more nuclear weapons, and once the Soviet Union deployed nuclear bombers and missiles, the top priority for the U.S. Strategic Air Command became the destruction— the instant the Red Army crossed the West German border—of as many Soviet bombers and missiles on the ground as possible.   Since then, the concept of such a prompt, all-out strike has become a dogma that warps the design of our strategic forces to this day, even though it had become impossible to disarm the Soviet nuclear forces with such a strike many years ago.

The obsolete dogma that our nuclear retaliation must be prompt is responsible for the Pentagon's insistence that we must maintain a large force of land-based missiles, with all the difficulty and expense this entails.   More dangerously, it perpetuates a vulnerable and hence a hair-triggered deterrent of thousands of missiles, both American and Soviet, sitting there like a thousand Chernobyls—till something, someday, goes dreadfully wrong.   The confrontation of these U.S. and Soviet missile forces has evoked a morbid fascination among many defense technicians.   By a banal and unrealistically abstract calculation—the so-called "missile exchange"—these technicians pretend to measure the "stability" of deterrence.

The Stalinist threat to Western Europe created other evil legacies for our nuclear strategy and forces.   To prolong the life, or reach, of our nuclear deterrent against the feared Warsaw Pact invasion, we deployed a great many shorter-range nuclear arms in Europe, especially in Germany.   All these nuclear artillery pieces, missiles, and nuclear-armed aircraft eventually, like a Sorcerer's Apprentice, acquired a life of their own.   They became "vital," had to be modernized, and gave birth to a totally incoherent doctrine— Flexible Response—which flatly contradicts the "stability" doctrine of the "missile exchange."

Given the contradictions and shortcomings of these strategic concepts, perhaps the time has come to pay some attention to Soviet criticism of our nuclear deterrence doctrine. Gorbachev called mutual deterrence a source of tension. As [former] Soviet foreign minister Shevardnadze put it, "nuclear deterrence inevitably perpetuates the totality of confrontational relations among states."

Defense Secretary Cheney has wisely requested increased funding from Congress for certain research and development projects—in particular, strategic defense—that will purchase us flexibility in terms of doctrine and enemies. What we now develop and build will have to serve our military strategy in the twenty-first century. For the foreseeable future, one must hope, America's nuclear strategy will continue to be an alliance strategy embracing and protecting a non-nuclear unified Germany as well as a non-nuclear Japan—but a strategy that can put behind us the "confrontational" bipolar relationship with the Soviet Union to which Shevardnadze referred.

Yet before we wax lyrical about the dawn of a new era, free of the danger of instant nuclear holocaust, we have to remember that Stalin's legacy is not so easily overcome. The laws of physics, to be sure, do not ordain that there must be two nuclear superpowers, dividing the world into "two sides" threatening each other indefinitely with mutual annihilation. It is habits of mind and bureaucratic inertia, in both Washington and in Moscow, that cling to the apocalyptic "two sides" confrontation Stalin inflicted on the world at the end of World War II.

Such inertia casts a dark shadow far into the next century. The Pentagon bureaucracy continues to disparage strategic defense, contrary to the policy of the President and Secretary Cheney; it keeps designing our nuclear forces to deter a [military] onslaught [from the East]—and thus favors nuclear weapons installed in the middle of Germany and hair-triggered missile forces. Stalin has been buried twice in Moscow, but his ghost lives on in the Pentagon.

NOTE

1. *Containment: Documents on American Policy and Strategy, 1945–1950*, ed. Thomas Etzold and John Gaddis (New York: Columbia University Press, 1978), pp. 302–6.

21   AMERICAN INTERVENTION IN THE THIRD WORLD: LESS WOULD BE BETTER

Stephen Van Evera

What policy should the United States pursue toward the Third World in the post–Cold War era?   Three harbingers suggest that the Bush administration intends to continue America's past interventionist policies.   First, a large chunk of the Bush administration's defense budget for fiscal year (FY) 1991 was allocated to forces optimized for Third World intervention, including fifteen aircraft carriers and eight light army and Marine divisions. The proposed budget for FY 1995 makes only modest cuts in these intervention forces.

Second, the Bush administration has continued four wars-by-proxy against leftist Third World regimes and movements, long after a Cold War rationale for fighting disappeared.   In Cambodia the administration supports a coalition dominated by the Khmer Rouge, which seeks to oust the Vietnam-installed Hun Sen government.   In Angola it has backed a violent rebellion by the National Union for the Total Independence of Angola (UNITA).   In Afghanistan it sustains a rebellion by seven *mujahideen* groups against the Najibullah regime.   In El Salvador it supports the right-wing National Republican Alliance (ARENA) government against the Marxist Farabundo Marti Front for National Liberation (FMLN).

Third, during the latter half of 1990 the administration deployed a large military force to the Persian Gulf, and it used this force in early 1991 to rout Iraq from Kuwait, which Iraq had seized on August 2, 1990.   By January 1991 this American force totaled some 515,000 troops, including some eight army and one and two-thirds Marine divisions, six aircraft carriers, roughly

This article is adapted from a chapter published in Joseph Kruzel, ed., *American Defense Annual, 1991–1992* (Lexington, MA: Lexington Books, 1991).   A fully footnoted version appears in *Security Studies* 1.1 (Summer 1991).   Earlier versions appeared in *Defense & Disarmament Alternatives* 3.3 (March 1990), and in *The Atlantic*, July 1990.

two thousand tanks, and fifteen hundred planes.   Over one-fourth of all American military personnel, and two-fifths of America's ground units, were deployed.

I argue here that widespread American intervention in the Third World made little sense even at the height of the Cold War, and it makes even less sense with that war's demise.   Accordingly, the United States should avoid further interventions in all but a few circumstances.   Iraq's invasion of Kuwait presented these circumstances; hence the Gulf deployment deserved support, although the Persian Gulf War was perhaps unnecessary, since economic sanctions also might have forced Iraq from Kuwait.   The case for the four proxy wars is much weaker, however.   These wars should be quickly ended, and intervention forces should be sharply cut.   Such cuts would save more than $30 billion per year.

INTERVENTION FOR NATIONAL SECURITY?

Throughout the Cold War, proponents of U.S. intervention have made two principal claims: that Third World interventions protect American security by preserving the global balance of power, and that interventions promote democracy, thereby promoting human rights.   Both arguments were false in the past, are false now, and would remain false even if the Soviet Union regained its strength and returned to an aggressive foreign policy.

The national security argument for intervention rests on three main assumptions:

1. The Soviet Union seeks an empire in the Third World.
2. It could gain such an empire, either by direct intervention or by sponsoring the expansion of proxies, unless the United States intervenes to stop it.
3. Such an empire would add significantly to Soviet military strength, ultimately tipping the world power balance in the USSR's favor, thus threatening American national security.

All three assumptions must be valid to uphold the security case for intervention.   If any fails, the global balance of power is not threatened, leaving no security problem for intervention to solve.   In fact, however, all three assumptions are defective.   The first assumption crumbled with the waning of Soviet expansionism under Mikhail Gorbachev.   Soviet tolerance of the 1989 democratic revolutions in Eastern Europe signaled the ebbing of Soviet expansionism worldwide, and perhaps its total abandonment.   Eastern Europe matters far more to the USSR than any Third World region; Soviet leaders who concede their empire in Eastern Europe cannot be planning to colonize much less valuable Third World areas.   Soviet cooperation against Iraq—an erstwhile Soviet ally—during the Persian Gulf crisis also illustrates the change in Soviet policy.   In short, there is little Soviet imperial thrust left for American interventions to blunt.

The second assumption fails because the Soviet Union lacks the capacity to colonize the Third World.   Today it can barely control its inner empire, as unrest in the Baltic republics, Transcaucasia, and Central Asia reveals. Overseas colonialism is unthinkable.

But even if the Soviets recovered their unity and their appetite for Third World empire, they could not seize it.   Soviet military forces are designed primarily for land war in Europe and for intercontinental nuclear war with the United States, not for Third World intervention.   This leaves the USSR with scant means to intervene directly.   Nor can the USSR gain empire by promoting leftist revolution or expansion by Soviet "proxy" states, because the centrifugal force of nationalism tears the bonds between proxy and master. As a result, Third World leftists tend to be unruly proxies, seldom following Soviet dictates except when pushed into the Kremlin's arms by American bellicosity.   This is underlined by the unfraternal relations among communist states and illustrated by the conflicts that have often flared between the Khmer Rouge and Vietnam, Vietnam and China, China and the Soviet Union, the Soviet Union and Yugoslavia, and the Soviet Union and Albania.   In fact, communists have fought each other as much or more than they fought others, indicating that Third World "Soviet proxies" are largely fictitious.

In addition, the USSR is evolving away from communism.   This further discredits fears that the Soviets can organize a transnational communist empire, since the leaders of the empire are themselves discarding the ideology that would allegedly glue it together.

The third assumption fails because the Third World has little strategic importance, hence even large Soviet gains in the Third World would not shake the global balance of power.   By the best measure of strategic importance—industrial power—the Third World ranks very low.   All of Latin America has an aggregate gross national product (GNP) less than half that of Japan.   All of Africa has an aggregate GNP below that of Italy or Britain. The aggregate GNP of the entire Third World is below that of Western Europe.   Modern military power is distilled from industrial power.   The Third World has little industrial power, hence it has little military potential, and correspondingly little strategic significance.   As a result, Third World realignments have little impact on the global power balance.

Moreover, the nuclear revolution has further reduced the Third World's strategic importance to a level far below even what its industrial strength might indicate.   Nuclear weapons constitute a defensive revolution in warfare.   They make conquest among great powers almost impossible, since a victor now must destroy almost all of an opponent's nuclear arsenal—an enormous task requiring massive technical and material superiority.   As a result, the nuclear revolution has devalued the strategic importance of all conquered territory, including Third World territory, because even huge conquests would not provide the conqueror with enough technical or material assets to give it decisive nuclear superiority over another great power.   Hence industrial regions that mattered greatly before the nuclear age now matter little, and Third World regions that formerly mattered little now matter even less.

Some interventionists assert that the Third World has strategic importance despite its lack of industrial power because the West allegedly depends on Third World raw materials, or because military bases in Third World areas allegedly have considerable strategic value. Both claims are much overdrawn. Oil is the only Third World material on which the West depends to any degree. The West imports many other materials from the Third World, but at modest additional cost all could be produced locally in the West, synthesized, replaced by substitutes, conserved and recycled, or acquired from alternative Third World sources if supplies from current producers were interrupted. Bases, too, can be replaced by longer-range forces, or moved to new locations, if a given country denies basing rights to the United States. Soviet bases in the Third World are vulnerable to Western blockade and destruction, since the West holds naval superiority. This leaves the Soviets unable to defend or resupply forces based overseas in wartime, hence Third World bases add little to Soviet military capability. Finally, the nuclear revolution renders such strategic arguments largely obsolete. Even if the United States depended heavily on Third World imports, and even if Third World bases mattered for conventional war, the American nuclear deterrent would still give the United States nearly absolute security from conquest.

The failure of all three assumptions creates a redundant, and therefore a very strong, case against intervention. Moreover, the latter two assumptions were false before the Gorbachev revolution, and would remain false even if that revolution were reversed. Hence the security case for intervention was very weak before Gorbachev appeared, and would remain very weak even if the changes he instituted were swept away.

In short, no national security justification exists for U.S. commitment to Third World intervention.

INTERVENTION FOR DEMOCRACY?

During the 1980s proponents of intervention supplemented security arguments with claims that American interventions promote democracy. This argument fails on both logical and historical grounds.

Deductive logic indicates that the United States lacks the means to implant democracy by intervention. Democracy requires suitable social and economic preconditions: a fairly equal distribution of land, wealth, and income; high levels of literacy and economic development; cultural norms conducive to democracy, including traditions of tolerance, free speech, and due process of law; and few deep ethnic divisions. Most of the Third World lacks democracy because these preconditions are missing. Moreover, it would require vast social engineering, involving long and costly postintervention occupations, to introduce them. American taxpayers clearly would not support extravagant projects of this sort.

The historical record shows that past U.S. interventions have generally failed to bolster democracy. These interventions have more often left dictatorship than democracy in their wake. Moreover, Washington has often subverted elected governments that opposed its policies, and many U.S.-supported "democratic" governments and movements were not at all democratic. Overall, this record suggests that the United States lacks the will and the ability to foster democracy.

The legacy of American interventions and occupations is not wholly undemocratic: Germany, Japan, Italy, Austria, and Grenada are significant exceptions. But these were easy cases: all had some previous experience with democracy, and all but Grenada were economically developed. Elsewhere the American record is bleak.

The United States governed Cuba, Nicaragua, Haiti, and the Dominican Republic in a generally undemocratic fashion during the intermittent occupations in the period 1898–1934 and then allowed brutal dictators to seize power after it left. South Korea has seen far more dictatorship than democracy since American forces arrived in 1945. Following the era of U.S. colonial rule (1899–1946), the Philippines experienced a corrupt and violent perversion of democracy and a long period of repression under Ferdinand Marcos's U.S.-supported dictatorship. Even in the post-Marcos era, violence has marred Philippine elections, and the threat of a military coup has hung over the elected government. Iran and Guatemala have been ruled by cruel dictatorships ever since the CIA-sponsored coups of 1953 and 1954. Chile is only now emerging from years of harsh military dictatorship under Augusto Pinochet, who was installed by a U.S.-supported coup in 1973.

Some would argue that the United States brought democracy to Panama in 1989 and Nicaragua in 1990, but the United States deserves less credit than appearance suggests. The legacy of the 1989 U.S. invasion of Panama is still uncertain. The Bush administration's invasion deposed dictator Manuel Noriega and installed an elected government in his place. However, the administration also installed a sinister Noriega henchman, Col. Eduardo Herrera Hassan, as the commander of the new Public Force (PF), the successor to Noriega's corrupt Panamanian Defense Forces (PDF). Herrera staffed the PF almost exclusively with former PDF members, raising the risk that corrupt military cliques will continue to dominate the country's politics. Moreover, by invading, the United States merely sought to undo a mess of its own making. The United States created and trained the PDF; then, in 1968, the PDF destroyed Panamanian democracy, installing a junta that later gave rise to the Noriega dictatorship. Overall, U.S. policy toward Panama has not fostered democracy.

The 1990 Nicaraguan elections have apparently put Nicaragua on the road to democracy for the first time in its history. The U.S.-sponsored *contra* war and U.S. economic sanctions contributed by pressuring the Sandinistas to hold earlier and freer elections than they otherwise would have. However, the social conditions required for democracy were created by the Sandinista revolution, over American opposition.   In 1979, when the Sandinistas took power, 50 percent of the adult population of Nicaragua was illiterate; land ownership was maldistributed (5 percent of the rural population owned 85 percent of the farmland, while 37 percent of the rural population was landless); and the country was terrorized by the Somoza dictatorship's brutal National Guard.   The Sandinistas reduced adult illiteracy to 13 percent, redistributed the land, and disbanded the National Guard.

Had the United States gotten its way, these changes never would have happened.   As the Somoza regime crumbled in 1979, the Carter administration tried to forestall a Sandinista victory by replacing Somoza while preserving his National Guard in power.   A National Guard–dominated regime surely would have left intact the old oligarchic social and political order—an order in which widespread coercion, voter ignorance, and vote fraud made elections meaningless.

The United States also gets mixed reviews for its role in arranging the 1990 Nicaraguan elections.   The Reagan administration preferred a military victory to any compromise solution, including one providing for elections.   It therefore disrupted the 1984 Nicaraguan elections by persuading the opposition not to run.   It also resisted the peace plan proposed by Costa Rican President Oscar Arias in 1987, which launched the process that led to the 1990 elections.   This resistance ended only when the Bush administration took office.   In short, the impetus for the Nicaraguan election process came from Central America against U.S. opposition, while the conditions for democracy were established by a social revolution that the United States sought to prevent.   Hence U.S. claims of authorship for Nicaraguan democracy ring hollow.

The undemocratic effects of American policies result partly from their pronounced bias in favor of elites.   The Carter administration's support for the Nicaraguan oligarchy was not unique; in many other Third World countries American policy has bolstered the power of local antidemocratic upper-class elements, who then blocked the social leveling that democratization requires.   In South Korea, U.S. policies favored the rightist elite from the early days of the postwar occupation.   In the Philippines the United States aligned itself with the upper-class *ilustrado* elite after seizing the islands in 1898–1899, and again when it recovered the Philippines from Japan in 1944–1945.   In Guatemala the CIA-sponsored Castillo Armas government (1954–1957) repealed universal suffrage and dispossessed peasant beneficiaries of earlier land reforms, leaving Guatemala among the most stratified societies in the world.   Throughout Latin America the Alliance for Progress, founded partly to promote social equality, was coopted by oligarchic governments that ran it for the benefit of wealthy elites.   As a result, the alliance in fact increased social stratification.

America's ambivalence toward Third World democracy is more starkly manifest in its recurrent subversion of elected Third World governments that pursued policies distasteful to the United States.   There have been eleven prominent instances since 1945 in which Third World democracies have elected nationalist or leftist regimes whose policies disturbed Washington. In nine of these cases—Iran (1953), Guatemala (1954), British Guiana (1953–1964), Indonesia (1957), Ecuador (1960–1963), Brazil (1964), the Dominican Republic (1965), Costa Rica (mid-1950s), and Chile (1970–1973)—the United States attempted to overthrow the elected government (or, in the Dominican case, to prevent its return to power), and in most cases succeeded. In the other two cases—Greece (1967) and Jamaica (1976–1980)—evidence of American subversion is less clear-cut, but is nevertheless substantial.

In short, American leaders have favored democracy only when it produced governments that supported American policies. Otherwise they have sought to subvert democracy.

American ambivalence toward Third World democracy is revealed by the thuggish character of many American Third World clients. America's client regimes in Central America are illustrative. The U.S.-backed governments of El Salvador, Guatemala, and Honduras hold regular elections, which qualifies them as "small and fragile democracies" in Ronald Reagan's view. But none pass the first test of democracy—that those elected control government policy. Instead, the army and police effectively rule all three countries; the civilian governments are hood ornaments on military vehicles of state. Civilian officials who defied the military would promptly be removed by assassination or coup. Knowing this, they obey the military. Moreover, the preconditions for fair elections—free speech, free press, and freedom to vote, organize, and run for office—are denied by government death squads that systematically murder critics of the government. The official terror has reached vast proportions in El Salvador, where the government has murdered 40,000 Salvadorans since 1979, and in Guatemala, where the government has murdered 140,000 since 1970. Fair elections are impossible amid such slaughter.

In sum, the United States lacks the means to institute democracy by intervention, and apparently lacks the will. There is little reason to expect more democratic results from future interventions. Accordingly, the advancement of democracy is an unpersuasive reason for intervention.

WHEN NOT TO INTERVENE: THE CASE AGAINST BUSH'S PROXY WARS

These criticisms of the case for intervention apply directly to the Bush administration's ongoing proxy wars. The Bush administration did not create these wars; they were inherited from the Carter and Reagan administrations. Nor is the United States solely responsible for past fighting; it became directly involved only after all four wars began. However, U.S. responsibility for past fighting is sizable, and the United States now plays a key role in sustaining the three wars where active fighting continues. (An uneasy truce has suspended the fighting in Angola, but a secure peace has not yet been achieved.) These wars have taken a huge human toll: 341,000 killed in Angola since

1975, including 320,000 civilians (thanks to the war, Angola has 50,000 amputees, the most per capita in the world); 64,000 killed in Cambodia since 1978; thousands killed in Afghanistan since the Soviets withdrew in 1989; and 75,000 killed in El Salvador since 1979. Such enormous violence requires a compelling justification, but the case for these wars is extremely thin.

Their main rationale vanished with the waning of Soviet expansionism. The Reagan administrations claimed that these wars were required to blunt the Soviet Union's "imperial thrust" in the Third World, in order to preserve the global balance of power. This rationale—dubious even during the Cold War, because there was little power in the Third World to add to either side of the balance, and little Soviet capacity to exert imperial control—wholly dissolved once the abatement of Soviet imperialism became clear, leaving these wars without strategic purpose.

Moreover, the administration's client groups are dominated by brutal elements who will rule by terror if they win on the battlefield. Democracy won't be helped, and human rights will be harmed, if the Bush policy succeeds.

In Cambodia the administration claims to oppose the return of the Khmer Rouge, while working to oust the Hun Sen government. But the Khmer Rouge are Hun Sen's only real competitors for power, and his most likely successors. In effect, then, the administration supports the Khmer Rouge's bid for power. These same Khmer Rouge killed over one million Cambodians when they held power during 1975–1978. In contrast, Hun Sen leads a pluralist, fairly popular regime that is accepted as legitimate in most of Cambodia.

UNITA leader Jonas Savimbi preaches democracy and capitalism to credulous conservative audiences in America, but he runs a brutal quasi-Stalinist autocracy in the territory he controls in Angola. He has murdered UNITA dissidents and once burned alive an entire family at a public bonfire as "witches." As a youth Savimbi was a communist organizer in Portugal, and UNITA defectors warn that he remains an unreformed Maoist. The training manual for UNITA leaders has a communist flavor, defining UNITA domestic policy as "democratic centralism," and UNITA's structure includes a Central Committee and a Politburo. UNITA also favors Savimbi's tribal kinsmen against others, leading one commentator to label his movement "nepo-Leninist." (Americans who mistook Savimbi for a supply-side conservative can probably blame Black, Manafort, Stone and Kelly, the high-powered public relations firm that Savimbi paid over $2 million to give him a suitably Reaganite public image.)

The Afghan *mujahideen* are a fractious group dominated by Moslem extremists and drug traffickers. The strongest *mujahideen* group, Hizbe Islami, is led by Golbuddin Hekmatyar, an extreme fundamentalist described by some Afghan specialists as an "Afghan Khomeini." His fundamentalist cohorts have launched a reign of terror among Afghan exiles in Pakistan, murdering those who criticize their views. Hekmatyar has also scornfully castigated the United States and its "immoral" society, even while the United

States lavished him with aid.   Another *mujahideen* leader, Nasim Akhunzada, was known until his death as the "heroin king" because he controlled the Afghan heroin routes to Iran.   In 1989 rebel-controlled Afghan areas exported seven hundred tons of opium, the raw material for heroin, making Afghanistan the world's second-largest opium producer, after Burma.   These "founding fathers" are not the type to build democracy if they win power.

The Salvadoran government is dominated by ARENA party founder Maj. Roberto D'Aubuisson and his military colleagues.   President Alfredo Cristiani is largely a figurehead who distracts the American Congress with moderate rhetoric while D'Aubuisson and the military run their savage war. D'Aubuisson is widely regarded as the mastermind of El Salvador's official death squads and was personally implicated in the 1980 murder of Archbishop Oscar Romero and the 1981 murders of two American labor officials. He also authored a plot to assassinate the U.S. ambassador to El Salvador, Thomas Pickering, in October 1984.

In short, victory by the Administration's clients would lead to rule by violent elements who have committed gross human rights abuses and have shown no commitment to democracy.

Why does war continue?   One would expect even an interventionist administration to cut off such odious groups once the wars they waged no longer served a strategic purpose.   But the Bush administration presses on with its wars.   Perhaps most striking, it has pressed on even after winning its main demands.   Its targets have conceded America's principal aims, but the administration won't take yes for an answer.

As the price for a settlement in Cambodia, the United States has long demanded that Vietnam withdraw the occupation forces it left in Cambodia after it overthrew the Khmer Rouge regime in 1978–1979.   Vietnam finally agreed and withdrew its forces in September 1989.   But then the Bush administration upped its demands, first insisting that Hun Sen include the Khmer Rouge in his government as coalition partners and later demanding that his government step down under a complex and expensive scheme involving an interim United Nations (UN) administration—a solution that would raise the risk of a Khmer Rouge return to power, since Hun Sen's regime is the main barrier in their way.   Meanwhile, the Hun Sen government has been prepared since late 1989 to accept internationally supervised elections conducted—as they were in Nicaragua, Namibia, and Poland—with the incumbent regime in office.   These three cases, and several others, show that fair elections are feasible under such conditions.   The administration has nevertheless rejected this solution, insisting instead on Hun Sen's prior departure. It also continued supplying the Khmer Rouge coalition armies, which forced Vietnam to counter by sending forces to Cambodia in the fall of 1989— thereby defeating America's main declared aim.

As the price for a settlement in Angola, the United States has long demanded that Cuba withdraw the troops it sent there in 1975 to bolster the new Angolan government.   In late 1988 the Cubans agreed to withdraw by July

1, 1991, and began leaving.   The Angolan government also offered to give amnesty to all UNITA members and to integrate UNITA personnel into the government.   But then, in September 1989, the Bush administration for the first time demanded that the government also hold elections as the price for peace.   This is a nice-sounding afterthought, but a pointless complication, because even foreign-sponsored elections will not bring real democracy to Angola; Angola is a poor country with a largely illiterate and deeply divided population, hence it lacks important preconditions for democracy.   In late 1990 the Angolan government accepted multiparty democracy in principle, and in May 1991 it finally accepted a U.S.-Soviet plan that would resolve the war through elections, to be held in late 1992.   Thus it appears that a peace premised on elections may be possible, and both sides also agreed to observe a cease–fire in the meantime.   However, even if the peace succeeds, Angola surely won't become a democracy; thus the Bush administration's late demand for elections merely prolonged a war that could have ended sooner.

In exchange for an Afghan settlement, the United States asked the Soviet Union to withdraw the invasion force it sent to Afghanistan in 1979.   The Soviets did so in February 1989, leaving behind an Afghan regime that offered moderate peace terms, including a broad coalition government and UN-supervised elections.   Elections cannot bring real democracy in Afghanistan, for the same reasons as in Angola—intense poverty, widespread illiteracy, and deep tribal divisions.   A peace based on power-sharing that reflects the relative military strength of the parties would probably prove more durable. Whatever the shortcomings of an electoral solution, however, the administration has impeded even that road to peace by demanding that the Najibullah regime step down before elections are held—a solution that Najibullah predictably rejects.

The United States said it sought to build a democratic political system in El Salvador.   The FMLN has progressively softened its demands and now agrees in principle with Washington's declared objective, pledging to lay down its arms if conditions for free elections are established.   The FMLN's main demand is the dismantling of the government death squads, to allow the opposition to organize and campaign without fear.   But the Bush administration has not pressed the Cristiani government to accept such a settlement. Until the November 1989 FMLN offensive, the administration opposed any settlement that would give the left a significant share of political power. Later it began to express more support for negotiations, but still failed to apply strong pressure on the government.   The two sides may eventually reach a settlement by themselves—they made substantial progress toward a peace agreement during early 1991—but American pressure could have brought peace earlier.

Why does the Bush administration wage these wars so stubbornly?   One theory holds that the administration has ceded control of Third World policy to the far right, in a bid to appease ultraconservatives for their exclusion from arenas of foreign policy decision making in which the stakes are higher for the United States, such as U.S.-Soviet relations.   The far right favors a *jihad* against all Third World leftists, even if this means aiding barbarians or wrecking the targeted societies.   To win this *jihad*, it will even use Marxist movements to destroy other Marxists if non-Marxist clients are not available—hence its peculiar willingness to back the Marxist Khmer Rouge and UNITA.   In contrast, American peace groups have shown little interest in these wars, except for the Salvadoran conflict; hence the administration can make more friends than enemies by fighting on.

WHEN TO INTERVENE: THE CASE FOR THE GULF DEPLOYMENT

The case for the 1990–1991 Persian Gulf deployment is far stronger than the case for these proxy wars.   Like them, the Gulf deployment did not protect American sovereignty or advance democracy, nor did it protect American prosperity.   The Gulf deployment did advance secondary American interests, however, and was justified for this reason.

Had Iraq gone unchecked, its seizure of Kuwait might have foreshadowed its seizure of the rest of the Arab Persian Gulf.   Iraq could have easily overrun the other Arab Gulf states (Saudi Arabia, the United Arab Emirates, Qatar, Bahrain, and Oman), especially if it had retained Kuwait's large resources and converted them to military use.   Iraqi expansion would have been eased by the common Arab culture that Iraq shares with the Gulf states; this common identity would have dampened popular resistance to Iraqi occupation, allowing Iraq to digest Arab conquests at modest cost and then move on to take more.   Moreover, an Iraqi campaign of this sort was not implausible.   Iraq has launched two wars of choice since 1980, and the ideology of the Iraqi Ba'ath party stresses the importance of achieving Arab unity, thus justifying a campaign of expansion against Iraq's Arab neighbors.

Had it seized the other Arab Gulf states, Iraq would have gained control of 20 percent of world oil production—a vast increase from the 4.4 percent that Iraq controls alone.   Iraq's GNP would have more than quadrupled. In short, an enlarged Iraq would have emerged far stronger than before.

This expanded Iraq would have remained a minor world power, too weak to directly threaten American security.   It still would have produced only 1 percent of gross world product (GWP), leaving it dwarfed in economic strength by the major industrial states.   (In contrast, the United States produces 27 percent of GWP; the North Atlantic Treaty Organization [NATO] states together produce 50 percent of GWP.)   With this small economic base, even an enlarged Iraq could not have built a military machine that could match the militaries of the industrial West. Iraq could have developed a modest nuclear deterrent and could have emanated power in the Mideast region under the umbrella provided by this deterrent. However, Iraq would have remained vulnerable to Western military power, because even a nuclear-armed state cannot build a robust defense against determined opponents with economies twenty-seven times larger, or fifty times larger, than its own. As a result, the Western countries could have managed any direct Iraqi threat to themselves.

An enlarged Iraq would have also gained some capacity to coerce others from its influence over world oil supplies. However, this capacity would have been partially offset by its military inferiority; had it used the oil weapon to threaten others' vital interests, they might have played their military card. Moreover, Iraq could not use the oil weapon without wounding itself, since it needs oil revenues just as oil consumers need oil.

Nor could an enlarged Iraq have extracted much wealth from the West by forcing a large permanent oil price increase. Such an increase would have triggered new non-OPEC oil production, alternative energy development, and wider energy conservation. These events would devalue oil held in the ground by current oil producers, including Iraq. Such considerations have led Saudi Arabia to pursue a moderate oil pricing policy; the same considerations would have compelled Iraq to adopt similar policies. Moreover, with just 20 percent of world oil production even an enlarged Iraq would have lacked the market power required to force more than a marginal rise in long-term oil prices. Had it cut its oil production completely, it might have caused a large oil price rise, but other producers would have harvested all the profits. Had it pumped enough oil to make money from the price rise, its own pumping would have kept that rise to a minimum. In short, the price of oil was not at stake in the Persian Gulf.

Thus Iraq's seizure of the Gulf would have posed little direct threat to American sovereignty or prosperity. Overall, an expanded Iraq would have become a dominant regional power but would have remained a minor world power, with little influence beyond the Middle East. It could not have jeopardized vital Western interests or taken the offensive against the West. Nor would its expansion have injured democracy, since the Gulf states are not democratic.

However, the United States does have secondary interests that would be jeopardized by unchecked Iraqi expansion and that were protected by the Gulf deployment. These include the protection of human rights, the preservation of peace among other states, the deterrence of terrorism, the prevention of nuclear proliferation, and the fulfillment of its moral commitment to Israel. If these interests are considered alone, each by itself can seldom justify the use of force, but here their cumulative importance is substantial, and Iraqi expansion would have threatened them quite directly. Hence the Gulf crisis was an instance where the limited use of force was appropriate.

Iraqi occupation forces cruelly violated the human rights of the residents of Kuwait. The United States has acquiesced to far more serious human rights violations by other governments, and American opposition to Iraq's lesser violations reflects a double standard. Nevertheless, the fact that the Gulf deployment ended these violations weighs in its favor. Iraq's aggression was unusually blatant—UN members have very rarely tried to conquer and annex one another—and American action to reverse it helps deter similar acts by others in the future; this bolsters peace. Iraq has sponsored international terrorism and has escaped punishment for this sponsorship; the Gulf crisis provided an opportunity to correct this oversight. Kuwait's financial resources would have allowed Iraq to intensify its quest for nuclear weapons, hence America slowed the Iraqi nuclear program and inhibited the regional spread of nuclear weapons by restoring Kuwait's freedom.

Most important, the U.S. deployment thwarted a serious threat to Israel's security and deflected a threat to the United States that derived from America's commitment to Israel. If the Arabs living to the east of Suez were united under a single government, Israeli security would be seriously jeopardized. These Asian Arabs are now ruled by eleven separate governments. This leaves them unable to act in concert, limiting their collective ability to threaten Israel. However, Israel might be unable to defend against a single Arab regime that controlled both the oil wealth of the Persian Gulf and the military power of the eastern frontline states. Such a state would command a net GNP many times that of Israel and might convert this economic superiority into military superiority.

If Iraq controlled the Gulf it would be well positioned to establish such an Asian Arab hegemony. Syria, Jordan, Yemen, and Lebanon would then be vastly outmatched by Iraqi power and might succumb to it. Like Bismarck's Prussia, Iraq would enforce national union.

If so, the GNP of this hegemonic Iraq would be 7.7 times that of Israel. In contrast, the frontline states that fought Israel in 1967 and 1973 held a GNP superiority over Israel of only 1.9 to 1, and the worst plausible "eastern front" that now might challenge Israel—a coalition of Syria, Iraq, and Jordan—holds a GNP superiority of only 2.3 to 1 over Israel. Thus an Iraqi hegemony in Arab Asia would threaten Israel with a far greater preponderance of resources than it has faced before. If it exploited this preponderance, hegemonic Iraq could probably gain conventional superiority over Israel, and might even find ways to threaten Israel's nuclear deterrent.

Moreover, such a hegemony would concentrate these resources in very hostile hands. The Iraqi Ba'ath party remains committed to the destruction of Israel, hence it seems quite plausible that Iraq would have turned against Israel once it gained dominance among the Asian Arabs.

The containment of Iraq also serves American interests, if the United States intends to sustain its security guarantee to Israel, as I believe it should. The United States could certainly contain even an Iraq that controlled Arab Asia.

However, America's security guarantee to Israel would then require greater American effort and involve greater risks. A hegemonic Iraq might have launched a renewed oil embargo to coerce the United States to halt security assistance to Israel. The United States could have weathered such an embargo, especially if it prepared properly beforehand, but an embargo would pose a major nuisance. A hegemonic Iraq also might have compelled the United States to rescue Israel in a future Arab-Israeli war, if it defeated Israel on the battlefield. This might have required the direct use of American forces, perhaps involving the United States in a regional nuclear conflict. The United States undoubtedly would have succeeded, but perhaps at a high price. These dangers were avoided by containing Iraq before it gained hegemony over its Arab neighbors.

By containing Iraq, the United States also sustained the possibility of an Arab-Israeli peace. Israel will not trade land for peace if it faces a serious military threat from the east, since territorial concessions involve some loss of military capability for Israel. Hence the containment of Iraq is a precondition for an Arab-Israeli peace. The possibility of an Arab-Israeli peace now seems remote, given the aggressive aims embraced by both sides. Nevertheless, both parties may someday pursue peace more seriously, so it seems worthwhile to preserve the conditions that peace requires. The Gulf deployment helped sustain these conditions by bolstering Israel's security.

The size of the Gulf deployment and the administration's decision for war in January 1991 can still be questioned, however. The administration chose to deploy a large force, in order to put strong military pressure on Saddam Hussein to concede, and to prepare an offensive military solution if he did not. In January the administration decided that it had waited enough and launched the war. However, a strategy of prolonged economic siege also might have forced Iraq to concede. Such a strategy would have required a far smaller force and cost fewer lives. It stood a good chance of success because Iraq is vulnerable to economic embargo and blockade: it heavily depends on revenues from oil exports, which supplied 42 percent of Iraq's GNP in 1989 and are easily interdicted. By one estimate a sustained siege would have reduced Iraq's GNP by 48 percent. Economic sanctions have often failed in the past, but previous economic sanctions have never been so punishing. Iraq would have resisted, but it seems doubtful that this resistance would have lasted for many years had the United States kept the pressure on. Such a siege strategy would have required a force adequate to defend Saudi Arabia from Iraqi attack and to blockade Iraqi ship traffic—perhaps 75,000–100,000 U.S. troops—but probably no more than this.

Administration officials rejected a long-siege strategy on grounds that the United States might have been unable to maintain unity in the international coalition required to enforce it. However, only a small coalition—including just Saudi Arabia, Turkey, and the United States—was required to prevent Iraqi oil exports. The politics of maintaining this small coalition seem manageable. Thus the goals of the Gulf deployment were worthy, but the size of the deployment seems excessive, and its offensive use seems unnecessary.

WHAT INTERVENTION FORCES DOES AMERICA REQUIRE?

The United States has no interests in the Third World that could justify a long and costly intervention. As noted above, the main arguments for past interventions—those positing that interventions protect national security or promote democracy—are not persuasive. Certainly no American Third World interest could justify another engagement as expensive as the Indochina war.

However, the 1990–1991 Persian Gulf conflict illustrates that the United States does have interests in the Third World that could justify the limited use of force. It also provides a useful yardstick for setting America's intervention force requirements, because a more demanding Third World contingency is hard to imagine: Iraq lies halfway around the world, it had the world's fifth-largest army, and it held the advantage of standing on the defensive, having already seized Kuwait. One analyst suggests that the 230,000 U.S. troops in the Gulf by early November 1990 were already adequate to retake Kuwait; and, as noted above, others argue that a siege strategy requiring only 75,000–100,000 troops might have sufficed to free Kuwait. The Gulf deployment thus provides a "worst plausible case" and sets a generous standard for meeting the requirements of that case, since a smaller force might have been sufficient to achieve American goals; hence it indicates a maximum requirement for intervention forces.

America's major interventionary forces are its lighter conventional forces— that is, those forces that are strategically mobile but are rather lightly armed. These include the army's light infantry, airborne, and airmobile divisions (comprising 6 of the army's 18 active divisions in FY 1990); the Marines' 3 amphibious divisions; supporting air force tactical airpower and air force and navy transport forces; and the navy's 15 aircraft carriers. Together these forces cost $102.3 billion in fiscal year 1990, or 34 percent of the $300 billion FY 1990 defense budget.

The Gulf deployment engaged somewhat less than half of America's light forces—only three and two-thirds light army and Marine ground divisions, and only 6 aircraft carriers. The "Gulf deployment" standard therefore suggests that at least half of America's light forces could be safely eliminated. Such a cut would leave the United States with a substantial capacity for Third World contingencies.

Specifically, the United States could cut four active army light infantry divisions and one active Marine division and still retain four active light divisions—an army airborne division, an army airmobile division, and two Marine divisions—for Third World contingencies. This four-division force matched the Gulf deployment with an extra one-third Marine division to spare. It substantially exceeds the American force deployed in the 1989 invasion of Panama (which utilized only one and one-half ground divisions) and is comparable to roughly half the peak American deployment in Vietnam—surely enough for any plausible future Third World contingency.

If the navy carrier force were cut from fifteen to eight carriers, the United States could still sustain a force of two to three carriers in combat for many months at a time and could surge a force of six or seven carriers into combat for a few months. Perhaps six carriers would be required to cover American sea lanes early in a Soviet-American confrontation—two carriers each for the Atlantic and Pacific sea lanes, and two more for the Persian Gulf or Northern Norway—hence an eight-carrier force should be adequate for this task. Experience suggests that a Third World contingency requiring more than six carriers is very unlikely. The six carrier Gulf deployment was America's largest carrier deployment anywhere since World War II. An eight carrier force could sustain a multi-month deployment of this size, although carrier crews would face the hardship of prolonged tours of duty.

Had these cuts been imposed on the FY 1990 defense budget, it would have dropped by 17 percent ($51.5 billion), to a total of $248.5 billion. Such sharp cuts should not be imposed in a single year, but could be phased in over several years. Instead, however, the Bush administration cut American light forces by only one army division during FY 1991 and has proposed additional cuts that will probably total one additional light army division, two light army reserve divisions, and one aircraft carrier by FY 1995. These cuts would produce a savings of $17.6 billion from FY 1990 spending levels if parallel cuts are made in supporting forces—a significant cut, but some $33.9 billion less than would be allowed by reductions to a Gulf deployment standard. American light forces would still total seven active light ground divisions (four army and three Marine) and fourteen aircraft carriers, some three light ground divisions and six aircraft carriers more than a Gulf deployment standard suggests. Thus the Bush budget for light forces substantially exceeds the likely demands of the Third World contingencies that these forces are designed to address.

Fewer dollars, but many lives, could be saved by ending the Bush administration's proxy wars in Cambodia, Afghanistan, and El Salvador. The administration's aid to its proxies totals only some $600 to $700 million per year, but this small expenditure is causing vast human suffering. If the Bush administration values human rights, it should stop these cruel wars as quickly as possible. Toward this goal, it should serve notice that its subsidies are ending and should press its clients to accept peace terms that each has been offered. If it did so, the fighting could soon be ended.

22 NOW THAT THE COLD WAR IS OVER, DO WE NEED THE CIA?

Loch K. Johnson

Espionage isn't what it used to be. Consider that for over forty-five years, the national security efforts of the United States have been designed to thwart the global expansion of the Soviet Union and its communist allies—the so-called containment doctrine.

The United States has deployed ships and soldiers around the world and aimed twelve thousand strategic nuclear warheads on targets from Moscow to Minsk. We have peered into the Soviet heartland with sophisticated reconnaissance satellites and ringed the perimeter of the USSR with electronic listening devices. Our spies have pilfered top secret documents from safes within the Kremlin itself.

Presidents have unleashed the Central Intelligence Agency (CIA) to fight communism in the back alleys of the world. Its weapons have included secret propaganda, political manipulation, economic disruption, and paramilitary (warlike) operations ranging from assassination plots against foreign leaders to large-scale "secret" wars.

On their side, the Soviets have done their best to spy on the United States and disrupt our attempts to influence global affairs. The KGB, the chief Soviet intelligence agency, proved to be a ruthless adversary in this hidden and undeclared World War III.

Now, suddenly, the CIA and the KGB have run into a hitch: the end of the Cold War. The opening of Soviet society (*glasnost*), coupled with the warming of relations between the superpowers, threaten to make intelligence agencies anachronistic.

The president of the Soviet Union, Mikhail S. Gorbachev, has promised to allow a large increase in the number of U.S. on-site military inspections in his country, and President George Bush has agreed to reciprocate. Once cut

Note: This chapter was written especially for this book. An earlier version appeared in the newsletter of the Foreign Policy Section of the International Studies Association in 1990.

off from the West by an iron curtain, today Moscow is practically as accessible to Americans as London and Paris.   Further, the Warsaw Pact—once a knife-point against the jugular of Western Europe—has been thrown into the furnace of history, replaced by upstart new regimes struggling for freedom and democracy.

These startling developments, predicted by no one, have led to clamors in the United States for sharply reduced spending on national security—a longing for a "peace dividend" in a time of budgetary stress.   Certainly much can be cut among large-item, strategic weapons systems, as the two leading military experts in Congress, Sam Nunn (D) of Georgia and Les Aspin (D) of Wisconsin, have spelled out.   Yet, as the war in the Persian Gulf has underscored, this nation will need to have a diverse (and, unfortunately, costly) array of conventional weapons at hand—from the smart bombs that so impressively invited themselves through closed doors in Baghdad to the modern tanks and airlift capability that may again be called on in the future to deter aggression in the Middle East or elsewhere.

Moreover, in the longing for a peace dividend in the aftermath of the Cold War, it should not be forgotten that the nation's intelligence budget merits protection.   The reason is simple: threats to the United States remain plentiful, even if the USSR is now a friend.   Too often these lingering dangers have been ignored as a result of America's fixation on the Soviet peril.

Although the intelligence mission ought to be retained as a budget priority, new ways of spending these resources are warranted.   No longer must the United States dedicate 50 percent of the strategic intelligence budget to intelligence operations against the Soviet Union, as was the case throughout most of the Cold War.   Now it must concern itself with other more pressing dangers, outlined below.

Naturally, the Soviet Union cannot be ignored, even in this new era of friendship.   It still maintains the largest army in the world, and its strategic missiles have lost none of their capacity to annihilate the United States within thirty minutes.   This concentrates one's attention.   And even during the first real test of U.S.-Soviet cooperation—inside the loose alliance (with other nations under the auspices of the United Nations) formed to repel Iraqi aggression against Kuwait in 1990–1991—strains were evident.   Gorbachev complained about the scope of the American bombing missions over Baghdad; and in February 1991, he advanced his own peace initiatives containing provisions that the Bush administration considered too lenient toward Iraq.

Despite the significance of the Soviet Union as a factor in America's relations with the world, consider how important it is for the United States to have information from overseas about other matters touching our daily lives—not always very gently.

It is hard to tell in advance what nation—large or small, friend or enemy—may pose a threat to our security in the future, as Iraq's bellicose behavior underscored.   It is clear, however, that the United States has sometimes been quite unprepared to react to dangers, often because its leaders lacked good information about global events.

For example: regardless of how one evaluates the U.S. military operations against Grenada (1983) and Panama (1989), the interventions were based on shoddy information. The chief rationale for the invasion of Grenada—an alleged threat against American medical students studying there—was never verified; neither the CIA nor any of America's other intelligence agencies had espionage agents on the island. (The medical school's administrators later denied any threat.) Upon landing, U.S. troops had to acquire maps of the island at local service stations, so lacking was the military intelligence.

In Panama, the American military commander leading the operation to apprehend its unscrupulous dictator, General Manuel Antonio Noriega, was astonished to find the Panamanian troops well armed with advanced weaponry—another dangerous intelligence failure.

Grenada and Panama are small nations located right next door to the United States. Harder still is the task of knowing what is happening in countries thousands of miles away. Islamic fundamentalists have held American hostages for years now (chiefly in Lebanon), but the United States still doesn't know their precise location or the plans of their captors. Nor did the United States have much information about where its prisoners of war were being kept in Kuwait and Iraq during the Persian Gulf War, the exact whereabouts of the Iraqi leader (Saddam Hussein), or much about the resolve of Iraqi troops hidden in bunkers—though much of the intelligence about Iraqi military movements was first-rate, pouring into U.S. decision councils from dozens of "platforms" (satellites and aircraft) gliding high above the sands of Iraq and Kuwait.

Iraq openly proclaimed that it has chemical and biological weapons; but the outside world knows little about its ability and intentions to use them. Nor do we know, with much precision, to what extent U.S. bombing during the Persian Gulf War managed to destroy the plants where they were manufactured. The proliferation of advanced weaponry around the world must be tracked more closely by American intelligence. Accurate data on the worldwide flow of weapons may lead, one hopes, to renewed international efforts in the United Nations (and elsewhere) designed to curb the sale of sophisticated arms, which have made regional disputes so dangerous to world peace.

Illegal drugs pose another threat to the United States. The Bush administration has declared the drug scourge Public Enemy No. 1. Every year some five thousand to six thousand ships ply the waters from Colombia and Peru to the United States, each carrying two hundred to three hundred containers (many with freight originating in nearby landlocked Bolivia). A comparable number of airplanes make this same trip annually. Efforts to monitor this transportation for contraband—not to mention the drug traffic from other countries (with Turkey high on the list)—presents an intelligence problem of staggering proportions.   So far, only about 10 percent of the illegal drugs are intercepted as they stream across U.S. borders.

Some would argue that America's declining economic strength presents the greatest threat to the United States since the decline of the Cold War.   They see an important new role for the CIA and other intelligence agencies in secretly gathering economic intelligence to share with American industry in its struggle against foreign competition—especially the Japanese.

Such a role would not be entirely new.   The CIA has been interested in knowing more about the decisions of the Organization of Petroleum Exporting Countries (OPEC) ever since 1973, when secret price fixing sent gasoline prices spiraling upward.   The CIA has also closely monitored Soviet crop production and oil supplies over the years, among other things.   Sometimes the relationship between the CIA and American industry has been startlingly close and controversial.   In the 1960s, for instance, the CIA joined in a secret alliance with a U.S. corporate behemoth, International Telephone and Telegraph (ITT), to overthrow the president of Chile, Salvador Allende, before he could move to nationalize the company's holdings (an operation that failed, though it probably helped to weaken Allende, who was eventually toppled by an internal right-wing coup).

Widespread economic spying on one's major allies is an even more contentious matter than covert interference in the affairs of smaller, developing nations.   Here intelligence experts, as well as chief executive officers in the private sector, are of two minds.

Some in each group argue for a greater CIA role, as part of a national industrial strategy.   If the CIA can help give American industry a competitive edge by finding out about trade deals and negotiating positions, so much the better.   Major companies already perform their own industrial espionage but, argues this side, they need help.   In addition, other nations—including U.S. allies—have been spying on U.S. companies for years.   (KGB activities of this sort have actually increased during 1990, according to former CIA director William Webster.)   So, continues the argument, it is time for Americans to use whatever means we have for discovering others' commercial secrets.

Others in the CIA, as well as inside the boardrooms of U.S. industry, are less quick to accept this espionage mission.   They worry about disrupting alliance relations if the spies are caught (as some inevitably are).   They are skeptical that the CIA is well equipped for this kind of espionage; and they believe that industry can handle this task pretty well itself anyway.   They wonder, too, how this information would be distributed.   Which industries would benefit in the United States?   Could the identities of the CIA's spies and their methods be kept secret?   Mostly, they see this approach as insignificant compared to the more deep-seated causes of America's ailing manufacturing capabilities.

This brief list of spy missions for U.S. intelligence barely scratches the surface.   Terrorism will continue to be a problem.   Indeed, experts fear that the war in the Persian Gulf may have as one of its end results the spawning of a whole new generation of anti-American terrorists operating out of the Middle East.   On another front—of obvious relevance to long-range security interests of Americans and everyone else on this small globe where all life is connected—some ecologists hope that the CIA can turn its impressive satellites toward monitoring the changing condition of the world's rain forests and other environmental concerns.

Beyond the list of collection targets lies the vital task of *analyzing* what all the information means.   Too often analysis has been the neglected stepchild of the intelligence agencies.   The new collection priorities will require the training of specialists to appraise the rising tide of information about once-ignored nations.   As former CIA Director William E. Colby observed in 1990, "When Cold War secrecy and contest made information hard to come by, except by fascinating secret operations and technological triumphs, and produced a demand for action-minded paramilitary and political warriors, the analysts took a back seat."   Now, he concludes, "The new era will put them where they should be: at the center of the intelligence process."

So, while some savings in the national-security budget should be possible in this new era of U.S.-Soviet *rapprochement*, the intelligence budget should be separated out from the weapons budget.   The United States needs more intelligence (and steady attention to its conventional capabilities for deterring aggression by renegade nations in the developing world); but the United States can safely reduce spending on strategic weapons systems.   This reduction can be carried out without undermining the still-necessary posture of mutual assured destruction (MAD).   The place to begin, as many authorities have advocated (America's premier statesman, George F. Kennan, among them), is with a 50 percent reduction in strategic nuclear warheads, carried out simultaneously in both the United States and the Soviet Union—all carefully monitored by "national technical means" (NTM, that is, modern surveillance instruments such as satellites), as well as by on-site inspections.

Budget-planners should make sure, however, that any increased funds for the CIA are channeled almost exclusively toward arms control monitoring and other information gathering, not into its "dirty tricks" department.   With few exceptions, the CIA's covert actions have done more to harm than to help America's interests abroad.   In contrast, the CIA in its role of information-gatherer has proven itself, despite the inevitable errors, indispensable to those who make decisions in Washington.

This is not to say that covert action should be abandoned altogether.   The United States needs to maintain a capacity for secret operations in emergency situations.   Indeed, members of the United Nations (UN) Security Council should consider the establishment of a UN-directed "SWAT team"—*small, multinational, acting under proper authority, and carefully supervised*—to conduct quick paramilitary strikes against chemical-biological (CB) and nuclear-weapons facilities in the hands of outlaw regimes and terrorist factions. When diplomatic initiatives fail to curb the outlaws, this approach may arguably serve as a better alternative—in extreme cases of CB or nuclear threats—than a full-scale military invasion, with all the loss of civilian lives that option usually entails.

"The winds and waves are always on the side of the ablest navigators," observed the great British historian Edward Gibbon. Skillful navigation depends on taking one's bearings carefully. Without a robust intelligence service able to monitor events around the world (not just in Moscow), the United States would find itself condemned to steerage beneath cloudy skies. The Cold War may be over, but the U.S. need for accurate information about the world remains acute.

23 INTERNATIONAL ECONOMICS AND U.S. NATIONAL SECURITY

Theodore H. Moran

I

The list of international economic problems that will trouble policymakers in the 1990s is long and diverse. Among the most important issues for U.S. national security are three that pertain primarily to relations among the developed countries: encouraging stability and reform in the Soviet Union, maintaining a cooperative U.S.-Japanese relationship, and avoiding vulnerabilities from the globalization of America's defense industrial base. Three more major issues facing the United States have a North-South dimension: reducing dependence on oil from the Persian Gulf, moderating the impact on the Third World of the prolonged debt crisis, and limiting the damage from the narcotics trade.

Clearly this list is not exhaustive; it could be lengthened without difficulty. Several issues that deserve emphasis in purely economic terms—from the outcome of the multilateral trade negotiations, to the competitiveness of American industry, to the future of the U.S. budget deficit—weave their way in and out of the entire list.

In the six primary areas examined here, U.S. national security policy in the 1990s faces a challenge of a different order than that confronted during the Cold War period: not clear and present dangers requiring great sacrifices, but dim and distant dangers calling for small sacrifices. The array of threats to American well-being on today's horizon is no less real than in earlier periods and in some cases may turn out to be even more troublesome. But meeting these threats will require a new kind of leadership: the management of the mundane.

Before turning to the broader theme of economic policy and the evolving strategic concerns of the United States, it is important to look closely at each issue on its own terms.

Note: One footnote has been deleted, and others have been renumbered to appear in consecutive order.

307

II

Does the United States have an interest in joining with other countries to provide large-scale financial support to the Soviet Union as that country struggles to transform its economy?

The deterioration of the economy in the Soviet Union has been so precipitous that it has become fashionable for experts to vie with one another in exposing new weaknesses.   In April 1990 the Central Intelligence Agency [CIA] calculated the Soviet gross national product [GNP] to be no more than half that of the United States.   Viktor Belking, a prominent economist from the Soviet Academy of Sciences, promptly pronounced the CIA figures too optimistic, asserting Soviet output was at most little more than a quarter of the American GNP.   The combination of shortages, inflation and regional blockages has made it difficult to assess even the current rate of economic decline with any accuracy.

The question of whether the major capitalist powers should provide assistance has taken on fiercely partisan overtones in the United States.   One side hopes such assistance might strengthen the effort to lead the Soviet Union in directions beneficial to the West.   The other side fears such assistance might prop up a decaying authoritarian state and provide succor to its military establishment, which otherwise would disintegrate and disappear as a threat.

There are three economic arguments as to why external assistance would be a good idea.   First, a supply of working capital, bridge financing, support for ruble convertibility, and infrastructure development is necessary before domestic markets and foreign investment can begin to work on their own. Second, outside assistance could take advantage of economies of scale in a coordinated effort to address multiple problems simultaneously.   Third, it could capture a unique opportunity to provide incentives to see that reforms stay on track.   The objective would be to help buffer the transition, since pain (higher prices, harder work, less job security, more unemployment) will come before any gain (greater investment, higher productivity, larger output).

The economic argument against external assistance, which so far has carried the day, is that the Soviet leadership has simply not yet made a firm decision in favor of transforming the economy to a market-based system. The Soviet Union is not like the other countries of Eastern Europe.   It has a low level of foreign debt ($48 billion), large gold reserves ($30 billion) and vast resources available for development (American oil companies, for example, report a sizable inventory of already discovered fields lying idle for lack of capital and technology).   In short, it is argued, the Soviet Union has the wherewithal to undertake determined action on its own.

Yet so far Soviet market reforms, at least until the 500-Day Plan, have been halting and indecisive.   State ministries continue to exercise monopolistic power as buyers and sellers of goods.   A plan to make the ruble convertible has yet to appear.   Therefore, foreign assistance at this time might well serve the Soviets as a substitute for making tough domestic choices.

The stakes are high.   A reinvigorization of the Soviet economy along market lines would add to European (and world) growth—incalculably more than would the resuscitation of Poland, for example, or Czechoslovakia, for which the industrial powers are willing to spend generous sums.   Stagnation and decline in the Soviet economy, in contrast, will constitute a great drag on European prospects.   Most ominous, of course, is the prospect that failure to integrate the U.S.S.R. into the Western economic order may result in chaos and disintegration in Russia and, ultimately, a return to a resentful and authoritarian Soviet regime, still in control of awesome military assets.   Then, indeed, there could be serious concern that "decaying superpowers do not go quietly into the night." [1]

External assistance for the evolution of the Soviet Union into a stable market-based confederation of republics with growing economic links to the industrial democracies would be a feat worthy of comparison with the original Marshall Plan.   Like the revival of Europe after the Second World War, it will depend primarily on courageous decisions made internally under highly uncertain circumstances.   But a successful outcome will almost certainly require external assistance of Marshall Plan dimensions as well, for support and reassurance.   For fundamental reform to work, there will have to be a major program of economic conversion and reconstruction lasting over an extended period of years—preferably in the form of loans under the auspices of the International Monetary Fund and the World Bank.   Of course, the effort may fail, but historians, looking back at the decade of the 1990s, will be astounded if the opportunity is allowed to pass with no attempt to seize it. . . .

For the idea of assisting the reconversion of the Soviet economy to be adopted, however, American leaders will have to persuade the public that such resources are better devoted to the Soviet Union than to competing— and worthy—causes at home.   That will be no easy task.

III

How should the United States approach the U.S.-Japanese relationship?   Should it be tougher or softer, more hard-line or more accommodationist in the 1990s?

The growth in Japan's economy between 1950 and 1990 represents the most rapid peacetime shift in relative economic status in the history of the world.   Such explosive change on the part of a single nation could not but cause substantial dislocation to other nations.   Helping to fuel resentment at the necessity to adjust, of course, is the fact that Japanese success is due in part to unfair trade practices, in particular the protection of Japan's local market from imports and the promotion of certain sectors for export-led growth.

The persistence of a large bilateral trade deficit with Japan has led to proposals that the United States shift to a tougher posture, demanding reciprocity in access between the two markets and threatening exclusion of Japanese products to the extent equal access is not achieved.   The argument on behalf of this approach extends beyond mere Japan-bashing; the contention is that only a "results-oriented" approach will reduce the trade imbalance with a partner for whom the abstract exhortation to "open markets" has no meaning.

The difficulty with this approach is that all Japan's unfair trade practices, taken together, block no more than $8 billion to $15 billion in potential sales, whereas the recurrent bilateral trade deficit ranges between $35 billion and $40 billion.   The fundamental cause of the imbalance lies in the disparity between savings and consumption in the two countries: the United States consumes more than it produces and does not save enough to build the additional productive capacity to make up the difference, leading to a trade deficit that supplies excess American consumption and inflows of foreign capital that make up for insufficient American savings.   Thus, even the most aggressive market-opening demands on the part of the United States would leave the largest part of the problem untouched, unless there is a simultaneous change in underlying U.S. behavior toward savings and consumption, including public consumption as embodied in the federal deficit.   Technically, macro-imbalances account for the entire deficit, with trade practices affecting only the composition of that deficit.   The correct focus for U.S. policy, of course, is equilibrium in the country's overall trade balance, not equality in each bilateral balance.   Threatening Japan with dire consequences cannot produce the desired results in the absence of a fundamental commitment to address America's own macroeconomic misalignment at the same time.

Moreover, the hard-line stance is likely to fuel resentment in Japan without producing relief.   The combination of growing Japanese anti-Americanism and a changing geostrategic environment, in which the need for the U.S. nuclear umbrella is disappearing, renders it no longer implausible that the United States might push Japan too far and even fracture the U.S.-Japanese alliance. . . .

American policy . . . faces the task of preventing the political process from tilting too far . . . toward Japan-bashing at one extreme or toward toleration of economic imbalances at the other.   The goal of preserving a close U.S.-Japanese political relationship requires a delicate balance of maintaining well-justified pressure against Japan's unfair trade practices while addressing—rather than avoiding—American responsibility for the fundamental economic misalignment.

IV

The third challenge to U.S. national security on the international economic agenda is the globalization of the defense industrial base.   Technological prowess and production sites for goods and services vital to the U.S. economy are spread more broadly across the globe than ever before. The Department of Defense has reported that the lead in developing one-quarter of the technologies most essential to American industry is held by non-U.S. firms, and a growing proportion of the products and components needed for defense come from abroad.

On the one hand, this globalization carries great benefits. It brings superior performance, innovation and lower prices for military as well as commercial purchasers. This is the aspect that traditional economic analysis tends to emphasize, celebrating the benefits of comparative advantage and dismissing concerns about the nationality of supplier firms or the location of production sites.

On the other hand, globalization does pose real threats, threats that could become more, not less, prominent as the Cold War recedes. A survey of post–World War II experience suggests that external domination of technology, goods and services may well lead to persistent attempts at meddling, manipulation and harassment in the recipients' sovereign affairs, even in peacetime relations among allies. Such interference has ranged from denial of computer technology to inhibit De Gaulle's *force de frappe*, to insistence on permission to reexport products that incorporate foreign inputs to designated areas (China, Cuba, several Middle Eastern states), to retroactive cancellation of licensing agreements (the Soviet gas pipeline case). Since the United States has frequently been the manipulator, it has largely ignored the prospect of experiencing the process in reverse, until now. There is a legitimate concern about American vulnerability as local industries crucial to defense disappear, and high-tech firms are acquired by foreigners.

One response is for the United States to turn in a neomercantilistic direction itself, protecting its own industrial base (as America has already done with steel, machine tools, even textiles), devising an industrial policy to support its own national champions (the joint public/private Sematech semiconductor research venture, the 1986 American-Japanese Semiconductor Agreement, a civilian Defense Advanced Research Agency), blocking foreign takeovers (Fairchild, Perkin-Elmer), and requiring the U.S. government to "buy American" (ball bearings, machine tools).

But the neomercantilistic response saddles American users of steel or machine tools or semiconductors with high-cost inputs, and reduces their competitiveness even further vis-à-vis foreign rivals. . . . Moreover, there is no evidence the U.S. government can pick "winners" for public support appropriately, or ensure that political forces do not divert such support to "losers" instead. How, then, can the United States cope with this dilemma?

In all cases of external interference, the threat from foreign dependence is genuine only when there is a concentration within a very few nations of external suppliers of technology, products or inputs. When sources of supply have been well dispersed internationally there has been no ability to control, to delay or to deny, and hence no real peacetime threat. As a rule of thumb, when there are more than four foreign companies or four foreign nations supplying more than fifty percent of the world market, they will lack the ability to collude effectively even if they wish to exploit or manipulate recipients. This "four-fifty" rule provides a useful guide for designing U.S. policies.

For American industries that are being "wiped out" by imports, those in which the sources of external supply are concentrated do represent a source of concern and should be eligible for legitimate "national security" trade protection; those in which the sources of external supply are deconcentrated do not. By this concentration test, semiconductor equipment manufactures would qualify for national security protection, textiles and footwear manufactures would not. Similarly, within an industry, subcategories of high-performance machine tools might be concentrated enough to justify protection, but measures to restrict imports of standardized cutters and grinders that have multiple suppliers would not be justified. This would provide for legitimate American security interests without incurring the costs of blanket protectionism.[2]

For American firms that have been targets of foreign acquisition, the degree of concentration in the world industry again provides the relevant screening measure. Even in cases in which a U.S. target firm is the only American producer of a given product, a foreign acquisition should be allowed to proceed by CFIUS (the Committee on Foreign Investment in the United States, an interagency body that advises the president . . .) so long as there are multiple external suppliers. If the external sources are concentrated in only a few hands, the acquisition should be blocked by CFIUS and, if need be, the U.S. parent firm granted national security protection. . . .

In sum, the security objective of maximizing efficiency and innovation in vital national industries while avoiding foreign dependence requires channeling popular protectionist and neomercantilistic instincts into those narrow areas in which foreign domination actually poses a genuine threat.

V

Turning to the North-South axis, the first question is: How can the United States use the domestic shock from the confrontation with Iraq to avoid even more severe energy shortages in future?

The Iraqi invasion of Kuwait . . . reawakened public consciousness to the extent of American dependence on imported oil. The restoration of stability in the Persian Gulf will provide only temporary relief, however, to the looming prospect of energy crises in the 1990s. In the absence of policy changes, the United States is likely to be importing between 55 percent and 65 percent of the oil it consumes by the end of the 1990s, and more than two-thirds after the year 2000. The previous historical high for import dependence was 47 percent in 1977; the figure for 1973 when the first oil crisis struck was 35 percent.

The price projections that accompany this growing dependence on imported oil vary widely, by more than 60 percent, due to uncertainties about the cohesion and strategy of the Organization of Petroleum Exporting Countries [OPEC] (imprudent price rises in the 1980s nearly destroyed the cartel). What is more certain is that the production volumes demanded from OPEC will rise substantially (from 22 percent to 39 percent greater than today by the year 2000), with increasing concentration in the Persian Gulf and Libya. The expansion of output from Saudi Arabia, the United Arab Emirates and Venezuela in response to the blockade of Iraq and Kuwait . . . revealed the narrow availability of excess capacity.   By the mid-to-late 1990s the number of major OPEC exporters will have shrunk, with Gabon, Ecuador, Algeria and even Indonesia and Nigeria consuming domestically much of what they produce.   Since 1985, 90 percent of the increase in world oil production has come from the Persian Gulf, a trend that will continue in the 1990s as non-OPEC countries reach a production plateau.

Adding to the energy vulnerability of the United States in the 1990s is the dilemma faced by electrical utilities as they seek to build the next generation of power facilities.   In the 1970s and 1980s electrical utility capacity was in oversupply, leading to low rates of new construction.   In the early 1990s electricity demand is overtaking production capacity at the very moment when there is strong opposition to the two principal sources of baseload output, coal and nuclear power.   As a result utilities are returning to oil, raising usage by more than 30 percent.   This supplements the demand for petroleum consumed in the transportation sector.

The United States and other industrial democracies are better off than they were during the oil crises of 1973 or 1979 since they have petroleum reserves to draw upon in a crisis.   In general, however, the prospects for energy vulnerability are growing ever more worrisome, especially given growing military capabilities for long-range destruction among the countries in the Persian Gulf.   Upheavals there could come to have a genuinely devastating impact on the international economy. . . .

Policy recommendations for reducing vulnerability to oil imports from the Persian Gulf would have to combine conservation with the promotion of domestic sources of supply (especially for electricity).   For conservation, the most efficient approach is to continue to raise energy taxes, which will still be lower in the United States than elsewhere (taxes reach $1.20 to $3.00 per gallon of gasoline in Europe and Japan).[3]   Energy taxes are appealing in revenue terms; each 10¢ increase in gasoline taxes, for example, generates approximately $6 billion in government receipts (allowing for the drag on the economy).   For environmental reasons (global warming, acid rain), some analysts recommend a more general carbon tax and a turn away from coal.

For promotion of domestic sources of supply, solar energy has long-term appeal, but nuclear power offers the only realistic alternative to coal for the next generation of utilities.

Both options have strong domestic opposition.   But difficult choices about substantially higher energy taxes and the resumption of nuclear plant construction are unavoidable if the United States is to decelerate the rate of growth of imported oil to a more moderate pace from the current headlong rush.

VI

The security implications of relations with the Third World are not limited to the energy supply from the Persian Gulf. What are broader U.S. concerns in regard to the less developed countries (LDC) as Cold War anxieties diminish?

With the exception of East Asia, the Third World is just ending a "lost decade" in which the attempt to pay off foreign loans with a net capital outflow of $20 billion per year from South to North has reduced per capita living standards by more than ten percent in real terms, producing a social setback greater than the Great Depression of the 1930s.

Any analysis of the causes of the debt crisis bestows an abundance of blame on all parties. Public and private borrowers sought, and commercial banks provided, funding for many dubious projects in the late 1970s. Then, the dramatic rise in U.S. interest rates from 9 percent to 19 percent in the period 1978–1981, followed by recession in the developed countries and the consequent collapse of commodity prices, left both LDC borrowers and bank creditors unexpectedly overextended. The interest expense in Argentina, Brazil and Mexico, for example, tripled, while the terms of trade dropped by almost ten percent.

Initially, the United States, in its "Baker Plan," gave priority to maintaining the viability of the international financial system by seeking to ensure the health of the commercial banks. The succeeding "Brady Plan" has for the first time permitted discussion of the concept of debt relief for the LDC borrowers. The Brady Plan combines a U.S. Treasury bond guarantee for the principal of new, discounted bonds plus IMF-World Bank guarantees for interest payments, in return for domestic policy reforms in the debtor countries. It has been expanded in 1990 to include the possibility of relief on debt owed to governments as well as commercial banks.

The case of Mexico has perhaps greatest salience. The United States welcomed the inauguration of Mexican President Carlos Salinas de Gortari, whose administration had more coherence and ideological commitment to market forces than any other in the past quarter century. Mexico, consequently, became the showcase for the Brady Plan. But at the end of long negotiations relying on voluntary participation by the banks, the magnitude of the relief in fact turned out to be quite small. . . . The outcome raises doubts about the utility of allocating scarce public resources to a program that fails to reduce the debt burden sufficiently to "jump start" an economy. . . .

Looking to the future, for Mexico to regain its economic momentum will require that it reach and sustain throughout the 1990s more favorable economic conditions than have yet been achieved. For Latin America as a whole to "grow out" of the debt crisis, economic expansion must average five to six percent per year through the late 1990s, replacing the current rate of less than two percent. Adding to the growing pessimism that this can happen is evidence that the potential boost that could come with further repatriation of "flight capital" is not likely to occur simply with the introduction of favorable LDC policy changes (since many are by now already in place), but only with the appearance of growth-induced profits themselves, creating a catch-22 for the prospects of sustained economic growth.

For other countries, such as Brazil and Argentina (there are 36 remaining countries eligible for assistance by the Brady Plan), postponement of debt repayment is taking place de facto, if only because their dire straits do not permit a Brady Plan negotiation of Mexican dimensions. The outcome is turning out to be the worst of all worlds, however, a slow-motion slide toward bankruptcy without the "new start" that actual bankruptcy proceedings afford.

The very "success" of the Brady Plan, which provides strong guarantees but only small debt relief, shifts the burden for turning around the LDC economies to the other side of the equation, trying to solve the debt problem via the expansion of trade. Here the outcome rides to a great extent on the results of the Uruguay Round of multilateral trade negotiations. The key market-opening initiatives for the Third World (with special importance for Mexico, Central America and the Caribbean as well as the rest of Latin America, involving textiles and apparel, leather goods, footware, ceramics, sugar, fruits and vegetables and other agricultural products) are highly sensitive. Concessions may be politically palatable to the developed countries only in a context that simultaneously includes breakthroughs on the issues of most benefit to them, such as services, intellectual property and unfair trade practices. In short, the Uruguay Round will have to be a major triumph to touch those areas of most importance to the Third World.

An alternative might be a free trade agreement with Mexico. But since a bilateral pact would offer Mexico many fewer compensating gains than would a global agreement, the price paid by the United States in politically sensitive labor-intensive industries would have to be significantly greater. Over the medium term, while higher oil prices may boost Mexico's growth prospects, the corresponding slower economic expansion (or recession) in the United States will stiffen resistance to trade liberalization. Extending the free trade idea to all of Latin America, as the Bush Administration has proposed, would attenuate the benefit for Mexico, and still be more costly to the United States and less beneficial to the recipients than a global approach.

Over the course of the 1990s, as Cold War preoccupations fade, American policymakers will not be able to relax their geopolitical concern about the economic and political fate of the Third World, especially Latin America.

They will have to develop new visions of mutually beneficial economic engagement persuasive enough to overcome short-sighted opposition to concessions on trade and debt.

VII

Finally, there is the pernicious problem of narcotics. To deal with the growing dimensions of narcotics trade, George Shultz and Milton Friedman have articulated the starting point of most economists when faced with a powerful cartel, namely, decriminalization as a means to eliminate the basis by which the cartel controls the market. This approach, Shultz and Friedman argue, would undermine the ability of producers and traffickers to reap such high profits and eliminate the incentive for drug pushers to get young people addicted.

The consequences, however, are more complicated than the proponents of decriminalization first envisioned. The outcome might be an expanded underclass of addicts, prone, in the case of crack cocaine, to particularly destructive, paranoid behavior.

On the other hand, the profitability of the current system is so great that even dramatically improved success in supply-side enforcement (interdiction of production and distribution) will only marginally offset the incentive for generating new sources. The prospect of providing alternative economic opportunities to woo Peruvian, Colombian and Bolivian peasants away from coca production appears dim when one considers that marijuana has come to be the largest cash crop of California's rich, fertile and irrigated agricultural regions, where alternative opportunities are abundant. It is not implausible, therefore, that narcotics traffic could proceed in its growth to nation-state-threatening dimensions, unless the current system of oligopoly pricing is eliminated. More generally, the drug trade may become the successor to the Cold War in providing resources to sustain worldwide terrorist activity.

To prevent this from happening, political leaders may have to let national security considerations tilt the highly sensitive domestic debate in the direction of decriminalization.

VIII

This survey of the international economic issues that will gain increasing prominence on the national security agenda as the Cold War recedes suggests an array of policy alternatives and preferred outcomes. Certain economic themes appear and reappear.

Continued improvement in the budget deficit, for example, is desirable in economic terms to help restore the balance between savings and consumption, to lower the cost of capital in the United States, to improve the competitive position of American companies and strengthen the defense industrial base in a period of globalization, and to re-equilibrate U.S.-Japanese relations and maintain trans-Pacific as well as trans-Atlantic political ties with post-1992 Europe as international economic competition intensifies.

The success of the Uruguay Round of trade negotiations would be favorable to diverse issues.   A successful outcome would not only improve trade efficiency and expand the range of comparative advantage, as economists are wont to argue, but play a central role in bolstering political stability for countries still struggling with the debt crisis.   [The Uruguay Round of negotiations ended in late 1990 without successfully completing its agenda, but efforts may be made to revive the failed talks—Eds.]   Success in multilateral trade agreements will likewise ease the pressure for more insulated neomercantilistic blocs in Europe, Asia and North America and help build the economic "substructure" to support the "superstructure" of ongoing political coordination among the industrial democracies.

Better macroeconomic performance on the part of the United States is not only an economic objective but also a growing strategic concern if the nation is to maintain a position of leadership in national security affairs worldwide. New resources are needed to pursue the option of offering assistance to Eastern Europe and the Soviet Union, as well as providing economic and military aid to allies in the Third World beleaguered by nearby enemies (the Middle East and Persian Gulf) or within their own borders (the narcotics-producing countries of Latin America).   The analysis of the relationship between the cost of capital and the competitiveness of American business suggests that future attempts to seek resources by raising the corporate tax rate would be counterproductive.   The requirement to balance savings and consumption carries a public policy preference to reward the former and penalize the latter.   The need to hold down the growth in energy usage in particular points to further boosts in the gasoline tax.   (There may be other candidates for new revenue as well, like a value-added or general consumption tax.)

Overall, the economics agenda gives national security strategists much to think about in considering relations with the major powers, the Soviet Union, Europe and Japan.   It also suggests, however, that the Third World will be the source of renewed preoccupation for the national security community for reasons that have nothing to do with U.S.-Soviet competition.   International economic policies that ignore the importance of restoring Third World growth and stability would bode ill for the longer term security environment.

Searching for solutions across all the topics from the economics agenda, there is a final conclusion that is greater than the sum of the parts: the distinction between high politics (vital interests affecting national security) and low politics (petty questions of economic dispute and rivalry among states) may be disappearing.   In the post–Cold War world, low politics is becoming high politics.

The traditional difference is that high politics involves clear threats to the nation, and therefore lends itself to the formation of domestic consensus, whereas low politics involves issues that are much more likely to be mired in domestic struggles for short-term partisan advantage. In the security environment of the future, dangers are likely to be more diffuse, the connections between them and the policies needed to respond to them more murky, and the need for sacrifice in order to advance national interests more opaque than in the period of bipolar antagonism.

The ultimate question for the United States in the post–Cold War era, therefore, may be one of governance: how to achieve the consensus and the continuity of domestic policy in the realm of low politics that are now required for America to continue as a great power into the 21st century.

NOTES

1. Z, "To the Stalin Mausoleum," *Daedalus*, Winter 1990, p. 297.

2. When "national security" trade protection is granted, the most appropriate form is a tariff. A tariff is less distorting than a quota, and the rents go to the home government instead of to the foreign firms. A voluntary restraint agreement (a common kind of quota) not only penalizes consumers but provides extra profits to external suppliers, strengthening their competitive position vis à vis domestic companies. The national security community should be particularly skeptical of proposals for managed trade. . . : the implementation of managed trade requires cartelization by foreign governments, which then apportion privileged access to the U.S. market among their own industries. . . .

3. For those who stress reliance on market signals, the argument for an energy tax is that the play of supply and demand among private parties creates a price that does not adequately reflect the potential social costs associated with concentrated dependence on a particularly volatile supplier; to the market price, consequently, should be added a "national security premium." For those concerned about a "level playing field" for U.S. competitiveness, an energy tax of up to $2–$3 per gallon of gasoline would simply match the burden borne by Asian and European firms.

24 POSTWAR ECONOMICS

Robert Kuttner

The Persian Gulf War has taken its economic toll.... What's more, in resurrecting a Pax Americana, the Bush Administration has complicated a host of nagging economic issues.

DEFICIT. The war has increased the real budget deficit ... by tens of billions of dollars, in all likelihood wiping out the $40 billion in savings for fiscal 1991 realized by the politically painful budget summit meeting of [1990].In addition, America's new, post-cold war military protectorate, along with the apparent success of our high-technology arsenal, has whetted the military appetite for new equipment suited to new missions in the third world. All of which has dashed hopes that a substantial peace dividend might finally reduce the deficit and free resources for domestic needs.

We have lived with the deficit so long that public opinion has become inured to it. Those who have warned that the deficit would wreck the economy have been discounted as Cassandras. But the economy bears the effects of permanent deficit—among them, higher interest costs for American businesses and consumers, a long-term dependence on borrowing from abroad and a fiscal paralysis that prevents Congress from addressing genuine domestic needs. Unfortunately, the cost never quite shows up as a highly visible cataclysm that would spur remedial action. Rather, it contributes to a slow bleed of economic vitality, which can be tolerated for decades as long as the opinion-leader class maintains its living standards and as long as Tokyo and Frankfurt keep lending us money.

GROWTH. ... Robust growth is unlikely to be restored. Our economy has become dependent on foreign investors for its capital, and on chronic deficit spending for stimulus. Structurally, the same sources of slow growth persist—too little savings, too little investment of public and private capital, money markets that prize short-run return, a deepening failure to replenish either physical infrastructure or human resources. ... Military victory [in the Middle East] contributes to a misleading military definition of American well-being: We are a superpower again, so all must be well.

ENERGY. In some respects, the conflict between Iraq and Kuwait was the fruit of a laissez-faire approach to energy. The immediate pretext for Saddam Hussein's invasion of Kuwait was an oil price war, brought on by Kuwait's cheating on its OPEC production allocations. This drove down the price of oil and deprived Iraq of anticipated export earnings that Saddam Hussein needed to pay for his previous war against Iran. Saddam, the economist C. Fred Bergsten has observed, then reacted "like an enraged commodities trader." The recent volatility in the price of oil has led to broader economic and political volatility in regions of the world as far flung as Mexico and Iran, not to mention Louisiana and East Texas.

Bush administration economists insist that the best energy policy is the free market. But pure supply and demand have never set the price of oil. Before . . . [August] 1990, Persian Gulf oil was selling for $12 to $24 a barrel but cost only about $2 a barrel to pump. Oil has always been cartelized, first by Western interests and more recently by OPEC. Oil is too vulnerable to price manipulation and too intimately connected to the high politics of national security for either consuming nations or producing nations to trust its price and supply entirely to the vagaries of markets. Industrial nations— other than the United States—have tax and pricing policies intended to discourage oil consumption. In 1985–86, when an oil price war wreaked political havoc from the Persian Gulf to the Gulf of Mexico, the Reagan administration, despite its stated freemarket principles, worked with the Saudis to enforce a target price of about $18 per barrel. Politically, any durable settlement of the Persian Gulf crisis will likely include a restabilization of the price of oil, even though this contradicts the Administration's stated (non-) energy policy.

PRICE OF PEACE. Since 1979, the Camp David accord has cost the United States at least $30 billion in stepped-up aid to Egypt and Israel. It has probably been worth the price. A new Middle East settlement will cost even more. The Egyptians and Saudis have called for a regional reconstruction program, which would include some redistribution from the richer Arab states to the poorer ones; almost certain to be reinforced by a new infusion of Western (read American) aid. The scale of an economic aid package for the entire region would dwarf the Camp David effort. And if the oil-rich Middle East can qualify for new aid, the rest of the third world (to say nothing of Eastern Europe) will undoubtedly clamor for more assistance, too. As always, dominion is not cheap.

TRADE TALKS. As the Persian Gulf crisis was coming to dominate the news, attention was mercifully diverted from one of the great foreign policy debacles of recent years—the collapse of the Uruguay Round of trade talks last December [1990]. When Reagan administration officials conceived the round of talks, which began with great fanfare in September 1986, the stated concern was a tangle of trade conflicts with Japan that were fueling protectionist sentiments at home. The new round was supposed to pry open Japanese markets; increase protection against technological piracy that was costing American exporters billions of dollars, and extend the reach of the General Agreement on Tariffs and Trade (GATT) to nontraditional areas like financial services and agriculture where the United States was thought to have advantage. In return, the United States was willing to give up some of its own protection of textiles and some farm products.

But by the time the round got going, it was virtually captured by American farm export interests. A combination of laissez-faire dogma and farm-bloc lobbying transformed the round into a donnybrook over agriculture price supports, in which we identified not Japan but the rather more open European Community as the prime culprit. . . . The United States held out for an implausible all-or-nothing deal: all price supports and export subsidies would have to be phased out by the year 2000.

We came away with nothing. Progress toward giving American exporters real protection against industrial piracy and against foreign dumping was squandered.

Now, our trade negotiators are working to bring the talks back to life. . . . But the same self-defeating, freemarket trade ideology still reigns.

The most serious economic cost of the war may be the distraction it created. President Bush tends to conduct policy with a very small inner circle of top advisers. Once the gulf became the main diplomatic concern, they lost interest in other pressing issues. . . .

The end of the cold war promised a long-overdue respite from the burdens of Pax Americana; at last the United States would be able to turn its attention to long-deferred domestic economic problems and revise its goals for the world economic system. But barely nine months after the Berlin Wall came down, the Persian Gulf war launched a second era of Pax Americana. With that war's end, attention seemingly can be redirected to the home front. But in this war, as in the cold war before it, there is no clean dividing line between war and peace. Thanks to the bitter enmities that will outlast the shooting war, the United States is likely to remain enmeshed in the region for many years.

And this reality, unfortunately, prolongs the misguided division of roles among the Western powers, in which we keep the peace while other wealthy industrial nations tend their economic gardens. Under this arrangement, American technology manufactures exceptionally precise missiles, while other nations take the lead in consumer electronics, machine tools, automobiles and the rest of the commercial economy.

Every one of our accumulated domestic economic problems is complex, and requires both Presidential attention and rare executive leadership, lest the policy simply default to the lowest common denominator of interest-group lobbying. The overhaul of the banking system, for example, ought to be directed to redesigning the financial economy to better serve the capital needs of the real economy. But with White House attention focused elsewhere, banking legislation is likely to be a narrow compromise between the interests of commercial bankers and investment bankers, large banks and small ones, the Federal Deposit Insurance Corporation and Federal Reserve and Treasury, rather than a coherent policy that serves the public interest. The systemic crisis in health costs similarly calls for a bold new approach, as do the permanent budget deficit, energy dependence and rotting public infrastructure. But all of these problems will continue to sputter along on automatic pilot as long as a new Pax Americana dominates Presidential attention. And they will afflict our economic health long after the shooting has stopped.

25 FREE TRADE AND PROTECTIONISM

Paul Krugman

When future historians list the achievements of the United States during the 45 or so years that it acted as the undisputed leader of the world's democracies, special emphasis is sure to be given to the creation of a relatively free and open world trading system. From about 1950 until the early 1970s, protectionist barriers to world trade came down steadily, and world trade grew rapidly. Nearly everyone thinks that this growth in trade was a good thing.

Yet there are now powerful forces in the United States working against free trade. Much of the argument for protectionism represents sheer interest-group politics: It comes from well-organized groups that are losing out to foreign competition and want protection, never mind the national interest. Yet not all the opponents of free trade are hired guns (and not all its supporters are disinterested, either). It's important to look at both the political sources of protectionism and its intellectual foundations.

THE POLITICS OF PROTECTIONISM

The basic rule of trade politics is that producers count more than consumers. The benefits of a trade restriction are usually concentrated on a relatively small, well-organized, and well-informed group of producers, while its costs are usually spread thinly over a large diffuse group of consumers. As a result, the beneficiaries of a trade restriction are usually much more effective politically than its victims.

The classic case in the United States is the import quota on sugar, which benefits a handful of domestic producers at a typical annual cost to consumers of $1 billion a year. This quota goes unchallenged, because the $5 average

Note: One footnote has been deleted, and the others have been renumbered.

annual cost per person is so small that probably not one voter in 200 even knows that the import restriction exists.

But if consumers offer no effective opposition to protection, why is U.S. trade relatively free? Because *exporters* advocate free trade. Exporters by definition want access to foreign markets and are as well organized as import-competing producers. For the past 40 years the United States and other advanced countries have used this fact to provide a framework for maintaining relatively free trade. Trade policies are not set unilaterally; they are negotiated between countries. In these negotiations, U.S. import restrictions must be traded off against the import restrictions of other countries, so that U.S. exporters become a powerful voice urging us to accept imports from other countries if they will accept our exports in return.

The source of new protectionist pressure is now obvious. When the United States is running a huge trade deficit, the exporters who want open markets are outnumbered by the import-competing groups who want protection. If in 1980 you had told trade specialists that America would run trade deficits of more than $100 billion for seven years on end, they would surely have predicted more, not less, protection than we have seen.

The relatively mild protectionist reaction so far is a tribute to the strength of free-trade ideology in the United States. The question is how long this can last. It may be useful to think of the United States as having a "protectionist overhang": a backlog of potential protectionist reaction barely held in check. Fear of this reaction is one of the main reasons for worrying about the trade deficit. If the trade deficit continues, sooner or later the persistent demands for more protection are likely to become irresistible.

But what would be wrong with that? Is protectionism really a fate to be greatly feared?

THE (LIMITED) EVILS OF PROTECTIONISM

Although most policymakers in Washington are convinced that protectionism is a bad thing, few of them have any clear idea why. In popular arguments against protectionism, the usual warning is that protectionism threatens our jobs—the Smoot-Hawley tariff of 1931, we are told, caused the Depression, and history can repeat itself.

Although protectionism *is* usually a bad thing, it is worth pointing out that it isn't as bad as all that. Protectionism does not cost our economy jobs, any more than the trade deficit does: U.S. employment is essentially determined by supply, not demand. The claim that protectionism caused the Depression is nonsense; the claim that future protectionism will lead to a repeat performance is equally nonsensical.

The real harm done by protectionism is much more modest and mundane: It reduces the efficiency of the world economy. To the extent that countries limit each other's exports, they block the mutually beneficial process by which

nations specialize in producing goods for which their knowledge and resources are particularly well fitted. They also fragment markets, preventing
firms and industries from realizing economies of scale. A protectionist country is usually less productive and thus poorer than it would have been under
free trade; a protectionist world economy almost always so. (See the accompanying box.)

Just how expensive is protectionism? The answer is a little embarrassing,
because standard estimates of the costs of protection are actually very low.
America is a case in point. While much U.S. trade takes place with few
obstacles, we have several major protectionist measures, restricting imports
of autos, steel, and textiles in particular. The combined costs of these major
restrictions to the U.S. economy, however, are usually estimated at less than
three-quarters of 1 percent of U.S. national income. Most of this loss, furthermore, comes from the fact that the import restrictions, in effect, form
foreign producers into cartels that charge higher prices to U.S. consumers.
So most of the U.S. losses are matched by higher foreign profits. From the
point of view of the world as a whole, the negative effects of U.S. import
restrictions on efficiency are therefore much smaller—around one-quarter of
1 percent of U.S. GNP.

Other countries are more protectionist than the United States, and in some
Third World nations wildly inefficient protectionist policies have caused major economic losses. Among advanced countries, however, protectionism at
current levels is not a first-class issue. Without a doubt the major industrial
nations suffer more, in economic terms, from unglamorous problems like
avoidable traffic congestion and unnecessary waste in defense contracting
than they do from protectionism. To take the most extreme example, the
cost to taxpayers of the savings and loan bailout alone will be at least five
times as large as the annual cost to U.S. consumers of all U.S. import restrictions.

If the costs of protectionism are so mild, why does the defense of free trade
loom so large on the public agenda? Symbolism and politics. Ideologically,
free trade is an important touchstone for advocates of free-market economics.
As [economist] Paul Samuelson once pointed out, comparative advantage is
one of the few ideas in economics that is true without being obvious. Politically, free trade is important as a counterweight to crude economic nationalism. So free trade has passionate defenders in a way that other, equally
worthy causes—such as economically efficient environmental regulation—
do not.

Even if protectionism isn't the most terrible thing in the world, however,
it is still a bad thing. Or is it? While the great weight of educated opinion
still condemns protection, there are some arguments in its favor.

PROTECTION AND THE TRADE DEFICIT

Arguments in favor of protection come in two basic forms. One argument
wants the United States to use the *threat* of protection to extract concessions
from foreign countries; those who use this argument are not advocating

THE COSTS OF TRADE CONFLICT

A hypothetical scenario may be useful for understanding what the costs of protection are, and why they are more modest than many people seem to think.

Let's imagine that most of the world's market economies were to group themselves into three trading blocs—one centered on the United States, one centered on the European Economic Community, and one centered on Japan. And let's suppose that each of these trading blocs becomes highly protectionist, imposing a tariff against goods from outside the bloc of 100 percent, which we suppose leads to a fall in imports of 50 percent.

So we are imagining a trade war that cuts the volume of world trade in half. What would be the costs of this trade war?

One immediate response would be that each bloc would lose jobs in the industries that formerly exported to the others. This is true; but each bloc would correspondingly gain a roughly equal number of jobs producing goods it formerly imported. There is no reason to expect that even such a major fragmentation of the world market would cause extra unemployment.

The cost would come instead from reduced efficiency. Each bloc would produce goods for itself that it could have imported more cheaply. With a 100 percent tariff, some goods would be produced domestically even though they could have been imported at half the price. For these goods there is thus a waste of resources equal to the value of the original imports.

But this would be true only of goods that would have been imported in the absence of tariffs, and even then 100 percent represents a maximum estimate. Our three hypothetical trading blocs would, however, import only about 10 percent of the goods and services they use from abroad even under free trade.

A trade war that cut international trade in half, and which caused an *average* cost of wasted resources for the displaced production of, say 50 percent, would therefore cost the world economy only 2.5 percent of its income (50 percent × 5 percent = 2.5 percent).

This is not a trivial sum—but it is a long way from a Depression. (It is roughly the cost of a 1 percent increase in the unemployment rate.) And it is the result of an extreme scenario, in which protectionism has a devastating effect on world trade.

If the trade conflict were milder, the costs would be much less. Suppose that the tariff rates were only 50 percent, leading to a 30 percent fall in world trade. Then 3 percent of the goods originally used would be replaced with domestic substitutes, costing at most 50 percent more. If the typical domestic substitute costs 25 percent more, then the cost of the trade conflict is 0.75 percent of world income (25 percent × 3 percent = 0.75 percent).

protection per se, but they are willing to use protection as a bargaining threat—a bluff that they are presumably willing to see carried out, at least occasionally.   The other argument takes protection to be an intrinsically good thing, at least in some cases.

The bargaining argument for protection is usually stated in the context of the problem of lowering the trade deficit.   The United States needs to reduce its trade deficit, say the advocates of this position; but driving down the dollar is ineffective [due to] foreign trade barriers and [because it] reduces American living standards.   So let's instead expand our exports by threatening to limit our imports: This will force foreigners to open their markets and allow us to reduce the trade deficit without the need for a much lower dollar.

The main problem with this proposal is that it won't work.   It is just not realistic to expect increased access to foreign markets to make more than a minor contribution to reducing the U.S. trade deficit, with or without U.S. pressure.   The reasons are both economic and political.

First, the economics.   When we talk about removing foreign barriers to U.S. exports, what do we mean?   Despite the rhetoric, there are only a few major legislated foreign programs that have a large identifiable impact on U.S. exports; most of these are in the agricultural area.   If Japan opened its rice market, or Europe canceled its agricultural support programs, this would help U.S. exports, but it would fall far short of curing our trade deficit.[1]

Meanwhile, there are political realities.   U.S. pressure is simply not going to force radical changes in economic policy abroad.   The major barriers to American exports are programs, like Europe's agricultural policy, with powerful domestic constituencies.   American pressure may induce marginal changes in these programs, but it is a fantasy to imagine that by getting tough we can force other countries to abandon them.   The U.S. economy is no bigger than Europe's, and not much bigger than Japan's.   Politicians in other countries answer primarily to domestic interests, just as ours do.   We cannot expect to bully Europe or Japan into doing things our way any more than they could expect to do the same to us.

Given these economic and political realities, the proposal to use the threat of protection to solve the trade deficit will, in practice, inevitably degenerate into the implementation of that threat.   To say that you favor using potential import quotas as a way to spur U.S. exports is, in the end, disingenuous: The result will almost always be fewer imports rather than more exports.

Indeed, however much they may talk about spurring exports, the advocates of a tougher trade policy seem much more interested in limiting imports. [Journalist] Robert Kuttner's own manifesto on trade policy, which advocates a broad system of "managed trade," takes as its model the Multi-Fiber Arrangement: an international treaty that purely and simply restricts trade in textiles and apparel.   That is, in the end he views protectionism not as a bargaining chip but as a permanent policy.

But what's so bad about that? We have just seen that the conventionally measured costs of protection are not very large. And there are intellectually respectable arguments suggesting that protection may, in some cases, actually be beneficial.

THE ECONOMIC CASE FOR PROTECTION

Economic theories matter, though not necessarily in the ways that their creators might have wished. In the 1970s public finance economists, Martin Feldstein prominent among them, worked hard to persuade the economics profession that flaws in the tax system distort incentives and retard U.S. economic growth. The result was to help create a climate of opinion in which supply-side economists could advocate radical tax cuts, leading to the massive budget deficits that Feldstein took the lead in denouncing. In the late 1970s and early 1980s a group of international economists—myself among them—similarly worked to persuade the economics profession that the principles of international trade needed to be rethought. This rethinking of international trade has won tenure and academic prestige for its leaders. But an unintended by-product of the effort has been to lend some new intellectual respectability to protectionism.[2]

Traditional international economics attributes international trade to underlying differences among countries. Australia exports wool because its lands are well suited to sheep grazing, Thailand exports labor-intensive manufactures because of its abundance of labor, and so on. The new international economics, while not denying the importance of this traditional view, adds that much international trade also reflects national advantages that are created by historical circumstance, and that then persist or grow because of other advantages to large scale either in development or production. For example, the development effort required to launch a new passenger jet aircraft is so large that the world market will support only one or two profitable firms. Once the United States had a head start in producing aircraft, its position as the world's leading exporter became self-reinforcing. So if you want to explain why the U.S. exports aircraft, you should not look for underlying aspects of the U.S. economy; you should study the historical circumstances that gave the United States a head start in the industry.

Why does this provide a potential justification for protectionism? Because if the pattern of international trade and specialization largely reflects historical circumstances rather than underlying national strengths, then government policies can *in principle* shape this pattern to benefit their domestic economies. As journalist James Fallows put it in a recent plea for a more aggressive U.S. trade policy, "Countries that try to promote higher-value, higher-tech industries will eventually have more of them than countries that don't."

Which industries should a country try to promote? One criterion is the potential for technological spillovers. Suppose that you believe that whichever country develops a high-definition television (HDTV) industry will find that its other industries, such as computers and semiconductors, gain an edge over their foreign competitors from their close contact with HDTV producers. Then it might be worth developing an HDTV sector—even if it requires a continuing subsidy due to costs that are persistently above those of foreign imports. This is an old argument, but it becomes much more attractive if the new theory is right, because the new theory suggests that the need for subsidy may be only temporary: Because comparative advantage is often created, not given, a temporary subsidy can lead to a permanent industry.

Another potential criterion for industry targeting has a sexy name: "strategic trade policy" (a term that is also loosely used to refer to the technological argument). A hypothetical example may convey its essence. Imagine that there is some good that could be developed and sold either by an American or a European firm. If either firm developed the product alone, it could earn large profits; however, the development costs are large enough that if both firms tried to enter the market, both would lose money. Which firm will actually enter? The answer may be determined by government intervention. If European governments subsidize their firm, or make it clear that it will have a protected domestic market, they may ensure that their firm enters while deterring the U.S. firm—and thereby also ensure that Europe, not America, gets the monopoly profits.

The strategic trade policy story (using the term to refer to both arguments) is not, at base, an argument for protectionism per se. It is really an argument for a limited government industrial policy consisting of carefully targeted subsidies, not for tariffs and import quotas. Yet it provides advocates of protectionism with a new intellectual gloss to justify their position, and it has been picked up enthusiastically by advocates of "managed trade." . . . If they do not argue that the United States should adopt a strategic trade policy, they at least claim that other countries—primarily Japan—have already done so, and that the United States needs to respond. As Kuttner puts it, "The New View radically alters the context of debate, for it removes the premise that nations such as Japan which practice strategic trade could not, by definition, be improving their welfare." There is a strong temptation for both politicians and intellectuals to run with this, to claim that all the old ideas about free trade should be thrown out the window.

In fact, however, none of the international economists responsible for the new trade theory has come out as an advocate of Kuttnerian trade policy. This is not because they are afraid to break the free-trade ranks. It is because the actual prospects for a successful strategic trade policy are not very good.

Once again, this is partly a matter of economics, partly one of politics. On the purely economic side, there just isn't any evidence that an aggressive strategic trade policy can produce large gains. Technological spillovers could be important, but they are difficult to measure. Take the example of HDTV. Many regard it as "one of the most, if not the most, crucial technological advancements" about to take place.[3] But a recent Congressional Budget

Office study concluded that "it is hard to believe that HDTV will . . . play a pivotal role in the competitiveness and technological development of the electronics sector. . . ." Never mind which side is right: Someone is very wrong. Reaching a practical consensus on which sectors really are strategic is certain to be extremely difficult—even without the interjection of interest-group politics.

As for the possibility of capturing monopoly profits through strategic trade policy, the result of a good deal of technical analysis of the prospects for such policy in particular industries over the past few years is fairly discouraging. The general conclusion of those who have tried to estimate the likely gains from strategic trade policies is that, while you can do better than free trade, the potential net gains are nothing to write home about—they are even smaller than the conventional estimates of the costs of protection. . . .

Meanwhile, there is political reality to consider. Given the uncertainty about what strategic trade policy should be, wouldn't any attempt at doing it turn into thinly disguised interest-group politics? Almost surely it would.

THE PROTECTIONIST PROSPECT

There is a better intellectual case for protection than there used to be, and the case for free trade is often overstated. Nonetheless, there is still a good case for free trade as a general policy—not as an absolute ideal, but as a reasonable rule of thumb. American interests would probably best be served by a world of free trade, with the temptations of strategic trade policy kept out of reach by international treaty. Unfortunately, that's not going to happen, for two reasons.

First, the other major players *are* engaging in strategic trade policy. Quite possibly they are doing themselves more harm than good. But it is extremely difficult to maintain a hands-off position in the United States when other countries do not do the same, especially when America is evidently in relative decline. The extent to which other countries are using strategic policy shouldn't be overstated, but the examples—Japanese protection of supercomputers, European promotion of aircraft—are too conspicuous to dismiss.

Second, the politics of free trade depends on a belief that market access is reciprocal—that open U.S. markets can be traded for open markets elsewhere. For most U.S. trade this has been and remains true. When we negotiated a free trade pact with Canada, it meant increased access for both sides; the same would be true if we could negotiate a similar pact with Germany, or even with Mexico. But free trade becomes very difficult to sustain politically if there is a widespread and growing perception that one of the main players is following different rules.

The problem of relations with Japan—the second largest market economy, one of America's principal trading partners, but an economy into which the United States finds it difficult either to export or invest—is not the most important issue we face, but it is one of the hardest to solve.

NOTES

1. There is a special issue of access to the Japanese market, which is less of a matter of identifiable restrictions than of the whole structure of Japan's economy. . . . But even if something could be done to remove the "structural impediments" to imports in Japan, it would not make a large difference to U.S. exports.

2. The "new international economics" is generally associated with several people: Princeton's Avinash Dixit, Tel Aviv's Elhanan Helpman, James Brander and Barbara Spencer of the University of British Columbia, and myself. The most widely read summary of the new ideas is a book I edited, *Strategic Trade Policy and the New International Economics* (MIT Press, 1986); a much more technical exposition is my *Rethinking International Trade* (MIT Press, 1990).

3. Statement by Senator John Glenn (D-OH).

26   ON THE ROAD TO RUIN
Walter Russell Mead

The United States has won the Cold War. But the United States has not won this war the way it won World War I and World War II. Each of those wars left the United States richer and thus, in the international arena, more powerful. During World War I we became, for the first time in our history, a creditor nation and a year later played the major role at the Paris Peace Conference; in 1945 we emerged from the war with the world's only healthy industrial economy and soon assumed the mantle of superpower.

The Cold War—the forty-five-year battle to thwart the expansionistic goals of the Soviet Union—is a different story. We have won the Cold War the way Britain won World War I; the Soviet Union has been defeated, but in the struggle the United States lost economic ground to our allies. We had a larger role in the world—economically and politically—in 1950 than we do in 1990. After the Second World War, we were in a position to establish a new world order—and we did. But the post–World War II era is over; the post–Cold War era is beginning. And while the post–World War II order was designed by the United States and served our interests, the new order is being created by others, and it threatens to lock the United States into long-term economic decline. In the era that followed the vanquishing of the Germans and the Japanese, there was no country to challenge the United States; our standard of living knew no precedent or equal. Now it is Japan and Germany who stand to map the post–Cold War world economy; in this new world, the United States may well be the Argentina of the twenty-first century.

It is too often forgotten that the American strategy after World War II had *two* pillars. One was, of course, the policy of containing Soviet expansionism in Europe and the Third World. However, in the years immediately following World War II, the primary goal of our diplomacy—the original foundation of our postwar strategy—was the creation of the international financial system designed at the conference of forty-four states and nations held at the New Hampshire resort of Bretton Woods. It was at Bretton Woods in

332

1944—more than in Warsaw and Budapest and Bucharest in 1989—that the United States won the Cold War.

In 1944 and the years that followed, Americans had three goals for the postwar economic order. *First,* we insisted that we would be in charge. As we had all the gold and all the goods, this seemed like a reasonable position to take, and those nations that considered it unreasonable were in no position to do much about it. Our *second* demand was for the creation of a truly global trading system. The wholly *international* economy was our idea—a bold, new idea. The nations of Europe had traditionally preferred their own trading blocs to a global system regulated by international rules of trade. Countries like England and France had grown by building overseas empires, carving up the world in a way that guaranteed each imperial power its own source of raw materials and its own markets. American strategists came to believe that such systems blocked economic growth and eventually caused wars. And they were right.

Colonial subjects fought for independence, and countries without colonies fought to get them. The imperial nations used protectionist tariffs to strengthen their own economies at the cost of their colonies and of their nonimperial trade rivals: In both 1914 and 1939, German militarists claimed that the European imperial "haves," Britain and France, were unfairly denying Germany its "place in the sun." Japan felt the same way in the 1930s about the "ABCD" (American, British, Chinese, and Dutch) powers who had divided up Asia and used their positions against Japan.

Even before the German and Japanese surrenders, the United States implicitly acknowledged that both Germany and Japan had a point. American officials stated, while the war was still being waged, that one of our war aims was the creation of an open international trading system in which all nations could participate on a free and equal basis. After the war, the United States pressed the generally reluctant countries of Western Europe to dismantle their colonial empires and admit the trade of all countries on an equal basis.

Of course, we did not attack the old empires simply out of a sense of fair play. We had powerful, less selfless motives. America is big, stretching from one great ocean to another. We make and consume such a broad range of products that we need markets and suppliers all over the world. History and geography make the United States an economic generalist; after World War II we were able to force all the would-be specialists to see things our way.

The *third* American postwar goal was the establishment of a growth-oriented world economy. Generally speaking, economic policymakers have to choose either slow growth with minimal inflation or faster growth with the risk of greater inflation. Compared with other major countries, the United States wants a little more growth, even if we have to take the inflation. Countries like Germany, on the other hand, are more willing to accept slow growth if it will keep the inflation rate at or near zero.

destroyed by the war. No one else had a merchant marine capable of handling such a flow of goods in international trade. We had accumulated an enormous gold reserve. We had the best-equipped army in the world and an unchallengeable navy and air force. We enjoyed an atomic monopoly, made all the more useful by our demonstration that we possessed the will to use the bomb.

These weapons have fallen from our hands. Our oil production is no longer adequate for our own uses. World markets in minerals and food are glutted. Our industrial economy has lost its supremacy—it is, at best, first among equals. We now owe foreigners more than Argentina, Brazil, and Mexico combined; Germany and Japan can set the value of the dollar.

This is the road to Argentina. Argentina is a rich country and in many ways similar to ours. Spacious skies cover its amber waves of grain; purple mountain majesties tower over its plains; it has oil and cowboys in the south and industry in the north. Its talented population is made up of immigrants and their descendants who came to the New World determined to build a better life for themselves and their children.

Fifty years ago, Argentina was part of the First World. It was a European society with living standards comparable to those of Canada and France. Today it is part of the Third World. Its economy alternates between hyperinflation and depression; its politics, between anarchy and dictatorship.

Last fall [1990], as Soviet-bloc communism collapsed, I was in Argentina and followed the story through that country's media. Newspaper stories in Buenos Aires headlined the events in Hungary and Poland "The Triumph of Capitalism." The same papers carried stories on the collapse of yet another effort to stabilize Argentina's money: 17 australs to the dollar in 1989; 1,800 in 1990. I could not help but think of the future, and of the dollar.

The future does not have to be this bleak. But we will have to change the way we think about foreign policy. For the last fifty years we have waged foreign policy in the spirit of Jeane Kirkpatrick and General Patton; now we need to move in the spirit of Ginger Rogers and Fred Astaire. Peace is a complicated dance in which partners change rapidly. It is a dance at which the United States has never excelled.

In the nineteenth century, we were proud of our wallflower status; we sipped lemonade and heaped scorn on the wrinkled and rouged coquettes waltzing gaily around the European ballroom. After World War I, when it was our turn to preside, we closed down the bar and told the band to play hymns. As Jane Austen might have predicted, the result was more rational but very much less like a ball. Our guests grew impatient; French premier Georges Clemenceau, hearing of Wilson's Fourteen Points, remarked that "The good Lord had only ten."

We went home in a huff in 1919, taking our hymns and our lemonade with us. In 1945, fear of the Soviet Union made everyone martially minded; under our leadership, the Concert of Europe played Sousa and there was at least as much marching as dancing. But now the martial mood is fading;

the nations are beating their swords into punch bowls and their spears into chafing dishes.

A new party is beginning, and we shall have to rouge, to dance, and to flirt with the best of them.   That will be harder today; our jewels are mortgaged and our gown is patched; we are not as young as we used to be and have put on a little weight.   We can't afford to stay home and sulk this time, and since we can't afford to pay the piper, we can no longer expect to always call the tune.

It will not be impossible to shine at the ball.   The Soviet Union is fatter and worse dressed than we will ever be, and its dance card is full. . . . There are plenty of partners willing to give us a whirl.   The national interest is the key to our position in this strange new world of peace.   Those interests have not changed much since colonial times: We want a world that is open to peaceful commerce, and one that is open to growth.

We can no longer impose these values on the rest of the world, but they remain persuasive.   France, for instance, does not want an insular Europe if it means German domination.   Korea feels the same way about Japan.   Our interest in growth continues to be shared by developing nations.

There is nothing inevitable about the future.   But to avoid a fate like that of Argentina, the United States will need to stop gloating about winning the Cold War and start to assess, soberly, its place in the global economy.   Of this I see little sign.

27   AGAINST "DECLINISM"

Joseph S. Nye, Jr.

Two years [1988] ago Paul Kennedy's *The Rise and Fall of the Great Powers* caught a wave of public anxiety about American decline and rode it to the top of the best-seller list.   When a serious work of history with more than a thousand footnotes starts selling in Stephen King-like quantities, you can be sure it has touched something in the popular mood.   For the fact is that despite the successful end of the cold war, Americans are feeling far from triumphant.   On the contrary, polls show public opinion about evenly divided between the two camps Kennedy calls "declinists" and "revivalists."   Events in the Persian Gulf will help determine which camp emerges the stronger. But a good case—if a necessarily provisional one—can be made that the first major post–cold war crisis has already weakened the declinists' case, and may end up strengthening the revivalists'.

Before August [1990], the belief in decline had already colored interpretations of current events.   A striking case in point was *Lignes d'Horizon*, a book published [early in 1990] in Paris by Jacques Attali, a key adviser to President François Mitterrand and the director-designate of the new multilateral bank for Eastern Europe, who thinks the American decline is so steep that the future will be dominated by a European bloc and a Japanese-led Pacific bloc.   At a more mundane level, a front-page article in *The New York Times* pointed to President Bush's inability to dominate the Houston summit of the advanced industrial nations as a sign of slipping American power. Such accounts show little sense of history.   Fifteen years ago, when economic summitry began, the United States was similarly unable to dominate.   The definitive study of the early summits—*Hanging Together* by Robert Putnam and Nicholas Bayne—concluded that though no other country could pick up the slack when American leadership faltered, the United States was not able to impose cooperation alone.   By exaggerating American dominance in the past, declinists find it easy to portray a diminished American present.

The same can be said of the economic picture.   Important industrial sectors such as consumer electronics and automobiles have slipped badly.   The household savings rate dropped from 8 percent in the 1970s to 5 percent in the 1980s; the government deficit subtracts another 3 percent. Since gross investment stayed roughly the same, the missing savings were made up by capital imports that transformed the United States into the world's largest debtor in absolute terms.

The declinists stress this negative side of the ledger, but there is another side. During the 1980s the American economy grew by 2.5 percent a year, above its historical average of 2 percent over the past century. Contrary to Attali's view of the United States as merely "Japan's granary," industry contributed the same one-fifth of the gross national product [GNP] as it did in the 1970s. Productivity in manufacturing rose by 3.5 percent per year in the 1980s, and absolute productivity (product per worker) remained higher than in Japan or Germany. The United States remains in the forefront of such high-tech industries as aircraft, chemicals, biotechnology, and computers. Moreover, some economists believe that the slower 1 percent rate of growth of overall labor productivity (i.e., in all sectors) is an underestimate that reflects the difficulty of measuring productivity increases in the service sector.

These seemingly contradictory strands can be aggregated by looking at the American share of the world product. The American share was artificially high at the end of World War II because the United States was the only major country to escape devastation. Over the next three decades, the war's effect eroded as other nations regained their economic health. But for the last decade and a half the American share of world product has held stable at about 23 percent of the total. In fact, if one uses purchasing power parities (which correct the current exchange rate of currencies for what the money will buy in a local economy), the American share of world product, and of the product of the seven summit nations, actually increased in the 1980s.

With the end of the cold war, the declinists soft-pedaled the theory of imperial overstretch that was at the heart of *The Rise and Fall of the Great Powers*: a vibrant national economy spreads its interests beyond its borders, then develops a political and military apparatus to defend those interests, and finally declines as the cost of the military machine undercuts national economic strength. As Kennedy ably showed, this has been the experience of many past empires, including the now moribund Soviet empire. But for the theory to apply to the American situation, the burden of defense should have increased over time. Yet even before the end of the cold war, the opposite was the case: defense was 10 percent of GNP in the 1950s, 6 percent in the 1980s, and falling toward a projected 4 percent by the mid-1990s.

The declinists turn this good news into bad. For example, Kennedy has written that the end of the cold war reduced "the significance of the one measure of national power in which the United States had a clear advantage over other countries"—the military. But this not only ignores American economic, scientific, cultural, and ideological strengths. It also misunderstands the past and present roles of military power. One reason the United

States was unable to boss around its allies in the past was that it was never a fully hegemonic power. Its military strength was balanced by Soviet military strength. Europe and Japan sometimes prevailed over the United States in intra-alliance bargaining because of Washington's greater concern about the Soviet Union.

The end of the cold war reduced but did not eliminate the role of military force. In Asia, many cleavages have nothing to do with the cold war. In Europe, many welcome the continued presence of a United States four times the size of Germany. Even a reduced American security guarantee remains of value to Europe and Japan as insurance against the uncertain future of the second Russian Revolution. And if the allies value an American insurance policy more than the United States does, it may do more for American bargaining power, ironically, than much larger forces did at the height of the cold war.

When Iraqi tanks rolled into Kuwait, they knocked two other props out from under the declinist case. One is the view that the world had entered a multipolar era in which economic power had replaced military power. In fact, it was the rapid mobilization of American military power that prevented Saddam Hussein from gaining control of 40 percent of world oil reserves and a stranglehold on global economic growth. The crisis also exposed the one-dimensional nature of the power of Germany and Japan.

The second count on which the declinists have been proved wrong is the U.S. success in organizing collective action against Iraq. In the Gulf crisis, it was important to move military forces to the region, but it was equally important to have United Nations resolutions defining Iraq's entry into Kuwait as a violation of international law and legitimizing the enforcement of sanctions. Without American leadership in the U.N. to define the issue as aggression, Iraq might have gotten away with defining its actions as the postcolonial recovery of a former province. This success shows that the United States is still the largest possessor of both "hard" power—the ability to command others, usually through the use of tangible resources such as military and economic might—and "soft" power—the ability to co-opt rather than command, to get others to want what you want.

The United States cannot stand alone as the world's policeman, or as Representative Pat Schroeder put it, "the world's 911." On the other hand, it is the largest country in the international system in terms of both hard and soft power resources; and if the largest power does not lead in organizing collective action, no one will.

Over the long term, America's hard and soft power resources will depend upon addressing such difficult domestic issues as the budget deficit, the savings rate, our educational system, and urban poverty. Military strength depends on a strong economic base. Cultural and ideological appeal depend on maintaining a healthy and open society. But there is no reason Americans cannot afford both Social Security and international security. Unlike Britain in 1914, the United States remains both the world's largest economy and its largest military power.   If declinist writings persuade the public to support domestic reforms, that will be all to the good.   But if they persuade Americans to become more protectionist and draw back from international leadership on the grounds that "a declining power can't afford it," they may create a self-fulfilling fallacy.   The moral for a post–cold war world is to beware of historians bearing false analogies.

28   A DECLINING EMPIRE GOES TO WAR

Paul Kennedy

Over [several] months [the Wall Street Journal] . . . offered many justifications for its strong support of America's decision to fight Saddam Hussein, and with the largest and most impressive display of force possible.

But perhaps the most remarkable new argument from the Journal came . . . in its editorial of Jan[uary] 18, [1991], "A Declining Power." The reported early successes against Iraqi forces, the wizardry of American military technology, the firmness and "moral courage" of the president in ordering the attack, would all help—so the editorialists hoped—to break the mood of self-doubt and defeatism that has existed among the country's elites since the 1960s. In proving that the U.S. was not a declining power suffering from "imperial overstretch," the easy battlefield victories in the Middle East might thus allow the nation to recover its self-esteem. Well, well.

We have come a long way since the Founding Fathers warned their countrymen against overseas entanglements, but whatever reasons were given for American interventions in earlier wars of this century—protecting freedom of the seas, responding to Pearl Harbor, stopping North Korean aggression— I do not think that the recovery of America's lost self-esteem was one of them.

To the historian of international politics, however, this reasoning has a very familiar and disturbing ring to it. For example, anyone dipping into the relevant chapters of John Elliott's masterly biography "The Count-Duke of Olivares" will discover Philip IV's great minister frequently justifying Spain's distant military interventions of the 1630s and 1640s on the grounds of "reputation."

'THE GREATEST VICTORY OF OUR TIMES'

True, there were many other reasons—strategic, dynastic, support of faithful allies—and most of them could be advanced at the same time, as occurred in 1634 and 1635 when fresh armies of Spanish troops were sent across

Europe to aid their beleaguered Austrian Habsburg cousins during the Thirty Years' War. But behind such deployments—which were just as impressive, with allowance made for time and technology, as the recent dispatch of U.S. forces to Saudi Arabia—there was also Olivares's firm belief that victories in the field would confound the domestic and foreign critics who spoke of Spain's decline.

When the news of the first battlefield success (at Noerdlingen, in September 1634) reached Madrid, therefore, Olivares declared it to be "the greatest victory of our times." Once again, Spain had proved its detractors wrong; because of its military prowess, it was still number one in international affairs.

Yet if one glanced at the non-military dimensions of power, a different picture emerged. Spain's industries had become less and less competitive, and it increasingly relied upon foreign manufacture. Vested interests fought, all too successfully, against any diminution of privilege and against all proposals to amend an inefficient and archaic tax structure. The social fabric was torn; beggars, unemployed laborers, the homeless, could be seen in city streets, while rural poverty was widespread. Above all, the country's debts were increasing from day to day, and Olivares was finding it ever more difficult to borrow from foreign bankers—or to get Spain's allies to share the burdens of war—so that the more the military operations continued, the more the country went into the red. Nevertheless, Madrid felt that the borrowings would have to continue, for without them the military endeavors would fade, and with it Spain's own reputation. And so, the show went on—for another few decades.

Before the critics rush in to declare that [George] Bush's America is not Philip IV's Spain, let me hasten to agree with them; of course it is different, just as every nation and century are different. But the point of this historical analogy is to remind readers what the theory of "imperial overstretch" is really about. Essentially, it rests upon a truism, that a power that wants to remain number one for generation after generation requires not just military capability, not just national will, but also a flourishing and efficient economic base, strong finances and a healthy social fabric, for it is upon such foundations that the country's military strength rests in the long term. The latter phrase is a critical one, and not well understood by those who think only of the present.

In those controversial pages of "The Rise and Fall of the Great Powers" that discuss the American condition, I observed that if the country allows a gap to open up between its capacities and its many obligations, it "runs the risk . . . of what might roughly be called 'imperial overstretch.' " Logically, therefore, it can seek to avoid that risk.

THE 'DECLINE DEBATE'

So much of the "decline" debate seems to be obsessed with where America is now; hence, no doubt, the rejoicings . . . at the way in which . . . military successes [against Iraq] supposedly prove that the U.S. is not "a declining power." My own concern is much more with the future, a decade or more down the road, if the trends in national indebtedness, low productivity increases, mediocre educational performance and decaying social fabric are allowed to continue at the same time that massive American commitments of men, money and materials are made in different parts of the globe. Like the late Victorians, we seem to be discovering ever-newer "frontiers of insecurity" in the world that we, the number one power, feel impelled to guard.

I do not want the U.S. to follow the path of imperial Spain and Edwardian Britain; but it is no use claiming that America is completely different from those earlier great powers when we are imitating so many of their habits—possessing garrisons and bases and fleets in all parts of the globe and acting as the world's policeman on the one hand, running up debts and neglecting the country's internal needs on the other.

The dilemma that the U.S. faces during the next decade in achieving a proper balance between ends and means—thus avoiding "imperial overstretch"—is awkward enough. But the last thing that is needed is for its people to be encouraged to seek its self-esteem on the battlefield. If the U.S. wishes to recover its "reputation," it might begin by repairing its inner cities, public education, crumbling infrastructure and multiple social needs, at the same time resisting the temptation to follow the path of Spanish grandees. The "sense of self-confidence and self-esteem" that Americans desire to see restored would be more appropriately felt in a democracy like this one if it rested upon evidence of the nation's health and strength rather than upon reported distant glories in war.

CONTRIBUTORS

David Calleo is Dean Acheson Professor and the director of the European Studies program at the Paul H. Nitze School of Advanced International Studies, Johns Hopkins University.

I. M. Destler is professor at the School of Public Affairs, University of Maryland, and visiting fellow at the Institute for International Economics.

Aaron L. Friedberg is assistant professor of politics and international affairs at Princeton University.

John Lewis Gaddis is Distinguished Professor of History at Ohio University, where he serves as director of the Contemporary History Institute.

Andrew C. Goldberg is vice president of Burson-Marsteller, New York, and a senior associate at the Center for Strategic and International Studies, Washington, D.C.

Selig S. Harrison is senior associate of the Carnegie Endowment and a former Northeast Asia bureau chief of the *Washington Post*.

Fred Charles Iklé was undersecretary of defense for policy in the Reagan administration and is currently a distinguished scholar at the Center for Strategic and International Studies, Washington, D.C.

Josef Joffe is foreign editor and columnist of the *Süddeutsche Zeitung*, Munich and was the 1990 to 1991 Beaton Michael Kenab Professor of National Security Affairs at Harvard University.

Loch K. Johnson is Regents Professor of International Relations in the Department of Political Science at the University of Georgia.

Charles W. Kegley, Jr., is Pearce Professor of International Relations at the University of South Carolina.

Geoffrey Kemp is senior associate at the Carnegie Endowment for International Peace. He served as special assistant to the president during the first Reagan administration.

Paul Kennedy is professor of history at Yale University.

Paul Krugman is professor of economics at the Massachusetts Institute of Technology.

Robert Kuttner is economics correspondent of *The New Republic* and a columnist for *Business Week*.

Jessica Tuchman Mathews is vice president of the World Resources Institute in Washington, D.C., where she also serves as its director of research.

Walter Russell Mead is a senior fellow in international economics at the World Policy Institute in New York City.

John J. Mearsheimer is professor and chair of the Department of Political Science, University of Chicago.

Theodore H. Moran is Karl F. Landegger Professor and director of the Program in International Business Diplomacy at the School of Foreign Service, Georgetown University.

Michael Nacht is dean of the School of Public Affairs, University of Maryland, and was acting director of the Harvard Program on U.S.-Japan Relations.

Joseph S. Nye, Jr., is Dillon Professor of International Affairs at Harvard University and served as the deputy undersecretary of state in the Carter administration.

Norman J. Ornstein is a resident scholar at the American Enterprise Institute in Washington, D.C.

Clyde V. Prestowitz, Jr., former counselor for Japan affairs to the U.S. secretary of commerce, is president of the Economic Strategy Institute and director-general of the Pacific Basin Economic Council.

Earl C. Ravenal, a former official in the Office of the Secretary of Defense, is distinguished research professor of international affairs at the School of Foreign Service, Georgetown University, and senior fellow at the Cato Institute.

John E. Rielly is president of the Chicago Council on Foreign Relations.

Mark Schmitt is a research associate at the American Enterprise Institute in Washington, D.C.

John W. Sewell is president of the Overseas Development Council and served previously in the U.S. Foreign Service and in the Research Bureau of the Department of State.

W. Y. Smith, a retired military officer, is president of the Institute for Defense Analyses.

Theodore C. Sorensen is a senior partner at Paul, Weiss, Rifkind, Wharton and Garrison in Washington, D.C., and served as an adviser in the Kennedy administration.

Ronald Steel is professor of international relations at the University of Southern California.

Robert W. Tucker is emeritus professor of American foreign policy at the Paul H. Nitze School of Advanced International Studies, Johns Hopkins University.

Stephen Van Evera is assistant professor in the Department of Political Science at the Massachusetts Institute of Technology.

Eugene R. Wittkopf is professor of political science at Louisiana State University.

Acknowledgments (continued from copyright page)

John Lewis Gaddis, "Toward the Post–Cold War World." Reprinted by permission of *Foreign Affairs*, (Spring 1991). Copyright 1991 by the Council on Foreign Relations, Inc.

Josef Joffe, "Entangled Forever," reprinted with permission. © *The National Interest*, Fall 1990, no. 21, Washington, D.C.

Robert Tucker, "After 1989: Continuity or Retrenchment?" Reprinted by permission of *Foreign Affairs*, (Winter 1991). Copyright 1991 by the Council on Foreign Relations, Inc.

John J. Mearsheimer, "Why We Will Soon Miss the Cold War," *Atlantic Monthly* 266 (August 1990): 35–37ff. Reprinted by permission of the author. John J. Mearsheimer is Professor of Political Science at the University of Chicago.

Earl C. Ravenal, "The Case for Adjustment." Reprinted with permission from *Foreign Policy* No. 81 (Winter 1990–1991). Copyright 1990 by the Carnegie Endowment for International Peace.

Theodore C. Sorenson, "Rethinking National Security: Democracy and Economic Independence." Reprinted by permission of *Foreign Affairs*, (Summer 1990). Copyright 1990 by the Council on Foreign Relations, Inc.

"Preserving the Global Environment: Implications for U.S. Policy," by Jessica Tuchman Mathews is reprinted from *Preserving the Global Environment*, edited by Jessica Tuchman Mathews, with the permission of W. W. Norton & Company, Inc. Copyright © 1991 by The American Assembly.

Aaron L. Friedberg, "Is the United States Capable of Acting Strategically? Congress and the President." Reprinted from *The Washington Quarterly* 14 (Winter 1991): 5–23. Aaron L. Friedberg, "Is the U.S. Capable of Acting Strategically?" by permission of the author and The MIT Press, Cambridge, MA.

Norman J. Ornstein and Mark Schmitt, "Post–Cold War Politics." Reprinted with permission from *Foreign Policy* No. 79 (Summer 1990). Copyright 1990 by the Carnegie Endowment for International Peace.

John E. Reilly, "Public Opinion: The Pulse of the '90s." Reprinted with permission from *Foreign Policy* No. 82 (Spring 1991). Copyright 1991 by the Carnegie Endowment for International Peace.

John Lewis Gaddis, "Coping with Victory," *Atlantic Monthly*, 264 (October 1989): 49–60. Reprinted by permission of the author.

Andrew C. Goldberg, "Challenges to the Post–Cold War Balance of Power," *Washington Quarterly* 14 (Winter 1991): 51–60. Reprinted by permission of the author and The MIT Press, Cambridge, MA.

Ronald Steel, "Europe After the Superpowers," *Sea-Changes: American Foreign Policy in a World Transformed*, pp. 7–21, ed. Nicholas X. Rizopoulos. Reprinted by permission of the author.

David Calleo, "American National Interests and the New Europe: The Millenium Has Not Yet Arrived." Based on an essay originally published in *The Crisis of Leninism and the Decline of the Left: The Revolutions of 1989*, Daniel Chirot, ed. Copyright © 1991 by the University of Washington Press.

Selig S. Harrison and Clyde V. Prestowitz, Jr., "Pacific Agenda: Defense or Economics?", Reprinted with permission from *Foreign Policy* #79 (Summer 1990). Copyright 1990 by the Carnegie Endowment for International Peace.

I. M. Destler and Michael Nacht, "Beyond Mutual Recrimination: Building a Solid U.S.-Japanese Relationship in the 1990s," abridged, with footnotes deleted, from *Intenational Security* 15 (Winter 1990/91): pp. 92–119. Reprinted by permission of the authors and MIT Press, Cambridge, MA.

"The Metamorphosis of the Third World: U.S. Interests in the 1990s" by John W. Sewell is reprinted from *The Global Economy: America's Role in the Decade Ahead*, edited by William E. Brock and Robert D. Hormats, with the permission of W. W. Norton & Company, Inc. Copyright © 1990 by The American Assembly.

Geoffrey Kemp, "Regional Security, Arms Control, and the End of the Cold War," *Washington Quarterly* 13 (Autumn 1990): 33–51. Reprinted by permission of the author and the MIT Press, Cambridge, MA.

W. Y. Smith, "Principles of U.S. Grand Strategy: Past and Future," *Washington Quarterly* (Spring 1991): 67–78. Reprinted by permission of the author and The MIT Press, Cambridge, MA.

Fred Charles Iklé, "The Ghost in the Pentagon: Rethinking America's Defense," reprinted with permission. © *The National Interest*, Spring 1990, no. 19, Washington, D.C.

Theodore H. Moran, "International Economics and U.S. Security." Reprinted by permission of *Foreign Affairs*, (Winter 1991). Copyright by the Council on Foreign Relations, Inc.

349

Robert Kuttner, "Postwar Economics," *The New York Times* March 24, 1991. Copyright ©
1991 by the New York Times Company. Reprinted by permission.

Paul Krugman, "Free Trade and Protectionism." Reprinted by permission of the Washington
Post Company from Paul Krugman, *The Age of Diminished Expectations: U.S. Economic Policy
in the 1990s.* Cambridge, MA: The MIT Press, 1990.

Walter Russell Mead, "On the Road to Ruin," Copyright © 1990 by *Harper's Magazine.* All
rights reserved. Reprinted from the March issue by special permission.

Joseph S. Nye, Jr., "Against Declinism," *The New Republic* October 15, 1990: 12–13.
Reprinted by permission of The New Republic © 1990, The New Republic, Inc.

Paul Kennedy, "A Declining Empire Goes to War," *The Wall Street Journal* January 24, 1991:
A 10. Reprinted with permission of *The Wall Street Journal* © 1991, Dow Jones & Company,
Inc. All rights reserved.